West-Nordic Constitutional Judicial Review

– A Comparative Study of Scandinavian Judicial Review and Judicial Reasoning

To Jóhanna, my inspiration

Tá ið danskurin steig sín fót á land
og vavdi okkum inn í týskan gand,
tá mistu vit burtur ongul og stein
og fingu kanska – deyðamein?
Regin Dahl

Kári á Rógvi

West-Nordic Constitutional Judicial Review

– A Comparative Study of Scandinavian Judicial Review and Judicial Reasoning

DJØF Publishing
Copenhagen 2013

Kári á Rógvi
West-Nordic Constitutional Judicial Review
– A Comparative Study of Scandinavian Judicial Review and Judicial Reasoning

1. edition

© 2013 by DJØF Publishing
Jurist- og Økonomforbundets Forlag

Illustrator: Eyvind Dalsgaard
Cover: Bo Helsted
Print: AKAPRINT, Tilst

Printed in Denmark 2013
ISBN 978-87-574-2915-2

Sold and distributed in Scandinavia by:
DJØF Publishing
Copenhagen, Denmark
Email: forlag@djoef.dk
www.djoef-forlag.dk

Sold and distributed in North America by:
International Specialized Book Services (ISBS)
Portland, USA
Email: orders@isbs.com
www.isbs.com

Sold in all other countries by:
The Oxford Publicity Partnership Ltd
Towcester, UK
Email: djof@oppuk.co.uk
www.oppuk.co.uk

Distributed in all other countries by:
Marston Book Services
Abingdon, Oxon, UK
Email: trade.orders@marston.co.uk
www.marston.co.uk

Content – Short

Content – Long

Figures

*

"New constitutionalism repudiates legislative supremacy, establishes fundamental human rights as substantive conditions on legislators, provides for judicial protection, and has fashioned a quasi-federal legal system out of treaty."
Martin Shapiro and Alec Stone Sweet, International Scholars

*

"As I understand constitutional theory, if you cannot simultaneously apply both Basic Law and Statute Law, you must prefer the former."
Peder C. Lasson, Norwegian Chief Justice

*

"A study will show that the right of review was made up to be used in the political game, in its origin and effect antiparliamentarian in character."
Jens Arup Seip, Norwegian Scholar

*

"The constitution-giver undoubtedly stands above the other powers of state, as well the legislative as the executive and judicial. The provisions of the constitutional law must, therefore, be categorised as higher legal norms above the regular laws."
Ólafur Jóhannesson, Icelandic Scholar

*

"Basic rights in the Basic Law, the ECHR, and the EU-law limit public power, including legislation. They solve the clash between state and citizen according to our cultural norms, as necessary preconditions for a just human life."
Torben Jensen, Danish Justice

*

"It is not alien to Danish tradition to use a dynamic style of interpretation and therefore not necessary for European impulses to leave the text of the Basic Law. Danish tradition is dynamic but the dynamics have consisted in restrictive interpretation."
Henrik Zahle, Danish Scholar and Justice

*

ABSTRACT

Thesis Summary

The subject of this thesis is West-Nordic judicial review. The three countries Norway, Denmark, and Iceland (and the dependencies Greenland and the Faroe Islands) share a common legal heritage due to history, politics, and academics.

The nineteenth century brought constitutional changes, most notably written Basic Laws, documents with equally legal and constitutional qualities. Like in so many other regions, accident and force prevailed in many respects, and one common issue was difficult to settle: What if instruments issued by the various branches of government appear contrary to the Basic Law? The question has many profound aspects. Do the Basic Laws themselves set up any specific review scheme? Can courts or other forums legitimately decide ultimately political disputes? Can the elected representatives be trusted to uphold the legal rights of the people?

A number of studies have engaged passionately in considering these somewhat philosophical matters. This study, however, proceeds on the basic premise that there is no single answer; different actors and factions propose different answers and solutions at different times. To lawyers, the prevailing course of events is most relevant. Have the adjudicating forums actually reviewed the constitutionality of laws – and how have they gone about it? Is there any difference between these related lands and, if so, what can explain the difference? And how can we then utilise such insights?

It turns out that there are many differences between polities even in this homogenous region, and there is much difference over time within each jurisdiction. All the three Supreme Courts have stated that, in principle, it follows from constitutional logic that they must ultimately set-aside or repair unconstitutional instruments, even parliamentary laws. But when and how varies.

This thesis explores the underdeveloped aspect of Scandinavian law of how the dynamics of dispute resolution have had profound impact in a region, where the constancy of law is assumed, and where the predictability of law is valued very highly. These dynamics, created by case law, legal reasoning, academic and political reactions may cause shifts in the constitutional norm structures.

The most significant impact in later years has been the creeping federalisation of Nordic law. Having been self-reliant nation-states in legal terms, these countries unexpectedly find themselves subject to review by courts that do not necessarily agree with Nordic attitudes to neither dogma nor methodology. For those practising Nordic constitutional law, including Supreme Courts, the scene is effectively changing into a quasi-federal constitutional arrangement where judgement on basic human rights can be appealed to the European Court of Human Rights, economic rights cases to the European Court of Justice or the EFTA Court. With these associations, Nordic law is being whirled into the vigorous supranational dynamics of those courts that are influenced by much of Europe abandoning judicial restraint and parliamentary supremacy; laws are being challenged all over Europe, and constitutional questions are integrated into political, ideological, and legal struggles.

In short, this thesis concludes that, philosophy aside; Nordic constitutional law does not flow easily from laws, comments and textbooks but is the complex product of several factors that now include the impact of the rights revolution, the federalisation of European law, and the judicialization of politics. This has momentous implications for the study and practice of constitutional law as the law is vigorously morphing, pending on which issues and arguments are raised – and *who decides*.

Acknowledgements

I would like to take this opportunity to thank a number of people:

Foremost, I thank my most gracious sponsors BP Amoco Exploration and Amerada Hess and their directors Hjarnar Djurhuus and Ben Arabo. Without their funding and encouragement, this project would not be possible.

I thank my supervisors at the University of Iceland Professors Eiríkur Tómasson, Björg Thorarensen, and Róbert Spanó for their time. Likewise, I am very thankful towards all other colleagues and friends at the University's Law School at Lögberg.

I will always be very much obliged to María Thejll, administrator at the Lagastofnun, who in innumerable ways has helped our little family with our stay in Iceland.

Furthermore, those learned colleagues at other law schools who took me under their wings and gave me opportunity to visit, in particular Professor Eivind Smith of the University of Oslo and professor Michael C. Dorf of Columbia Law School.

Fellow PhD-students at various institutions have been a great support, especially Ingvill Plesner.

Crucially, Mike Karlsson and Ágúst Þór Árnason of the University of Akureyri School of Social Science and Law at the University of Akureyri have given me the opportunity to try out my theories on their students.

Moreover, my fellow editors of the Faroese Law Review, particularly Jógvan Elias Winther Poulsen and Bárður Larsen have been very helpful.

Among legal practitioners, Stephen Lamb, Esq. has provided invaluable advice on language and style, and Halgir Winther Poulsen, Esq. has been inestimable with his relentless critique.

For helping me to get back to editing the book for publication my most heartfelt thanks to judge Niels Waage and the good people of the San Cataldo institution, www.sancataldo.dk.

Numerous other people have helped me by giving me advice and opportunities but for fear of forgetting anyone, I shall refrain from mentioning them all.

Acknowledgements

I thank the West-Nordic case reports, Retstidende, Ugeskrift for Retsvæsen, and Hæstiréttur www.haestirettur.is for access.

Plentiful friends and family have been supportive throughout without getting into the project itself but by helping out so many other ways.

Thank you all!

Kári á Rógvi[1]

1. Born in the Faroe Islands 1973. Formal education: cand. jur. Københavns Universitet (five-year law programme, Copenhagen) 1998, LL.M. Aberdeen University 1999, Advokateksamen (Danish Bar Exam) 2004, Ph.D. Háskóli Íslands (Iceland) 2009. Has practiced law, worked as legal secretary to, later deputy Chairman of Faroese Constitutional Committee, Faroese Member of Parliament, Dean of Faculty of History and Social Sciences, Currently Senior Lecturer in law at the University of the Faroe Islands and Chair of the Board of the Faroese Labour Law Tribunal. Lives in Argir, Faroe Islands, a married father of three and ardent sheep farmer.
    Thesis previously provisionally published by Háskóli Íslands.

Preface on Scope

The following is a monographic work forming part of a PhD project that further consists of a series of public lectures, university teaching, courses, and related work. The public defence was held in March 2009 at Háskóli Íslands (The University of Iceland). The thesis has been edited in early 2012 and revised in light of the defence and considering new material. My thanks to my opponents Eivind Smith and Guðmundur Alfreðsson, who made the defence a spirited occasion. The thesis[1] shall:

- Present a *theory of constitutional judicial review*, its concepts, conditions, dynamics, and mechanics. Constitutional judicial review will be analysed in a wider context with focus on how review actually is conducted by review forums, the factors that may facilitate or impede review and, particularly, on federal formations, human rights, and legal culture.
- *Apply the theory to the development of judicial review in the West Nordic countries* with emphasis on relevant formative periods and recent developments.
- In application, *analyse the legal reasoning of the selected cases* and their dealing with or exposure of relevant aspects of judicial review, especially the contemporary quasi-federal formations.
- Moreover, as appropriate suggest *alternatives methods* for reading, understanding, and using judicial review as law and as part of the wider constitutional discourse.

---

1. The thesis is written in English for the purpose of a wider debate. All Nordic sources are translated by Kári á Rógvi unless otherwise indicated. Numbers in notes usually refer to pages. Case details are listed in tables.

On Reading the Thesis

This thesis is probably best read by appreciating (or at least being aware of) its structure.

A brief summary of the parts follows:

Part on ...	Contains ...	The main parts being ...	Using the outline ...
Introductions	Formal information	Summary Acknowledgments Scope Contents Tables of Cases Method	
Theory ... *... and Application*	The main body of work	Concepts and Conditions Dynamics Mechanics West Nordic Review Norwegian Review Danish Review Greenland and Faroese R Quasi-Federal Review	 {Summary} {Review in development} {Early Cases} {Previous Practise} {Recent Review}
Legal Reasoning	Some critique		
Alternatives	Some suggestions		
References	Sources other than cases		

Introductions give the formal constraints and purposes of the thesis.

> The *summary* introduces the entire thesis, as every major element is likewise summed up in exactly one page.
>
> *Acknowledgements* are my brief thanks (as words are not adequate).
>
> *Scope* explains the purposes and limits of the thesis.
>
> *Contents* are a detailed list of all headlines with their page numbers.
>
> *Method* explains more carefully *how the thesis is written.*
>
> *Tables of Cases* contain all the cases used, listing the raw material of the thesis. For details of a case, flip back to this part.

Theory and Application is my contribution to the legal scientific body.

> *The three Chapters on Theory* provide the scholarly framework for analysis.
>
> *The six Chapters on Application* apply the theory to the subjects within our scope. Note that they all contain a *summary,* followed by a survey

of *judicial review in constitutional developments* in a given jurisdiction, followed by a rough periodic division into *early cases, previous practise,* and *recent review.*

Legal Reasoning contains a critique of the legal sources and the legal science in this area.

Alternatives are a somewhat normative outline of what could be done instead.

References give details on scientific and theoretical sources; their names are shortened in notes.

On Method

The aim of this thesis is to formulate a theory of judicial review applicable to West-Nordic judicial review and reasoning. The pros and cons of judicial review are well known to most people interested in the subject. Conversely, this thesis *is not on what ought to be*. Rather, the focus will be on *what constitutional judicial review actually is in the West-Nordic countries*.

The method developed and then applied shall be an analytic way of describing constitutional law as it is and provide others with the tools to better understand and analyse aspects of constitutional judicial review and West-Nordic case law in general, constitutional or otherwise.

The method is based on the basic presumption that '*new constitutionalism*'[1] is prevailing in our time, awarding supremacy to human rights and other substantive constraints over legislative omnipotence and that it "has fashioned a quasi-federal, legal system" out of treaties.[2]

Furthermore, the best way of analysing the actual state of constitutional judicial review is to apply theories on constitutional judicial review developed by a number of scholars of various jurisdictions, in particular professors Alec Stone Sweet, Martin Shapiro,[3] Henrik Zahle,[4] Eivind Smith,[5] and Michael C. Dorf[6] on case law dynamics, precedent, and historical developments.

---

1. Martin Shapiro and Stone Sweet, Alec "Law, Courts, and Social Science" in *On Law, Politics and Judicialization* (2002b) 1.
2. Shapiro and Stone Sweet (2002b) 1.
3. Their most important collective effort for this study is Martin Shapiro and Alec Stone Sweet *On Law, Politics, & Judicialization* (2002c).
4. His most important work for this study is Henrik Zahle *Praktisk retsfilosofi* Christian Ejler's Forlag (2005).
5. His most important work for this study is Eivind Smith *Høyesterett og Folkestyret* Universitetsforlaget (1993).
6. So many of his works have been important for this study, like Michael C. Dorf "Create Your Own Constitutional Theory" 87 *California Law Review* (1999) 593 and Michael C. Dorf "Legal Indeterminacy and Institutional Design" 78 *New York University Law Review* (2003) 875 but also his many often deconstructive analyses on www.findlaw.com/writ. My hope would be to continue this project of fully analysing

The writings of Shapiro and Stone Sweet are especially helpful in understanding the dynamics of third party dispute resolution, quasi-federal formation, the potential communication through judicial review across jurisdictions, and the judicialization of constitutional law and politics. Henrik Zahle (re)introduced concepts of legal dynamics and justice into Danish legal scholarship.[7] Eivind Smith has done a lot of work on Nordic judicial review both historic and prospective. His work has been very influential in the rediscovery of the potential of judicial review often in a comparative perspective.[8] Judicial review can be seen as taking constitutions and rights seriously,[9] treating constitutional texts as the positively enacted legal texts applicable as any others. Smith's theories are especially helpful in understanding the particular Nordic context and the re-emergence of judicial review within it. Michael Dorf's writings have inspired me to create my own theory.[10]

The fundamental choices and perspectives in viewing judicial review are reflected inside the title page of the thesis (see those quotations). The best view is to look closer at what present day *new constitutionalism* judicial review is and explain it (Shapiro, Stone Sweet). Older theories often either rely on the super-positive properties of constitutional norms (Lasson) or simply emphasise the supremacy of elected assemblies (Seip). Both the latter approaches come across as either somewhat naive or too passionate for a lawyerly approach. Simply preferring the constitution over statue or merely dismissing the legal properties of constitutions as anti-parliamentarian are both over-simplifications, based on 'ought' rather than 'is.' Others have focused more on the power to constitute a polity as part of the political-constitutional structure (Jóhannesson) and that the basis for Nordic review includes a European dimension that can be viewed from both a narrow doctrinal point and a broader legal cultural perspective (Jensen). The full view of West-Nordic law includes seeing its deeply traditional and dynamic properties that have transformed constitutional norms away from enacted text contrary to the popular belief of constancy in law (Zahle).

West-Nordic constitutional law with a collective effort like Michael C. Dorf *Constitutional Law Stories* Foundation Press (2004).

7. Henrik Zahle "Grundlovens menneskerettigheder: Sammenstødet mellem legalistiske og dynamiske retstraditioner" in *Grundloven og menneskerettigheder* Jurist- og Økonomforbundets Forlag (1997). Henrik Zahle *Omsorg for retfærdighed* Gyldendal (2003).
8. Eivind Smith *The Constitution as an Instrument of Change* SNS Förlag (2003c) and Eivind Smith and Olof Petersson *Konstitutionell demokrati* SNS Förlag (2004).
9. Ronald Dworkin *Taking rights seriously* Harvard University Press (2002)
10. Dorf (1999).

Analyses of new constitutionalism[11] have revealed *changing constitutions*[12] and *dynamic constitutions.*[13] Judicial review has been adopted by a number of *new democracies*[14] but studies show that even older *constitutional cultures*[15] can apply, then disregard, and later rediscover judicial review. In particular, constitutions seem apt as *instruments of change*[16] and *transition.*[17]

For all these purposes, constitutional judicial review proves to be a crucial *medium*[18] of *discourse.*[19]

This thesis seeks to develop in the context of West-Nordic academic law two approaches that should prove beneficial. *The first* is better understanding the *dynamic properties* of constitutional law as it develops through case law. *The second* is better understanding the *quasi-federal and quasi-constitutional properties* of supranational law created by such regimes as the European Union (hence EEC or EU) and the European Convention on Human Rights (hence ECHR), making jurisdictional sovereignty 'differently' relevant for the practice of law.[20] This is not to say that sovereignty is irrelevant, far from it. Unfortunately, however, conceptual-formalist attitudes have obscured the advent of new regimes with constitutional and federal properties, as "[the ECHR] differs from most other [conventions by a real court where people

11. For a good critical account of new constitutionalism see Ran Hirschl *Toward juristocracy* (2004).
12. Jeffrey Jowell and Dawn Oliver *The Changing Constitution* (2004).
13. Richard H. Fallon, Jr. *The Dynamic Constitution* Cambridge (2004).
14. Tom Ginsburg *Judicial Review in New Democracies. Constitutional Courts in Asian Cases* Cambridge University Press (2003).
15. Eivind Smith "Constitutional Cultures: The Constitution between Politics and Law" in *The Constitution as an Instrument of Change* SNS Förlag (2003a).
16. Smith (2003c).
17. See Preamble and §§ 1 and 94 of draft Faroese Constitution in Stjórnarskipanarnevndin *Stjórnarskipan Føroya* (2006).
18. Henrik Zahle writes, "The legal reality has thus become relative. When several individually "correct" but not mutually reconcilable understandings of the law must be managed the need arises for a frame that makes possible a coexistence of the irreconcilable perceptions of basic constitutional issues." Henrik Zahle "Hjemmestyret i dansk forfatningsret – en fredelig pluralisme" in *Retsforhold og samfund i Grønland – en antologi* Ilisimatusarfik (1998) 59.
19. For ways of measuring and improving discourse in West-Nordic context see Pernille Boye Koch *Forfatningskontrol – fremtidige perspektiver og udfordringer* DJØF Jurist- og Økonomforbundets Forlag (2002) from 95, from 210, and particularly from 260. See also Richard H. Fallon, Jr. ""The Rule of Law" as a Concept in Constitutional Discourse" 97 *Columbia Law Review* (1997) 1.
20. Alec Stone Sweet "Islands of Transnational Governance" in *On Law, Politics and Judicialization* (2002b) 323.

can bring suit against their nations-state]."[21] Kaarlo Tuori writes that these new systems of law both outside and sometimes within the nation-state "have a common attribute: they witness to the nation-state's reduced importance as uniting factor of the legal system ... But at the same time we must remember the opposite harmonising tendencies," concluding that, "the role of legal science will become more important [with] new tasks."[22]

These new tasks create a need for a more relevant and focused methodology to provide students, scholars, and practitioners with the tools to predict and apply 'new constitutional law.' The method used here borrows from realist and critical legal studies as well as from historical approaches. The most influential strain however, is what can be called *political jurisprudence,*[23] understanding the inherently political nature of constitutional law, where the task of judicial review is to draw a line between "politics" and the "political law" of the Constitution,[24] resulting in the *judicialization*[25] of constitutional law and politics. This obviously requires a practical understanding of the dynamics of case law.[26]

Applying these general theories on constitutional judicial review to the West-Nordic countries poses certain challenges. *First,* persuading Nordic lawyers that the same *fundamentals apply* and that Nordic law is inherently functioning in the same way as, say, French or American law. (This is perhaps 're-persuading,' as Nordic legal theory used to teach that the law of different polities are 'in many elements the same').[27] *Second,* explaining how, consistent with said similar elements, that Nordic constitutional law is *continuously changing* irrespectively of the constancy of constitutional documents. *Finally,* arguing that accepting the political and dynamic nature of present day West-Nordic constitutional law is *necessary to understanding* it,

21. Eva Smith "Foretager Højesteret en selvstændig fortolkning af Den Europæiske Menneskerettighedskonvention og Strasbourg-domstolens praksis?" *Juristen* (2001) 54 at 54.
22. Kaarlo Tuori "Den (post)moderna rätten mellan harmonisering och fragmentering" in *Senmodernitetens historiska och komparativa konstruktioner* Corpus Iuris (2006) 26.
23. Martin Shapiro "Political Jurisprudence" in *On Law, Politics and Judicialization (2002).*
24. Anita Usacka ""Strict" or "Liberal" Interpretation? Comments on Latvia" in *The Constitution as an Instrument of Change* (2003) 227.
25. Alec Stone Sweet "Judicialization and the Construction of Governance" in *On Law, Politics and Judicialization* (2002c).
26. Stone Sweet (2002c) .Zahle (1997) 59.
27. Ditlev Tamm *Retshistorie. Danmark – Europa – globale perspektiver* DJØF (2005) 164.

predicting it, and practising it. This approach has been summed up as "the opposite [of] 'willing suspension of disbelief' as a tool of understanding."[28]

The Danish scholar Henrik Zahle has called this a "de-mystification" of law realising that the "usual methods [apparently leave] the interpreter in a situation of choice [ultimately asked] to make sub-political decisions [because of lacking agreement or knowledge] on the political level. Legal interpretation becomes the framework of political decision."[29]

The West-Nordic countries are eminently suitable for such a study as old and new constitutionalisms are battling each other and the constitutional law thus is in transition.[30] However, this study will show that West-Nordic constitutional law has displayed dynamic properties best explained in terms of political jurisprudence and judicialization at previous stages of their history and that the outlined methodology is apt also for re-examining the history of judicial review and is crucial for understanding the outset of present day judicial review in its hermeneutic setting.[31]

The term West-Nordic[32] shall for our purposes[33] cover Norway, Denmark, and Iceland, and the dependant countries Greenland and the Faroe Islands. Traditionally, Denmark and Sweden have dominated the West- and East-Nordic regions respectively and their legal traditions have evolved somewhat differently. Through Nordic co-operation and not least supranational developments, the two traditions may be converging but this study is limited to the West-Nordic tradition based on original Danish hegemony of legal teaching comparable to English influence in its dominions. The Danish legal tradition came to dominate the dependent realms and lands of Norway, Iceland, Faroe

---

28. Shapiro and Stone Sweet (2002b) 21.
29. Henrik Zahle "Den fortryllede ret: fortolkning af autoritative tekster" in *Senmodernitetens historiska och komparativa konstruktioner* Corpus Iuris (2006) 41-43.
30. Henrik Zahle writes, "The legal reality has thus become relative. When several individually "correct" but not mutually reconcilable understandings of the law must be managed, the need arises for a frame that makes possible a coexistence of the irreconcilable perceptions of basic constitutional issues." Zahle (1998) 59.
31. The great modern breakthrough of hermaneutics in Danish law can rightly be attributed to Peter Høilund *Den forbudte retsfølelse* Munksgaard (1992).
32. Helgadóttir uses the phrase 'Nordic' to designate Norway, Denmark and Iceland though admitting the term usually has a wider scope Ragnhildur Helgadóttir *The Influence of American Theories on Judicial Review in Nordic Constitutional Law* Martinus Nijhoff (2006) 1 note 1.
33. In cultural terms, Norse may signify the Nordic countries, not counting Finnish-speakers and Inuits, as well as earlier settlements outside the present Nordic area. In linguistic terms Icelandic, Faroese and New Norwegian are considered West Scandinavian, Book-Norwegian, Danish, and Swedish East Scandinavian.

Islands, and Greenland. Consequently, these countries are fit for a comparative study,[34] as their legal philosophical tradition is similar but their constitutional development differs. At times, the phrase Scandinavian shall be used, not as term of geography but rather reflecting the political, cultural and academic reality that place as well Danish, Icelandic, Greenlandic and Faroese law solidly in Scandinavia, geography notwithstanding.

Constitutional judicial review has undergone several transitions in Nordic legal culture. Today, the realms of constitutional law, politics, and international law are interacting, increasing the potential of clashes between statutory law and potentially superior norms, testing and challenging the methods used to resolve the issues – "the law is under transformation."[35]

It may seem plain that a study of judicial review should for the most part be an analysis of court judgements. Nonetheless, to many Nordic lawyers the reasoning of judicial decisions is not where they usually look for authoritative expressions of law. To outsiders this may seem puzzling, surely cases are where we get the law restated and applied to real world circumstances. However, for historical and ideological reasons the pervasive perspective for more than a century in Nordic scholarly theory and teaching have to a very high degree underrated and even misrepresented the importance of case law. Typically, Jens Peter Christensen in his useful book on the Danish Judiciary as the third branch of governments quotes very few cases, *none* in the section "Judge-made legal principles" (case law, it seems, is not even the primary source for ... case law!).[36]

To paraphrase Torstein Eckhoff, *Nordic Courts are unlikely to admit to their restatement of law and much less outright rulemaking, and Nordic law schools are even less likely to point out such activity.*[37]

---

34. On the comparative method see Mark Tushnet "The Possibilities of Comparative Constitutional Law" 108 *The Yale Law Journal* (1999) 1225; Ruti Teitel "Comparative Constitutional Law in a Global Age" 117 *Harvard Law Review* (2004) 2570; and Vicki C. Jackson and Mark Tushnet *Comparative Constitutional Law* Foundation Press (1999).
35. Torben Jensen *Højesteret og retsplejen* GAD jura, Thomson Information (1999) 51 (on "internationalisation").
36. Jens Peter Christensen *Domstolene – den tredje statsmagt* (2003) 34-36.
37. Torstein Eckhoff writes, "*It is often claimed that the courts have played a particularly great role in the development of law in England and the U.S.A. However, I doubt whether there is any significant difference between those countries and the Nordic. The difference lies, probably, more in the greater interest in the courts' lawmaking in England and the U.S.A. than in our countries. They write textbooks and hold classes on it – while consigning legislation to footnotes. And their courts are much more like-*

This study tries to rectify perspective by focusing more on court judgements. Nonetheless it draws upon the general theories already mentioned as well as two recent books, '*Forfatningskontrol*'[38] by Pernille Boye Koch and '*The Influence of American Theories on judicial Review in Nordic Constitutional Law*'[39] by Ragnhildur Helgadóttir. Especially the former is more focused on *legal writings* on judicial review than on actual *judicial review*.

The focus on institutional writers and theory, even when discussing judgemade legal principles and judicial review, probably tells us a lot about the West-Nordic legal culture; legal writings are in many ways the *meta-source* of law,[40] the controlling medium that provides access to the other sources of law, with preparatory works filling that function if no comments exist. This is in stark contrast to common law traditions (including such new common law cultures as EU and ECHR law) where *court judgements* are the meta-source. The difference is that though both types of cultures of course recognise 'constitutions' and 'statutes' as valid legal norms, they differ in approach to ascertaining what these actually mean. The Nordic lawyer will quote a scholar and a textbook,[41] and the English-speaking lawyer a court and a case as respectively the institution and the written source most likely to determine or sum up the issue. Likewise, the Nordic lawyer will turn next to the preparatory

ly to admit that they are contributing to the development of the legal system." Torstein Eckhoff "Domstolenes Rettskapende Virksomhet" 27 *Úlfljótur* (1974) 274 at 276.

38. Koch (2002).
39. Helgadóttir (2006).
40. Harking back to the medieval tradition of teaching Roman law by study of learned comments that became a source of law themselves Tamm (2005) 62.
41. Probably on the far scale of the scholarly-inclined method is the thesis "On Expropriation" by Icelander Gaukur Jörundsson, who appears to rely on scholars as his primary source and cases merely underscoring scholarly views. The book has no table of cases, though it does cite many. Jörundsson begins most chapters with a short presentation of the issue, for instance in one chapter saying that "some other limitations than taxes have a special positions in the legal system [but] scholars are mostly more reserved on [these compared to taxes.]" He then lists the names, works, and views of some eleven Norwegian, Danish, and Icelandic scholars. Gaukur Jörundsson *Um eignarnám* Bókaútgáfa Menningarsjóðs (1969) from 143. Even the final conclusion of the thesis refers to, "the mentioned scholars pointing out ... (For example ...)." Jörundsson (1969) 404. An interesting parallel is the classical Danish treatise on family law: "The opinions of the learned are very different on this point ..." Niels Hemmingsen in 1572 as quoted in Tamm (2005) 174. The method seems rooted in canon law and undoubtedly has its merits if the ultimate arbiter is swayed by greater number of institutional writers or texts, as has been the principle at both old Icelandic and Roman law.

works issued by the government agencies that both propose and later administer legislation, whilst the English-speaking lawyer looks to a case law based textbook that explains how the courts have applied, tested, and interpreted legislation.

There are obvious flaws in observing *judicial* review only through the scholarly comments that are both removed from and somehow competing with the actual judgements by the courts themselves. In that respect, this study focuses more on the primary source (though scholars shall get their due). This is not only a matter of perspective but also a question of sources of law. Nordic law is being drawn into new legal systems like the EU[42] and ECHR with their *autonomously forming traditions with common law properties* in viewing law through case law reasoning. We are likely to witness a gradual change of perspective where court judgements will become more relevant as a meta-source of law. This will be especially so if the Nordic teachers of law start to "write textbooks and hold classes" on case law and the Nordic courts become "more likely to admit that they are contributing to the development of the legal system."[43]

This new reality is reflected in the method of this study. Different sources of law will have varying weight in all the diverse circumstances relevant to us but the fundamental issue at stake is that of West-Nordic constitutional judicial review. Consequently, we shall focus on how courts that hold jurisdiction in the West Nordic countries have exercised, are exercising, and likely will exercise review based on constitutional norms. As Husa and Mattei put it, "the main shortcoming of scholarship of constitutional law has been to excessively focus on the understanding and explanation of the written law. Likewise, this is precisely why there is the need for comparative or at least non-nationally oriented study of constitutional law."[44]

Moreover, these shortcomings include a lack of focus on the dynamics of reasoning and political participation (political in the wider sense of 'governance' and 'policy') of the several courts that now decide constitutional cases and provide non-national and non-written (i.e. non-enacted) sources of law. By contrast, the "political jurist begins with what any fool could plainly see if his eyes were not beclouded by centuries of legal learning: that judges and courts are an integral part of government and politics."[45]

42.   Ruth Nielsen and Christina D. Tvarnø *Retskilder og retsteorier* DJØF (2005) 22.
43.   Eckhoff (1974) 276.
44.   Jaako Husa *Nordic Reflections on Constitutional Law* (2002) 22.
45.   Shapiro and Stone Sweet (2002b) 22.

To ensure that the reader has particular expectations to theory and application, these specific questions shall be posed at the outset:

- What is the *most relevant definition* of constitutional judicial review for legal practitioners?
- Is constitutional judicial review *a general phenomenon* common to the several cultures?
- What are the key *concepts* of constitutional judicial review?
- What are the *conditions that trigger or hinder* constitutional judicial review?
- How do the *dynamics* of constitutional judicial review work and affect a given legal order?
- How do the *mechanics* of constitutional judicial review typically function?
- To what extent are these factors *present in the West Nordic countries*?
- How is *quasi-federal* constitutional judicial review presenting itself in this context?
- What are the effects of these developments on West Nordic *judicial reasoning*?
- Are there indications of *shifts in the constitutional norm structures* in this context?
- What use do *comparative approaches* to constitutional judicial review offer in this context?
- Which *alternatives* can be suggested to strictly judicial constitutional review?
- What is the likely *future* of West Nordic constitutional judicial review?

Constructing a Theory of Judicial Review

Summary of Theory of Judicial Review

Constitutional judicial review is part of West-Nordic law. The pros and cons of that are not the subject of this study. Rather, we shall construct a workable theory of how to analyse judicial review universally but with particular reference to review in the West-Nordic countries.

We shall start with the *concepts* and *conditions* of judicial review. The former refers to the central phenomena of judicial review, the norm structures, the institutions, the constitutional frameworks that set the scene for constitutional judicial review in the wider sense, the latter the factors that commonly initiate, increase, or reduce the activity of constitutional judicial review and its effects.

Then, we shall proceed to the *dynamics* of judicial review. The context of constitutional review is often potently laden with unresolved issues and inherent contradictions in constitutional text, tradition, and precedent. Judicial review often provides the occasion for resolving these issues facing the several polities. Though legal developments have always been part of legal analysis, recently developed theories have come closer to providing the methodology to observe, analyse, and predict constitutional developments, the changes in law that occur through judicial review.

Furthermore, we shall look at the *mechanics* of judicial review. The more prosaic elements of judicial review relate to the *who, how,* and *where* of judicial review. As review is institutionalised to some extent and restrained by procedure, understanding the options available in precedent as well as pending cases is a necessary skill in analysing and using review.

These three first major elements will be explained in the following and form the first chapters of the study. Based on this theory, we shall apply it to West-Nordic judicial review and examine review cases in light thereof. Integrated into our reading of cases shall be the final two major elements of judicial review theory.

Legal history and the *history of review* are crucial to providing an adequate perspective on current constitutional law as moulded by review. The way courts are performing review is very much a product of the past; history also provides us with examples of concepts, conditions, dynamics and mechanics differing from today's setting but shedding more light on leading cases, where to look for comparative angels, and clues to future developments.

Ultimately, *legal reasoning* as formulated in judicial review gives us straight from the judges' mouth the final words that determine how all the other factors result in the actual state of the law. Therefore, a suitable theory is needed for analysis of West-Nordic legal reasoning in case law.

Constitutional judicial review is performed at the overlap of law and politics, reflecting the legal and political properties of constitutional documents and traditions. Intriguingly, constitutional review not only lies at the intersection between the judicial and legislative powers but also has distinctly *rule-making properties*.

In summary, constitutional judicial review is best analysed through this framework of concepts, conditions, dynamics, mechanics, history and reasoning.

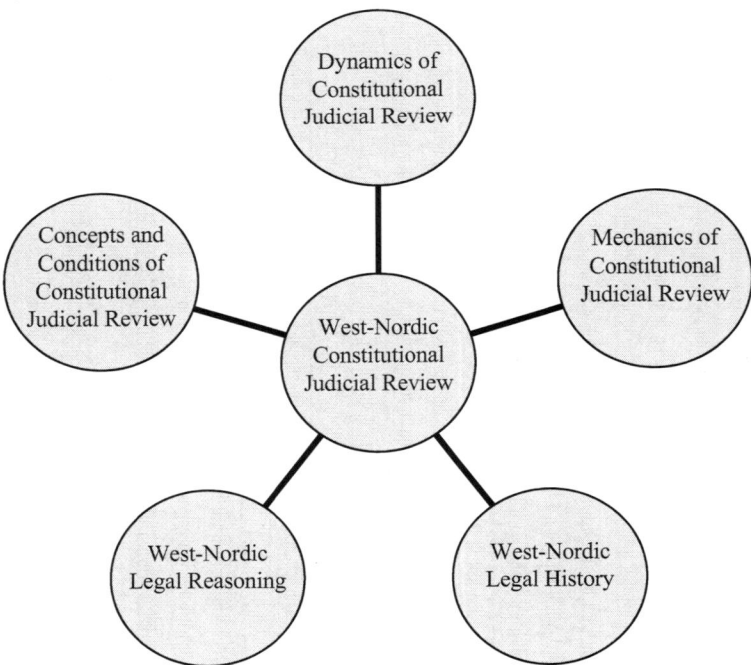

Figure A: Constructing a Theory on Judicial Review for a West-Nordic Context

A note on Normative Theories on Judicial Review

A lot has been written on judicial review. Regrettably, most of it is "setting forth the pros and cons on the power to declare laws unconstitutional" – as observed by Mike Dorf.[1] This is odd for two reasons. First, because courts are not about to be stripped of that power and, consequently, writing essays urging courts to retreat, therefore, seem somewhat quixotic.[2] Second, it would seem a more practically-minded as well as a methodically more challenging approach to study how judicial review actually works and how to deal with it in terms of practical lawyering.[3]

West-Nordic legal writings include innumerable examples of ghastly and wholly unsupported normative expletives like claiming that one "cannot come to another Result than a Rejection of the Extreme American Teaching that it is the Courts, which are supreme Authorities in Constitution-Interpretation-Questions."[4] Such statements are wholly unpersuasive and reveal a lack of understanding of law in general, Nordic constitutional law in particular, to say nothing of the nuances and actual comparative values of foreign law.

Alas, because so much of West-Nordic theory is devoted to preferences, much scholarly theory becomes tracing and restating normative theory[5] or focus on alternatives.[6] Pernille Boye Koch, for instance, narrates the developing attitudes to constitutional judicial review in Danish legal theory,[7] and then analyses a number of alternatives, and concludes based on discourse theory

---

1. Dorf writes, "*In many constitutional law courses, the professor spends about half the semester setting forth the pros and cons of "judicial review," the power of American courts to declare laws unconstitutional. This is fun, to be sure, but not very important as a practical matter, because the issue has been settled since 1803: American courts have this power, and no one is taking it away from them anytime soon.*" Michael C. Dorf "The Five-Minute Law School: Everything You Learn In Your First Year, More or Less" *FindLaw's Writ* (2005).
2. A good example of this is Jens Elo Rytter "Går menneskerettighedsdomstolen for vidt?" 88 *Juristen* (2006) 9.
3. Shapiro and Stone Sweet (2002b). Martin Shapiro and Stone Sweet, Alec "Testing, Comparison, Prediction" in *On Law, Politics and Judicialization* (2002d).
4. Quoted in Koch (2002) 24, a typical example of the normative, self-reliant, and uninformed style Danish scholarly pronunciations on the issue, notice the "it must be concluded" style, the logical fault of conclusion without any premise.
5. See Koch (2002) and Helgadóttir (2006) for accounts of West-Nordic normative theory on judicial review.
6. Koch (2002).
7. Ibid. from 14.

what, on balance, is the best option for future constitutional control or oversight.[8] This is undoubtedly valuable as history of legal writings and suggesting suitable criteria for *alternatives to law as it is* but the main implications are normative, historic or future, stating what others previously thought the law *ought to have been* or what the future law *ought to become*.

Our aim shall be to look at actual present day (or past day) constitutional law and how to analyse it. Abandoning normative theory for the multi-layered, dynamic jurisprudence of constitutional judicial review is a pursuit that may contribute to advance law as an analytical academic discipline, understanding the phenomenon rather than taking sides. Thus, this study of judicial review is written to engage academics, students, and practitioners alike in a discussion on *how* judicial review works, *how* judicial review affects the existing norm structures and power balances, and *how* to make the most of judicial review in a practical context, preferring descriptive analysis to prescriptive normative statements.[9]

---

8.   Koch (2002) 260-62.
9.   Alec Stone Sweet *Governing With Judges* Oxford University Press (2000) 5.

The Concepts and Conditions of Judicial Review

Understanding the Concepts and Conditions of Judicial Review

The term *Constitutional Judicial Review* implies an action with three components. First, the review is based on a superior legal norm – *constitutional* – the archetype being a written Constitution. Second, the review is performed by an independent forum – *judicial* – the archetype being a Supreme Court. Third, an action of evaluation – *review* – the archetype being (considering) invalidation of a statutory law.

The *superior norm* may alternatively be international law, supranational law, a (quasi-)federal constitution, as well as concepts of justice, natural law, human rights, or other system of (un)written norms that are awarded superior legal status. The competing norms may form a neat hierarchy or form polycentric relationships that award them different relative status in different situations or by different reviewing institutions. The discourse over constitutionality is potentially prolonged. Different arguments can be made and several of them can be 'right,' at least in the sense that they are vindicated by some important writer, court or other institution of government. In West-Nordic context, the most relevant norms are the national Basic Laws and European basic rights.

The *forum* may alternatively be international, supranational, or (quasi-) federal courts, special tribunals or committees, offices charged with determining the constitutionality of bills. (Arguably, scholarly writings may serve the function of review forum, as their pronouncements on constitutionality are respected as authoritative legal determinations, but their role in reviewing legislation shall not be investigated here). In West-Nordic context, the most relevant forums are the national Supreme Courts and the European Courts, the ECHR Court, and the ECJ.

The *evaluation* may be any kind of assessment overriding or limiting the inferior act or considering doing so. It may be authoritative interpretation in light of the supreme norm, prospective pronouncements, orders, or hints to reconsider legislation as well as full, partial or particular invalidation, as long as they are a result of legal application of supreme norm, may constitute review. In West-Nordic context, the most relevant evaluation is often evident as various flexible techniques, subtle alternatives to setting-aside parliamentary instruments.

These factors can be varied immensely. Review takes on many forms from abstract a priori review initiated by the parliamentary opposition in the forum of the French Constitutional Council; to prejudicial submission by a Member State court to the ECJ when a party alleges that their individual (directly effective superior) rights according to EU Treaty have been violated; or as a point of defence raised by a party when appealing a criminal conviction to a West-Nordic Supreme Court.

Although many cases concern the powers of branches or bodies of government, the most commonly raised issues in constitutional review are related to the rights and freedoms of individuals or groups outside government, claiming various limits to government (legislative) powers. The great Danish judge, Torben Jensen, explains this very well: "*As a legal positivist dogmatic definition, [basic rights] can be defined as the rules that according to the Basic Law, the European Convention on Human Rights, and the EU-law limit the public exercise of power, including the power of legislation. As a legal ideological definition, they can be defined as rules to solve the clash or limits of competence between state and citizen, and to some extent between the several citizens, that according to our cultural norms and human value system are viewed as necessary preconditions for a just human life in a democratic culture.*"[1]

Judge Jensen explains very well several aspects of present day judicial review. On the one hand, that the deeper reasons for constitutional review relate to prevailing values pertaining to just human life and democratic culture in a given polity. On the other hand, that today's review viewed soberly in the positivist tradition of describing the dogma of *valid law*, entails analysing all the super-norms that have the effect of limiting the power of legislation in the polity in question. This understanding of the interaction between values and law, offered by Judge Jensen, is a much-needed perspective when developing the legal skills needed for the reality of new constitutionalism.

We shall further digest it by using the approach of realism and political jurisprudence, which is still solidly within the tradition of focusing on the de-

---

1.   Torben Jensen "Domstolskontrollen med overholdelse af grundrettigheder" 1995 *UfR* (1995) B241 at 241 with note 5.

scriptive and analytical, not normative. As Shapiro and Stone Sweet write: "Political jurisprudence has given a central place to 'values,' but values treated as the attitudes of judges or the policy preferences of actors in the legal process. It has been positivist in this sense of being concerned with the 'is' rather than the 'ought,' but including in the 'is' the values that political actors in fact hold, as well as a concern for questions of what difference those values in fact make to political action and policy outcomes."[2]

By contrast, the 'rump-realists' of the misleadingly called *Scandinavian realist* tradition have descended into the kind of conceptual jurisprudence that they originally derided.[3] Law is a science making sense of social and cultural phenomena, its concepts and definitions are only approximations that do not compel reality. To paraphrase, *constitutional judicial review would smell just the same by any other name.*[4] The critique of natural law was in many ways well founded – law is often anything but natural – but insisting on conceptual restraints on the issue of constitutionality is just another way of deductive reasoning from unpersuasive first principles.

When discussing constitutional judicial review, focus is often on the dramatic consequences of invalidating laws. In the words of Alec Stone Sweet, "*Constitutional Review* is the authority of an institution to invalidate the acts of government – such as legislation, administrative decisions, and judicial rulings – on the grounds that these acts have violated constitutional rules, including rights."[5]

However, a wider term than "invalidate" is probably better, as it implies expressed annulment ergo omnes, whereas many courts will merely interpret the instrument differently or use other flexible techniques for the wider effect

2. Shapiro and Stone Sweet (2002b) 11.
3. Sverre Blandhol has coined the phrase "restrealister" – 'rump realists' or 'rest realists' – for those hanging on to Scandinavian realism. Sverre Blandhol "Formalisme, pragmatisme, realisme: Teori, metode og grunnlovsforståelse hos Castberg, Knoph og Ross" in *Grundlagens makt. Konstitutionen som politiskt redskap och som rättslig norm* SNS författningsprojekt (2002) Blandhol provides a very insightful view of the search for scientific certainty and the (social democratic) political undertones of the misnamed Scandinavian realists in Sverre Blandhol *Juridisk ideologi – Alf Ross' kritikk av naturretten* DJØF; Jurist- og Økonomforbundets Forlag (1999).
4. The archetype 'rump realist' Sv. Gram Jensen introduces his book on legal theory with a quotation from Shakespeare's Romeo and Juliet on a 'rose smelling just as sweet by any other name' – yet one of the main components of his legal theory is applying mathematical reduction to legal concepts, for instance claiming to eliminate the meaning of 'duty.' Svend Gram Jensen *Almindelig retslære* DJØF (1989) 57. See also comments in Høilund (1992).
5. Stone Sweet (2000) 21.

and formally limit the judgement to the parties before it.[6] Constitutional Review is thus the authority of an institution ultimately to invalidate *or otherwise limit, reinterpret, or amend* acts of government based on a superior legal norm.

We shall concentrate on the review of statutes and other laws on the highest level of legislation pursuant to a constitutional order in relation to constitutional norms. The usual narrow definition of a constitution in the Nordic context is 'a superior written law of a given nation-state.' However, this definition is essentially linguistic, attached to the Nordic-language phrases meaning 'Basic Law,' or romantically dualistic, claiming that the law of these sovereign entities is wholly autonomous and everything outside them international or foreign – and never the twine shall meet.

As suggested by Judge Jensen, relevant definition must capture the federal dimension. Our wide definition is 'a valid superior legal norm that constitutes superior institutions, overriding procedures, and enforceable rights.' Documents like the ECHR, the EEC/EU Treaties and possibly others fall under the scope of this definition.[7]

This wider definition of the term constitution works in tandem with a wider definition of federation, as 'an association of higher-order polities with a legally arranged division of powers between centre and associates,' adding that 'a quasi-federation may be limited by subject matter, by lack of institutional framework or in other ways appear incomplete.' This definition obviously treats the ECHR-regime as a polity with federal properties, with the Convention and the Court being the foremost elements of this 'incomplete federation.' As a polity, the EU is more complete but may still lack the attributes that some would require of a 'full federation.' To avoid contention over definitions, reference to the ECHR and the EU shall be made as quasi-federations.[8]

The particular subject of this study is constitutional judicial review as exercised by the courts that have jurisdiction over the West Nordic Lands, notably the Supreme Courts of Norway, Denmark, and Iceland and the European Courts. The courts are exercising constitutional judicial review in the wide

---

6. Smith (1993) 74.
7. The EEA, EFTA, and WTO are examples. See for instance Stone Sweet (2002b) These polities hold potential federal properties as they have formulated superior written norms, have created accessible courts that can interpret them and States committed to respecting the decisions. The States may run away but whilst members they cannot hide.
8. Shapiro and Stone Sweet (2002b).

sense when they determine whether the laws enacted by the Parliaments are compatible with the Basic Laws and the enforceable treaties. Crucially, from the point of view of someone wanting to challenge a given law, review based on the supranational documents is a form of constitutional judicial review readily available.[9]

The quasi-federal complements to national constitutional judicial review present themselves in the following way. States commit themselves to respect an international instrument but, unusually for such instruments, also submit to the jurisdiction of a supra-national forum regarding the interpretation of the instrument, providing for direct individual complaints. If the State in principle sees the world as dualistic, a law may be enacted that is formally a statute but in reality a supplement to the constitution, which attributes superior status to this 'federal dimension' relative to other regular laws, thus creating an intermediate sphere of law[10] between Constitution and statutory law. As the international forum gains influence the instrument in effect becomes a judiciable superior norm that may even trump national constitutional law.[11]

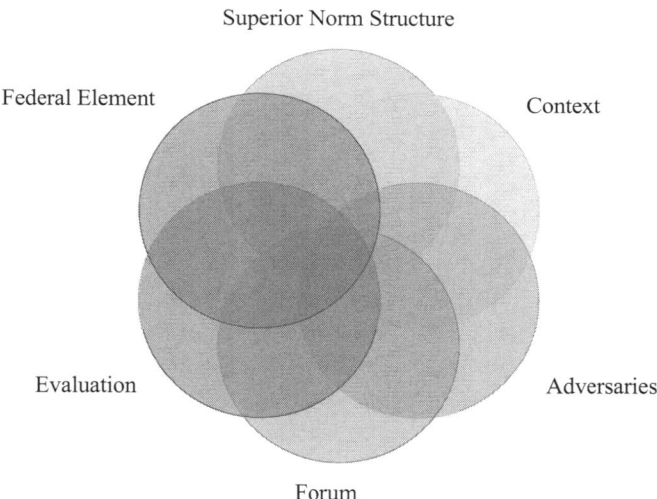

Figure B: Concepts and Conditions of Constitutional Judicial Review

---

9. As evident in Jensen (1995).
10. Martin Shapiro and Stone Sweet, Alec "Constitutional Judicial Review" in *On Law, Politics and Judicialization* (2002a) 138.
11. Factortame is the classical ECJ case on this point.

Figure B illustrates how constitutional judicial review is best analysed. The *superior norm structure* is the basic law, tradition, or directly applicable international law that potentially trumps a given statutory law. The *forum* is the institution that may have jurisdiction to review; its powers and procedures are often crucial to legal strategy in review. The *context* includes the wider constitutional and legal cultural setting. The *adversaries* are parties that are able to bring constitutional cases to review. The *federal element* relates to the wider power structure, federal review is likely to alter the balance of legitimacy. The *evaluation* is the available particular techniques of reviewing that affect the outcome and likelihood of review.

More on Conditions for Review

The state of West-Nordic judicial review as elsewhere is the product of several factors.[12] We shall survey some of the prevailing factors that increase or decrease the likelihood of constitutional judicial review, focusing on written constitutions, federal formations, human rights, legal writings, and comparative influence.

Written Constitutions are an obvious factor as they create the potential for conflict of norms. In the words of Icelandic professor Ólafur Jóhannesson: *"The constitution-giver undoubtedly stands above the other highest powers of state and political bodies, as well the legislative as the executive and judicial power. The provisions of the constitutional law must, therefore, be categorised as higher legal norms above the regular laws."*[13] The word 'constitution-giver' is here contrasted to the usual often-used 'lawgiver' (singular noun) that features so prominently in West-Nordic legal writings and who's putative will and intentions are attributed prevailing legitimacy. The neat point is that the 'constitution-giver' deserves even more respect, thus undermining the logic of deference to 'lawgiver' as well as the simplistic 'three branches' view of the constitutional pantheon.

The potential for conflict between superior and inferior norm is universal[14] and not restricted to 'Western' legal culture.[15] Written constitutions are not

---

12. Eivind Smith "Grunnlovens makt (eller avmakt)" in *Grundlagens makt. Konstitutionen som politiskt redskap och som rättslig norm* SNS författningsprojekt (2002) 21.

13. Ólafur Jóhannesson "Nogle ord om den stilling, islandsk ret tager til spørgsmålet om gyldigheden af forfatningsstridige love" 6 *Úlfljótur* (1953) 3 at 4.

14. For an example from another corner of the world, Jim Yardley writes, *"Faced with a conflict between national and provincial law, Judge Li had declared the provincial*

absolute conditions, as even English courts assumed that "the common law will controul Acts of Parliament, and sometimes adjudge them to be utterly void" as stated by Chief Justice Coke in a judgement in 1610, his writings inspiring later American assertion of fundamental law.[16] Principles of government and justice may show the same properties, as traditional constitutional principles are part of the deep structure of any constitutional system. No polity, however progressive, can bear the change of everything all the time. Tradition is somewhere safe to start or to return; "we take our bearing from tradition."[17] The constitutional text in question may also be a quasi-federal or the intermediate sphere of human rights and administrative principles that is not quite constitutional yet trumps other legislation.[18]

When they are enacted, written constitutions may codify existing traditions or reflect a will for change, either empowering review based on old principles or break with established tradition.[19] Written constitutions may also be revitalised with a return to its true meaning or emphasis on a particular provision over others previously favoured,[20] thus creating new dynamics.[21]

Constitutional change in the form of a new written constitution or amendments can set in motion dynamics of its own. "New constitutional texts often turn out to give the citizens opportunities that were at first not intended. As

law invalid. In doing so, she unwittingly made legal history, setting in motion a national debate about judicial independence in China's closed political system. "For the first time, a judge announced a local law or regulation was void," said Xiao Taifu, a member of the Beijing Lawyers Association, which petitioned the central government on Judge Li's behalf. "It was historic. For the legal process in China, it was a first, and it carried deep meaning." Yardley, Jim *"Rule by Law. A Judge Tests China's Courts, Making History"* New York Times 28 Nov. 2005.

15. Regarding the prospects for judicial review in China see also Michael C. Dorf "What a Chinese Height Discrimination Case Says About Chinese (and American) Constitutional Law" *FindLaw's Writ* (2004).

16. Berhard Schwartz *A History of the Supreme Court* Oxford University Press (1995) 5 with note 9. Also Tamm (2005) 84.

17. Zahle (2003).

18. Shapiro and Stone Sweet (2002c).

19. Smith (2003a) 23.

20. Consider both the U.S. civil rights cases that were built on very old constitutional provisions on equality and process that were in light of recent developments weighted differently in relation to other provisions on state powers and implicit recognition segregation, etc. See Mark Tushnet "Making Civil Rights Law. Thurgood Marshall and the Supreme Court 1936-61" Oxford University Press (1994).

21. Consider French Constitutional Council's rediscovery of human rights found in the 1776 Declaration and in the 1948 Preamble in *CCD Case 82-146*.

the provisions become more familiar, it is likely that they will more frequently be used in legal arguments. In the long run this influences the way courts reason – and the results of judgements."[22]

Federal Formations are a particularly relevant factor, as they create multiple layers of law and shift the issue of legitimacy – a recent national statute can seem more legitimate than the old constitution but it may appear as an anomaly in a larger context. The majority locally or nationally may be the minority in federal context, inverting the counter-majoritarian aspect. When a polity enters federal arrangements or comes into existence by the federal disintegration of a previously unitary state,[23] this provides for further opportunity for review. Federalism is a particular variant of constitutionalism with increased potential for conflict of norms and thus judicial review.[24]

Federations hold the potential for review but may develop in different ways. Consider if *van Gend en Loos v. Netherlands* (ECJ Case 22/62) had not been decided in light of the 'spirit of the Treaty' to have direct effects, the entire political and economical development of Europe would have been different. Arguably, judicial review is part of what makes the EU a quasi-federation rather than just another forum for discussion and non-binding resolutions like, say, the Nordic Council and other regional entities that have not achieved the same effective transformation to an autonomous legal order with enforceable laws. That the EU through a gradual process has become a (quasi)federation and the ECJ its supreme/constitutional court is almost conventional wisdom.[25] Even famously formalistic Finnish scholars now talk of the "transformation process of the ECJ into a *de facto* constitutional court."[26]

On international or supra-national human rights as those of the ECHR, Danish scholar Rytter writes, *"The practically most important question is whether some of these rights – despite that they are not given independent constitutional status – still have such an effect in national law that they can be said to have a kind of "quasi-constitutional" status. [They do] if they by national courts in normal cases have the same effect as constitutional rights*

---

22. Smith (1993) 29.
23. Kári á Rógvi "Except by some Action not provided for in the Instrument itself" 2 *Faroese Law Review* (2002) 193.
24. Vicki C. Jackson "Narratives of Federalism: of Continuities and Comparative Constitutional Experience" 51 *Duke Law Journal* (2001) 223.
25. Jowell and Oliver write, "The legal doctrine of sovereignty has been modified by British membership [and] the concomitant importation into the UK hierarchy of norms of the doctrines of primacy and direct effect [developed by the ECJ]" Jowell and Oliver (2004) vi-vii.
26. Husa (2002) 21.

[and if] case law from international control bodies [in] national court practice is consistently upheld by national court regardless of [national law]."[27]

The quasi-federal and quasi-constitutional qualities of the EU and ECHR regimes are there irrespectively of where ultimate sovereignty rests. Assuming the Members States of both these quasi-polities are still sovereign and assuming that their membership is rightfully categorised as "international law," they may ultimately "be able to change the interpretation adopted by the courts,"[28] and otherwise defy or leave the obligations of membership.

However, in the short to medium (to quite long) term, this is extremely unlikely to occur, especially with regard to the conformist West-Nordic countries. Put differently, "the difference [compared with national constitutions] is only that international human rights with "quasi-constitutional" status must yield in the (normally hypothetical) case that the lawgiving power consciously sets [them] aside."[29] The latter option would have "grave foreign policy implications."[30] Thus, the possibility of non-compliance is retained in principle, but not in practice, compliance with quasi-federal decisions is thus in practise the trumping value of the system and therefore the practical state of the law.

As the youngest West-Nordic nation to be recognised at international law, Iceland can be assumed to attach greatest value to formal sovereignty and substantive independence in real terms. However, it has amended its bill of rights in effect more closely to resemble the ECHR provisions. Ironically, this may attach Iceland closer to the ECHR, as ECHR case law becomes potentially more to the point as precedent, and as non-compliance with ECHR law or judgements becomes potentially unconstitutional nationally as well. As Professor Eiríkur Tómasson explains, "In the wake [of the amendment of the rights provisions, even] though the ECHR has, formally seen, the same validity as other general laws it follows that its provision may be legally superior to other comparable sources because of [the constitutional provisions although the wordings may differ].[31] In case the "Nation's Highest Court [defies] precedent of the ECHR Court, that Court is not empowered to formally quash the judgement [though it] will be substantively trumped by the Court

---

27. Jens Elo Rytter *Grundrettigheder* Thomson (2000) 113.
28. Jonas Cristoffersen "Folkeretskonform grundlovsfortolkning" in *Politik og jura. Festskrift til Ole Espersen* Thomson (2004) 257.
29. Rytter (2000) 113.
30. Jens Elo Rytter *Den Europæiske Menneskerettighedskonvention – og dansk ret* Thomson (2006) 37.
31. Eríkur Tómasson *Réttlát málsmeðferð fyrir dómi* (1999) 16.

[because] Iceland will be [bound at international law to correct it]."[32] This indirect superiority has led to major changes in criminal procedural law as the ECHR Court overruled the judgement of the Icelandic Supreme Court.

Herein lays the point of using the phrase quasi-federal in reference to particularly the ECHR-regime in this thesis. The options of secession or noncompliance[33] notwithstanding, the idea that the West-Nordic countries will actively defy ECHR case law is 'normally hypothetical' in all foreseeable future. Consequently, the ECHR rights as perceived by the ECHR court or national courts will have 'such an effect in national law that they have "quasi-constitutional" status.' They are, in effect, *quasi-federal.*

The West-Nordic countries have been drawn into federal formations by stealth through, "the influence [on judicial review that follows] from judgements against [them] several times in the ECHR Court in Strasbourg. Harmonisation with the EU legal system will presumably act in the same direction."[34] This was not anticipated and certainly not easily deducible or predictable from the textual sources but is due to complex developments. In case of the Nordic countries, the Strasbourg Court and the Luxembourg Court, "*both have increasing importance not only for the development of the norm sets that they have been charged with upholding but also for the legal developments in the individual member states. It is likely that their activities will affect attitudes to legal limits to political action and the role of the courts in Norway as well. The almost unconditional signing up to the ECHR Court's role in our political life can hardly but work in the same direction.*"[35]

Human rights hold the twin potential of increasing the number normative conflicts and increasing the number of potential adversaries that may refer their disputes to judicial review. Human rights both as part of constitutions, traditions, federations but indeed also as manifest in international conventions provide the most frequent occasions and most spirited debate over judicial review. As Eivind Smith puts it, "The extent of review depends on e.g. the reference norms that the constitutional courts can build on, [notably] extensive catalogues of rights [furthermore] international norms have increasingly

---

32. Tómasson (1999) 17.
33. Expressly reserved according to Danish preparatory works and theory, though envisaged to occur "not ... very often" Rytter (2006) 37 and 40.
34. Smith (1993) 29.
35. Ibid. 40.

stronger affect."[36] In the West-Nordic countries, it is in the "area [of] human rights that judicial review of statutes ... is most significant."[37]

Scholarly theory as we have already noticed may filter the way that lawyers view the various sources of law. New ideas and solutions may come through legal writings,[38] but scholarly theory may be both wrong, distorted, or by design or fault trying to influence as well as explain law. Finding out which of us theorist are right and not merely righteous, explaining the law and not merely expressing personal views is difficult.[39]

A particular fault in legal writings on constitutional law may be that lawyers lack the proficiency in the political, philosophical, sociological, and historical aspects of constitutional law. Lawyers may not appreciate the interaction between legal and political aspects of constitutional law.[40] Scholars and judges do not always speak the same language, as "the scholars have not always been great Justices, and the great Justices have not always been scholars."[41] Therefore, the textbook may provide an overly legalistic view and miss the 'cultural values' that judges favour in cases.

What view lawyers have of judicial review will depend on their 'legal upbringing' for example, according Lars Oftedal Broch, "In the last part of the nineteenth century, the practise of "setting aside" statutes infringing upon the Constitution was well established. In the following period of more than 100

36. Smith (1993) 37.
37. Smith (1993) 18.
38. Ragnhildur Helgadóttir writes, "Changing ideas concerning constitutional interpretation and the role of the judiciary began to appear in Icelandic court opinions around 1950. It is likely that the jurisprudential changes occurred mainly on the basis of the evolving Norwegian and Danish theory, influenced by American theory. This is likely because of the lack of Icelandic theory in the early years of the republic and the corresponding reliance on Danish and Norwegian theory. A majority of the Justices had studied in Denmark and the U.S." Helgadóttir (2006) 141.
39. For an interesting perspective on Scandinavian realism see Gregory S. Alexander "Comparing the Two Legal Realisms – American and Scandinavian" *The American Journal of Comparative Law* (2002) 174. For a further analysis of what lead Scandinavian legal writings off the beaten path see Blandhol (1999) and for an absolutely wonderfully written critique of American theoretical activism see Bork Robert H *The Tempting of America – the political seduction of the law* Touchstone (1991).
40. Eivind Smith Grundlagens makt. Konstitutionen som politiskt redskap och som rättslig norm SNS författningsprojekt (2002) 7.
41. Schwartz (1995) 265.

years, generations of jurists have been brought up with judicial review of leg-islation as part of their basic understanding of the legal system."[42]

Figure C: Concepts and Conditions – Examples Overview

Figure C provides an overview of the following examples. *Norm Structure* is/are the superior legal norm(s) in question. *Federal element* is the collective jurisdiction. *Forum* is the court or other reviewing institution. *Adversaries* are the parties or other initiators of proceedings. *Effects and techniques* are the forms of evaluation.

	Concept 1 Norm Structure	Concept 2 Federal Element	Concept 3 Forum	Concept 4 Adversaries	Concept 5 Effects and Techniques
Example 1	United States Constitution	United States, newly formed federation	United States Supreme Court	Citizen v. executive government	Constitution reinterpreted, law set-aside
Example 2	Norwegian Basic Law	None	Norwegian Supreme Court	Citizen v. government	Constitution reinterpreted, restricted, law upheld
Example 3	Danish Basic Law ECHR	ECHR functions as federal constitution	Danish Supreme Court - ECHR Court	Gov. v. citizen, then citizen v. government	ECHR explained, violation found
Example 4	Icelandic Constitution	ECHR case is controlling precedent	Icelandic Supreme Court (ECHR)	Government v. citizen (prosecution)	Doctrine changed
Example 5	EEC Treaty	EEC Treaty functions as federal constitution	Belgian court asks for ECJ prejudicial precedent	Citizen v. Citizen (prejudicial)	EEC Treaty reinterpreted, prospective precedent

Comparative Influence may work in the same way as legal writings to per-suade judges, practitioners, and writers. The potential for comparative influ-ence is so significant that otherwise independent courts may in practice be-

---

42. Lars Oftedal Broch ""Strict" or "Liberal" Interpretation? Comments on Norway" in *The Constitution as an Instrument of Change* (2003) 242.

come co-ordinated.[43] The West-Nordic countries, however, have probably been relatively little influenced by comparative materials. Eivind Smith writes that, "With some exception in case of Denmark, there is no basis for assuming that the Nordic examples have significantly influenced the development of judicial review in Norway, nor the debate."[44] However, comparative influence in constitutional law seems to be increasing.[45]

We shall now consider comparative examples to illustrate these points.

Example 1: The Concepts and Conditions of Marbury

The case ***Marbury v. Madison*** (5 U.S. 137 (1803)) arose in the United States in the formative period, shortly after the new Constitution was enacted and the young Union of former colonies was still on shaky grounds having recently won by war the right of self-determination and the Constitution succeeding the now defunct Articles of Confederation. The context was highly political as the loosing federalist faction only dominated the Supreme Court and the winning democratic-republican faction was ready to ignore the Court's ruling on a highly political controversy. Marbury was one of the judges that the federalist had wanted to appoint just before their term of office expired but he was denied his papers by the new Secretary of State Madison.

Norm Structure. The opinion of the Court delivered by Chief Justice Marshall used principles of justice established in case law and extolled by the institutional writer Blackstone to thoroughly thrash the acts of President Jefferson. However, the federal Constitution was used as the basis for setting aside the statute that gave the Court jurisdiction thus avoiding overriding the President.

Federal Element. This was the beginning of the application as superior law of probably the most famous federal constitution and federal judiciary in the world. The United States became a federal system of law with both vertical and horizontal divisions of power not least because of Marbury.

---

43. Martin Shapiro "Towards a Theory of Stare Decisis" in *On Law, Politics and Judicialization* (2002) Shapiro and Stone Sweet (2002d).
44. Smith (1993) 25.
45. Ragnhildur Helgadóttir writes, "*[The convention has also had some impact on constitutional interpretation and on the practice of judicial review. When the Convention was incorporated into Danish law, the Ministry of Justice stated its opinion that this should not lead to increased lawmaking on the part of the Danish courts. This did not turn out to be an accurate prediction. One of the consequences of importing the ECHR into Danish law is that Danish Courts have to use methods of interpretation which are different from those they use when working with domestic law.]*" Ragnhildur Helgadóttir "Not so in America" – *The Influence of American Theories on Judicial Review in Nordic Constitutional Law* Unpublished (2004) 345.

Forum. The federal judicial branch could just as well have focused only on technical adjudication of federal law but instead this case laid the foundation for judicialization of constitutional discourse.

Adversaries. The amazing feature of American constitutional law more than two centuries ago was that it allowed an individual to challenge his federal government and to be told that he almost defeated it – but for a technical bar of jurisdiction.

Effects and Techniques. The judgement carefully argued that the legal order of the United States was built on the rule of law with legally superior norms including both the written constitution and principles of justice. The true genius in technique was to avoid a clash between the branches of government by stretching the interpretation of the statute that provided jurisdiction to make it appear unconstitutional and thus inapplicable – but at the same time expounding the principles of justice, the superior legal standing of the constitution, and the seemingly inescapable power of review.

(*Additional*) As a note to Nordic readers who may not have read the case,[46] it must be stressed that the case was only incidentally on judicial review of statute. The judgement was mainly condemning the President's administration (of statutory and common law) and probably only used judicial review (setting aside a procedural law) to avoid awarding a remedy that might have been ignored thus resulting in constitutional crisis. As a piece of legal writing, *Marbury* is simply awe-inspiring. The text is crystal-clear and reads rather like a Grisham novel. The basic facts revolved around the political rivalries of two bitterly opposing parties, the elitist Federalists, wealthy urban northerners who favoured strong central powers, and the populist Republicans, farmers and southerners who favoured decentralisation. The Federalists had been in power since the revolution as the case for establishing great central powers was strong and their celebrated leader George Washington drew widespread support for the party. The Republicans, however, had a larger natural following and their leader Thomas Jefferson, the main author of the Declaration of Independence, also enjoyed broad support.

In the elections of 1800, the transition of electoral power finally happened. John Adams was defeated by Jefferson by a handsome margin and his allies elected to Congress with substantial majority in both Houses. Transition in the U.S., however, comes gradually and both the outgoing Federalist President and Congress had several weeks to finish off their terms in power. Among the ra-

---

46. Case may be found on www.findlaw.com. For a very good comment see William E. Nelson *Marbury v. Madison* (2000).

ther curios and desperate measures undertaken were an Act to establish more judges and the use of the enabling provisions to appoint these judges, who became known as the 'midnight judges' due to their appointment so late in the term.[47] The Constitution has somewhat conflicting provisions on the issue, providing both for life tenure of judges and legislative powers to create or abolish courts other than the Supreme Court. The matter became further complicated due to the time-pressure involved. Working hard on the eve of inauguration, President Adams signed a number of commissions for justices of the peace of Washington D.C. John Marshall was at the time both Secretary of State and Chief Justice; he received the signed commissions from the President but failed to deliver them all before his time in office ran out.

Subsequently, the new Secretary of State, and principle author of the Bill of Rights, James Madison refused to deliver the remaining commissions and President Jefferson succeeded to reverse the legislation that created the offices. However, Marbury, one of the judges whose commissions were signed but not delivered, sued Madison for release of the appointing document. Madison and Jefferson would probably not have respected any court order, they even got the entire 1801 session of the Supreme Court suspended, reducing the effectiveness of the last Federalist stronghold in the federal government. When *Marbury* was finally heard, the outlook seemed straightforward: either Marshall backed down and let Jefferson be vindicated or he would order Madison to deliver the commission, which Madison would openly refuse, leaving both the Supreme Court and the Federalists humiliated. Apparently, a lose-lose situation for Chief Justice Marshall.

Marshall delivered a unanimous Supreme Court Opinion (the collective reasoning was his invention). The first part deals with the issue of Marbury's position. Relying very much on the institutional writer Blackstone's Commentaries, which were extremely revered and even described as "a runaway bestseller"[48] in young America, Marshall explains Marbury's rights to his commission, adding citation of an English case from the 13th century to indicate the firm line of precedent on the point. Only in the shorter second part does Marshall regret that the law that provided the Court with original jurisdiction in the case was contrary to the Constitutional provision on jurisdiction. "It cannot be presumed that any clause in the constitution is intended to be without effect," Marshall opined, and as it was "emphatically the province and duty of the judicial department to say what the law is," including if "two

---

47. Nelson (2000) 54.
48. Akhil Reed Amar *The Bill of Rights* Yale University Press (1998).

laws conflict with each other, the courts must decide on the operation of each." Thus, he concluded that "a law repugnant to the constitution is void, and that courts, as well as other departments, are bound by that instrument."[49]

Marshall thus cunningly avoided outright conflict but still got to scold Madison and Jefferson and create a firm precedent for judicial review. However, it must be stressed that judicial review did not come as a surprise, review was widely expected, and "several early decisions of the Supreme Court assumed the power of judicial review without anyone paying much attention."[50] It might likewise all have ended there, but Marshall was to preside over the Supreme Court until 1835, "forging a remarkable unity among the Justices of his Court, including those appointed by his former political opponents."[51])

Example 2: The Concepts and Conditions of Johansen

The case *Johansen v. Norway* (Rt. 1918-401) came up in Norway in the early 20th century. For several decades, Supreme Court case law had established and applied constitutional judicial review including wide-ranging doctrines of property rights. Parliament wanted to limit the windfall profits that proprietors received from the development of railways, waterways, and hydropower.

Norm Structure. The Norwegian Basic Law had been in force since 1814 but the majority of the Supreme Court relied on legal writings and principles of democratic theory in judging its significance and connotations. Notably, it disregarded the previous case law of the Court itself.

Federal Element. The case had no federal element but may have persuasive comparative elements.

Forum. The Norwegian Supreme Court is one of the oldest continuous European Courts and certainly has the longest tradition of judicial review resulting in setting aside statutory law.

Adversaries. The Norwegian legal system gives all citizens the right to challenge their government.

Effects and Techniques. The Court used constitutional theory to justify overruling previous case law on both the relevant doctrine and judicial review itself. The effect, beyond allowing the intended legislation, was to reduce the relevance of judicial review and consequently the Basic Law as superior positive law. Thus, one century of active review was followed by half a century of deference.

49. *Marbury v. Madison per* Chief Justice Marshall.
50. Fallon, Jr. (2004) 10 with note 13 citing cases.
51. Ibid. 20.

Example 3: The Concepts and Conditions of Jersild

The case *Jersild v. Denmark* (ECHR 1994) originated in Denmark where the Supreme Court upheld a conviction of journalist Jersild for disseminating racism when conducting a TV interview with socially deprived bigots. Jersild then sought recourse to the ECHR and his case was heard by the ECHR Court.

Norm Structure. The case was first adjudicated based on the Danish Basic Law that per traditions and prevailing legal writings does not include substantive freedom of expression. The case was then measured up to the ECHR that conditions restriction of expression on their necessity.

Federal Element. The ECHR began as an international treaty in the wake of the Second World War that stated a minimum of human rights, upon which a number of European countries could agree. To the Nordic countries, these seemed as already fulfilled and perhaps somewhat conservative compared to the more collectivist Nordic welfare agenda. For a long while, this treaty was like most others a question of international law with little effect in the member states. Today, the treaty is so often applied, especially after being incorporated and thus directly applicable that it now has quasi-federal quasi-constitutional properties. In the *Jersild* case, the relevant provision had a more substantial content.

Forum. Unlike most treaty systems, the ECHR established forums for dealing with human rights disputes. The ECHR Commission and Court came to function as forums for adjudicating and effectively reviewing national law based on the conventions text and the dynamically evolving interpretation of it. In case of *Jersild*, the forum consisting of judges from different legal and cultural backgrounds decided that it was against the convention to curtail the press in said manner. The Danish Supreme Court in its judgement deferred to the unclear will of the legislature and the interpretation of the prosecution service but it is otherwise increasingly likely to consider ECHR case law.

Adversaries. The ECHR system allows any citizen of the member states to apply and have his case heard after exhausting national remedies. Not all cases reach the Court but tens of thousands of cases are pending. As ECHR law becomes more a part of member state legal culture, the citizens can effectively use ECHR law in the national courts.

Effects and Techniques. The ECHR judgement laid down further criteria for deciding whether a restriction of expression is necessary, thus making it easier for national courts to decide ECHR compatibility on their own, though the ECHR Court could be more apt at formulating tests and other means of determining ECHR compatibility.

Example 4: The Concepts and Conditions of Ægisson

The case *Ægisson v. Iceland* (Hrd.1990.2) concerned an Icelandic citizen who challenged the organisation of the Icelandic justice system where police, prosecution, and judicial functions were collectively held by the Sheriffs.

Norm Structure. The Icelandic Constitution formed the basis of the Icelandic Supreme Court's judgement.

Federal Element. In effect, however, the case was decided by reference to the ECHR that has come to function as a quasi-federal constitution for the Iceland and other member states. The Supreme Court had decided a number of cases with reference to fair trial but in all the cases dismissed the ECHR argument summarily.

Forum. The case was decided exclusively by the Icelandic Supreme Court but effectively it was decided by a binding on-the-point precedent as another case on the same issue had been decided unanimously by the ECHR Commission – an example of a quasi-judicial reviewing institution. Iceland had agreed to pay compensation and the government asked Parliament to approve legislation to change the procedures that the Supreme Court had previously endorsed with reference to the will of the "lawgiver." Thus, Ægisson is a good example of the dependency of national forums on ECHR case law.

Adversaries. Ægisson demonstrates how a citizen can challenge the State, even in the national court, even without implementation or constitutional enactment of ECHR law.

Effects and Techniques. The ECHR system introduced a new view on the sources of law into the Nordic region. Normally, the ECHR commitment could have been dismissed by reference to preparatory works stating that all legislation was assumed to be in conformity and that the judiciary was to restrain itself and to legal writings claiming that Parliament can repeal any legislation, including ECHR accession. However, the purpose-driven, case-law-based dynamic interpretation of the ECHR won the day as both non-compliance and withdrawal from the ECHR regime were effectively ruled out as too embarrassing and politically untenable. The importance of legal culture is nonetheless apparent in the reluctance to bring and decide cases accordingly.

Example 5: The Concepts and Conditions of Defrenne

In *Defrenne v. SABENA* (ECJ Case 43/75), a Belgian airline hostess claimed that paying her a salary that was lower than the equivalent for male workers doing the same job was illegal according to the equal pay provision of the EEC Treaty.

Norm Structure. The EEC Treaty had become a superior legal norm in the Member States.

Federal Element. Although not a federation formally, the EEC is effectively a (quasi)federation with the federal layer having grown all relevant branches of government. The Member States remain sovereign and can leave the arrangement but as long as they are in, the system is quasi-federal with the Treaty functioning as a quasi-constitution. In the *Defrenne Case*, the Treaty provision on equal pay was held directly applicable as a rights provision with horizontal effects between one citizen of a Member State and another citizen of the same state.

Review Forum. The ECJ has taken initiative and effectively reviewed a huge proportion of both EU and Member State legislation. Through prejudicial procedure, the ECJ can control any unsettled issue of EU law and does explain them in decisions that are very lengthy and principled compared to Nordic decisions.

Adversaries. All citizens, including companies and other legal entities, can effectively insist on EU review in national courts with recourse to the EU Court(s), making the EU (EEC) probably the largest federations with effective rule of law and judicial review in history. EU law is directly applicable even in controversies between nationals of the same country.

Effects and Techniques. As said Treaty provision had been ignored by lawyers and courts alike for a number of years, the Court decided to issue a prospective ruling as to the law. Only future (or already initiated) cases of equal pay based on sex could be brought. Thus, the ECJ overcome one of the great obstacles to courts applying neglected constitutional provisions, back payment or other retroactive effects that may make the courts reconsider an otherwise just decision.

Judicial Review in Constitutional Developments

For each of the jurisdictions, we shall look at judicial review in constitutional developments. Our focus will be on what has facilitated or hindered judicial review and the general outline of how review may appear in constitutional developments. Our particular focus will be on the nature of review dynamics and what their implications.

In a nation state's legal order, constitutional judicial review may appear thus:

Figure D: The Developments of National Constitutional Judicial Review

(1)	(2)	(3)	(4)	(5)
Nat. State >	Constitutional Norm >	National Court >	Case Law >	Triadic Rulemaking

By a constituting act (1), (the people of) a nation state may enact (2) a constitutional document that – often apparently unwittingly – becomes judiciable and legally supreme within its substantive scope. The constitution provides for (3) courts of law to adjudicate interpretive disputes. This leads to (4) case law that (5) becomes the basis for further interpretive disputes and results in triadic rulemaking (that is lawmaking by a third party deciding a controversy between two adversaries), supplementing the original constituting act.

In case of the Nordic countries, this process has been hindered, reversed, or become dynamically restrictive by certain factors:

Figure E: The Developments of West-Nordic Constitutional Judicial Review

(1)	(2)	(3)	(4)	(5)
Nat. State >	Constitutional Norm >	National Court |F|	Case Law |F|	Triadic Rulemak.

By a constituting act (1) a nation state enacts (2) a constitutional document that in principle becomes judiciable and legally supreme within its substantive scope. The constitution provides for (3) courts of law to adjudicate interpretive disputes. This may lead to the next stages, however, certain factors act as filters to prevent or hinder the full emergence of (4) case law or hindering case law from becoming (5) the basis for further interpretive disputes resulting in triadic rulemaking.

Consider briefly some of these factors. Danish law in particular provides an excellent filter for the prevention of dissemination of rulemaking case law. From its creation, the Danish Supreme Court functioned under a ban against publishing the reasoning of judgements. The ban on reporting was only gradually lifted. Still only a fraction of the opinions of the learned opinions are published and reported. This can be very easily be observed by comparing cases from the Danish Højesteret to similar cases form the Norwegian Høyesterett. Danish reporting of judgements is mostly long on the narrative and seemingly "without any wish to state the law as principally as possible."[52] Furthermore, prevailing legal ideology emphasised the illegitimacy of constitutions as the metaphysical workings of the dead[53] and that constitutional judicial review was consequently democratically illegitimate.

Constitutional developments in a quasi-federal legal order can be represented thus:

Figure F: the Developments of Quasi-Federal Constitutional Judicial Review

(1)	(2)	(3)	(4)	(5)	
Nat. State >	Supranat. Norm >	Supranat. Court >	Case Law >	Triadic Rulemaking	**A**
Nat. State >	Interm. Law >	National Courts >	Case Law >	Triadic Rulemaking	**B**

On the upper parallel **A**, by a sovereign external act (1) a nation state accedes to (2) a supra-national norm that (often inadvertently) becomes judiciable and legally supreme within its substantive scope. Furthermore, the norm provides for (3) a court of law to adjudicate interpretive disputes concerning the norm. This leads to (4) case law that (5) becomes the basis for further interpretive disputes and result in triadic rulemaking, norm shifting through the process of third party dispute resolution.

On the lower parallel **B**, by a constitutional internal act (1) a nation state enacts (2) an intermediate law, implementing the supranational norm, that (often inadvertently) becomes judiciable and legally supreme within its substantive scope. Furthermore, the intermediate law, as all statutes, can be brought before (3) the courts of law to adjudicate interpretive disputes concerning the intermediary law. This leads to (4) case law that (5) becomes the basis for further interpretive disputes and result in triadic rulemaking.

The current West-Nordic situation seen from the point of view of the citizen wanting to challenge a law is an amalgamation of the previous figures:

52. Preben Stuer Lauridsen *Om ret og retsvidenskab* Gyldendal (1994) 145.
53. On the "dead" view Smith (1993) 324.

Figure G: The Developments of Quasi-Federal West-Nordic CJR

(1)	(2)	(3)	(4)	(5)	
Nat. State >	Supranat. Norm >	Supranat. Court >	Case Law >	Triadic Rulemaking	**A**
Nat. State >	Interm. Law >	National Courts >	Case Law >	Triadic Rulemaking	**B**
Nat. State >	Constit. Norm >	National Courts >	|F| Case Law	|F| T. Rulemaking	**C**

On the **A** parallel (1), a nation state accedes to (2) a supra-national norm that becomes judiciable and legally supreme within its substantive scope. The norm provides for (3) a court of law to adjudicate disputes. This leads to (4) case law and (5) triadic rulemaking through third party dispute resolution.

On **B** the parallel (1), a nation state enacts (2) an intermediate law, implementing the supranational norm, that becomes judiciable and legally supreme within its substantive scope. (3) The courts of law adjudicate disputes. This leads to (4) case law and (5) triadic rulemaking.

On the **C** parallel (1), a nation state enacts (2) a constitutional document that becomes judiciable and legally supreme within its substantive scope. The constitution provides for (3) courts of law to adjudicate but certain factors act as filters to hinder (4) case law and/or (5) triadic rulemaking.

When it comes to the techniques and results of review, courts can both set aside and re-interpret. Eivind Smith uses this graphic illustration on the Retroactive Clause of the Norwegian Constitution.[54]

Figure H: Techniques and Effects of Judicial Review

	Re-interpretation	Setting aside
Principle	x	
Provision	x	X

The figures shows how a constitutional principle will likely not lead to the overruling of an inferior instrument but can be used to justify re-interpretation, amending the instrument through interpretation to fit with the

---

54. Smith (1993) 101.

principle. A constitutional provision is more likely to lead to either of these techniques being used but presumably more likely to lead to the latter.

Figure I: Dynamic Techniques and Effects of Judicial Review

		Re-interpretation	Other effect	Setting aside	Restricting
Principle, Provision, Discovery	+ Dynamic	X	X	x	
	÷ Dynamic	(x)	(x)	(x)	x

The figure shows how constitutional principles, provisions, or 'discovered' fundamental principles[55] will lead to different techniques and effects pending the dynamic developments in that particular jurisdiction. If the dynamic development is positive or expansive ("+ Dynamic"), the effect may be re-interpretation or setting aside, or it may take on various other techniques that the different polities develop. If the dynamic development is negative or contractive ("÷ Dynamic"), the various techniques will fade, even to the point where the court is essentially over-looking or restricting the Constitution as a source of law.

Figure J: Restrictive or Expansive Dynamics

Interpretive traditions	*Jurisdiction*	*Ideology*
Dynamically expansive	European (from around 1960)	(Post)-Modern rights
Legalistic, dynamically restrictive	Danish (until around 1990)	Parliamentary-traditional
Selectively dynamically expansive	West-Nordic (presently)	Substantive rights
Dynamically expansive	Norwegian (before 1900)	Natural rights-traditional

55. Among the creative techniques of control used by courts in review, finding fundamental principles as yet unknown is classic, for instance privacy in the US, right to life in Germany and fundamental principles in France, Alec Stone Sweet "Constitutional Politics in France and Germany" in *On Law, Politics and Judicialization* (2002a) 189-90, 195.

Figure J is developed from a model by late Danish scholar Henrik Zahle.[56] The figure illustrates *interpretive techniques* that are or were used in various jurisdictions in different periods. Interestingly, Norway (as will be demonstrated) has changed interpretive paradigms several times and Denmark at least once. West-Nordic law now depends on two different traditions.

Nordic and European Developments in Particular

The West-Nordic Constitutions do not address the issue of constitutional judicial review directly. They do not have explicit provisions awarding preeminence to the 'general will' of parliamentary statutes, and they do not establish clear review authority.

Central- to West-Nordic tradition is the enormous reverence for "the lawgiver" ("lovgiver" in modern Danish) a concept apparently used since medieval times ("legifer" in old Danish,) "stemming from contemporary European legislative ideology."[57] The reference (and deference) is very rarely to people, nation, or majority; the singular *lawgiver* is given this respect, irrespectively of changing majorities or circumstances. This is even more interesting given that drafting new legislation has been the province of the central administration since medieval times.[58]

Constitutional judicial review in the West-Nordic countries is rather opaque due to a number of factors most notably that judgements have not been available for extensive periods even in the democratic era and only in limited form.[59] Even in later years, the legal reasoning of the Icelandic and Danish Courts have remained short and summary and thus inaccessible and obscure in the field of constitutional law with even the Norwegian reasoning being somewhat guarded.

The relative strength in all Scandinavian countries of textbooks and preparatory works as meta-sources of law coupled with a certain tradition of departmentalism that lets Parliament decide the constitutionality of its Acts for itself leaves constitutional case law as a strange subset of law that may (at times) be disregarded both in form and in substance. We have already heard

---

56. Zahle (1997).
57. Tamm (2005) 107.
58. Ibid. 153.
59. Ragnhildur Helgadóttir writes, "... *treaties in general carried great authority in Nordic law at the time. That was due to a number of factors, including the fact that Danish and Norwegian Supreme Court opinions were not published until late in the 19th century, the opinions' inaccessibility and, perhaps, remnants of the distrust of precedent that characterised the absolute monarchy.*" Helgadóttir (2006) 26.

the point made on "Extreme American Teaching."[60] Nordic law may thus not entirely deserve a self-understanding as "legal thinking that is more *pragmatic* (lacking formalism, deductive and scholarly nature, i.e. not so-called Juristenrecht."[61] Rather, there is an informal deference to the lawgiver.

Historically, the West-Nordic countries were ruled by the conglomerate monarchy centred in Copenhagen in Denmark and thus most often referred to as Denmark and Danish, though it further comprised several German states, at times Sweden, and even Baltic polities. For our purposes, the relevant evolution of law starts at the time when absolutism gives way to a conflicting array of constitutionalism, democracy, and nationalism. The three nation states of Norway, Denmark, and Iceland are forged and then spun off from this conglomerate polity, as are the emerging lands of Greenland and the Faroe Islands, all of which share 'Danish law' as base of their legal-cultural tradition[62] and nineteenth century constitutional language as their superior normative provisions.

Like the United States, the West-Nordic countries emerged as constitutional polities without an explicit answer to the question of how to deal with allegedly unconstitutional instruments. Absolutist tradition, political ideology, and constitutional role models thus had to slug it out in a tug-of-war over the issue. Like in much of Western Europe, the West-Nordic countries experienced and profound constitutional change from clear division of power to parliamentarism. This was called *negative parliamentarism* in the case of all the West-Nordics, meaning that the executive governments must not have a majority of Parliament against it. This change occurred contrary to clear constitutional provisions through intense constitutional strife and was unsettled for decades before being variously codified in later constitutional amendments. The prevailing tendency following the advent of parliamentarism was to allow the 'common will' as expressed by parliamentary statutes to prevail in case in determining constitutionality. Parliamentarism has integrated the political branches "in a way that makes an active role by the courts less likely."[63] When Western Europe after the Second World War turned towards various federation schemes to restore constitutionalism, establish integration, and protect human rights, the West-Nordic countries initially moved in the opposite direction with Iceland pursuing sovereignty and independence, Norway remaining outside the European Communities (later Union) and

---

60. Quoted in Koch (2002) 24.
61. Husa (2002) 174.
62. Tamm (2005) 215.
63. Smith (1993) 18.

Denmark not sharing the feeling that unrestricted parliamentarism had failed during the War.

Thus, the West-Nordic countries face the post-modern world with their constitutional order unravelling. Somewhat unwillingly and unknowingly, they are becoming federated to systems where judicial review is a core component. Somewhat reluctantly, they are having second thoughts about both departmental constitutionalism and the 'rule of statute.' Somewhat perplexed, the legal milieu is having to reconsider its position on case law in general and constitutional judicial review in particular.

Following the Second World War, two different reactions to the conflicts between nations and gross mistreatments of insular minorities led to an unexpected upsurge in judicial review. The creation of the European Communities, later European Union, and the European Convention of Human Rights resulted, to some degree unexpectedly, in the creation of two quasi-federal regimes. Unlike other international regimes, these both had clearly worded judiciable provisions, including crucially individual rights. In addition, both created superior courts to adjudicate disputes and both courts developed doctrines that effectively made them the super-supreme courts adjudicating the two quasi-constitutions. The member states remained sovereign and free to leave these arrangements, but as long as they stayed, there was no escaping the constitutional judicial review of these institutions. For the West-Nordic countries, these implications probably contributed to Norway and Iceland remaining outside the EU. However, the EFTA and EEA regimes that they joined have some of the same quasi-federal properties, and both Norway and Iceland with Denmark joined the ECHR. A clear manifestation of the new legal reality is the prominent marble plaque displayed in the Supreme Court Building in Oslo – giving equal treatment in aesthetic physical display to Old Norse Law, the 1814 Constitution, and human rights.[64]

Meanwhile, for various reasons, many European countries, including Italy, Spain, Germany, and France turned to judicial review to an extent previously unseen. The factors that triggered judicial review included new written constitutions, superior status human rights, federal arrangements, and less scholarly resistance. Most intriguingly, France, who had been the die hard stronghold of the 'general will' and opposition to case law, established a court-like constitutional council, initially to supervise the constitution that increased the powers of the president and did not contain any human rights clauses.[65]

---

64. Stephan Tschudi-Madsen *Norges Høyesterett* Aschehoug (1998) 137.
65. John Bell *French Constitutional Law* Oxford University Press (2001).

Through a series of intriguing developments, the council developed one of the most intense case-law-based judicial review systems yet known. Moreover, the regular courts, still formally barred from applying the constitution, have developed their own practise of reviewing statutes based on higher status statutes and case law. Elsewhere, the Eastern European countries emerged from behind the iron curtain and established their own forms of strong judicial review.

This has also meant that: "the process of *constitutionalizing* of European law has not only begun, it is irreversible."[66]

Turning the focus back on the West-Nordic countries, the superiority and influence of supra-national courts have initiated a process towards greater scrutiny of legislation and changing style of legal reasoning.

In the Baltics, constitutional judicial review of legislation with courts having the last word on constitutional interpretation was not explicitly enacted as parts of the constitutional revival following the collapse of communism. As should be expected, however, it soon presented itself in concrete controversies. Egidijus Kuris sums it up thus: "None of these countries explicitly mentions constitutional interpretation *per se* as a function entrusted to the courts. Like the US Supreme Court in Marbury, the Constitutional Courts of Latvia, Lithuania, and Estonia have self-assumed the function of constitutional interpretation, sometimes openly stating that it is for the court to interpret the constitution."[67]

The constitutional revival of the Baltics created a new vocabulary for political discourse and provided the basis for judicialization of politics. Estonia probably had the strongest tradition of constitutionalism, legality, and justice. In the words of Liia Hänni: "I would even say, justice has been our religion. Even the harsh totalitarian regime could not extinguish what could be termed "a cult of justice.""[68] The institutions of Legal Chancellor and Court of Constitutional Review have particularly worked to refine and clarify the Constitution and the powers of the other institutions, the Estonian Legal Chancellor may hear interpellations from parliamentarians, thus providing "one more channel of dialogue."[69] Especially, the procedure of interpellation (recourse) to the Legal Chancellor by opposition lawmakers has forced the ruling coali-

---

66. Stone Sweet (2000) 1.
67. Egidijus Kuris "Judges as Guardians of the Constitution: "Strict" or "Liberal". Interpretation?" in *The Constitution as an Instrument of Change* (2003) 193.
68. Liia Hänni "Constitutional Arguments in Political Decision-Making: Estonia" in *The Constitution as an Instrument of Change* (2006) 56.
69. Hänni (2006) 61.

tion to defend its proposals and actions in light of constitutional principles. Constitutional case law, including the practice of the Legal Chancellor as well as recourse to fundamental principles such as legitimate expectation and equality, has become the "gold reserve of the political debates held in the Riigikogu."[70]

In Latvia, the new Constitution has likewise become a very potent political weapon.[71] Similarly in Lithuania, where: "It is noteworthy that constitutional arguments have a profound effect on political culture and political language. Interpretation by the Constitutional Court and the way the Court argues become examples to be followed as well a goal for political discussions. If politicians want the Constitutional Court to settle their dispute, they have to learn how to remodel their political dispute into a legal one. That way, ideological disputes are turned into constitutional disputes."[72]

The Two Ideal Types

There appear to be two main ideal types of liberal-democratic constitutions that permeate legal writings, judgements, and political opinions. The first may be called the *legislative supremacy* constitutional model, the second the *higher law* constitutional model.[73]

Either the superior norms are adjudicated by some instance or they will remain dependant on the good will of the majority.[74]

The most obvious arguments for judicial review are usually centred on the superior status of constitutional norms and the need to abide the highest law. As justiarius Lasson put it: "if you cannot simultaneously apply both Basic

---

70. Ibid. 61.
71. Gunars Kusins "Constitutional Arguments in Political Decision-Making: Latvia" in *The Constitution as an Instrument of Change* (2003) 68.
72. Andrius Kubilius "Constitutional Arguments in Political Decision-Making: Lithuania" in *The Constitution as an Instrument of Change* (2003) 71.
73. Stone Sweet (2000) 20-21.
74. Bernhard Gomard writes, "*Restraint is, of course, natural when considering whether the state's highest authorities have remained faithful to the provisions in the Basic Law regarding their organisation and operations. Another question is if it is desirable continuously in line with court practice so far to consider the provisions regarding freedoms or human rights as flexible standards, which are not normally taken into consideration as data in interpretation or more free creation of law, and which are hardly ever seen as violated by any legislation that can muster a majority in the Folkething, so that the protection of the individual and minorities, which is inherent in these provisions, to a large extent becomes dependant on the good will of the majority.*" Bernhard Gomard "Et retspolitisk program for dommerskabt ret" in Højesteret 1661-1986 G.E.C. Gads Forlag (1986).

Law and Statute Law, you must prefer the former."[75] The most obvious counter arguments focus on the superior power of the people's elected representatives and the need to abide by the people's will (as expressed by elections of said representatives). As Bickel puts it, "judicial review constitute[s] control by an unrepresentative minority of an elected majority."[76]

The counter-argument to the counter-majoritarian angle is that a legally relevant constitution is an instrument for change whose principles the majority may endorse although elections may lead to specific or incidental violations of those principles. When courts point out that aspects of a certain popular policy actually infringes constitutional principles, at least partially, the majority may well pause, see the point and amend its ways. Thus, there may be "good reasons for pointing out that weakening the weight of constitutional arguments may equally be corrupting the constitution's potential as an instrument of political action."[77]

Writers typically follow one of two approaches that seem to divide into the *legalistic* and the *equitable* methods. The first path implies taking a strict and textual or impartial stand, sticking to what is formal law. The second path implies taking a balanced hermeneutic stand, trying to solve conflicts for the best.

Interestingly, the legalistic approach gave rise to judicial review in both the United States and Norway; the first two countries on each side of the Atlantic to have judicial review arise from judgements. The words of Chief Justice Marshall and Chief Justice Lasson are remarkably similar in this respect. Furthermore, their wording fits rather neatly with ideal of the judge simply announcing the law (including supreme law) as Hamilton, for instance, put it in Federalist 78.[78]

---

75. *Wedel-Jarlsberg* (6 UFL (1866-67) 165) 172.
76. Alexander M. Bickel writes, "*The root difficulty is that judicial review is a counter-majoritarian force in our system. There are various ways of sliding over this ineluctable reality [claiming to be] enforcing, in behalf of "the people," the limits that they have ordained for the institutions of a limited government, deny[ing] that judicial review constitute[s] control by an unrepresentative minority of an elected majority.*" Alexander M. Bickel *The Least Dangerous Branch. The Supreme Court at the Bar of Politics* Yale University Press (1986) 16.
77. Smith (2003a) 23.
78. Publius (Hamilton) writes: "*[In a republic [the standard of good behaviour for the continuance in office of the judicial magistracy] is a no less excellent barrier to the encroachment and oppression of the representative body. The judiciary, from the nature of its functions, will always be the least dangerous. The complete independence of the courts of justice is peculiarly essential in a limited Constitution. Limitations of*

This illustrates the paradox of democratic constitutionalism. Is the general will best expressed in the constitution or in the statute? Claiming that the multitudes of legislative instruments somehow follow from the general will is somewhat stretched and, arguably, if any law is within the power of the people to grasp and support it may be the constitution. Equally arguably, however, constitutions are often very old and abstractly stated, far removed from present-day legislation by representatives that have actually faced the voting electorate. (Suggesting the balanced solution of extensively using referenda and electing judges is usually a non-starter in polite scholarly discussion).

As we shall explain below, the reason why the legalistic approach, counter-intuitively perhaps, led to or justified, judicial review is because of a clear rule-to-rule conflict. The more difficult task for the judge is to consider the situation where the constitutional provision or norm in question has the characteristics of standard, especially a vague one. If the constitution properly ratified calls for equality[79] or freedom of expression, what is the judge to when faced with statutory bans on contraceptives or racist views when these bans appear unequal or restrictive?[80] Unsurprisingly, judges often have to take into account "other considerations"[81]

What judicial review can do at its best is to ensure the wider constitutional discourse through its constitutional dialogue with the legislature or other constitutional bodies. Especially taking the view that constitutions contain conflicting principles that need to be weighed against one another and suggesting that the legislative process has failed in considering certain principles or may have weighed them wrongly can create dialogue. Judicial review can through a discourse work for "society's and the citizen's best if for example parliament asserts its position and scrutinizes better what laws and resolutions that it sanctions really entail."[82]

---

this kind can be preserved in practice no other way than through the medium of courts of justice, whose it must be to declare all acts null and void. Without this, all the reservations of particular rights or privileges would amount to nothing.]" Publius (Hamilton) "Federalist No. 78: The Judiciary Department" in *The Federalist Papers. Mentor edition* (1999) 434-35.

79. The concept of equality is very often under-theorised Michael C. Dorf "The Unanimous Supreme Court Decision in The Iowa Gambling Case; When Is a Difference Also Inequality?" *FindLaw's Writ* (2003).
80. See such cases as *Griswold* and *Jersild.*
81. Dr. RV. Bergens Tidende (Rt. 1994-0348) pr. Judge Backer.
82. Fredrik Sterzel "Ett kvartsekel efter "det författningslösa halvseklet": Har Sverige nu en författning?" in *Grundlagens makt. Konstitutionen som politiskt redskap och som rättslig norm* SNS författningsprojekt (2002) at 95.

Every arrangement of constitutional review, including judicial review, will have its inherent costs.[83] When exercising judicial review, some middle ground might be sought out, either by procedural limitation or in limiting the substantive range but whatever model is chosen, say reinforcing the representative elements of government by focusing on upholding procedural constitutional provisions, although it is likely prone to attacks from some quarters.[84]

As indicated by the focus on *constitutions as law* (trumping statutes) or *statutes as general will* (trumping constitutions), the Nordic debate has overwhelmingly focused on the philosophical rule-against -rule clashes between these two sources of law. The subtleties of standard-against-standard[85] conflicts have hitherto been rather neglected in Scandinavian theory. A number of discussions seem to miss the point because this distinction is not realised or not sufficiently theorised. Smith opines that "an important side of the courts' task is to apply firm provisions in light of changing ideological, social and economic circumstances, [especially concerning] "standards" that leave to the courts to provide the further content of the discretionary words and phrases."[86] This insight, that constitutions are often deliberately open-ended and include a popularly sanctioned mandate for the courts to develop constitutional law in a discourse with the public and their representatives conducted through judgements, legislation, and elections, providing 'further content' to

---

83. Cass R. Sunstein *One Case at a Time – Judicial Minimalism* Harvard (1999). Mark Tushnet "Following The Rules Laid Down: A Critique of Interpretivism and Neutral Principles" 96 *Harvard Law Review* (2004) 781. Eric M. Fink "Post-Realism, or the Jurisprudential Logic of Late Capitalism: A Socio-Legal Analysis of the Rise and Diffusion of Law and Economics" 55 *Hastings Law Journal* (2004) 931.
84. Johan Hart Ely writes, "The elaboration of a representation-reinforcing theory of judicial review by insisting that it can appropriately concern itself only with questions of participation, and not with the substantive merits of the political choice under attack. In saying that so clearly, I have set myself up for a familiar form of attack. " You'd limit courts to the correction of failures of representation and wouldn't let them second-guess the substantive merits? Why, that means you'd have to uphold a law that provided for_____!" John Hart Ely *Democracy and distrust. A Theory of Judicial Review* Harvard University Press (1980) at 181.
85. Kathleen M. Sullivan "The Justices of Rules and Standards" 106 *Harvard Law Review* (1992) 22 For a slightly more entertaining approach to the rules and standards discussion see Leo Katz "Playing By, With, Around, Under, and Above the Rules: An Essay For and About Fred Schauer" in *Rules and Reasoning – Essays in Honour of Fred Schauer* Hart Publishing (1999).
86. Smith (1993) 337.

constitutions, is probably the best available way of reconciling the two ideal types.

As opposition to constitutional judicial review has been historically dominant in the Nordic countries, we shall look a little closer at the argument that the People or their Parliament must be sovereign in matters constitutional. The opposition to judicial review is often based on the idea that statute represents the general will, a concept developed by philosopher Rousseau.[87] Less to the point, the view expressed by Montesquieu that the judge must only 'express the law' ("la bouche qui pronounce les paroles de la loi"[88]) is taken to mean the favouring of literal application of statute over any form of judicial rulemaking, including application of constitution. (Actually, Montesquieu's views of the judge are best understood as being favouring an independent incorruptible judiciary that the Executive cannot reach, including lay judges drawn from the people with very limited discretion, thus prompting clear and exhaustive legislation.[89] Thus, Montesquieu was more anti-discretion than anti-review. John Locke[90] whose writings are more to the point on separation of powers also seems to have overlooked judicial review and was likewise relying more on lay than learned, rather juries than judges).

The French Constitution Art 66(2) sums up the traditionally continental view accordingly, "The judicial authority, guardian of individual liberty, shall ensure the observance of this principle as provided by statute." Note the phrase '*as provided by statute;*' French tradition sees the functional separation of legislature and judiciary as fundamental but the substantive determination of '*individual liberty*' is by the scheme of things left to Parliament to determine in the form of general statutory law. However, the creation of the Constitutional Council proved to be advent of enforceable restraints on plenary powers.[91]

However, French constitutional law, like Nordic constitutional law, can only be understood as the product of the constitutional text and later developments seen in hermeneutic perspective. French law nowadays as both ab-

---

87. Tamm (2005) 233.
88. Smith (1993) 53.
89. Tamm (2005) 245.
90. "Locke's *Second Treaties* was roundly panned by critiques, who saw it as a flimsy pretext to bring back the characters from the *First Treaties*." Jon Stewart *America (the Book)* Warner Books (2004) 7.
91. Bell (2001) 139.

stract constitutional review as performed by the Constitutional Council[92] and review based on the semi-constitutional status of human rights legislation.[93]

Realising that French constitutional law changed dramatically as a result of very minor institutional amendments and subsequent developments helps us to clear away two profound misunderstandings. First, that legislative supremacy is an integral part of the philosophical foundations of democratic constitutionalism. It is not, formal and substantive alike may fit well with democratic constitutionalism. Second, that basic rights present themselves as easily applicable and unambiguous rules. They are not, taken seriously they will require difficult value-laden decisions.

Usually, the only philosopher quoted[94] by Nordic lawyers is Montesquieu, whose ideas are paraphrased to favour a separate but restrained judiciary. Actually, Montesquieu was not addressing judicial review in his voluminous ramblings on this and that. His 31 Books on the Spirit of the Laws is sometimes like Politica by Aristotle, sometimes a strange weather report, and in its most celebrated part it is haphazardly plagiarising John Locke[95] with idealised misrepresentations of the English constitution and its supposedly three branches of government.[96] He described the executive as Locke did the federal branch, and the judicial as Locke did the executive branch, revealing that he contemplated balance of power neither originally nor profoundly. This badly researched plagiarism prompted a translator's note in the 1770 Danish translation. (Interestingly the only Danish translation available before 1998, indicating that De l'Esprit was more known from reference than reading.).[97] Montesquieu was generally rationalising a system of natural law piecemeal from various observations, legends, and prejudices. For instance viewed it as against nature and reason for women to head households; they could however, head empires, moderate or despotic regimes, especially in cold climates where their late maturity and temperance would give them an edge, but naturally not oriental regimes, where even slight emancipation would lead to

---

92. Stone Sweet (2002a).
93. Stéphanie Lagouette and Lassen, Eva Maria "Menneskerettigheder i forfatningen: Billeder af fransk og dansk forfatningshistorie" in *Grundloven og menneskerettigheder* Jurist- og Økonomforbundets Forlag (1997).
94. Stýrisskipanarálitið 49, iko, A3.
95. Gorm Toftegaard Nielsen "Magtadskillelseslæren – er domstolenes uafhængighed en menneskeret eller en dommer-ret?" in *Grundloven og menneskerettigheder* Jurist- og Økonomforbundets Forlag (1997) 313.
96. Book 11m Chapter 6, Danish translation Charles Louis de Secondant de Montesquieu *Om Lovenes Ånd* G.E.C. Gads Forlag (1998) 167. Tamm (2005) 241
97. Toftegaard Nielsen (1997) 313.

"streams of blood."[98] If any, his ideas of legal supremacy were those of the natural order under given circumstance; thus, the only philosopher known to most Nordic lawyers supported the opposite of legislative supremacy.

The second misunderstanding means that many do not realise to what extent judges and others similarly positioned make policy choices, that "justices, like presidents and congressional representatives, make policy choices according to their own policy preferences, given institutional constraints."[99]

Often, the power of reviewing bodies to decide 'within institutional constraints' is assumed to be only an American phenomenon. Actually, the older American tradition, possibly a common West-Germanic tradition, as that of popular review based on long held principles.[100] *Judicial* review was largely seen as illegitimate, as when a number of Rhode Islands' judges did: "disclaim and totally disavow any the least power or authority, or the appearance thereof, to contravene or controul the constitutional laws of the State."[101] Americans in line with European enlightenment philosophers favoured juries as the ultimate arbiters of law as well as facts.[102] Judicial review was invented and developed in America around the same time as in Norway and is today much more restrained than many European variants.

Thus, supremacy of principles over positive laws is arguably more European than American. To better understand the change that constitutions un-

---

98. Book 7, Chapter 17 and Book 16, Chapters 2 and 9. Danish translation, Montesquieu (1998) 120, 282, and 287. Apparently Denmark's own Ludvig Holberg, natural law professor and renowned playwright, took a more stringent view, Tamm (2005) 248.

99. Stone Sweet (2000) 26.

100. Larry D. Kramer provides a fascinating example, "*July 2, 1798. During a debate in Congress over whether to adopt the Alien Act – which gave the President unilateral power to imprison or deport aliens, even in peacetime – Edward Livingston reproached its supporters. "If we are ready to violate the constitution we have sworn to defend, will the people submit to our unauthorized acts? Will the states sanction our usurped powers? Sir, they ought not to submit. They would deserve the chains which these measures are for them if they do not resist." Responses to Livingston's admonitions were immediate and widespread. Public meetings denounced the Alien and Sedition Acts and declared them null and void. Federalists responded by pleading that judgement of constitutionality be left for the courts, a position their opponents fiercely denied. To say that "a decisions as to constitutionality of all legislative acts, lies solely with the judiciary, is removing the cornerstone on which our federal compact rests; it is taking from the people the ultimate sovereignty." Larry D. Kramer The People Themselves – Popular Constitutionalism and Judicial Review* Oxford University Press (2004) at 4.

101. Kramer (2004) 68.

102. Ibid. 3.

dergo without their formal amendment procedures being observed,[103] in particular the morphing rights provisions,[104] Scandinavians should read more American sources and get better informed.

Furthermore, Nordics favouring 'pure' and 'positivist' legal theory need to understand that thinkers like Kelsen did not by their writings negate the existence of judicial review but rather provided us with an early insight into the legislative functions that judges would be wielding if allowed to perform judicial review. To paraphrase, if you want constitutions as positive super law, you might sensibly recognise the legislative aspects of review and deliberately design the institutional restraints, for instance creating special constitutional courts and preferring abstract a priori review as in many European countries today.[105]

To return to Nordic theory, Eivind Smith quotes Jens Arup Seip as being typical of those that saw judicial review as necessarily antiparliamentarian. According to Seip, "A study will show that the right of review was made up to be used in the political game. In its origin and in its first effect it was politically reactionary and clearly antiparliamentarian in character. It was a stick on purpose thrown into the wheel of democracy, a last-ditch effort, behind the back of the Storthing, by the dethroned class of civil servants."[106] The simple Seipian view does not withstand scrutiny but seems to have led its own life, distorting the proper understanding of the history of review. Even the 'stick' metaphor appears ill fitting, as "It is seldom wise to set a wheel in motion without retaining a minimum of mechanisms to stay the course and – if necessary – to reduce the speed."[107] Nordic theory must also recognise that review can be based on "superior norms outside the Basic law [e.g.] "international law," including newer development in court practice."[108]

Thus ends our discussion of the two ideals of the judiciary's role in democracy. Both are wrong if they claim that there is the only one compatible with democracy. Actually, you can have democracy without review as well as

---

103. One intriguing discussion the Amar engages in of relevance to Scandinavians is if should consider the constitutions amended by other means than those formally available, see Akhil Reed Amar "The Concent of the Governed: Constitutional Amendment Outside Article V" 94 *Columbia Law Review* (1994) 457 and Joanne Mariner "The Supreme Court, The Constitution, and Precedent:Some Comments on the Amars' Analysis" *FindLaw's Writ* (2003).
104. Amar (1998).
105. Shapiro and Stone Sweet (2002c).
106. Smith (1993) 13.
107. Ibid. 14.
108. Ibid. 115.

with review – and even review without democracy or review without courts or judges. Likewise, you may have an independent judiciary without extending it powers to perform constitutional review. Importantly also, review by courts or other institutions are likely to arise more as consequential developments where other choices are made and constitutional review comes to be in ensuing events. However, review is double-edged and does not only protect against overbearing legislators, it becomes a form of rulemaking of its own.

Lawyers had best stay away from choosing either ideal as their learned opinion. Rather, a number of variants of constitutional review are possible and have their consequences. Lawyers must study them all, in particular be able to see where their own jurisdiction is at any given moment.

The Dynamics
of Judicial Review

Understanding the Dynamics of Judicial Review

Law is a dynamic phenomenon. The dynamic properties make 'law' a product of the interaction between various legal sources and the people competing within the framework that the law governs. Danish scholar Henrik Zahle explains that, "The law is created through practice, as it is by the legal decision in the actual situation that the state of the law is determined. Often, the decision-making [person] must choose, the judge for instance has to pick a side in an old discussion of interpretation that is decided by the court making its decision. In such situations, what is *law* is not *found*, it is created."[1] This insight tells us that law is *choice* within a certain framework, "and by recognising this creative aspect of the legal decision and thereby in the legal practice, it must also be recognised that e.g. "Danish law" or "EU law" is not something that is existing as a given and determined entity but something that is shaped day by day and step by step."[2]

When reading West-Nordic literature, there is sometimes a feeling that the opposite view is prevalent. References to US law, to EU law, to ECHR law and other systems of law seem often to attribute legal dynamics, especially in a court and case law context, as particular to those 'foreign systems of law,' alien to West-Nordic law. However, the better view is that the polycentric, practice-driven, dynamic properties of law are also attributable to West-Nordic law, in particular our field of interest, West-Nordic constitutional law.[3] Even latter day Scandinavian positivists are

---

1. Zahle (2005) 332.
2. Ibid. 333.
3. Henrik Zahle writes *"In my opinion, which I shall document further in the following, the usual understanding of the relationship between the European impulse and the Danish tradition is based on a fundamental misunderstanding concerning human rights. It is not alien to Danish tradition to use a dynamic style of interpretation and it*

now belatedly recognising the dynamics of law and the choices facing lawyers.[4]

Understanding the dynamics of case law is crucial. For some time, this has been understood when dealing with such systems of law as the ECHR, which "the ECHR Court interprets resolutely dynamically."[5] However, the full comprehension of dynamics, not just as an undercurrent but a way of dealing with dogmatic questions of law, is crucial to lawyers' (not least Nordic) giving their best view of the law as it stands; predicting the outcome of disputes is our subject in the following.

It may be in the interest of lawyers and part of their self-understanding to claim that law is constant and flows from sources that they are uniquely equipped to understand and that the methods of analysing other human institutions cannot be applied to law. "The lawyer scholar is still a lawyer. Lawyers are ... defenders of courts [that] rely for their institutional legitimacy on their reputation for independence and neutrality."[6] Accepting that courts have a choice as Zahle does, especially in the cases where there is doubt and dispute as to the best interpretation, means accepting that courts are to some degree making decisions about policy, "a group of men seeking to make good decisions about public policy."[7] However, even in the United States, often seen in Scandinavian conventional wisdom as the embodiment of political adjudication, this realisation has "[typically been grudging]."[8]

To Anglo-American lawyers, accepting law as 'created in practice' is probably easier than for Scandinavians, as judgements function as their meta-source of law but even lawyers of the common law tradition may think of cases and the 'case law' expressed by them as statements of what the law was all along, applied to a particular set of facts. The tendency to view good law as the kind of firm and longstanding practice that leads to inevitable results is understandable and probably as old as the study of law. However, research shows that even medieval law was "not static"[9] but subject to a dynamic dis-

---

is, therefore, not necessary to produce European impulses to leave the text of the Basic Law. The Danish tradition is, on the contrary, dynamic. The Danish dynamics have, however, consisted in limiting or restrictive interpretation." Zahle (1997) 363.

4.   Peter Blume "Juristen i det usikre retsystem" 84 *Juristen* (2002) 182 and Svend Gram Jensen "Om Lovfortolkningen, Retsbegrebet og Juridisk Metode" 84 *Juristen* (2002) 69.
5.   Rytter (2006) 61.
6.   Shapiro and Stone Sweet (2002b) 6.
7.   Ibid. 12.
8.   Ibid. 5.
9.   Tamm (2005) 96.

course. Nonetheless, valuing the constancy and predictability of law and denying the legitimacy of judges and other institutions to make law, may create the comfortable illusion that law is settled, easily predicted by lawyers, and ultimately found and inexorably applied by judges.

Yet, the dynamics of law and judicial rulemaking through the necessary choices are, inescapably, a universal phenomenon of human behaviour from Danish constitutional law[10] to international trade law,[11] from informal legal systems[12] to quasi-federal supranational structures.[13] Objecting to judicial rulemaking may be warranted in case of frequent policy changes or unprincipled amendment of black-letter-law. But the "objection, however, even if it has force against a court's retrospective change or overruling of clearly established law, seems quite irrelevant in hard cases since these are cases which the law has left incompletely regulated and where there is no known state of clear established law to justify expectations."[14]

The choice faced by judges in practice can lead to different dynamics, as noted by Zahle, "Danish dynamics have consisted in *limiting* or *restrictive* interpretation."[15] The choice facing judges is not *either* to make law instead of politicians *or* not to make law but rather *which* law they want to make, in favouring lawgiver over basic-law-giver, reconciling them, or clarifying either or both. As Dworkin puts it regarding American judgements finding laws unconstitutional, "the Court would have made law just as much if it had [refused to hold a statute unconstitutional]. It would have made law by establishing as a matter of precedent that the [relevant] clause does not reach that far."[16] Judges are a form of specialised third chamber of parliament whether they like it or not.[17]

Thus, understanding and predicting the dynamics of case law are a crucial skill for lawyers. This is so regardless of whether the dynamics are expansive, say reading increasingly more into ECHR human rights provisions, or restrictive, for instance disregarding, or limiting human rights provisions of the Danish Basic Law. The dynamics of constitutional law obviously depend on

10. Zahle (1997) 374.
11. Stone Sweet (2002b).
12. Stone Sweet (2002c) 56.
13. Alec Stone Sweet and Brunell, Thomas "The European Court and Integration" in *On Law, Politics and Judicialization* (2002).
14. H. L. A. Hart *The Concept of Law* Oxford University Press (1997) 276.
15. Zahle (1997) 363.
16. Dworkin (2002) 132.
17. Stone Sweet (2000) 204.

the extent of choice faced by the judge. The room for textual interpretation, the precedent already created, the access that interested parties have to contending the issue, as well as the constitutional setting, including federal elements, are among the factors that influence the dynamics. We have already in the section on the conditions of judicial review dealt with some of these factors.

Looking at constitutional text as a point of departure, some elements are worth remarking on. Legal standards will be by their nature more indeterminate than legal rules. ECHR standards referring to what is "necessary" invite a choice that refers back to the ideal types of democracy. As it stands, such an open-ended standard (in enforceable treaty or constitution) forbids anything that is not "necessary." An institution charged with ruling on the issue, assessing whether a statute is, at law, *necessary* has the basic choice between 're- strictive dynamics,' deferring to someone else (often a small transient elected majority not terribly focused on the issue) or 'expansive dynamics,' deciding necessity for itself (and thus to some degree overruling elected officials). In both cases, the standard of necessity will somehow be explained and developed, the central point being that its full meaning is not determinable beforehand and will most likely be gradually clarified – with or without you.

The "discussion of interpretation" that Zahle talks of is created by all sorts of uncertainties. In our constitutional context, the room for contention arises from the potentially numerous inconsistencies between constitutional and statutory texts. Both groups of texts raise their own interpretive issues and two texts that both can mean different things to different people at different times can obviously conflict on some points. This will be especially true, as differences in values and perceptions change. A Norwegian judge today may view the 1814 Basic Law differently than a judge back then; an Eastern European ECHR Judge may see freedom of the press in a different light than a Danish judge with no personal experience of censorship and overt state propaganda.

The dynamics set in motion these choices in law, especially if related issues are successively contended by interested parties, are best described by the theories on the judicialization of governance through the triad, developed by professor Alec Stone Sweet.[18]

We shall look at and adapt to our purposes this particular tool of political jurisprudence.

---

18. Alec Stone Sweet "Path Dependence, Precedent, and Judicial Power" in *On Law, Politics and Judicialization* (2002).

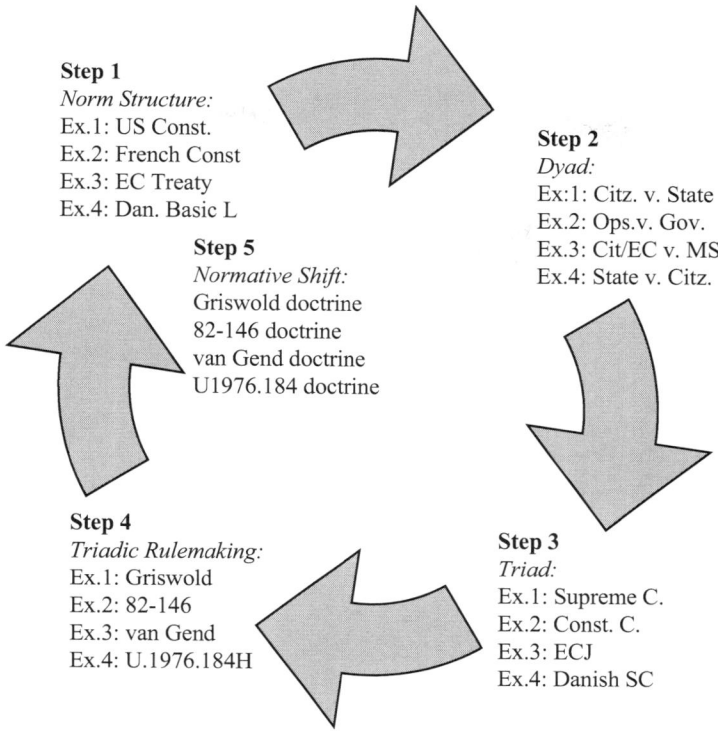

Step 1
Norm Structure:
Ex.1: US Const.
Ex.2: French Const
Ex.3: EC Treaty
Ex.4: Dan. Basic L

Step 2
Dyad:
Ex:1: Citz. v. State
Ex.2: Ops.v. Gov.
Ex.3: Cit/EC v. MS
Ex.4: State v. Citz.

Step 5
Normative Shift:
Griswold doctrine
82-146 doctrine
van Gend doctrine
U1976.184 doctrine

Step 4
Triadic Rulemaking:
Ex.1: Griswold
Ex.2: 82-146
Ex.3: van Gend
Ex.4: U.1976.184H

Step 3
Triad:
Ex.1: Supreme C.
Ex.2: Const. C.
Ex.3: ECJ
Ex.4: Danish SC

Figure K: Triadic Dynamics

Figure K illustrates the triadic dynamics.[19]

We shall now look closer at the examples contained in the previous figure.

---

19.   Stone Sweet (2000) 13.

Figure L: Triadic Dynamics – Examples Overview

	Step 1 Norm Structure	Step 2 Dyad – two opponents	Step 3 Triad – third party decides	Step 4 Triadic Rulemaking	Step 5 ... Shift in Norm Structure ...
Example 1	United States Constitution.	Citizen claim State violates federal Constitution	US Supreme Court decides case	US Supreme Court finds 'marital right of privacy'	Constitution now includes *privacy*
Example 2	French Constitution	Opposition claim Government violates Constitution	French Constitutional Council decides case	Constitutional Council uses 'declaration of human rights'	Constitution now contains *human rights*
Example 3	European Economic Community Treaty	Citizen claim State violates EC Treaty	European Court of Justice decides case	European Court finds EEC law has 'direct effects' & 'individual rights'	Treaty now has *direct effect, individual rights*
Example 4	Danish Basic Law	State prosecutes Citizen who claims unconstitutionality	Danish Supreme Court decides case	Court sees 'no hinder' to searches without prior warrant	Basic Law now is *no hinder* to disregarding rights

Example 1: The Dynamics of Griswold

The case ***Griswold v. Connecticut*** (381 U.S. 479 (1965)) arose in the State of Connecticut. Since the late 19th century, legislation in most states of the Union had restricted what can be termed as reproductive freedom.[20] In Connecticut, this meant a ban on prophylactics that could be used in having 'non-reproductive sexual acts,' it even meant that married couples were forbidden to use any drug or instrument that would prevent conception. Mr. Griswold, a director of Planned Parenthood, disregarded the law and helped people obtain contraceptives to avoid pregnancy. Along with a medical professor he was charged with being complicit to the crime; Griswold felt this was unduly restrictive and challenged the law. The law was already largely ignored but when contraception was offered freely to poor people in metropolitan clinics, catholic prosecutors were pressured to initiate proceedings especially around

---

20. Lucinda M Finley "The Story of Roe v. Wade: From a Garage Sale for Women's Lib, to the Supreme Court, to Political Turmoil" in *Constitutional Law Stories* (2004) 362.

election time; this gave the case a subtext of equality that may have been decisive.

Step 1. The Norm Structure. The United States Constitution contains a number of provisions on various aspects of the freedom of its citizen from interference from the federal government, clauses on equal protection, due process, self-incrimination, and 'other rights retained by the people.'[21] These freedoms have been gradually extended by case law to oblige the several States to respect these rights. The Constitution was, however, silent on both the particular issue of contraception (for married couples or otherwise) as well as being silent on the more abstract terms of "reproductive freedom" or "privacy" – or for that matter "government powers over procreation."

Step 2. The Dyad. Griswold and the State of Connecticut were both subject to the United States Constitution and Griswold could rely on the Constitution and its principles when the Connecticut government agents prosecuted his violation of the statute.

Step 3. The Triad. Connecticut and its agents were not persuaded by Griswold's arguments. The jurisdiction of the federal courts meant that Griswold could challenge the federal constitutionality of the statute in question in a forum not controlled by the State. Ultimately, the Unites States Supreme Court settled the matter by holding that "[Griswold and other] have standing to assert the constitutional rights of the married people. 2. The Connecticut statute forbidding use of contraceptives violates the right of marital privacy which is within the penumbra of specific guarantees of the Bill of Rights."[22]

Step 4. Triadic Rulemaking. However, the United States Supreme Court did not just hold this as a straightforward application of law, it did so on the reasoning that the case "concerns a relationship lying within the zone of privacy created by several fundamental constitutional guarantees."[23] One concurring Justice stressed that the ninth amendment had been enacted because James Madison and other founding fathers found that it might follow by implication that rights not mentioned would be insecure. For his part, "Although the Constitution does not speak in so many words of the right of privacy in marriage, I cannot believe that it offers these fundamental rights no protection."[24] One dissenting Justice, however, opined this was an "uncommonly silly law" but could find not find constitutional support for invalidating it.[25]

21. United States Constitution Amendments.
22. *Griswold v. Connecticut* main holding.
23. Ibid. per Justice Douglas (Opinion of the Court).
24. Ibid. per Justice Goldberg.
25. Ibid. per Justice Stewart.

The different opinions demonstrate how the decision was a matter of *choice in interpretation*. Of course, the decision was made within the institutional and factual limits of the case and the context of the United States Constitution – and all the judges sought respectfully to justify it by numerous references to earlier cases and preparatory work – but by choice and conscience, the Court discovered a general principle and a particular right.

Step 5. Shift in Normative Structure and Repeating the Process. Following *Griswold*, the doctrine of *privacy* (extended to the non-marital) was now a part of United States constitutional law. The primary norm was still the same Constitution but a shift in the norm structure had occurred and the "penumbra" of various clauses were found to contain a principle of privacy from which could be deduced at least the particular freedom of using contraceptives within marriage.

The shift in the normative structure led to further dyadic conflicts between citizen and States. Among the numerous cases, *Roe v. Wade* (410 U.S. 113 (1973)) represents one expansively dynamic shift of the norm structure. In that case, the principle of privacy was extended so that, "For the stage prior to approximately the end of the first trimester, the abortion decision and its effectuation must be left to the medical judgment of the pregnant woman's attending physician."[26] This right is, of course, not an obvious feature of the constitutional text but an extension of *Griswold* consistent with, but not necessarily deducible from, the discovered principle of privacy. Another extension was that of *Lawrence v. Texas* (000 U.S. 02-102 (2003)) that held a statute invalid when it sought to ban "individual decisions concerning the intimacies of physical relationships," (or "sodomy" *per* Justice Scalia) similarly based on privacy as form of protected liberty. Both cases discussed *Griswold* and other norm shifting cases.

The later cases have in common that the *Griswold* understanding of the Constitution becomes the normative basis for the dyadic dispute, the same courts have jurisdiction and decide the dispute based on the morphed constitutional norm. In doing so, the courts further shift the norm structure, often through fits and starts. For example, *Lawrence* overruled *Bowers v. Hardwick* (478 U.S. 186 (1986)) otherwise considered controlling on the point; the US Supreme Court thus decided in 1986 not to extend the principle to physical intimacies but some seventeen years later, with such laws becoming rarer, older and less consistently enforced, the Court was persuaded to further broaden the concept of privacy.

---

26. *Roe v. Wade* (410 U.S. 113 (1973)) holding 3(a).

Example 2: The Dynamics of CCD Case 82-146

The case *CCD Case 82-146 (1982)*[27] arose in the French Republic. France has had a volatile constitutional tradition ever since the late 18th century. The current constitutional structure is referred to as the Fifth Republic, as previous constitutional structures have broken down. The current Constitution was enacted in 1958 with the expressed intention of limiting constitutional review to a priori review of parliamentary instruments in order to "ensure a strong executive by keeping Parliament within its constitutional role," respecting a strong executive branch, particularly the President.[28]

The main innovation of the Fifth Republic was to strengthen the executive branch, President, Prime Minister, and Government vis-à-vis the legislative branch, Senate and Deputies. To this end, the Constitution provided for a Constitutional Council, to which President, Prime Minister, Speaker of the Senate, and Speaker of the House of Deputies could appeal statutes after their enactment by Parliament but prior to their promulgation and entry into force.[29] Constitutional review by a specialised Council was thus incidental to strengthening the executive.

The French Constitution true to the principle of statutes being the instrument of the general will,[30] has no provisions on human rights or other formal or substantive limitations on the power of government vis-à-vis the people or individuals. However, the Preamble of the Constitution refers both "to the Rights of Man and to the principles of national sovereignty as defined by the Declaration of 1789, confirmed and complemented by the Preamble to the Constitution of 1946."[31] (Fourth Republic).

Step 1. The Norm Structure. The French Constitution is silent on equality in general and in particular on the distribution of council seats among parties and among people of either sex in local elections. The majority Government proposed a statute providing for different principles of seat distribution for smaller and larger municipalities. Furthermore, the statute provided for at least 25 per cent of the candidates on municipal election lists to be of either sex; this was done to promote female participation in elections.

Step 2. The Dyad. The opposition disagreed with the governing coalition, alleging that different councils were treated differently and, furthermore, that

---

27. Cases are available at www.conseil-constitutionel.fr; in English on
    www.conseil-constitutionel.fr/langues/anglais/essential.htm
28. Bell (2001) 16, 19.
29. French Constitution, Article 46(5).
30. Declaration of Human and Civic Rights Article 6.
31. French Constitution, Preamble (1).

legal distinctions based on sex were inherently unequal treatment. This argument was raised in the Houses of Parliament.

Step 3. The Triad. When the coalition enacted the law despite the objections, the opposition alleged unconstitutionality. This would not have amounted to much in legal terms had it not been for the constitutional amendment that allowed sixty Members of either House to challenge a statute before the Constitutional Council.[32] Due to terms of office, the Council was largely appointed by the previous coalition, the current opposition, but functioned independently; neither party controlled and both were committed to respecting its decisions. The Council upheld the statute as to distribution of seats, as it was applied equally to all councils in the provided categories. However, on the gender requirements, it held that "The provisions of section 4 of the Act Amending the Electoral Code ... are unconstitutional." other parts of the Act were also declared unconstitutional whilst some parts were held constitutional and some issues not considered as rightly raised.

Step 4. Triadic Rulemaking. This was no straightforward application of the Constitution but required the Council to refer to "universal, equal, and secret" suffrage in Article 3 of the Constitution and "Article 6 of the Declaration of Human and Civic Rights: "All citizens, being ... equally eligible to all high offices ... without other distinction than that of their virtues and talents."[33] The Council then deduced that, "It is clear from a combined reading of these provisions that ... these constitutional principles preclude any division of persons entitled to vote or stand ... It follows that ... a distinction [made] between candidates on grounds of sex ... must be declared unconstitutional."[34] In typical French manner, this is considered self-evident and demonstrated in terse logical reasoning but there is no denying that the Council *made a choice* both in *discovering* the Declaration as the source of law and in its *interpretation* of the applicable principles.

Step 5. Shift in Normative Structure and Repeating the Process. The decision paved the way for a wide range of different claims and created a completely different constitutional culture in France. Since then almost all controversial legislative instruments have been challenged, including most budgets.[35] In *CCD Case 2001-454* (2002), the Council further refined its approach by holding that "The following are constitutional [said provisions] subject to

32. Stone Sweet (2002a) 189.
33. CCD Case 82-146 point 6.
34. Ibid. points 7 and 8.
35. Stone Sweet (2002a) 189.

the reservations set out in paras. 13 ... 24 and 25."[36] This enabled the Council despite the French tradition only to decide cases with a brief result to *explain the Constitution* through its reservations and thus create, in effect, binding constitutional precedent through case law. This inspired lower courts to en-force statutory rights as trumping other laws. Thus, an unenforceable 'small c' constitution without substantive constraints on government power became a 'capitol C' Constitution with expanding rights that can be forcefully relied on both in abstract controversies prior to promulgation of laws by the opposi-tion – and by individuals following when laws have come into force by rely-ing on the explanations of the Council and the priority awarded to human rights statutes.

Example 3: The Dynamics of van Gend en Loos

The case *van Gend en Loos v. Netherlands* (ECJ Case 22/62 (1963)) arose in the EEC Member State of the Netherlands. For ages, but especially since the 1930s, tariffs and legislation in most European States had restricted and hin-dered the free flow of goods, thereby reducing both freedom and welfare. In the Netherlands, this meant that import tariffs were placed on imports of chemical products. This happened despite the Netherlands joining the EEC ostensibly to cap and then to reduce duties and trade restrictions. When the customs nomenclature was amended, the product in question was placed in a different category and, in effect, burdened with a higher duty. The trading company of van Gend en Loos found this unduly restrictive and challenged the amended law. The case raised the wider issue of the effectiveness of EEC law, as Members States were already showing signs of giving in to protec-tionist pressure and were ignoring the EEC Treaty as much else international law.

Step 1. The Norm Structure. The European Economic Community Treaty proscribed new "customs duties and charges having equivalent effect."[37] What this meant was far from clear, however. Arguably, the Treaty was ex-pressing intentions of States that were relevant as political statements but would require active implementation to become effective; the States' being sovereign meant that non-compliance or delayed observance was a distinct option. In particular, re-categorising a product seemed to raise an interpretive issue that the Member States and its agencies were best placed to determine. The norm structure was thus in place but its relevance was unclear.

36. CCD Case 2001-454 main holding.
37. EEC Treaty Article 12.

Step 2. The Dyad. van Gend en Loos and the Member State of the Nether-lands were both subject to the EEC Treaty and the company could rely on the Treaty and its principles when the Netherlands government agents prosecuted their violation of the national trade regime.

Step 3. The Triad. The Netherlands and their agencies were not persuaded by van Gend's arguments. However, the jurisdiction of the European Court of Justice meant that van Gend could challenge the EEC compatibility of the laws in question in a forum that neither of them controlled. Ultimately, the European Court of Justice settled the matter by holding that "1. Article 12 of the Treaty establishing the European Economic Community produces direct effects and creates individual rights, which national courts must protect. 2. In order to ascertain ... regard must be had to the duties and charges actually ap-plied by the Member State in question at the date of the entry into force of the Treaty. 3. Such an increase can arise both from a re-arrangement of the tariff resulting in the classification of the product under a more highly taxed head-ing and from an increase [in rate]."[38]

Step 4. Triadic Rulemaking. The European Court of Justice did not just hold this as a straightforward application of law, rather it did so on the rea-soning that the EEC was "a new legal order of international law for the bene-fit of which the States have limited their sovereign rights."[39] This entailed that, "the spirit, the general scheme and the wording ... must be interpreted as producing direct effects and creating individual rights which national courts must protect."[40] The ECJ does not allow dissent and the Court has chosen the quaint French style of presenting an argument so it that appears necessarily to lead to the one unavoidable conclusion. However, the choice made is still clear as the case at hand and numerous others have shown. The Members States disagree among themselves, with their citizen and the European Com-mission, and the Court itself disagrees with its Advocate General, indicating choice within a given institutional arrangement. Of course, the decision was confined by the wording of the EEC Treaty and was sought justified by refer-ences to logical deductions from the EEC scheme and spirit but, ultimately, by choice or conscience, the Court *discovered* a general principle and a par-ticular right. The Court could have narrowly held that the Members State courts were obliged to re-examine the EEC-law implications or other such words of deference; instead, it chose a sweeping statement that centred on the

38. *van Gend en Loos v. Netherlands* main holding.
39. Ibid. point 3.
40. Ibid. point 5.

direct, individual and enforceable nature of EEC law and the easily applied rule-based test of the difference in actually paid duty.

Step 5. Shift in Normative Structure and Repeating the Process. Following *van Gend*, the doctrines of *direct effect* and *individual rights* were now part of European Economic Community quasi-constitutional law, initiating the "Constitutionalization of the Treaty System."[41] The primary norm was still the same Treaty but a shift in the norm structure had occurred and the "spirit" of various clauses were found to contain a principles of direct effect and individual rights from which could be deduced at least the particular freedom not having an increased burden of import duty due to re-categorisation of a product in the import nomenclature.

The shift in the normative structure led to further dyadic conflicts between citizen and Member States where time and again these principles and the implied principles of *supremacy* and *estoppel* prohibit "public authorities from relying on national law to justify their failure to comply with EC law."[42] Among the numerous cases, *Van Duyn* (ECJ 41/74 (1974)) established direct effect for directives. *Von Colson* (ECJ 14/83 (1984)) and *Marleasing* (C-106/89 (1990)) established and clarified *indirect effects*, and *Francovitch* (ECJ 1991 (C-6 and 9/90 (1991)) *government liability* for failure to implement community directives. All of these relied and to varying degree cited and discussed the earlier norm shifting cases.

The later cases have in common that the *van Gend* understanding of the Treaty becomes the normative basis for the dyadic dispute, the same Court has jurisdiction and decides the dispute based on the changed quasi-constitutional norm. In doing so, the Court further shift the norm structure.

Example 4: The Dynamics of Radio Search – UfR.1976.184H

The *Radio Search* (UfR.1976.0184H) case arose in Denmark. For ages, the Danish King and his agents has restricted the freedom of the subjects, for instance searching their houses and premises without procedural safeguards. This practice was continued by the democratic government even long after the Basic Law provided for such freedoms. A brave citizen, whose name is strangely withheld in the report but referred to as "T,"[43] refused access when the Directorate General of Post and Telegraph Provision wanted to gain access to his licensed private radio without at court issued warrant; the purpose was to control compliance with administrative regulations.

---

41. Stone Sweet and Brunell (2002) 263.
42. Ibid. 264.
43. *Radio Search* 184 referred to as "T" –abbreviation of Danish for "defendant".

Step 1. The Norm Structure. The Danish Basic Law contains a specific provision on the Freedom of the Person, including a Searches Clause that provides that searches cannot be performed unless authorised by prior warrant or by special exceptions in statute.

Step 2. The Dyad. T and the Danish agencies were both subject to the Danish Basic Law and T could rely on the Basic Law and its principles when the Danish government agents prosecuted her alleged violation of the statute by refusing access.

Step 3. The Triad. The Danish administration was not persuaded by T's arguments. The jurisdiction of the Supreme Court meant that T could challenge the constitutionality of the statute in question in a forum that the State did not control. However, the Danish Supreme Court settled the matter by holding that "The judgement of the Eastern High Court shall in force remain,"[44] thus upholding the conviction below.

Step 4. Triadic Rulemaking. However, the Danish Supreme Court did not just hold this as a straightforward application of law, it did so on the reasoning that, "the defendant's use of the equipment was conditioned on [certain terms, including inspection at any time.]"[45] The Court then referred to the argument of the Prosecutor of the Realm that the statute did not authorise searches of houses "but even if the provision in the Basic Law § 72 [the Searches clause] may be assumed to encompass inspections of the concerned kind, the provisions is found not to be of hinder to such as the present, by empowerment in statute provided, rules [on inspection on the pain of fines.]"[46] Just to untangle the prose: 'it is not certain whether the Basic Law protects against unwarranted searches of this kind but even if it does, it does not hinder searches authorised in law – such as this one – that we recognise when we see them.'

One concurring judge stressed that the Basic Law § 72 would have precluded the search absent the statute if the purpose was such inspection but otherwise found the statute as a legal basis "sufficiently clear for the provision of such rules in a regulation [for] a limited purpose and a natural condition."[47]

One dissenting Judge, however, opined that according to "the overwhelming opinion in theory and practice" the freedom from unwarranted searches was applicable also outside the core area of criminal investigation. He then

44. Ibid 185, main holding.
45. Ibid. 185 per majority.
46. Ibid. 185 per majority.
47. Ibid. 185 per Justice Spleth.

demonstrated briefly that in other areas, the legal basis for similar searches was stricter and sounder.[48]

The case is a good example of restrictive dynamics,[49] where a statute authorising a regulation is held to be sufficient basis for exemption form a constitutional principle.

Step 5. Shift in Normative Structure and Repeating the Process. Following *Radio Search*, the doctrine of *no hinder* and the limiting of the Basic Law provisions to their narrowest core were now integrated parts of Danish constitutional law. The primary norm was still the same Basic Law but a shift in the norm structure had occurred and the various clauses were found either not "to encompass" the freedoms allegedly encroached by various government regulations or through the principle of "no hinder," not to limit the particular power exercised.

The Danish courts did not even consider allowing the search itself and use but create a 'forbidden fruit' doctrine to limit the use of its outcome when not court authorised. "The possibility that there should not be imposed a fine when the courts have not provided prior warrant is not discussed. A dynamic restrictive constitutional interpretation!"[50]

The shift in the normative structure was probably followed by further dyadic conflicts between citizen and Danish authorities but is difficult to follow given the limited use of precedent and sparingly reasoned judgements. However, a number of restrictively dynamic cases, further limiting the Basic Law can be cited[51] and some will be analysed in the later part on Danish Review.

The Dyad and Triad

Whenever the conditions of "two individuals and at least a rudimentary normative structure"[52] are met, there is a *dyadic contract* that can lead to a dispute based on that normative structure. When a dispute occurs, the two parties will refer to the shared normative structure to give weight to their arguments and try to achieve a favourable outcome.

When the two parties exist and dispute without one of them being able forcefully to coerce the other, the two parties may be able to agree on a solu-

48.   Ibid. 185 per Justice Thygesen.
49.   Zahle (1997) 369.
50.   Ibid. 369.
51.   Ibid. 365.
52.   Stone Sweet (2002c) 60.

tion, or the conflict will simply remain active. However, in many settings, recourse is given to a third party that is accepted as a resolver of such disputes.[53]

In constitutional law, we can see this in many settings. We saw it in *Griswold* when the citizen Griswold and the State of Connecticut shared the same normative structure, namely the United States Constitution, and Griswold was able to take the dyadic dispute to the United States Supreme Court – that Connecticut effectively respected. Likewise, in *CCD Case 82-146*, the French opposition disagreeing with the governing coalition on the application of the French constitutional norm structure was able to take the dispute to the Constitutional Council – to whose authority both sides submitted. Furthermore, in *van Gend*, a Dutch businessperson and the Dutch customs agency disagreed on their shared EEC law; their dispute was decided by the European Court of Justice that was granted jurisdiction by EEC Treaty – and effectively respected by the Netherlands. Finally, the Danish radio amateur and the Danish radio agency shared the Danish Basic Law as their common normative structure but could not agree on its application in their dispute over radio law searches. Their conflict went before the Danish Supreme Court, whose authority both respected.

Triadic Rulemaking

The Norwegian historian Sandmo writes that, "The development of society nurtured the legislation, legislation gave birth to court cases, and the court cases became the subject of great debates both in the Storthing and in the legal milieu."[54] This insight takes us to the dynamic process of moulding positive law through case law.

Most courts will claim that they are only applying the law and, for the most part, they probably are following what seems to be the most persuasive or even imperative reading of the law. However, when solving the interpretive issues and explaining how they perceive the law, the courts restate the substantive normative content of the law in a way that purports to be true also if a similar question was raised. "In telling us why, normatively, a given act should or should not be permitted – [the triadic entity] has made rules of an

---

53. Ibid. 61.
54. Erling Sandmo *Siste Ord. Høyesterett i norsk historie 1905-1965* (2005) 124.

abstract, general, and prospective nature. This is so to the extent that the decision has clarified or altered rules that comprise the normative structure."[55]

The triadic instance explains how the norm structure must generally be understood in a certain way and that the general principle leads to the solution in this particular case.[56] Put differently, "triadic rule-making constitutes a discourse about how people ought to behave. Because rules, reasoning about rules, and the application of particular rules to particular conflicts constitute the core of this discourse, precedent follows naturally. Precedent helps legitimize TDR [Third-Party Dispute Resolution] by acknowledging rule-making behaviour."[57]

Triadic rulemaking can be seen in our examples. In *Griswold*, the Court interpreted the Constitution so that *privacy* was stated as being part of the normative structure, thus providing a principle from which the solution in the case at hand could be derived. In *CCD Case 82-146*, the Council discovered the *equality* doctrine in the ancient Declaration that the Constitution referred to and interpreted it to mean a ban on gender distinction in law, thus providing a general rule from which a solution could be deduced. Furthermore, in *van Gend*, the principles of superiority and direct effect were used to provide a principled solution. Finally, in *Radio Search,* the Danish Supreme Court discovered the principle of *no hindrance in cases like these* thus providing a general rule that could be applied.

What increases or reduces the use of triadic dispute resolution is known as the dispute resolver's calculus.

Figure M:The Dispute Resolver's Calculus

Figure M illustrates how courts, which become successful in attracting disputing parties, always try to choose a middle ground. Position A.1 would be full victory for party A, and B.1, likewise, victory for party B. Position A.2 represents how far the decision could go and still seem legitimate to A. Like-

---

55. Stone Sweet (2000) 17.
56. Stone Sweet (2002c) 62.
57. Ibid. 64.

wise, position B.2 is a as far a B finds a legitimate decision can go.[58] As shall be demonstrated, the courts that become involved in dynamic dispute resolution and generate triadic rulemaking are the ones most apt at explaining how a balance was struck, thus encouraging the parties or those of similar beliefs to try again.

Triadic rulemaking is a fact of West-Nordic law not least through the immense influence from EU law. In his great work on the influence of EU law on Danish administrative law, Niels Fenger writes, "The independence of the Courts in relation to the legislative power is most clearly manifested in the direct constitutional review where [the statute] is set aside as unconstitutional. Just as often, the independence will show itself indirectly as the courts – in order to further their understanding of the constitution – interpret [the statute by deviating from the legislature's intentions or by interpreting the provision not as necessarily best fitting with the constitution but with its basic ideas]."[59]

That courts are "adding to legislation"[60] and that there is a certain issue of the legitimacy of judicial rulemaking relating to "from where their power comes"[61] are well-established notion in West-Nordic law. What is perhaps underdeveloped is analysing law in light of the realisation that the courts do make rules and that they do feel empowered to do so by constitutions, treaties, and, increasingly, the dynamics of their own case law.

West-Nordic law is indeed developing dynamically. Niels Fenger writes that the "ECHR [influences] in the same way in non-EU areas." According to him, Danish Courts are gradually asserting themselves as responsible for adjusting Danish Law to ECHR law, citing *TV-Stop v. Denmark* compared to earlier cases as a particular example.[62]

Thus, triadic rulemaking is a source of law in constitutional law as well as in other fields that need to be recognised, analysed, and applied as well in practice as in theory. The neatness of the 'three branches of state' notwithstanding, the inevitability of triadic rulemaking and its peculiarities, particularly its subtlety and its discreet and indirect manifestations must be fully analysed by any serious scholar of constitutional law.

---

58. Shapiro and Stone Sweet (2002c) 16.
59. Niels Fenger *Forvaltning og fælesskab* (2004) 826.
60. Sigurður Líndal *Um lög og lögfræði. Grundvöllur laga – réttarheimildir Hið* íslenzka bókmenntafélag (2002) 302.
61. Líndal (2002) 309.
62. Fenger (2004) 835-36.

Normative Shifts

Having appreciated triadic rulemaking, the process whereby an independent arbiter will add something to the law as it applies it to a given case at hand, another realisation follows, namely that this auxiliary legislation will not only be relevant in that particular dispute but potentially in future controversies of a similar nature. All actors in a given jurisdiction will "gradually be placed under the authority of the dispute resolver or, more precisely, under the authority of an evolving set of behavioural norms, as managed by the third party."[63] To put it differently, when a given constitutional principle is explained and applied, the next case is likely to use the explanation and application as its starting point rather than just the original principle or provision. The case becomes law and the large number of cases become the combined case law that sometimes adds to the written law or at least decides its ambiguities but at other times more or less replaces the original norm. In all these instances, we can speak of a normative shift, at mutation of the norms through this dialectic process.

Legal norms can shift through their usage and perception, for instance, because the same or similar norms have been interpreted differently by respected instances,[64] including differences in interpretation over time. This entails that: "constitutional judges will increasingly behave as sophisticated legislators, and that legislators will act as constitutional judges do."[65] This should be no surprise to Scandinavians, as Danish Chief Justice Niels Pontoppidan warned in an interview in 1996 that "in an area such as property rights, where there a balance must be found between protection of the property of the individual and society's need for regulation, [it] becomes a question of political attitudes. If the courts did not show restraint in such situations, we would end as a kind of Supreme Folk Thing."[66] In said interview, there was very clear

---

63. Stone Sweet (2000) 3.
64. Weekendavisen "Grænser for magt" 26 February 1999 quoted in Christensen (2003) 19, Danish Chief Justice Niels Pontoppidan is quoted of saying *"There is a mutual influence between the international courts and the national courts. Especially the ECJ and the ECHR have had great influence. In the international courts, we can see the emergence of a practice with a more free style of interpretation emphasising 'present-day conditions' rather than historic interpretation. To some degree this rubs off on national practise as a trend."*
65. Stone Sweet (2000) 3.
66. Weekendavisen "Domstolene vil få mere magt" 28 June 1996 quoted in Christensen (2003) at 20.

sense of a normative shift, that the law was evolving without being formally amended.

As regards the dynamics of the ECHR, Danish scholar Jens Elo Rytter explains that what happens is that, "the starting point is always the phrasing and context of the right," however, ECHR methodology means that "phrasing should not stand in the way of a freer purpose driven interpretation [with] the purpose and "spirit" of the right not seldom decisive."[67] Notice the discomfort with the word "spirit," the explaining away of the spirit of the laws in Danish theory has definitely obscured its perception of dynamic developments such as that of the ECHR. A less ideological phrase could be "the broad point of the law," for people uncomfortable with the spiritual side of law.

Ultimately triadic rulemaking and the dynamic normative shifts mean that, "A state of the law that has been consistent with the ECHR can become contrary [as the] result of a dynamic development in the ECHR Court's practice."[68] Likewise any other constitutional scheme can expand, regress, or morph in various ways through this process, making law less predictable but also less static, less certain but also less rigid, less an instrument of status quo and more an instrument of change.

For those studying the dynamics of the law, the most interesting period will often be the initial period after a new written source of law is promulgated and is then frequently adjudicated or otherwise interpreted. This is often known as the *formative period.*[69] However, new formative periods can occur either when a provisions or principle is rediscovered or when important factors prompt new dynamics. This may be called a *period of renewed dynamics.*

The dynamic properties of constitutional law, including in particular the quasi-federal quasi-constitutional ECHR law as it affects West-Nordic national constitutional law, shall be a main point of focus in our further discussions.

---

67. Rytter (2006) 60.
68. Ibid. 62.
69. On this concept Tamm (2005) 35. See also Jensen (1995) 241.

The Mechanics
of Judicial Review

Understanding the Mechanics of Judicial Review

Ultimately, all law is useless unless it can be applied. Understanding how judicial review is actually exercised is crucial to understanding how to use it, why it has developed, or why despite otherwise promising indications it has halted in its tracks.

We shall now consider a number of the important mechanics or institutional and procedural aspects of constitutional judicial review.[1]

Figure N: The Mechanics of Judicial Review

Forum	**Jurisdiction**	**Parties**	**Timing**	**Extent**	**End Status**
General	Original	Citizen	A priori	Abstract	Disapplication
Specialised	Appeal	Institutions	A posterior	Concrete	Deference
Federal	Prejudicial	Politicians		For all	Correction
Quasi-federal	Supervisory	Supervisory			Flexible tech.

(Table to be read thus: **Terms in bold** is a class of mechanics that includes following instances).

Forum indicates the nature of institution where review is performed. The forum may be a general forum for legal disputes, such as the ordinary courts. The forum may be a specialised institution such as a constitutional court, constitutional council, or ombudsman[2] that is charged with dealing with constitu-

---

1.   Koch (2002) from 135 to 209 systemises the typology. See also Henning Koch "Folkesuveræniteten og domstolsprøvelse" *Juristen* (2000) 281.
2.   Jens Elo Rytter "Grundrettigheder som almene retsprincipper" *Juristen* (2001) 121.

tional issues or subdivisions thereof. The institution may be federal or quasi-federal with some form of jurisdiction over several subordinate polities.

Jurisdiction indicates how the forum is empowered. A forum may have original jurisdiction as the forum where such matters are referred at first instance and often final as well. It may be have appeal jurisdiction with the implication that other proceedings must occur prior to it and that procedural rules may bar a case from reaching it. The forum may decide matters prejudicially, providing another forum with the legal interpretation needed for deciding on the facts at hand. The jurisdiction may also be supervisory, as it may not decide the original case but rather the underlying legal issue meaning that it may not directly decide the case of a litigant or even the constitutionality of the disputed instrument but rather pronounce on the issues raised an initiate a process elsewhere.

Parties indicate who can raise an issue. Ordinary citizen may or may not be allowed to raise constitutional issues or classes of issues, including international, supranational or quasi-federal if the federation has its own judiciary or equivalent.[3] There may be corporations and institutions allowed to or barred from suits on constitutionality. Politicians or political bodies may have special or exclusive right to raise issues. Likewise, supervisory institutions, like ombudsmen, federal or quasi-federal institutions may have special rights or even obligations to raise constitutionality.

Timing indicates when in the lifetime of an instrument the adjudication occurs. Review may occur before the instrument has even formally come into force. It may instead happen after promulgation and effect.

Extent indicates how far the effect of review extends.[4] Review may be abstract in deciding if the instrument or parts of it are unconstitutional per se, regardless of actual effect or use. It may instead be concrete in relating to a particular controversy where both higher norm and competing instrument may apply to the same factual situation. In the latter case, the holding may be limited to the parties of the dispute or be extended in general to the provisions or entire instrument as such, for all potentially affected legal subjects.

---

3. Karin Åhman writes, "*It was only after loosing three cases regarding access to court review that new rules were introduced to avoid that Sweden would be condemned again. The judicial review statute was enacted as a direct reaction to e.g. Sporrong and Lönnroth. The lawgiver had chosen between a continued partial oversight of Swedish legislation and a more general solution and chose the latter method.*" Karin Åhman "Rättighetsskydd i praktiken – skydd på papperet eller verkligt genomslag?" in *Konstitutionell demokrati* (2004) 196.
4. Smith (1993) 39.

End status indicates what the ultimate status of the reviewed instrument is. The instrument may in some way be declared invalid even partially so, or just be disregarded by that particular branch of government. It may instead be lifted to trump the presumed higher norm in an act of deference to another institution. The instrument may also be allowed to stand but only after interpretation in light of the higher norm. In addition to such authoritative interpretation, a number of other flexible techniques may be used in review, such as prospective application, remand to other court or legislature, or by creating multifactor tests or other supplements to the higher norm or instrument in question.

Figure O: Review Mechanics – Examples Overview

	Forum	Jurisdiction	Parties	Timing	Extent	End Status
Ex. 1	French Constitution-al Council	Original	Political factions	A priori	Abstract	Law partially set-aside. Correction
Ex. 2	ECHR Court	Supervisory, Quasi-appellate	Citizen and National Government	A posteriori	Concrete, semi-abstract	Ruling set-aside. Partial clarification.
Ex. 3	Danish Supreme Court	Appellate	Citizen v. Government	A posteriori	Abstract	Act upheld. Reservation. Expansion

Example 1: The Mechanics of CCD Case 2001-454

The French case of *CCD Case 2001-454 (2002)* provides an excellent example of *forum*, namely a special body set up independently to decide on constitutionality. Its membership appointed for overlapping periods by the political branches, thus often representing the former regime, has the insight, savvy, and motivation to deal with political issues. The Council's *jurisdiction* is original and exclusive; it is the only forum for deciding constitutionality in the French system (this being a formal truth modified by the semi-constitutional status of human rights legislation and the effective review by the European Courts). There are no *parties* to the proceedings, as no one's legal interest or status is at stake. However, a question may be raised by the President, Prime Minister, House or Senate Speakers or 60 members of either House of Parliament, seeing it their interest to initiate proceedings. In reality, the controversy is between various political factions, as all major political players, including the parliamentary opposition, can raise the issue of constitutionality. In this case, a law granting wider autonomy to the territory of Corsica was challenged as vesting powers in the territory that could only be vested in the national executive. As to *timing* and *extent*, the Council decides constitutionality before the law comes into effect and does so in the abstract. However, in this case, the Constitutional Council decided that some provisions were indeed unconstitutional but others were left standing "with the reservations set out at paras. 13 [and] 24 and 25."[5] Thus, the challenged law was severed and partially upheld, partially set-aside, and partially corrected to conform to the Council's reading of the constitution. The *end status* of both constitution and law were consequently decided and altered.

Example 2: The Mechanics of Bergens Tidende

The ECHR case **Bergens Tidende v. Norway (2000)** provides another good example of *forum* for review, namely a supranational body set up independently to decide on conventionality. Its membership appointed by now close to fifty countries often among judges most likely to support the human rights agenda thus independent of governments and with high motivation to deal with political issues. The ECHR Court's *jurisdiction* is formally original in the sense that it hears cases not as a formal appeal but as arbiter of the ECHR dispute arising after the national matter has ended and without powers over the national case. However, it has effectively appellate aspects as the national case record is used as basis for the cases and the citizen is in effect appealing the ECHR aspects of her case. The *parties* to the proceedings are the applicant and his nation-state, in this case the paper Bergens Tidende and a journalist alleging that Norway violated their rights in allowing their conviction for libel when reporting a matter of general interest. Thus, millions of people can raise the issue of conventionality but with that procedural delay. National courts are often unsecure on ECHR law and ECHR case law is often very narrow and particular, creating limited or ambiguous precedent. As no ECHR 'district courts' exist to provide injunctions and ECHR law unlike EU law does not require national injunctions, thousands of cases are pending. They may be decided eventually but there is a clear need for more general pronouncements higher up and less delayed application lower down the ECHR chain. The Norwegian courts seem to develop this role increasingly, not least because the extended reasoning means that the contrast between na-

---

5.   *CCD Case 2001-454* main holding Article 2.

tional judgement and ECHR Court judgement becomes clearer. As to *timing* and *extent*, the ECHR Court decides compatibility after the law has taken effect and has been tested by all competent national instances and does so in the concrete, here going through the nitty-gritty of the reports on an allegedly negligent plastic surgeon mistreating female breasts. However, the reasoning makes clear that the ECHR Court makes general pronouncements on ECHR principles but the effect on national law is left to others to infer within the famed margin of appreciation.[6] Thus, the challenged law (libel doctrine) was partially set aside but only given the very particular set of facts as the Court read the ECHR, the *end status* of both super norm and law were consequently affected but not without substantial room for further clarification – and litigation.

Example 3: The Mechanics of Norup Carlsen
The Danish cases *Norup Carlsen I* (UfR.1996.1300H) and *Norup Carlsen II* (UfR.1998.0800H) provide a more traditional example of review *forum*, a national Supreme Court of general jurisdiction. Its membership picked mostly among career judges and bureaucrats, it is functionally independent of the governments but not particularly motivated to tackle legal issues with political connotations. The Danish Supreme Court's *jurisdiction* is appellate, sometimes directly from the High Courts functioning as trial courts, in cases originating at lower trial courts only so by special leave from an appeal board. The *parties* may be anyone with a legal interest within the Realm. In this case, Norup Carlsen and others had challenged the expansion of the EEC/EU Treaty.[7] However, in accordance with precedent, the Eastern High Court dismissed the case as not constituting a proper controversy. This was overruled by the Supreme Court that provided for a very liberal access to test the abstract constitutionality of Danish law, including Acts of Accession to treaty regimes conferring power upon international structures. Thus, as a matter of principle, millions of Danes and presumably others with some legal interest in Denmark may challenge laws in the abstract; what is more, this appears to be possible based on general issues rather than danger of individual loss. As to *timing* and *extent*, the Supreme Court generally decides on constitutionality after laws have come into effect but with this step moved forward the time of review, thus reducing the potential impact of setting aside an Act (of Accession); furthermore, the Court took on an abstract testing of the ac-

---

6. *Bergens Tidende v. Norway* (ECHR 2000).
7. *Norup Carlsen II.*

cession to Treaty, thus increasing the potential scope of review. In the end, however, the Court found the particular act within the relevant provision of the Basic Law but set up certain conditions and presumptions that clearly indicate that there are limits to what the Supreme Court will condone, especially regarding its own powers.[8] Thus the challenged law was upheld but conditionally so and with the *end status* of constitutional doctrine greatly changed to provide very wide access to review and an altered standard of review.

We shall now elaborate to some degree on the mechanics of judicial review and ask, *who decides?*

Older constitutional documents seem either not to have considered that – deliberately or unintentionally – unconstitutional instruments could be issued, or they provided legislative rather than judicial procedures to avoid them.

The West-Nordic constitutions originally provided for bicameralism and royal ascent, meaning that an instrument would be considered by different representative bodies as well as by the unelected monarch with a duty to uphold the constitutional order. Since then, bicameralism has been reduced to a formality in Norway and abolished in Denmark and Iceland, and the active monarch has been replaced by a passive custodian seldom occasioned into action. Parliamentarism means that the same majority controls both main political branches of government and can pass almost any measure unless there is a rare rebellion of coalition backbenchers. In addition, whereas in old times the State had to use prosecution thus giving the citizen the advantage of procedural rights, including in Norway and Denmark unpredictable juries, nowadays the State gets its way through its bureaucracy and forces the citizen to bring its suits to a reluctant judiciary.

This is worth noting. The original (Nordic) scheme of constitutional review through a cumbersome legislative procedure with and rigorous trial of fact, has been replaced by a manageable unitary legislative-executive government with review left to a somewhat uneasy trial of law.

In such jurisdiction, the general courts will be called upon to set aside statutes or other instruments as unconstitutional. When the constitutional documents are silent on the question of judicial review, for these historical reasons, it becomes incumbent upon the courts to take a position on constitutional judicial review. When they do allow such suits, constitutional review becomes in the jargon diffuse,[9] that is to say, part of the general workload of courts otherwise dealing with more everyday issues.

---

8. *Norup Carlsen II.*
9. Koch (2002).

In polities where the need for or tradition of judicial review has become more accepted, a specialised system may be set up. Many recent Eastern European countries have elected some version of a constitutional court from the example of Austria and later Germany, the system that Hans Kelsen invented to create constitutional but not (strictly) judicial review to fit better with parliamentary traditions.[10] The East-Nordic countries have introduced specialised committees into their parliamentary procedures.[11] Most interestingly, some supra-national structures have made their arrangements more legally effective through courts of law. The ECJ and the ECHR are both highly specialised courts dealing almost exclusively with reviewing inferior instruments. The advantages of specialised courts include the ability to deal with a number of cases and questions with theoretical and practical knowledge and understanding of constitutional, wider legal, historical, political, and cultural issues.[12] Most European constitutional courts exercise abstract review with their judgements taking effect erga omnes.[13]

Letting ordinary courts decide constitutionality means that the parties do not have to wait for a specialised court hearing the issue on ultimate appeal but it also risks leaving important general questions to be argued by parties and decided by judges not fully representing or understanding all implications.[14] The EU system provides for a best of both worlds approach in letting the general court decide on the facts whilst the ECJ pronounces on EU law when asked.

The West-Nordic countries have largely adopted the departmentalism model. Taking from the continental tradition that the judiciary is only the mouth that pronounces the phrases of the law, the West-Nordic countries have developed courts dependant on detailed directives that "cannot exactly have encouraged to viewing the highest courts as wielding any kind of active "branch of government.""[15]

Some jurisdictions will submit constitutional issues to the people; however, this rarely happens in the West-Nordic countries except for EU expansion.

---

10. Martin Shapiro and Stone Sweet, Alec "Abstract Review and Judicial Law-making" in *On Law, Politics and Judicialization* (2002) 343.
11. Thomas Bull "Riksdagen som grundlagstolkare" in *Grundlagens makt. Konstitutionen som politiskt redskap och som rättslig norm* SNS författningsprojekt (2002) 143.
12. Michael C. Dorf "No Federalists Here: Anti-Federalism and Nationalism on The Rehnquist Court" 31 *Rutgers Law Journal* (2000) 741.
13. Smith (1993) 34.
14. Koch (2002).
15. Smith (1993) 53.

This probably says a lot about opposition to judicial review on the grounds that it is undemocratic – if a referendum is shunned the real grievance is likely other than democratic considerations. Some recent constitutions categorise constitutional review and other forms of control and oversight as a special sub-category of constitutional powers. The Swedish form of Government talks of the control powers, including constitutional judicial review.[16]

Assembly oversight bears the risk of the review becoming too partisan with legitimate concerns unreasonably thrashed as political as well as the procedure being misused for political purposes. However, when the issue is the value judgement behind appointments or other priorities, parliamentary oversight may relieve the courts of some of the issues they would rather avoid.[17]

Another variant is to deal with the issues explicitly in parliament, thus avoiding judicial second-guessing of whether the politicians aware of the constitutional implications of an instrument. Unfortunately, this may turn to perversion of both political and judicial procedure with the ministry of justice or the parliamentary secretariat (often formally the Speaker) deciding issues of constitutionality without any hearings, adversary process, or published reasoning, creating an unpersuasive assumption of constitutionality for some instruments and depriving others instruments the opportunity to be argued in plenum or in court. This procedure has been criticised by the Norwegian Supreme Court.[18]

Constitutional issues will not go away just because there is no access to review. In countries with very reluctant courts, judicial writings can have the function of review with institutional or influential writers taking on the role of courts elsewhere. Issues of constitutionality become issues of the theory of constitutionality[19] and the courts in their efforts to be restrained end up deferring to the professors instead.[20] Interestingly, such 'theoretical constitutional review' can set in motion its own dynamics with rulemaking and normative

16. Swedish Form of Government Chapter 12.
17. Koch (2002).
18. *Knutsen v. Wiig.*
19. See Koch (2002) in general.
20. Oftedal Broch writes, "*Professor Knoph put forward the thesis that the prohibition should be perceived as a legal standard thus embodying a large degree of discretion. He claimed to find support in case law but his thesis no doubt worked as a kind of self-fulfilling prophecy. The judge in [Borthen v. Norway] quoted in some length Knoph's book on Legal Standards, before concluding that only retroactivity which was "clearly unreasonable or unjust" would violate the Constitution.*" Oftedal Broch (2003) 247-48.

shifts and a need for a study of the development of law through theoretical review, as is very apparent in much Nordic writing on law.[21] Alternatively, the excessive use of preparatory works will lead to deference to legal sources only slightly considered by Parliament and in reality further deference to other less restrained entities.[22]

The West-Nordic countries have largely adopted the departmentalism (or compartmentalism) model. Taking from the continental tradition that the judiciary is only the tongue that pronounces the phrases of the law, the West-Nordic countries have developed courts dependant on detailed directives that "cannot exactly have encouraged to viewing the highest courts as wielding any kind of active "branch of government.""[23]

By contrast, the European Courts have been acting like true branches of government. Straightforward supremacy may originally have been rejected in the case of the EU as it originally was with the US.[24] Nonetheless, supremacy became the most practical solution. Even in the case of the ECHR, near effective supremacy can be observed by the reactions of the member states, in the case of Sweden: "Some situation demand legislation and others that court practice must be changed. Another method to comply with a judgement is that the government uses its powers in RF 11:6 to control [the inferior agencies]."[25]

Today's administrative states have a range of specialised courts, tribunals, and instructions that may be called upon to deal with constitutional issues or aspects. Defining a court may be attempted in formal terms for instance as follows: "Defining the concept of 'court' is actually not a simple task. As a sort of basic conditions, which can of course be criticised, can be seen the following: 1) independence of judges, 2) pre-existing legal rules, 3) adversary process and 5) dichotomous decisions. However, because the conditions are quite rough, one should perhaps speak of certain general feature of 'courtness.'"[26] We shall for our purposes stick to looking for general 'courtness' rather than fitting candidates with said criteria, missing one criteria, say inde-

---

21. Jörundsson (1969) is a prime example.
22. "The Folkething has before enacting the Statute been aware of the question of comparability with §81 of the Basic Law, so that the Folkething has decided the issue of constitutionality. The Court finds support for this assumption in the Defence Secretary's preparatory remarks to the Bill." *Military MD* (UfR.1976.395-2V) per Varde Court, endorsed by Western High Court.
23. Smith (1993) 53.
24. Kramer (2004) 86.
25. Åhman (2004) 195.
26. Husa (2002) 124, note 8.

pendence or adversary process, may be more indicative of an flawed case of courtness than of no courtness at all.

The issue is adjudicated in several instances. This can negatively be distinguished from investigative procedure.[27] In *W. M. v. Denmark* (ECHR 1992), the then ECHR Commission ruled that an investigative parliamentary sub-committee established by the Danish Foreign Affairs Committee did not fall within the ambit of Article 6 ECHR, thereby it was not a court obliged to provide fair trial procedures. In *PROSA v. Denmark* (ECHR 1996), the Danish Labour Law Tribunal, *Arbejdsretten,* was found to be a court.

This survey shall for the sake of brevity focus on West-Nordic Supreme Courts and the ECHR Court with others included as appropriate. For future research, a number of institutions may appear just as relevant, especially in sub-categories of constitutional review.

---

27. Jon Fridrik Kjølbro *Den Europæiske Menneskerettighedskonvention – for praktikere* Jurist- og Økonomforbundets Forlag (2005) 251.

Applying the Theory to West-Nordic Review

Application Summary

West-Nordic constitutional judicial review has developed over the years. The constitutional documents of 1814, 1849, and 1874 respectively provided the legal framework for the clash between superior and inferior norms. However, the wider constitutional set-up had crucial effects. The constitutional documents were caught up in the fight between King and Parliament and later between modernisers and traditionalists. In Norway, the Basic Law become a revered symbol of national independence and to some degree an effective legal instrument with enforceable rights and balance of power provisions. In Denmark, the Basic Law may have achieved a comparable symbolic status but the formative period created a lasting suspicious bias against its legal supremacy. In Iceland, the struggle for national independence overshadowed individual rights for a long time and emphasised the supremacy of the legislature even more than in the others.

West-Nordic review has developed dynamically ever since the enactment of the respective documents. However, access to judgements have been severely restricted, either as reasoning was outright forbidden, later restricted in various ways, or because legal culture favoured the view that courts only applied law, thus making the study of and writing on case law less relevant than the loftier principles and authoritative sources supposedly guiding the judges.

The issue of compatibility between statute and constitution surfaced at different stages in the constitutional developments of the three countries. Apparently, an underlying assumption was that Parliament and King (or President) would deal with constitutional questions in the abstract. The constitutions furthermore lacked provisions suitable for effective review; with many rights provisions either stating that such and such right could only be limited by law or by providing open-ended standards. This lent support to the notion that as long as the legislative process at least considers the constitutional standard and observes all procedures, it is constitutional.

None of the countries has an explicit legal basis for judicial review but in them, all the presumption of review was created and developed by the courts themselves and legal writings.

All three countries have gone through phases considering issues such as the extent of property rights and the rise of the administrative state. In them all, a doctrine of parliamentary supremacy in economic regulation evolved. However, the Supreme Courts have shown deference to legislation, administration, and legal writings even on other constitutional issues. Several periods have demonstrated reversed and restrictive dynamics, where the importance of constitutional provisions and previous case law has been progressively reduced.

Following World War II, West-Nordic countries joined in the ECHR but due to assumptions of compatibility and traditional deference, its quasi-federal effects were delayed by several decades. With Demark joining the EEC (EU) and with national review increasing in Norway, judicial review was revitalised from the late 1970s. Increasingly, review through ECHR, EU, and EEA brought pressures; Iceland responded to ECHR pressure by reviving its own constitution accordingly, Norway most effectively adopted case law and all responded with harmonising legislation.

Today's West-Nordic constitutional judicial review is still restrained nationally but active in matters of personal rights, especially European (inspired) rights.

West-Nordic Review

In the following, we shall survey and analyse West-Nordic judicial review. First, the selected constitutional (and quasi-federal) provisions shall be presented. Then a section on each jurisdiction shall analyse selected cases. Each section shall start with a convenient summary. For each country, judicial review is set in context within constitutional developments. Then selected cases are analysed grouped in historical periods.

The approach is based on the premise that surveying judicial review historically is, as noted by Danish scholar Ditlev Tamm, to understand the law fully we need to understand it "from its root."[1]

The hypothesis of the survey is that by observing judicial review in various periods and dealing with selected issues, the dynamics of dispute resolution may become apparent, as will the concepts, conditions, and mechanics of judicial review.

All three countries have in common that their constitutional documents are silent on constitutional judicial review. By contrast, the Swedish Form of Government (the foremost of the four Swedish constitutional documents) is more explicit: "If a court or other public body finds that an instrument is contrary to a provision in constitution or other higher norm or that relevant usage has been significantly disregarded in its enactment, the instrument cannot be applied. If [Parliament] or the Government has enacted the instrument, the application can only be avoided if the error is obvious."[2] The tone of the Swedish constitutional text probably summarises Nordic attitude in general. Unconstitutional instruments should not be applied but if the highest political forums have issued them, the error must be obvious, effectively giving those bodies license to bend and develop the constitution for themselves. The provisions also points out that the forum may be a court or other body, the superior norm constitution or other higher norm or usage.

However, the West-Nordic jurisdictions have no precise Swedish-style provision on which to base their review. Instead, they have dealt with these

1. Tamm (2005) 15.
2. Swedish Form of Government Chapter 11 § 4.

issues differently from time to time, and from issue to issue. As we shall see, the law as it effectively presents itself in cases and controversies to the individual citizen trying to use it and the court trying to apply it, is not predictable from the traditional Scandinavian method of using 'the sources of law' to find 'valid law.' Nordic law is a dynamic phenomenon with case law expressing the true state of the law at a given time. Thus, lawyers, judges, scholars and the wider society need to recognise that their constitutions and their law are a gradually changing product of circumstances and need to be analysed as the trajectory of these dynamics rather than as a constant available from initiated exegesis. This may not sound revealing to many realists and critical students of law elsewhere but it points to the need for a new methodology in the study of West-Nordic law.

Constitutional Text

The constitutional texts of the three countries contain provisions that have proven more relevant than others have to the development and exercise of judicial review. Provisions on the balance of power, the powers of legislature and judiciary, general principles such as retroactivity, specific rights such as property rights and freedom of expression or assembly.

Figure P: Provisions on Powers, Balance of Power

Selected constitutional provisions by polity.

Norway

Form of Government clause

Basic Law 1814

§ 1. The Kingdom of Norway is a free, independent, and indivisible Realm. Its Form of Government is limited and hereditary- monarchical.

Current

§ 1. The Kingdom of Norway is a free, independent, and undividable Realm. Its Form of Government is limited and hereditary monarchical.

Legislative Power clause

Basic Law 1814

§ 75. It is rightly for the Storthing to: give and repeal Laws, impose Taxes ...

Current

§ 75. It is rightly for the Storthing to: give and repeal Laws, impose Taxes ...

Legislative Procedure clause

Basic Law 1814

§ 76. Any Law shall first be proposed in the Odelsthing ... If the Bill is there passed, it is sent to the Lawthing ... [If rejected returned with or without amendments ... If twice rejected, the full Storthing decides by 2/3 of its Votes.]

Current

§ 76. Any Law shall first be proposed in the Odelsthing ... If the Bill is there passed, it is sent to the Lawthing ... [If rejected returned with or without amendments ... If twice rejected, the full Storthing decides by 2/3 of its Votes.]

Overriding Veto clause

Basic Law 1814

§ 79. [... but is a Bill also by the 3rd regular Storthing ... enacted unaltered ... then it becomes Law, even if the King's Sanction is not forthcoming ...]

Current

§ 79. Has a Bill of Law been enacted unaltered by two Storthings [following elections] ... then it becomes Law, even if the King's Sanction is not forthcoming ...

Judicial Opinion clause

Basic Law 1814

§ 84. The Storthing can require the Opinion of the Supreme Court on legal Issues.

Current

§ 83. The Storthing can require the Opinion of the Supreme Court on legal Issues.

Denmark

Form of Government clause

Basic Law 1849

§ 1. The form of government is limited- monarchical. The Monarchy is hereditary.

Current

§ 2. The form of government is limited- monarchical. The Monarchy is hereditary [according to the Act of Succession].

Division of Power clause

Basic Law 1849

§ 2. The legislative Power is vested in the King and Realm Day in Union. The executive Power is vested in the King. The judicial Power is vested in the Courts.

Current

§ 3. The legislative power is vested in the king and the Folkething in union. The executive power is vested in the king. The judicial power is vested in the courts.

Legislative Procedure clauses

Basic Law 1849

§ 48. Any of the Things is entitled to propose and for its Part enact Laws.
§ 56. When a Bill is rejected by one of the Things, it can no longer be considered by the same Thing in the same Session.
§ 57. [Bills enacted by the Things must be reconciled. Joint Committee Proposal basis for Decision in each Thing].

Current

§ 42. When a Bill is passed by the Folkething, one-third of the Members may [within three days insist that it be submitted to a referendum] ...

Iceland

Form of Government clause

Constitution 1874

§ 1. [In matters pertaining to Iceland according to the Icelandic Constitutional Statues Act 1871] ...

Constitution 1944

§ 1. Iceland is a republic with a parliamentary form of government.

Current

§ 1. Iceland is a republic with a parliamentary form of government.

Division of Power clause

Constitution 1874

§ 1. ... the legislative power is vested in the king and the althing in union, the executive power is vested in the king, ant the judicial power is vested in the courts.

Constitution 1944

§ 2. The althing and the president of Iceland control the law-giver's power together. The president and other government authorities control the executive power in accordance with this constitution. The courts control the judicial power.

Current

§ 2. The althing and the president of Iceland control the law-giver's power together. The president and other government authorities control the executive power in accordance with this constitution. The courts control the judicial power.

ECHR

'Form of Government clause'

Article 1. Obligation to respect human rights The [ECHR Parties] shall secure within their jurisdiction the rights and freedoms of [the ECHR].

'Division of Power clause'

Article 19. To ensure the observance of the engagements undertaken by [the ECHR Parties], there shall be set up a European Court of Human Rights.

'Legislative Power clause'

Preamble. Considering [the Universal UN Declaration], the [effective observance of Rights], the [greater unity between Council of Europe members], [justice is best maintained by common understanding and observance of rights] ... take the first steps for the collective enforcement of certain rights ...

Preamble Protocol No. 1. ...
collective enforcement of certain
rights and freedoms other than
those already included ...

Figure Q: Provisions on Various Principles

Selected constitutional provisions by polity.

Norway

Retroactive clause

Basic Law 1814	Current
§ 97. No Law may be given retroactive Effect.	§ 97. No Law may be given retroactive Effect.

Denmark

Fiefs clause

Basic Law 1849	Current
§ 98. No Fiefs or [Feudal Trusts] can for the Future be established; it shall be provided how the now existing shall be transformed to free Property.	§ 84. No Fiefs or [Feudal Trusts] can for the Future be established.

ECHR

Fair Trial clause	Effective Remedy clause	Equality clause
Article 6. In the determination of his civil rights and obligations or of any criminal charge against him, everyone is entitled to a fair and public hearing within a reasonable time by an independent and impartial tribunal established by law. Judgement shall be pronounced publicly but the press and public may be excluded from all or part of the trial in the interest of morals, public order or national security in a democratic society, where the interests of juveniles or the protection of the private life of the	Article 13. Everyone whose rights and freedoms as set forth in this Convention are violated shall have an effective remedy before a national authority notwithstanding that the violation has been committed by persons acting in an official capacity.	Article 14. The enjoyment of the rights and freedoms set forth in this Convention shall be secured without discrimination on any ground such as sex, race, colour, language, religion, political or other opinion, national or social origin, association with a national minority, property, birth or other status.

parties so require, or the extent strictly necessary in the opinion of the court in special circumstances where publicity would prejudice the interests of justice.

Everyone charged with a criminal offence shall be presumed innocent until proved guilty according to law.

Everyone charged with a criminal offence has the following minimum rights ...

Figure R: Provisions on various Rights

Selected Provisions. Underlined heading used in main text.

Norway

Freedom of Expression clause

Basic Law 1814   *Current*

§ 100. Printing Freedom shall be in Place. No-one can be punished for any Publication of what Content it may be ... unless he with intent and publicly has shown, or incited others to, Disobedience towards the Laws, Disrespect for the Religion, Decency, the constitutional Powers, Insurrection against their Orders, or statement of false or libellous Accusations against Anyone. Open and honest Expressions on the Government of the State and any other Subjects are allowed Anybody.

§ 100. Printing Freedom shall be in Place. No-one can be punished for any Publication of what Content it may be ... unless he with intent and publicly has shown, or incited others to, Disobedience towards the Laws, Disrespect for the Religion, Decency, the constitutional Powers, Insurrection against their Orders, or statement of false or libellous Accusations against Anyone. Open and honest Expressions on the Government of the State and any other Subjects are allowed Anybody.

Freedom of Commerce clause

Basic Law 1814   *Current*

§ 101. New and lasting Limitations of the Freedom of Commerce shall not be imposed on Anyone in the Future.

§ 101. New and existing Limitations of the Freedom of Commerce shall not be imposed on Anyone in the Future.

Property clause

Basic Law 1814

§ 105. If the Need of the State requires that Anyone must part with his movable or immovable Property for public Use, then he shall have full Compensation from the State Treasury.

Current

§ 105. If the Need of the State requires that Anyone must part with his movable or immovable Property for public Use, then he shall have full Compensation from the State Treasury.

Human Rights clause

Basic Law 1814

Current

§ 100c. It is incumbent upon the State's Authorities to respect and secure the Human Rights. Further Provisions on the Implementation of Treaties on this shall be provided by Law.

Denmark

Freedom of Expression clause

Basic Law 1849

§ 91. Anyone is entitled to by Printing to make public his Thoughts, though under Liability before the Courts. Censorship and other preventive Measures can never again be introduced.

Current

§ 77. Anyone is entitled to by print, in writing or speech to make public his thoughts, though under liability before the courts. Censorship and other preventive measures can never again be introduced.

Freedom of Commerce clause

Basic Law 1849

§ 88. All limitations in the free an equal Access to Commerce, which not are based on the general Welfare, shall be revoked by Law.

Current

§ 74. All limitations in the free an equal access to commerce, which not is based on the general welfare, shall be revoked by law.

Searches Clause
Basic Law 1849

§ 86. The Dwelling in inviolable. House-searches, Confiscations, Investigations of Letters, and other Papers in addition to breaches of the post-, telegraph- and Telephone-secrecy must, where no Law enables a special Exception, only happen following a Court order.

Current

§ 72. The dwelling in inviolable. House searches, confiscations and investigations of letters and other papers in addition to breaches of the post-, telegraph- and telephone-secrecy must, where no law enables a special exception, only happen following a court order.

Property clause

Basic Law 1849

Current

§ 87. The Right of Property is inviolable. No one can be compelled to part with property unless the general welfare requires it. It can only happen according to law and against full compensation.

§ 73. The right of property is inviolable. No one can be compelled to part with property unless the general welfare requires it. It can only happen according to law and against full compensation ... [Any question on expropriation can be reviewed by the courts.]

Iceland

Freedom of Expression clause

Constitution 1874

Constitution 1944

Current

54. gr. Every man has the right to make public his thoughts on print; though shall he be liable for them before court. Censorship and other restrictions of the print freedom may never be introduced.

Every man has the right to make public his thoughts on print; though shall he be liable for them before court. Censorship and other restrictions of the print freedom may never be introduced.

73. gr. All are free to have their opinions and beliefs.
Every man has the right to make public his thoughts but he shall be liable for them in court. Censorship and other comparable restrictions of the freedom of expression may never be provided by law.

Freedom of Commerce clause

Constitution 1874

Constitution 1944

Current

51. gr. All those limits that hinder commercial freedom and the equality of men to commerce and are not built on common interest shall be revoked by law.

All those limits that hinder commercial freedom and the equality of men to commerce and are not built on common interest shall be revoked by law.

75. gr. All are free to pursue the commercial trade they choose. These freedoms may be subject to limitations though common interest is required.
In laws shall be provided for men's rights to negotiate for their employment rights and other rights related to commerce.

Property clause

Constitution 1874	*Constitution 1944*	*Current*
50. gr. The right of property is sacrosanct. No one can be compelled to part with property unless the general need demands; for this, orders of law are required and full worth will be compensated.	The right of property is sacrosanct. No one can be compelled to part with property unless the general need demands; for this, provisions of law are required and full worth will be compensated.	72. gr. The right of property is sacrosanct. No one can be compelled to part with property unless the general need demands; for this, provisions of law are required and full worth will be compensated. [Laws can limit foreign right to some property].

Human Rights and Equality clause

Constitution 1874	*Constitution 1944*	*Current*
		65. gr. All shall be equal before the laws and enjoy human rights without regard to sex, religion, beliefs, national origin, skin colour, association or other position.

ECHR

Freedom of Expression clause

Article 10. Everyone has the right to freedom of expression. this right shall include freedom to hold opinions and to receive and impart information and ideas without interference by public authority and regardless of frontiers. This article shall not prevent States from requiring the licensing of broadcasting, television or cinema enterprises.

2. The exercise of these freedoms, since it carries with it duties and responsibilities, may be subject to such formalities, conditions, restrictions or penalties as are prescribed by law and are necessary in a democratic society, in the interests of national security, territorial integrity or public safety, for the prevention of disorder or crime, for the protection of health or morals, for the protection of the reputation or the rights of others, for preventing the disclosure of information received in confidence, or for maintaining the authority and impartiality of the judiciary.

Presumption of Innocence clause

Property clause

Protocol No. 1. Article 1. Every natural or legal person is entitled to the peaceful enjoyment of his possessions. No one shall be deprived of his possessions except in the public interest and subject to the conditions provided for by law and by the general principles of international law.

2. The preceding provisions shall not, however, in any way impair the right of a State to enforce such laws as it deems necessary to control the use of property in accordance with the general interest or to secure the payment of taxes or other contributions or penalties.

Norwegian Review

Summary of Norwegian Review

Norwegian constitutional judicial review has the longest history of the entities surveyed. Norwegian review has developed dynamically throughout the period from 1814 to present. Crucially, Norwegian review has throughout been the most open and accessible. Furthermore, Norwegians have shown a respect for *the Basic Law* as a symbol of nationality and good government that has lent authority to the scrutiny of laws. The result is a familiarity with judicial review, sophistication in its execution, and a high level of legitimacy for constitutional review in Nordic context.

In Norway, the issue of compatibility between statute and constitution surfaced early and became part of the wider political discourse. Sometimes, the review cases dealt with very narrow constitutional issues but especially the general constitutional ban on retroactive laws became a basis for widening the field of constitutional controversies that could be reviewed.

The legal basis for judicial review was long disputed but was expressly endorsed by the Supreme Courts in the majority opinion in a case concerning retroactivity and officers' rights. The opinion clearly favoured the Basic Law as positive law trumping incompatible statutory law. This stance in turn led to a number of issues being raised and constitutional doctrines being developed by the Court, based on constitutional text and principle, and applying the Court's precedent.

The Supreme Court even involuntary, yet loyally, became part of the triumph of Parliamentarism, as the Justices accepted being part of the special impeachment Court of the Realm that pushed constitutional law and deposed the Government Ministers appointed without the confidence of the Storthing. Indeed, the Supreme Court was an important part of the constitutional discourse of the Norwegian State striving to build its structure, identity, and independence.

The rise of the administrative state brought with it inevitable tension with previous constitutional case law. Progressive economic legislation proved irreconcilable with developed doctrine on protected rights. In the end, the

Court accepted the new doctrine of parliamentary supremacy in economic regulation. This Nordic 'switch in time' apparently initiated reversed dynamics, fewer cases were contested on constitutional grounds and the Court showed great deference to legislation, administration, and conceptualist theory even outside the field of economic regulation. During World War II, the Norwegian Supreme Court took the heroic stance of resigning rather than upholding unconstitutional laws enacted by a collaborating legislature, thereby denying legitimacy to the Nazi regime, consolidating its own position as constitutional guardian.

Judicial review was somewhat revitalised in the 1970s with new dynamics that distinguished more between various levels of constitutional scrutiny depending on the rights in question and their impact. During this revival, the European Convention on Human Rights also had its impact. Norway was well suited to receive this quasi-federal review with its tradition of judicial reasoning, precedent, and flexible review techniques. Many issues have been tested in light of ECHR principles, leading to a gradual change towards more case law based constitutional jurisprudence.

Today's Norwegian constitutional judicial review is restrained in matters political but vigorous and sophisticated in matters of personal rights, especially European rights.

Review in Norwegian Constitutional Developments

The Norwegian Supreme Court has functioned since 1815. In many ways, however, it is like the Danish Supreme Court a successor to the old Danish-Norwegian Supreme Court and can thus trace its history back to 1661 and even to further predecessors. With Europe's oldest functioning written constitution, enacted 1814, and a long judicial tradition, the Norwegian Supreme Court is in many ways an impressive court.

Constitutional judicial review has been a feature of Norwegian jurisprudence for a long time. Its development has been dynamic and cyclical, rising and falling according to pressures and circumstances. Review of some kind has existed throughout the country's constitutional development.[1] Review has been exercised in hundreds of cases.[2]

1. See generally Niels Rune Langeland *Siste ord. Høgsterett i norsk historie 1814-1905* Cappelen (2006) .Smith (1993) and Sandmo (2005).
2. Smith (1993) 83.

Constitutional Origins

Norway has been a monarchy since the early middle ages. Norway is historically, in terms of jurisdiction, the amalgamation of four Norse lands, whose four courts survived to some extent to this day, creating a potential for a legal discourse amongst sophisticated interdependent actors. By the late 14th century, through a Union of Crowns, the Kingdom of Norway became tightly associated to Denmark and other principalities with the Monarch functioning as the *arch-king*[3] of a diverse union.

In the late 17th century, Absolutism was introduced in Denmark and Norway, which each got constitutional documents, called the Lex Regia,[4] establishing a constitutional order with a common Supreme Court. The Court served to demonstrate just and orderly government by the King and its Justices were generally excellent lawyers.[5]

The Supreme Court became a part of the constitutionalism that developed around the monarchy, uniting the two Kingdoms and their dependencies in the practice of law and justice. Many ideals of natural law and justice became common to these lands. In addition to the Lex Regia, the Norwegian Code and the Danish Code represented impressive efforts to make all positive law available, and the teaching of law at the University of Copenhagen with emphasis on natural law and Roman law was both unifying and created ideals of constitutionalism and justice, the ius commune.[6] In the words of Ditlev Tamm, "prior to 1800 the law crossed borders," and for a long time "national law studies were missing." This contrast with today when "not the law but lawyers must be able to cross borders between jurisdictions."[7]

It seems fair to say that Nordic lawyers previously were educated as in the USA today in 'typical and ideal law' and then went back to their jurisdictions, applying national and local law according to an acquired broader perspective. The 20th century Nordic lawyer became educated in national law, ideally memorised almost all positive legislation before being further educated in the traditions of their particular field of practice, creating very different

---

3. King Christopher III of Denmark (often called Christopher of Bavaria) used the title *archirex* to connote his position as the prince of the three Nordic Kingdoms and of the duchies of Northern Germany, most notably Schleswig and Holstein. Gyldendal *Navne i Danmarkshistorien 1000 kvinder og mænd fra Danmarks Historien* Gyldendals leksikon (2000) 79.
4. Tamm (2005) 199.
5. Jensen (1999).
6. Tamm (2005) 156.
7. Ibid. 45.

strata of law and very narrow perspectives. Nowadays, we are – as this book hopefully demonstrates – edging back to a wider perspective.

Norway was a dormant State throughout this period. In principle, the Treaty of Bergen 1450[8] established a union of equals but in practice, power was centralised in Copenhagen with the Supreme Court but one integrated branch of government. Norway was abruptly awoken from its constitutional slumber by developments at the end of the Napoleonic Wars. The King of Sweden sided with the allies, wanting compensation for the loss of Finland to the Tsar of Russia. The King of Denmark-Norway was on the losing side with France and had to cede Norway to Sweden according to the Treaty of Kiel.[9] The Danish-Norwegian King urged his Norwegian subjects to accept this arrangement necessary for "peace in the Nordic region"[10] and the Swedish King claimed the country accordingly.[11]

This did not go down well with the Norwegians; Sweden had, in earlier times, conquered parts of Norway, this therefore amounted to treachery by the King in Copenhagen, whom Norwegians generally seem to have afforded loyalty and legitimacy.[12] With the help of Christian Frederic, cousin of Frederic VI of Denmark-Norway and viceroy on his behalf, members of the Norwegian establishment organised a Constitutional Conference at Eidsvoll, cite of the old Things, resulting in the Constitution of 17 May, still celebrated as National Day of Norway. Christian Frederic, claiming that, "the free Norwegian People can on its own determine its Destiny,"[13] was elected King and this thus reconstituted polity held out against Swedish military assault. Eventually, not least for financial reasons, the Norwegians accepted the Swedish King but they would not budge on Norway's statehood, independence, and constitution. The compromise was a revised Constitution of 4 November 1814 stating that Norway was "united with Sweden under one King."[14] Chris-

---

8. Zakarias Wang "The Constitutional Status of Greenland and Faroe" 2 *Faroese Law Review* (2002) 159 at 164. See also Zakarias Wang "Upprunin til stjórnarskipan Grønlands og Føroya" 5 *Faroese Law Review* (2005).
9. Mads Tønnesson Andenæs *Grunnloven vår* (2001) 111-120.
10. Andenæs (2001) 121.
11. Ibid. 122.
12. Johs. Andenæs *Statsforfatningen i Norge* Tano Aschehoug (1998) 35.
13. Andenæs (2001) 123.
14. Ibid. 166, Basic Law § 1.

tian Frederic returned to Denmark and incidentally later became King Christian VIII of Denmark.[15]

Although the King would now reside in Stockholm, this still amounted to a major victory for Norwegian independence and constitutionalism. "No-one outside Norway would have thought it the least unreasonable if the Basic Law had shared its destiny with the short-lived Kingdom. Instead the Basic Law emerged so to speak unharmed from the negotiations on the union."[16] The conventional view of the time, anyhow, was that a King should head the executive government, give ascent to legislation, and conduct foreign policy. This was already reflected in the Eidsvoll Constitution; trading one King for another was not necessarily a defeat. Legislative power passed to the elected Storthing, the entire judiciary and the administration below cabinet level were solidly Norwegian, as were the armed forces. The State of Norway was up and running again.

Constitutional Strife

The Norwegian Supreme Court became a crucial part of the struggle to ensure Norway's newfound independence.[17] The Supreme Court used its powers to defend the provisions of the 1814 Constitution, which soon was referred to as the Basic Law, underscoring its status as positive, enforceable law. The high point of the "Patriotic Supreme Court" was the case *Frederiks Universitet v. Gjerdrum* where the Court held that banning or hindering 17 May celebrations as being "unwanted" by the King was "completely unwarranted"; the police might warn against "Disorder ... but not make the lawful Act unlawful."[18]

A longstanding dispute between the King, who apparently contemplated the use of force,[19] and his Norwegian subjects was over the Freedom of Expression clause, § 100 of the Basic Law. The King tried both to use legislation predating the Basic Law and to issue "additions" to that legislation without the full consent of the Storthing.[20] The Supreme Court held in several cases, most notably the *Peterson v. Aars* of 1823 and the *Allum v. Bjerre-*

---

15. Andenæs (1998). Apparently, Christian Frederic was suggested for the Swedish Throne when Bernadotte was eventually elected. Had he succeeded, there might have been a Nordic Union with entirely different dynamics.
16. Langeland (2006) 185.
17. Ibid. 192, in general from 185.
18. Ibid. 221-22. Case not in file.
19. Ibid. 194.
20. Ibid. 195.

gaard case of 1824, that the old regulation of 1799 on the press could not be applied against § 100's provision on free opinions on the State's government.[21] Thus, the Supreme Court established that statutes had to be enacted constitutionally properly and that, constitutional procedure notwithstanding, statutes would be substantively limited by the Freedoms of the Basic Law. "The active use of the Basic Law pointed forward to ... judicial review."[22]

As views on government changed, the Norwegians gradually wanted more autonomy, more power in the hands of the Storthing, and less government from Stockholm. Through a long constitutional struggle, Norway was finally free from its union with Sweden in 1905. The Basic Law had created a constitutional structure that facilitated a gradual transition over almost a century. In the end, Norwegian support for independence was almost unanimous[23] and support for a Danish royal prince as new King overwhelming.[24]

Before getting that far, however, the Storthing was able to force through a number of constitutional changes outside the amendment procedure provided by the Basic Law. Most notably, the executive was first divided into a government in Stockholm and another in Oslo,[25] and later Parliamentarism triumphed as it later did in the other Nordic countries with the King accepting that his Government had to have the confidence of the elected Parliament.[26]

If viewed legalistically, everything significant that happened in Norway from 1814 to 1905 was unconstitutional, disobedience to the King and disrespect for the Constitution. Perceived more analytically, we see a dynamic development that allowed the political forces to shift and shape the Norwegian constitution without bloodshed and without disintegration of the State. A detailed account of developments falls outside our scope; instead, a particular look a judicial review is relevant. Suffice it to say, that constitutional judicial review was but one aspect of law that Høyesterett helped to develop.[27]

When the progressive forces in the Storthing started to demand Parliamentarism, the view of most lawyers, not least the stern Supreme Court Justices seemed to be that this was unconstitutional and illegal. However, the political branch showed a remarkable understanding for the dynamics of constitutional adjudication. Norway had a special procedure for impeachment, probably in-

---

21. Ibid. 203-05. Cases not in file.
22. Ibid. 211.
23. Some 370,000 votes to 184. See Andenæs (1998) 48.
24. Andenæs (1998) 48.
25. Ibid. 45.
26. Ibid. 45.
27. Smith (1993) 65.

spired by the British and America models and adopted by Denmark as well, whereby Government Ministers would be impeached by the lower house and judged by a panel including members of the upper house and of the Supreme Court. This special Court of the Realm would effectively decide the constitutionality of Parliamentarism.[28]

In Norway until recently, the elected Storthing (the Great Thing) elected the Lagthing with the remainder becoming the Odelsthing. Usually, the parties and factions would be roughly proportionally represented in the Lagthing but now the progressive Left Party used its majority to elect only its own members. The sitting Prime Minister was then impeached for ruling without the confidence of the Storthing, the case was referred to the Court of the Realm, where the Supreme Court Justices voted to acquit according to the letter of the law, and the Members of Parliament who made up the majority voted to convict. The learned Justices could have disrupted the proceedings by walking out or by signalling that they would rule otherwise if a case were brought before the regular courts. However, they accepted the political ploy, sitting patiently with the "unprincipled bastards,"[29] convicting the ministers and thereby lent legitimacy[30] to judicial precedent providing that it was an impeachable offence to govern contrary to the popularly elected Parliament.[31] These examples of review were crucial in Norwegian constitutional developments. They also show that special institutions may serve the function of review forum.

This level of sophistication in understanding judicial politics perhaps reveals that the Norwegian elites were well versed in legal and constitutional method. Certainly, the Eidsvoll Constitution itself revealed understanding of government theory and foreign regimes somewhat comparable to the constitutional process in Philadelphia a few decades before. The Eidsvoll process was perhaps the whole process from Declaration of Independence to Constitution and first Congress in one sweeping effort. This could not have been done without an educated and cultured elite supported and trusted by the consent of the governed.[32]

---

28. Andenæs (1998) 172-73.
29. Langeland (2006) 539.
30. Smith (1993) 334.
31. Fr. Brandt *Samling af mærkelige Højesteretsdomme i Tidsrummet 1815-1835* (1855) 539-44.
32. Andenæs (1998) from 38.

The Supreme Court in Context

Our interest centres, of course, on the presence and understanding of judicial dynamics. Historically, Norway was established by uniting the various autonomous Norse Lands that were organised around the Things, functioning as both legislative and judicial bodies. The great four Land Things were Gulathing, Frostathing, Eidsivathing, and Borgarthing,[33] whose names are still reflected in the Norwegian Appeal Court Structure. Of course, it is difficult to say how much more than the names were continued from the old Things. However, the existence, even in Danish times under one common Supreme Court, of four Appeal Courts of equal standing may provide Norwegians with a practical knowledge of judicial dynamics.

Courts on the same level in a judicial hierarchy tend to feel persuaded by each other's cases and to communicate indirectly through reports and lawyers, who submit persuasive precedent from the sister courts. Such cybernetic communication[34] is always somewhat disorganised but it seems likely that the vast Norwegian Realm led to a diverse tradition. Local judges rode circuit explaining the law to the locals, appeal cases were heard by four different courts, and some cases reached Copenhagen, all leading to extensively reasoned and written opinions and dynamic development of difficult legal issues, such as clashing provision, including legislation ill fitting with tradition or the cosmopolitan background of the lawyers educated in Copenhagen. The tradition inherited from the Danes was one of "close expert community that mainly functioned under wraps."[35]

In 1814, a Norwegian Supreme Court had to be hastily established.[36] Although Norwegians had sat as prominent members of the Union Supreme Court in Copenhagen,[37] the new Norwegian Supreme Court may owe as much to the tradition of the Norwegian Appeal Courts. At any rate, several important factors were present at the same time. A new written Constitution, a newly formed Supreme Court, the importance of maintaining a distinct legal system in a federal arrangement with Sweden, and the beginning of the teaching of law in Norway itself. All these factors are likely to have led to a

33. Tamm (2005) 98.
34. Shapiro (2002) .Martin Shapiro and Stone Sweet, Alec "Judicial Law-making and Precedent" in *On Law, Politics and Judicialization* (2002) from 103, 107-09
35. Langeland (2006) 358.
36. Ibid. 25.
37. Ibid. 21-22. For a very engaging account of the old Court in Copenhagen see Ibid. 15-21.

dynamic development independent of Swedish law and away from Danish law. Norway was chartering its own legal course.

One Danish tradition that the Norwegian Supreme Court continued was not publishing reasoned judgements. By design, this was originally a way for the absolute government to avoid being petitioned based on equality and precedent.[38] This no longer stood to reason but habits are hard to shed. Private reporting seems to have been occurring with for instance the controversial Fr. Brandt, professor of law and extraordinary Supreme Court Justice, leading the way.[39] In 1844, for instance, the weekly Norsk Retstidende reported that the Supreme Court had decided a case regarding Oslo's bakers, noting the important legal issues involved.[40] The paper could not fully report Supreme Court reasoning but it was possible to notify the legal milieu of the case and to print both the lower court reasoning and the parties' arguments before the Supreme Court in a later issue.[41]

Partial publishing and four consecutive resolutions by the Storthing eventually led to the Court releasing its opinions for full publications.[42] The pressure from the progressive forces to let the people know the reasoning behind the judgements was eventually formulated as a choice for the Supreme Court; either the Court would be compelled to support its conclusions with published reasons or it had to publish the votes (opinions) of the Justices. The Court chose the latter, and from then on, Norwegian Supreme Court judgements have been uniquely accessible. The "trueborn child of the [absolutism was at last fully] on equal terms as an independent branch of government."[43]

Unlike the terse logic and formal statements of the Danish and Icelandic Courts, Norwegian judgements provide an insight to hearts and minds of the Justices. Norwegian opinions are written in the first person, usually with the first voting judge presenting the issues and then explaining, '*My* view of the case,' expressly stating that, '*I* find this so and so.' This mode is perhaps more akin to the individual opinions of the House of Lords (now Supreme Court of the United Kingdom) than that of the Supreme Court of the United States, where the majority often agrees on an Opinion of Court. Norwegian opinions are often long yet disarmingly personal, as the Justices "... have got accustomed to the system of individual votes and now seem to take pleasure

38. Jensen (1999).
39. Brandt (1855).
40. Rt. 1844-704.
41. *Rolfsen v. Petersen* (Rt. 1845-513).
42. Tschudi-Madsen (1998) from 29.
43. Langeland (2006) 358, 361.

in it by writing sometimes most lengthy opinions!"[44] This is the logical development set in motion by most "giving reasons requirements,"[45] deliberations and publications create a body of case law that further develops the norm structure.

Reflecting the solid international legal education of the time, issues of justice were featured in early Norwegian Supreme Court Jurisprudence. The Basic Law was seen as not only specific rules but also more as giving voice to higher principles of justice as expressed by judge Langberg, rendering his opinion "as well because of common Justice as according to the [Constitution]."[46] This mindset probably proved an important factor in establishing Norwegian judicial review.

Introduction to the Early Period

As the point of this study is to observe West-Nordic judicial review and analyse it based on universal theories that can explain developments at different times and in different countries, we shall take a closer look at some of the "Early Norwegian Cases," meaning cases from 1814 to 1905. These cases may to some seem old and irrelevant but closer inspection will reveal how several factors are involved, which seem parallel to present-day conditions. For instance, trans-national concepts of justice and human rights appear to have had equal importance back then as they do now, albeit perhaps in different shapes. Furthermore, the dynamic development of the constitutional norms through case law demonstrates that judicial rulemaking is not something inherently alien to the West-Nordic tradition. On the contrary, judicial dynamics are the original Nordic way of dealing with the contradictions inherent in democratic government based on principled written constitutions containing procedures and substantive rights and other restraints on the representative government. Moreover, the late 19th century saw much constitutional discourse; the Court would review statutes, the Storthing answered with new legislation and open debate on constitutionality, which led to scholarly

---

44. Eivind Smith "Courts and Parliament: The Norwegian System of Judicial Review of Legislation" in *The Constitution as an Instrument of Change* SNS Förlag (2003b) 174.

45. See in general Shapiro and Stone Sweet (2002c). For the need for more reasons to be given in a Scandinavian context see Peter Garde "Og ingen formummet Skjelm – Bemærkninger om domsmandsanonymitet, dissensret og -plikt" 84 *Juristen* (2002) 43.

46. *Blom v. Aars* (SmH.132 (1822)) per Judge Langberg.

debate and new cases. The quality of the discourse was enhanced by the law professors in Parliament and by Justices writing articles.[47]

Judicial review in this period is seen by some as reactionary misuse of power by the "dethroned class of public officials"[48] who had lost their grip on power to the democratic forces when the King accepted parliamentarism at the end of the 19th century. This, however, may not be a fully analysed perception.[49] The better view is that ideals held by the elite that wrote the Eidsvoll Constitution were, of course, embedded in that document and enforced when raised in controversies before the Court. A number of cases dealing with the Officers' Clause of the Basic Law probably reinforced the perception of class activism but said provision left little room for interpretation. Most importantly, the majority of Norwegian Justices saw the Basic Law as superior to statutes and judged accordingly. Especially, the change from self-reliant to salaried officials and general legislation superseding individual privileges, contracts, and exemptions led to many controversies.[50]

These early cases shall be divided between *Early Sportel Cases,*[51] dealing with a particular legal problem raised by the Norwegian civil servants when the reconstituted State undertook to restructure its administration.[52] These cases led to the more general *Early Retroactive Cases*, where the ban on retroactive laws became contested in several controversies; to this day, the Retroactive clause of the Basic Law is the most disputed. The *Officers' Cases*[53] relied somewhat on the precedent created by the aforementioned groups and the Officers' Clause;[54] this group of cases gave rise to explicit recognition of review. The *Trading Rights Cases*[55] created a material normative shift through judicial rulemaking, as the protection against retroactivity was extended very far. Comments will be made to the individual cases.

Introduction to Middle Period

In the late 19th and early 20th century, judicial review increased in use, and a number of other provisions of the Constitution were used as basis for the ex-

---

47. Langeland (2006) from 347.
48. Smith (1993) 13.
49. Smith (1993) 168, 172, and 179.
50. Langeland (2006) from 309.
51. A sub-group of the Officers' or Civil Servants Cases. Smith (1993) 131.
52. Langeland (2006) 310.
53. Smith (1993) from 131.
54. Langeland (2006) from 342.
55. Helgadóttir (2006) from 60, uses the phrase "vested rights" rather than "protected rights" and "trading rights".

ercise of review.[56] As the early cases demonstrated, however, judicial review relied very much on individual rights, which eventually came into conflict with the collective efforts and technical developments.[57] Just as the progressive factions had struggled over Parliamentarism, so they would push to limit the protection of property rights and the various rights discovered in connection with retroactivity.

In particular, what might be seen as windfall profits, which landowners reaped from hydroelectric power or from roads and railroads being constructed on their land, was a thorn in the side of the progressive politicians. Other interventionist economic legislation aimed at calming the market forces, protecting domestic markets, and so forth, was obviously at odds with established judicial doctrine, which was gradually challenged.[58] The first three decades of the 20th century saw a number of such cases, ending in reversal of doctrine in favour of allowing economic regulation.

Not only doctrine came under attack, however, a number of opinions openly disputed the authority of the Supreme Court to review legislation,[59] revealing that, in Norwegian jurisprudence, all questions can apparently be revisited and precedent may be overruled. The result was that "a strengthened self-consciousness around the right of review [but] a reluctance to use it. [Only the Court's] minority would use it in difficult cases ... The development made right of review more of a principle than a part of practise. That way, it also ceased to be a political problem."[60]

Several political initiatives were undertaken to limit judicial review even further.[61] However, in 1926, the Storthing apparently decided the longstanding debate on constitutional judicial review by explicitly accepting its existence with the Plenary Act. Since 1905, the Norwegian Supreme Court had functioned with two chambers, which was practical for expediting the caseload but potentially unfortunate for development of case law doctrine. In particular, the chambers increased the likelihood that a few Justices might exercise judicial review, setting aside statutes without support from the full Court. The Plenary Act provided which cases were to be handled by the full Court, including cases concerning unconstitutionality and reversal of precedent. This law led to less dynamics in case law and to fewer instances of active judicial

---

56. Smith (1993) 207.
57. Langeland (2006) 508.
58. Ibid. 509.
59. See for instance Chief Justice Thinn in *Johansen v. Norway* (Rt. 1918-401).
60. Sandmo (2005) 138.
61. Ibid. from 138.

review.[62] "The Plenary Act had a paradoxical effect: On the one side, it made it more difficult for the Supreme Court to set aside new laws, on the other, this was the first and final legislative recognition of the right to review. It simultaneously affirmed and weakened the right to review."[63]

The Plenary Act together with the fight against review in the name of economic policy resulted in the decline of review; less than a decade after the Act was promulgated judicial review had come to a halt. This development "based on the viewpoint of economic intervention [not constitutional amendment],"[64] has some similarities with that of the United States, where comparable doctrines had developed. There, the confrontation between the New Deal policies of F.D. Roosevelt and the Supreme Court ended when "a switch in time saved Nine."[65] Faced with relentless pressure from both President and Congress, the Supreme Court eventually gave in but much later than in Norway. For similar reasons both the Norwegian and US polity developed in similar direction in terms of judicial review.[66] Thus, Norwegian jurisprudence seems not to be so much inspired by US doctrine as predating it.[67]

During the economic depression of the 1930s, the Supreme Court seems to have allowed the Storthing to regulate the economy relatively freely, with the "last case clearly setting aside" decided in 1931 as a rather technical judgement on Udall rights that could be circumvented with another technical statute.[68] The decline of review affected all substantive areas, however, and not much review is recorded during this period. By this time, scholarly theory was changing from studying common principles and universal sources of rights and justice to Scandinavian realism and statutory positivism.[69] Terms like realism and positivism may be misguided in case of Scandinavia.[70] Realism is more properly used for analytical theory that accepts doctrines such as judicial review but examines them realistically. It is perfectly possible to be staunchly anti-natural law, pro-democratic, and willing to embrace constitutional review as resulting from the positive law status of the Constitution, re-

---

62. Sandmo (2005) 46-52.
63. Ibid. 52.
64. Smith (1993) 189.
65. Schwartz (1995) 234.
66. Smith (2003b) 172.
67. Smith (1993) 189. Helgadóttir may view the two more closely linked see Helgadóttir (2006) 204 and elsewhere.
68. Smith (1993) 218-19.
69. In general Blandhol (1999).
70. Gregory Alexander "Comparing the Two Legal Realisms – American and Scandinavian" 50 *The American Journal of Comparative Law* (2002) 241.

alistically viewing constitutional judges as negative legislators that are countering the positive legislators in Parliament.[71] Scandinavian legal ideology from the depression and almost to the present day has been wedded to government by experts, nurturing a conceptualist view of law including constitutionalism according to which a Basic Law is merely an inspiration from legislators and its rights provisions so indeterminate that as concepts are outside the realm of law.

The Second World War brought with it a brutal Nazi occupation of Norway. The Norwegian Supreme Court refused to co-operate and resigned en masse.[72] Following the War, the Supreme Court dealt with the issues of criminal charges brought against collaborators and Germans soldiers and continuous disadvantages faced by the collaborators.

For decades after the War, the Court appears to have been largely restrained, showing great deference to the Storthing, not least the preparatory works prepared by administrators and experts, who increasingly came to hold the initiative in new legislation. When issues of interpretation arose despite the extensive motives behind the legislation, textbooks came to play the role of precedent in earlier times. The textbook view in turn became that judicial review was unlikely to be applied again to substantial extent.[73]

However, constitutional judicial review was never completely wiped out; the potential for review may have restrained legislation to some degree, and flexible techniques like interpreting a statute in light of the Basic Law were always at hand.[74] In the 1970s, stagflation and dismal council estates[75] had weakened the belief in unrestrained planning and expert rule. In a series of cases, the Supreme Court began to apply the Basic Law again, developing distinctions between various levels of scrutiny depending on the provisions. This period is probably influenced by the increasing focus on international human rights as well.

The dominant theory was that issues pertaining to the political branches and their powers would be largely left to Storthing and Government to fight over among themselves. By contrast, individual rights deserved the full protection of the Court, with economic rights enjoying a middle category.

This leads to our second grouping of cases, the *Previous Practice*. The body of Norwegian Supreme Court cases dealing with constitutionality is

---

71. Shapiro and Stone Sweet (2002a) 147.
72. Andenæs (1998) 51.
73. Smith (1993) 42.
74. According to some the flexibility was sometimes stretched too far Smith (1993) 71.
75. The metaphor is persuasively used by Blandhol in Blandhol (2002)

enormous, especially compared with the other West-Nordic countries. We shall therefore survey only a number of them to gain an insight into the changing dynamics from the end of the classical review era to its resurgence up until around a decade ago. We shall look at the *Economic Regulation Cases*, concerning the battle between earlier rights doctrines and the new progressive regulation of the economy. Then, the *War Cases* provide an insight into legal reasoning under extreme circumstances. Finally, the *Review Revival Cases* deal with a number of issues tackled by the Supreme Court from the 1970s to the 1990s.

Introduction to the Recent Period

The attention shall then lastly turn to recent Norwegian constitutional judicial review. During the last decade, Norwegian judicial review has vastly expanded. Constitutional developments and the upsurge in review activities both based on the national Basic Law and the international sources such as ECHR have all laid the groundwork for quite some review activity in recent years.[76]

Our focus will remain on the various factors that increase or lessen the use of judicial review as well as on the reasoning and techniques used in review. Of particular interest is, of course, how the Norwegian Supreme Court continues to deal with the quasi-federal dimension of constitutional law and the methodical challenges it faces in reconciling West-Nordic conceptualist theory and fidelity towards textbooks and preparatory works with the overtly dynamic and case law based approach of the ECHR Court.[77]

Like the early and previous parts, the survey of recent case law shall be divided in to a number of sections based on the main subject matter of the controversy. We begin with *Freedom of Expression, Association, and Religion Cases*, groups of cases of increased importance. Second, we look at the *Property and Economic Rights Cases*, groups of controversies treated dynamically different over the years now being refined with relatively little European influence. Third, we shall look at *Recent Retroactivity Cases*, this special breed of Norwegian cases that have undergone much refinement through the ages. Fourth, we shall take a particular look at *Proportionality*. Fifth, we shall move into the *Rights of the Accused* focusing on presumption of innocence. Sixth and finally, we shall examine some of the numerous cases on *Double Jeopardy* that have been flooding the Norwegian Supreme Court.

---

76. Smith (1993) 284.
77. On the development in Norwegian Supreme Court methodology see Rytter (2006) 42.

Norwegian case law demonstrates that constitutional principles have manifested themselves even to the point "that the customary constitutional law has a *formal* position in the doctrines of sources of law."[78] However, there are three levels of scrutiny, as we shall see in cases like *Kløfta*. Individual liberty will be most vigorously guarded; economic rights are afforded a lesser degree of protection; and as to the workings of the other branches of government, the courts will largely defer to Parliament.[79]

Recent Norwegian theory displays a familiarity with judicial review, yet often fails adequately to explain the dynamic and quasi-federal qualities of Norwegian review.

However, some seem fully to appreciate the dynamic and the discourse created by ECHR membership. For instance, on the debate of the competing imperatives of freedom of the press and freedom of the person, it has been suggested that Norwegians could argue consistent with ECHR case law that Art 8 and Art 10 ECHR should be balanced, abandoning earlier Norwegian textbook positions.[80] Likewise, Professor Jørgen Aall, comments on presumption of innocence cases with a very precise analysis. First, that the field of contention between criminal acquittal and civil suit is that where the lack of factual evidence, rather than lack of intent or other, is the reason for acquitting. Second, that Norwegian legislation could pre-empt any conflict by going beyond Art 6 (2) ECHR, proscribing civil suit in case of acquittal for lack of factual evidence in the criminal case, thereby "affecting the ECHR Court's assessment in future cases."[81] This sums up the constitutional reality of review today, human rights provisions will to a great extent be interpreted by the ECHR Court; Norway has to make its democratic choices with the constraints of ECHR case law, including participating in and pushing the dynamic development of the ECHR norms.

Another interesting view of this was presented by the Gulathing Appeal Court in its petition regarding a major survey on power in Norway. The Court noted that the official report said "the internationalisation in form of the ties on legislation by Norwegian authorities through the EEA-agreement and EU's rules together with the incorporation of human rights," leading to a weakening of popular democracy and a strengthening of the courts. This,

78. Husa (2002) 149.
79. Oftedal Broch (2003) 245.
80. Bjørn Borvik "EMK artikkel 8 og vernet mot æreskrenkingar" *Tidskrift for rettsvitenskap* (2003) 246 at 304.
81. Jørgen Aall "Uskyldspresumsjonen etter frifinnende dom" *Lov og Rett* (2003) 249 at 253, 256.

however, could be justified by ideals of the "democratic rights state," and urged more courts to "uphold and control" the rights created when transferring legislative power. Gulathing further noted that interest in participating in jury and magistrate service pointed to an "optimistic picture of the future of people power," despite dwindling participation in party politics.[82]

Norwegian constitutional judicial review is clearly a product of accident and force. The silence of the Basic Law has allowed different theories to arise. In favour of review, people like professor Bredo af Mogenstierne, who opined that, "The Basic Law is to be regarded as the Proxy Power to the legislating Powers, which they cannot exceed without that Decision losing its legal Force. [T]he Occasion that the legislating Powers of State have disregarded the Basic Law cannot release the Courts from the Duty to follow it."[83] Opposing, people like professor Skeie found that, "the Norwegian legislative power stands lower than any other European legislature ... [in matters of the constitutionality of economic legislation to declare the legislative power bound by prejudicial voting in a criminal case, heard for a couple of hours and decided under dissent can only be called: constitutional caricature.]"[84] Depending on the politicians, professors, and judges,[85] and the laws, cases, and issue before them, the varying views on review powers have had differing impact.

Consequently, judicial review in Norway has undergone some interesting twists and turns since 1814 that seem to prove the point that neither is an obvious solution provided by the Basic Law, nor is there any consistent doctrine developed by the Supreme Court. The Norwegian word "prøvningsretten" indicates "the right to review" rather than the "power" or "duty" to do so, it also has a slightly apologetic ring to it, as it is never contrasted to the "lawgiving right" or "the right to behave unconstitutionally" but always to the "lawgiving power." Judicial review in Norway is probably best viewed as "a much wider phenomenon than a legal theoretical question of jurisdiction. The right to review seems anchored in certain cases; it rises with them and fades away with them. [The] strong normative constructions [lost] their supporting strength

---

82. Terje Einarsen "Domstolene – de nye maktsentra?" *Rett på sak* (2004) 26 at 26, 27.
83. Sandmo (2005) 122.
84. Ibid. 125.
85. "[T]he view on [the intensity of review] has changed among different judges and court panels." Smith (1993) 159.

[facing] legislation and change of climate. It can therefore be fruitful to talk of [several] rights of review with differing historical basis ..."[86]

Early Cases

Early Sportel Cases

The first reported case on judicial review *Blom v. Aars* (SmH.132 (1822)) was handed down without being announced as such, as the reasoning was not initially reported,[87] the short published result of the judgement did not mention the Constitution. However, a private report, the Brandt report, published in 1855[88] reveals that the judicial milieu probably knew a lot about the legal reasoning, as may have been the case also in earlier times regarding the Norwegian Appeal Courts.[89] The Brandt report states that, "In the Supreme Court the Appellants referred to the Precedent of 17 September last ..."[90] That earlier case, however, is not included in the report. Later research has revealed the full reasoning.[91]

Blom v. Aars was initiated by Jan Blom, President of the Corporation of Trondhjem together with the widow of its Bailiff Jonas Udbye. Their personal income had been secured by so-called "sportel," an arrangement whereby certain offices were financed by fees or part of fees levied on various activities, and after expenditure, the remainder would serve as their personal income. The system may date back to feudal times and was probably seen as practical in times before improved communication and transportation but was being gradually dismantled. In this case, the officers had the right to a certain proportion of the proceeds from public auction of the copper processed at Røraas. As the legislation on copper plant was amended, the producers could tender their copper without involving the officers in question, contrary to a decree of 1796.[92]

---

86. Brandt (1855) 538.
87. Its reasoning was later partially reported, however, through the (unofficial) reporting of the later case *Dahl v. Norway* (Rt. 1854-093) that relied on and referred to *Blom v. Aars* extensively.
88. Fr. Brandt *Samling af mærkelige Højesteretsdomme i Tidsrummet 1815-1835* (1855).
89. On precedent prior to 1863 Smith (1993) 174 with note 46.
90. *Blom v. Aars* 134.
91. Smith (1993) 134, note 15.
92. Ibid. 132.

The Court minority remarked that the claim was not forcefully pursued and thus lost due to passivity; and judge Kiøning further remarked in passing that the opposite result risked hindering devises for the common purpose.[93] Thus, this early case dealt with the same themes of balancing individual rights and government powers, the minority favouring the priorities of the representative government, choosing a restrictive interpretation of rights provisions and imposing procedural burdens on citizen challenging statute.

The majority, however, accepted the views of judge Langberg that "as well because of common Justice as according to the 105th Article [Property clause] of the Constitution as well as the 97th Article [Retroactive clause]," the judges were "only to determine the Consequences of a Statute on the Rights of Private Citizen."[94]

The statute left the question of compensation open, and the majority of the Court then used the Constitution as guidance for its statutory interpretation. This may arguably be categorised as constitutional judicial review using creative techniques,[95] setting aside the law through over-interpretation rather than over-ruling.[96] The government and minority both denied that there was any margin for interpretation; however, the majority chose to expand the statute's scope to include such rights as were mentioned by the Constitution – and part of common justice. The approach taken probably shows one of the earliest European examples of 'finding' fundamental principles, using creative techniques of control[97] to discover rights or remedies that are not immediately apparent. The full opinions were not known until much later and may thus not have had the full impact on the perception of constitutional law that they could had they been published in full early on. However, the 1855 Brandt report at least clearly refers to both the use of precedent[98] and to the applied sections of the Basic Law – § 105 combined with §§ 22 and 97 – regarding Officers, Property and Retroactivity.[99]

In sum, the case probably opens a window to the Norwegian constitutional case law. First, on the abstract constitutional level, the Constitution as a document is given legal force and is seen as exemplifying principles of justice that are also awarded legal relevance. Second, as to the merits of the case, the

---

93. Ibid. 134.
94. Ibid. 134.
95. Shapiro and Stone Sweet (2002a) from 189.
96. "These features have independent interest" Smith (1993) 159.
97. Stone Sweet (2002a) 189.
98. *Blom v. Aars* 134.
99. Ibid. 133.

statute is seen as an instrument that must be compliant with said principles and is thus interpreted as being so; to the extent that Storthing wanted to clash with the Courts' understanding of the Constitution by eliminating or reducing compensation. The Supreme Court used its power to review and set the law aside but only in terms of the results of the particular case. Presumably, Norwegian law could, at this point in time, be accurately restated to include a construction of statutory law to include compliance with relevant constitutional rights as well as recognised principles of justice. This indicates a very sophisticated initial approach that might even today be seen as a possible balanced approach. Third, however, the case reveals a disagreement that was later to become something of a schism as to methodology regarding the relative weight of 'private rights and justice' and the 'common purpose,' on the one hand an inclination to use precedent and natural justice, on the other a deference to parliamentary priorities and a high bar for individual suits.

In 1833, in ***Morgenstjerne v. Petersen*** (SmH.504 (1833)), the issue of civil servant duties was contested again. Chancery Council Morgenstjerne (represented by Lasson, the later Chief Justice) was ordered to sit as an extraordinary judge in a case concerning official misconduct. The indicted officials were convicted and ordered to pay cost, including salary for the commissioned judges. The judgment of cost, however, was reversed on appeal and Morgenstjerne humbly petitioned for a salary from the State for the 17 sessions involving 41 business days as well as expenses, amongst other reasons "in Analogy of the BL § 105,"[100] the Officers' Clause. The parties reportedly argued about the legal effect of the Supreme Court judgement in the main proceedings and Government Attorney Petersen relied on a theory that the State had a wide discretion in ordering people in any official position to assume any duty that may arise.[101] The Supreme Court is reported to have dealt explicitly with the extent of duties and to have found the duty in question far to have exceeded any incumbent position and ordered an assessment of the appropriate salary at the State's expense.[102] The report refers to further case law.

Though the case is not fully reported as to the constitutional issue, it shows that constitutionality was raised as legal basis in several ways. Precedent is assumed relevant, perhaps even binding, and other principles of justice, found by using constitutional principles as examples, starting points of interpretation.

100. *Morgenstjerne v. Petersen* 505.
101. Ibid. 506.
102. Ibid. 507.

In *Zeier v. Stang* (SmH.626 (1835)), the question was framed even more as a rights issue. Attorney Zeier was ordered to sit as judge in a case against a misbehaving priest. Zeier refused to sit without pay and, consequently, he was prosecuted for his insubordination. The prosecution claimed in the Supreme Court that, "whereas provision of the Code of Norway cannot be above the Basic Law, there are numerous Analogies that one is obliged to assume public Duties not less without than against Payment."[103] Prosecutor Stang then referred to jury duty and other such participation in legal proceedings. The Supreme Court upheld the lower court judgement that had dismissed the case as it was "a Consequence of as well the Nature of the Case as those in our Legislation incorporated Basic Principles" that an officer's duties could not be extended in this manner.[104] All three instances seem to have dealt with the finer points of Mr. Zeier's status as an officer of the court, the nature of his duties as such and the nature and burden of his added commission. The report refers to further case law.

The case shows again how the principles mentioned in the Basic Law are applied as law, not just at principles for parliamentary consideration. The Basic Law, as well as other principles that be deduced from it, seem to be assumed to trump statute, so the issue becomes more one of interpretation, is there or is there not a clash, as statutory law will only stand if the Basic Law is silent.

Early Retroactive Cases

The case *Young v. Norway* (Rt. 1841-274) brought other provisions into play. The late entrepreneur Jørgen Young and his son had issued deeds and mortgage documents that the state alleged were not or were inadequately stamped, and duty therefore owed. The case revolved around the Retroactive clause, the Taxation clause, and the proper understanding of the concept of "Law" (Lov).[105]

Because this was still prior to the full publication of Supreme Court reasoning, the report only refers to the reasoning of the two lower courts and to the arguments made by the parties. However, it seems clear[106] that the Supreme Court held with the trial court that the Retroactive clause meant that documents issued prior to the Stamp Duty Resolution could not be levied with the duty even if they in fact were stamped after the enactment of the

103. *Zeier v. Stang per* Prosecutor.
104. Ibid. *per* Appeal Court.
105. *Young v. Norway.*
106. On different readings of the case Smith (1993) 124-27.

Resolution. The Supreme Court seems to have endorsed that the term "law" in the Retroactive clause should be understood wider than "statutes." The official result of the case to "uphold the trial courts judgement"[107] appears enigmatic; however, the extensive account of some 40 pages of lower court holdings and party arguments[108] may still have had significant impact on the legal environment as indirect source of Supreme Court case law.

The case may signify that the legal relevance of the Basic Law was broadening; the Supreme Court was interpreting the concepts of the Basic Law and making them applicable in different categories of cases.

In ***Rolfsen v. Petersen*** (Rt. 1845-513), the Retroactive clause was extended to protect a number of bakers who had been baking bread contrary to a new regulation. Apparently, they had previously been admitted as "Burghers" (Borgere) by the Corporation of Christiania (Oslo), and at the time, their privileges extended to baking bread with hired help.[109] The report is again sketchy,[110] but it devolves that the parties "documented" earlier Supreme Court cases and other cases are cited by the report.[111] Furthermore, the Supreme Court appears to have held that "Anyone that prior to 1839 was a Burgher had in this Quality the Right to run a Bakery; this Right could not by later Law be deprived him against the Basic Law § 97, and it was completely unwarranted to distinguish between whether he had used it or not."[112] The report notes that legislation since the Basic Law had routinely used retroactivity to the beginning of the fiscal year, in which it was enacted. This practice was apparently overruled.

Surprisingly, the case seems not to have dealt with § 101 that proscribed future "Limitations in the Commercial Freedom." Rather, it seems to have centred on whether the Retroactive doctrine could be extended to previously issued privileges.

The case probably illustrates a normative shift resulting from third party dispute resolution and judicial rulemaking. The *retroactive doctrine* of the earlier cases is gradually extended to more issues. However, the case may also indicate that neither legal community nor wider public seemed to appreciate the full potential of this, demonstrated by the very particular use of constitutional provisions and the surprisingly infrequent controversies, assuming

---

107. *Young v. Norway.*
108. Ibid.
109. *Rolfsen v. Petersen* (Rt. 1845-513) 514.
110. On various readings of the case Smith (1993) 121.
111. *Rolfsen v. Petersen* 513, 515.
112. Ibid. 519.

that baking bread in Oslo was not the only commercial activity to be regulated in this period.

Officers' Cases

In **Dahl v. Norway** (Rt. 1854-093), we again see the role of precedent in the evolving Norwegian jurisprudence. The report opens with the words that "In this case, the claim was based on the Supreme Court's Precedent of 10th December 1822 in a similar Case [*Blom v. Aars*] ... to which was added a later Supreme Court judgement of 24th September 1823 [and an older precedent of 1819]."[113] The reference to *Blom v. Aars* is followed by a very extensive summary of the legal reasoning in that earlier case.[114] The quoted reasoning is mostly that of the Appeal Court in *Blom* but it nevertheless reveals that extensive copies were available to the parties and that the Appeal Courts seemed more accessible to the public than the Supreme Court. The report indicates that the Appeal Court had dealt with *Blom* head on, considering the combined scheme of Retroactivity, Officers, and Property. The very extensive reporting continues through two issues of Norsk Retstidende and no less than 15 pages, including not only the said precedent but also lower court opinions and party arguments in the present case.

This well-argued case appears to be Norway's possibly first class action test case. The report explains that "Several Probate Officers who [lost Sportel income by a new succession statute] agreed to occasion decided by Judgement to what extent they on this Occasion had a Claim for Damages from the State Treasury and chose [to present judge Dahl's case for] the Question of Principle that they want settled."[115] The trial court found for Dahl, explicitly referring to the contractual relationship between civil servant and state that the § 97 Retroactivity clause precluded from overriding, as "this View is presumably also approved by the Supreme Court [in *Blom*]."[116] The Appeal Court found that neither a complete reduction of Sportel income could be accepted nor could "the Individual's Interest hinder Measures aimed at the Need of the Whole."[117] However, in light of the evidence it found insufficient grounds for assessing whether a significant loss would occur given that it may be set off against other income.

---

113. *Dahl v. Norway* 93, 98.
114. Ibid. 93-96.
115. Ibid. 97.
116. Ibid. 105 *per* trial court.
117. Ibid. 107 *per* appeal court.

In the end, the Supreme Court upheld the trial court verdict of a very specifically calculated money amount. The reasoning is not fully reported but the winning party had referred to the Officers' Clause countered by the government on grounds of the Legislative Powers clause.

The case probably shows the level of sophistication now achieved by litigators in arranging a test case on behalf of a presumably considerable class of local judges. Further, it cements the importance of precedent in settling questions of law for all similar cases, indicating that judicial rulemaking was now taken for granted, the *Dahl doctrine* was assumed to be valid ergo omnes as a binding statement of the balanced law in this particular field.

Moving a further decade along, we encounter *Wedel-Jarlsberg v. Norway* (6 UfL (1866-7) 165).[118] The case centred on a familiar theme, the Officers' Clause but now the full legal reasoning was published, as the Supreme Court had agreed to publish its votes, thus ending 200 years of the Griffenfeldt silence from 1661. The case is the first to provide the full insight that is still lacking in the other West-Nordic countries almost a century and a half later.

The Officers' Clause provided for potent combination of factors. The first sub-clause enabled the King to terminate senior civil and military officers having only regard to advice by the cabinet and submitting their pension rights to the Storthing. The second sub-clause provided that junior Officers' Could only be terminated by court judgement and "nor against the Will be moved." Though possibly rooted in an effort to limit somehow the King's executive powers, the latter clause had the ring of an individual rights provision. The level of indeterminacy was low, junior officers 'could not be moved;' the clause was thus more of a rule than a standard, leaving little room for interpretation.

Lieutenant-Captain Ferdinand Wedel-Jarlsberg was a junior officer who would not be moved and was closely related to the founding fathers of the Basic Law. At the Eidsvoll Conference, Count Johan Caspar Wedel-Jarlsberg attended as a delegate of Jarlsberg County. Serving as an officer of the navy with peacetime station in Oslo, the younger Wedel-Jarlsberg was ordered to serve as master of rolls drafting young men mostly for the land forces. Though accepting to be sent to serve at sea, Wedel-Jarlsberg could not accept this added position that he nevertheless executed for a total of 21 months before suing the State for compensation.

Associate judge Løvenskiold gave the first opinion of record detailing the relevant facts extensively, noting that the added duties were "quite exten-

---

118. See comments by Smith (1993) from 146.

sive," at times four to five hours a day, his previous duties in drafting new servicemen persisted, making these "Businesses ... completely new."[119] Løvenskiold went on to discuss the interpretation of a relevant statute and a Supreme Court case as to its core scope. However, turning to § 22 of the Basic Law, the Officers' Clause, the judge opined, "it follows from this, I say, that an Officer is not obliged to without Compensation to accept Businesses that are completely new."[120] Further, the opinion noted that case law had established that officers appointed special commissioners should be compensated for that and, "many Times over" that the income from an office cannot be reduced without compensation. This led to the conclusion that "I believe it follows from the present State of Law that safeguards the citizen against Inequity that when the Courts find a Breach upon an Officer's Rights it is their Duty to step in and give Compensation."[121] Løvenskiold then returned to precedent, discussing *Dahl v. Norway* and e contrario *Lützow v. Norway* (2 UfL (1862-3) 200),[122] stating he "agreed with the Plurality" in the latter that had not awarded compensation because the duties in question were essentially more of the same, not of a "new Kind" outside the contractual relationship established. Returning to the role of the judiciary, the opinion went on, "I think that the Courts do not herby disregard the Reverence for the lawgiving Power ... when the lawgiving Power, which like any other human Power can make Mistakes, has overlooked that an Officer's [duties cannot be increased] without Compensation. Then the Courts have the Right to step in, – supposedly only in clear Instances, but such one is present here." Judge Løvenskiold ended his opinion by declaring that the case was one of legitimate doubt, therefore court costs should not be levied, and dismissing another case referred to by the Government Advocate, before concluding that the appeal verdict, which awarded a monetary amount to be assessed at the Governments expense, should be upheld.[123] The somewhat rambling opinion of Løvenskiold gives a glimpse into how a Nordic collegial court really functions. The Norwegian Supreme Court's choice of public "voting" i.e. publicly stated opinion over formulating reasoned judgement gave rise to a dramatically widened difference between the already forming branches of the West-Nordic tradition, with Norway developing genuine case law, and Denmark

---

119. *Wedel-Jarlsberg v. Norway* 167.
120. Ibid. 168.
121. Ibid. 169.
122. "[T]he case warrants interest as link in the development of judicial review in Norway." Smith (1993) 141.
123. *Wedel-Jarlsberg v. Norway* 169.

and Iceland developing a more convoluted kind, leaving restatement and balancing of law largely to theory.

Next to render his opinion was Associate judge Blich, who offered a few remarks on the need for military officers to follow orders and without much explanation found there was no violation of the officers' rights that warranted disregarding legislation that "the Courts must respect."[124]

Thereafter judge Andresen who found the issue to be one of an analogy of § 22's ban on officers being "moved" and that unconstitutionality must be incontestable for a law given by competent authorities to be disrespected. He disputed any contractual aspects and insisted that the statute had rightfully authorised the King to order his naval officers.[125]

Judge Hallager and auditor general Dirids joined Løvenskiold without any opinions of their own.[126] Judge Tomle disagreed with Løvenskiold, making it an even split before Chief Justice Lasson was to give his vote. Tomle joined the Andresen opinion but added that he felt it incoherent to uphold the law itself but at the same time order compensation for the ramifications of its application. In his opinion, compensation could not be determined by independent assessment, the King or the financing State Authority had to sole power, such matters were "outside the Competence of the Courts."[127]

When Chief Justice took the floor, Norway already had established judicial review, though some apprehension could still be detected among Supreme Court Justices. No case had succinctly established whether Norway as a constitutional democracy favoured upholding constitutional right and limitations over the general will, the previously (insufficiently published) case law had more repaired expansively construed statutory law to comply with constitutional law, assuming legislative intent to do so, avoiding the question of the intended clash between statutory and constitutional law.

Neither block of three Justices was eloquently persuasive, though Løvenskiold was certainly thorough and had dealt with both the law at hand and the issue of judicial review head on. Lasson opened his relatively short opinion of just under a page in the report by stating his essential agreement with the first vote. Then dealing with the constitutionality of the act he opined, "[whether] the contested § in the Law of 1857 really intended to [deprive] Compensation, I do not believe it can be said with Certainty. The Basic Law § 97 says evidently that no Law must be given retroactive Force. This Commandment

124. Ibid. 169.
125. Ibid. 171.
126. Ibid. 171, 172.
127. Ibid. 172.

concerns the lawgiving Power as well as the other Powers of State."[128] Chief Justice Lasson then went on to assume that when the statute was not expressly contrary to the Basic Law, it had to be read so that "this Commandment must therefore be assumed in the Longest to be observed."[129] Some naval officers would have received their commission knowing the terms of the 1857 act so the statute was naturally silent on this point.

The Lasson opinion went on to say that the appeal verdict should be upheld "even if one must assume that the lawgiving Power [intended no] Compensation."[130] This followed from earlier Supreme Court cases "whose Principle is perfectly applicable here."[131] He also cited *Lützow*, claiming that the plurality reasoning meant that, "if the Businesses in Question had been material and new to him, then the Judgement would ... precisely have gone in the other Direction." Like the first opinion, Lasson felt that, "it cannot be done in accordance with the Basic Law [adding] heterogeneous Businesses at will because one requires private Laws for this despite Basic Law § 97, the Principle in § 105 [Property] and the Analogy of § 22."[132] In Lasson's opinion, if 'Basic' and 'private' law clashed, the issue was to be decided, "clearly, only on the constitutional-legal Question. What shall the Supreme Court decide when there faced with at once Basic-Law and private Law? Then it has, as far as I know the Teaching of Constitutional Law, commonly been decided that to the extent that one cannot oblige the Courts to deem by both Laws at the same time, then they must necessarily prefer the Basic Law."[133]

Immediately after stating this 'higher positive law status' of the Constitution, Lasson went on to explain how this favouring of the higher law was to be performed, "in the least offensive and most indirect Way [not denying] the Law Effect."[134] This mode, in the opinion of the Chief Justice, was more natural and more suitable for the individual than, "the Holiness that the Government-Advocate wanted to ascribe to the lawgiving Power in its private-lawgiving Undertaking even if this stands in Conflict with the Basic Law."[135] Finally, Lasson dismissed the contention by some of the other opinions that the assessment of compensation made the matter unsuitable for judgement,

128. Ibid. 172.
129. Ibid. 172.
130. Ibid. 172.
131. Ibid. 172.
132. Ibid. 172.
133. Ibid. 172.
134. Ibid. 172.
135. Ibid. 172.

clearly the language of § 105 indicated compensation "determined by assessment."[136]

Before the Supreme Court rendered its judgement, judge Løvenskiold added that he "absolutely agreed" with the Chief Justice's remarks that "at the Courts the Basic Law must be placed higher than the private Law," regretting not making this adequately clear in his own opinion.[137]

The case is interesting in so many respects. By this judgement and especially the Lasson opinion, Norway had as the first European country adopted full-fledged judicial review. Justiarius Lasson became the Norwegian Chief Justice Marshall,[138] even if previous cases could be said to rival *Wedel-Jarlsberg* as the Norwegian *Marbury*. The case reveals how important precedent was and seemed to have been for some time in the reasoning of the Court, indicating that both politicians and commentators like Fredrik Brandt[139] were right in insisting on the publication of 'the votes.' Further, the reasoning seems strongly to indicate that Norway had, in contrast to Denmark, established 'appeal on the record' with the Supreme Court concentrating on the law and dealing with fact only as it corresponds with the 'legal facts' as described by law, leaving matters of evidence and monetary assessment to the lower courts.

One interesting point is Lasson's reference to the 'constitutional-legal Questions' ("statsretlige Spørgsmaal") and 'Teaching of Constitutional Law' ("Statsretslæren"). Relying on ostensibly established doctrine for this solution of superior-inferior norm conflict seems somewhat surprising, given the controversy even among the Justices and this allusion to theory not backed by citing any institutional writers. Lasson clearly indicated that constitutional questions and law were to be restated by the courts, not legal writings nor parliamentary considerations.

Thus, Norway had its Marbury moment incident – including a published and rather thorough reasoning – and the court built on this precedence, creating a body of case law elaborating the judicial review under the Norwegian constitution. Like in Marbury, the reasoning stresses that the courts were bound by the higher instrument, rather than outright invalidating the repug-

---

136. Ibid. 173.
137. Ibid. 173.
138. Smith (1993) 148.
139. Brandt was quite a character with "distinct dissents;" in 1867, he was only made extraordinary associate Justice, as the Supreme Court disliked him for his "notorious lack of collegiality" and resisted his full appointment. See Langeland (2006) 514 with note 18. See also the introduction to his report – Brandt (1855)

nant law. On the more technical side, there is a confident use of the term *plurality* that in common law jurisdictions means the largest group voting and not necessarily an outright majority. A further survey of older unpublished opinions outside the context of constitutional review might shed further light on this and other interesting aspect of judicial decision making, as it implies much room for elaborate and sophisticated reasoning.

In ***Hansson v. Norway*** (8 UfL (1868) 393),[140] Judge (Sorenskriver) Hansson was appointed warden of a local gaol that took prisoners from two other districts apart from his own. This was pursuant to a statute providing that the King was to appoint a "suitable Man" to manage local gaols according to circumstances for a salary. Hansson objected to having this added to his duties.

Voting first of a seven-judge panel, judge Hansteen carefully narrated the case and noted that the issue of adding "whatever new Businesses" to the duties of officers was "decided" by Wedel-Jarlsberg. However, *Lützow* had established that "not every Expansion of Businesses" warranted compensation. The question was then "when one does not want to break with earlier Precedents" to "draw the Borderline between" the two as a "Distinction must by the said cases" be made. The opinion then noted that a 1793 statute has provided "in both Realms" that judiciary officers were to supervise the gaols. After careful consideration of the facts, judge Hansteen found that although carefully itemised, the added duties were not more than what the judge could expect and found for the State. However, the question was a legitimate issue and undoubtedly and imposition given Hansson's age, who was to incur no costs for bringing the case.[141]

Judge Hansteen then turned to the Government-Advocate who "in his Reference to earlier Supreme Court Cases and especially [*Wedel-Jarlsberg*] has used Expressions and in the Whole expressed himself in a Way whereby he has disregarded the Reverence that that this Court according to the Supreme Court Act § 12" was due. The impertinent lawyer had suggested that said case would not be so decided, "by a really learned Man," as the issue was "to Despair clear in the opposite direction," asking what logic would apply the Basic Law's provisions regarding the executive to the legislative. In addition to much more of the same, the lawyer had ended with the line, "the lawgiving Power cannot desist writing Laws just because the Supreme Court writes Judgements apparently negating its Existence."[142] Government-Advocate Dunker was fined the considerable sum of 25 Dollars for "disre-

---

140. Smith (1993) from 143.
141. *Hansson v. Norway* (8 UfL (1868) 393) 396.
142. Ibid. 396.

garding the Respect and Reverence that he owes the Supreme Court."[143] The resentful Dunker published a note in the case report, lamenting over several pages the "modern Ideas on the Prerogatives of Public Officials," the "Right of the Courts to assist those who show Disobedience against valid Laws."[144]

Judge Andresen, who had headed the dissent in *Wedel-Jarlsberg*, agreed to the result but noted that he found the underlying discussion by the trial court and the parties to be misguided. He could not read into the earlier plurality a doctrine to the effect that in case of conflict between statute and Basic Law, the "the Private Law should in Accordance with the Principles of the Basic Law be declared void." Furthermore, "although a Plurality occasionally has promoted this Doctrine," it was not warranted to assume that it "should be received among the standing Doctrines of Law." Andresen added for good measure that Norwegian Supreme Court judgements are not provided with 'Ratio' ("Præmisser"), the opinions are published but no official reasons issued.[145] judge Andresen's opinion was joined by three other justices, thus forming the majority as to reasoning.[146]

The case demonstrates the dynamics of constitutional case law. First, the Court seems to have been in full agreement that its own precedent was relevant even to the point of courteous deference. Second, however, the reasons behind the earlier cases are debatable and distinguishable, as no official ratio is provided. Thirdly, declaring statutes invalid was still not established doctrine, rather to amend, construe or disregard them when dealing with individual controversies.

Trading Rights Cases

Norway had its share of *property cases*, dealing with the Property clause of the Basic Law. We shall look at one such ordinary expropriation case before examining the more interesting *trading rights cases*, as the latter demonstrate better the dynamic judicial rulemaking through case law. The case of **Kristiania v. Jensen** (Rt-1880-278) dealt with an old problem in expropriation law: how to balance the individual right to compensation against the advantages that proprietor gets form the investment in public infrastructure, e.g. you may lose some land but gain access to a better road.

---

143. Langeland (2006) 344-47.Smith (1993) 149.
144. Dunker "I Anledning af ovenfor meddelte Votering" 8 *Ugeblad for Lovkyndighed, Statistik og Statsøkonomi* (1868) 397.
145. *Hansson v. Norway* 396-97.
146. Ibid. 397.

The case concerned the application of a statute that enabled the municipality of Kristiania (Oslo) to seize parts of individual properties in the city for roads. The statute provided under certain conditions that a proprietor would get no compensation for part of his residential property needed for city roads. When dealing with a particular street most residents gave up their part of the widened road but one proprietor complained about the seizing of land as well as the damage to his remaining property; by agreement with the council, his land was transferred on the condition of having the damage surveyed and the case referred to the courts.[147]

The municipal court upheld the survey performed and awarded damages for both land expropriation and injury to remaining property. The municipal court held that the statute only directly regulated establishing new roads through takings or expansion of existing municipal roads, not as in this case expansion of private roads open to public traffic. It would be unjust to take without compensation such a private property. The municipal council appealed. The Supreme Court held that proprietor was entitled to compensation for both land and injury to remaining property.[148]

Judge Ph. Hansteen wrote the leading opinion, stating that the case was analogous to the provisions on new streets but nevertheless fell outside the statute and had to be dealt with as 'non-statutory.' The underlying presumption of the statute was that no compensation was due as the proprietors would not suffer any loss from the establishment of city streets because of the improvement of and value added to the properties. However, if this presumption could be rebutted and an injury demonstrated, "I believe that an assumption must be added to the statute as implicit, and according to the principle of §105 of the Basic Law self-evident, that compensation has to be awarded." Hansteen referred to an analogous provision in another statute providing for uncompensated taking of road-building materials in forests and undeveloped land unless the proprietor thereby suffered a discernable loss.[149] Then he added that if this presumption was not added, the statute would infringe too closely on §105 of the Basic Law, "but to imagine any such, especially concerning a statute having been the subject of such careful consideration, so much debate and scrutiny by knowledgeable men, as this law, would surely be unwarranted."[150] Lastly, he referred to a treaty by professor Aschehoug on

147. *Kristiania v. Jensen.*
148. Ibid.
149. Ibid.
150. Ibid.

this wider issue and concerning the injury to remaining property found an earlier case (Rt-1875-712) to be "binding precedent."[151]

All other judges but one joined the opinion but they decided on putting the conclusion differently. In the words of judge Andresen to ensure that it immediately meets the eyes that the reasons are different from that of the lower court.

Extraordinary judge Bull found the best interpretation of the statute was that no compensation for the taking of land was intended, that this was fully considered by the preparatory works and that the advantages of gaining new roads in all events would exceed any loss. Bull, however, would allow damages for injury to remaining property. It is interesting to note that judge Bull notes that a "plurality" had already formed wherefore he formed no conclusion of his own.

The case shows several interesting aspects of Norwegian judicial reasoning. First, the technical approach has a certain American or common law feeling to it considering issues like plurality, binding precedent and how to make the reasoning stand out to the reader. Second, the sources of law include justice, the finding supplementary non-statutory law, and the principles of the Basic Law. Thirdly, the whole tone of the judgement seems to be that of constitutional discourse with a subtle put down of the 'knowledgeable men' who had drafted the statute but still restrained enough to issue a narrow judgement rather than a sweeping invalidation of the statutory law at hand. Lastly, we see how theory in legal writings is entering the opinions, here adding weight to the judgement of the Court but later through dynamics of their own becoming more important than precedent.

The case *Lind v. Heffermehl* (Rt. 1882-229) dealt with the Retroactivity clause taken very far. Clearly relying on previous case law, the merchant Lind and others refused to abide by new statutory provisions affecting their stockpile of paraffin-oil and petroleum. Their storage was originally built legally outside the city but was now due to urban sprawl well inside the city of Oslo. Lind and partners claimed, relying on Basic Law § 97, that they could continue to maintain a larger storage within the city than the statute allowed.[152]

The seven-judge panel was overwhelmingly opposed to the idea that the Retroactivity clause could hinder safety regulation that seemed to them all as sensible and they thus upheld the conviction. However, the bench split over

---

151. Ibid.
152. *Lind v. Heffermehl* 229.

the reasoning and implications. Some Justices voiced their opinion several times not least over the doctrine of previous cases. A minority maintained that Lind and company could claim compensation. Extraordinary judge Professor Brandt even wondered "if not in this Instance the Accused could rightfully have refused to obey the Law as the Order they received was not accompanied by an Offer of Compensation," that they "completely undoubtedly" were entitled to.[153] However, the majority did not agree and the issue of compensation instead of acquittal was not raised by the defendants. Judge Løvenskiold suggested a distinction between "Commerce obtained by special Licence" issued to a "Person or Class of Persons" and "Commerce conducted in Accordance to regular provisions of Legislation." In the latter case, "the Legislation must have a very extended Empowerment to reduce existing Rights."[154] However, this point was not further developed, an example of a proposed sophisticated distinction that fell by the way, not generating further dynamics.

The case again demonstrates the dynamics of triadic rulemaking. First, parties will rely on case law. Then, Courts will have to decide how far to extend a doctrine. However, it requires a high level of sophistication on part of the lawyers representing parties who want to extend doctrine too far into uncomfortable territory. Had the parties acknowledged a reasonable public policy objective in moving dangerous stockpiles, but claimed compensation for their individual inconvenience is having a previous licence amended and demonstrated the cost of compliance, they might have successfully extended the doctrine. Such is the folly undistinguished analysis.

A few years later in **Marstrander v. Nikolaysen** (Rt. 1887-793), merchant Marstrander challenged new alcohol licence legislation according to which he was indicted for illegally selling alcoholic beverages. The merchant had a licence as an innkeeper and continued to sell beer to his customers after the introduction of alcohol licences. The Court agreed through several detailed opinions that there was no particular right to sell alcohol awarded to innkeepers and that the activity Marstrander engaged in, consequently, was simply unregulated commerce.[155]

The judgement without doing so explicitly apparently endorsed the Løvenskiold opinion in *Lind v. Heffermehl* on specially licensed commerce being more protected than generally regulated commerce. However, the case also indicated what was to come, namely a confrontation over the issue of

---

153. Ibid. 233.
154. Ibid. 232.
155. *Marstrander v. Nikolaysen* 795 per Justice Reimers.

those rights that were in *Lind* referred to as "Commerce obtained by special Licence."[156]

Huun v. Nikolaysen (Rt. 1888-200) featured the same Government-Advocate prosecuting a similar case. The town council of Hasslo enacted by-laws whereby the selling of alcohol should be forbidden except for those who obtained a licence from the council. Trader Huun was found having maintained small stock of foreign wine without the proper license. Local trial court ruled as a matter of law that Huun was licensed as a Trader by royal letter patent to "Small-sale of Wine of foreign Production." The county governor found "of Interest to see a higher Courts verdict," and the case was by special permission referred to the Supreme Court.[157]

First voting judge Hansteen observed that the trading letter was made conditioned on "those in Legislation provided or later provided Conditions." The elderly trader claimed that the Basic Law § 97 proscribed later restrictions of his trading rights. Judge Hanssteen opined that statutes such as the one that authorised the council bylaws were not proscribed by the Retroactive clause, as they were regulating commerce in a way consistent with "the common Need." Further, the legislative history revealed that "one was ... not unmindful" that the new provision would restrict older rights. Concerning the "Precedent" *Marstrander*, the opinion considered it to "go in the same Direction" and voted to convict but with the smallest permissible fine.[158]

The second voting judge Bachke did not agree; "the present Incident [was] concerning an Individual's specially awarded irrevocable Right."[159] As to the issue of protection by the Basic Law § 97, "I refer to the Development, which is given in Professor Aschehoug's Work on the Norwegian State-Constitution after 1814, 3. Volume, pages 258-65." In addition, Bachke found the council in the previous year to have taxed Huun based on continued sales of beverages.[160]

On a vote of 5 to 2, the Supreme Court found for the prosecution in accordance with Hanssteen's opinion.[161]

The case is interesting mostly for its 'battle of methods.' First, parliamentary considerations are taken into account referring to legislative history and preparatory work. Secondly, scholarly theory is used more directly; we saw it

---

156. *Lind v. Heffermehl* 232.
157. *Huun v. Nikolaysen* 200.
158. Ibid. 202.
159. Ibid. 202.
160. Ibid. 203.
161. Ibid. 204.

introduced in *Kristiania v. Jensen*, reported eight years earlier, by now Norwegian legal writings is cited with approval in a constitutional case. Thirdly, precedent is still applied but only rather vaguely. Lastly, when examining the language of both constitution and statute, there is an absence of external sources that could have been invoked like the philosophy of the founding fathers, comparative materials, or the principles of justice that earlier cases had found, indication the potential for more restrictive dynamics when dealing with pervious doctrine.

With **Jensen v. Norway** (Rt. 1890-455),[162] it finally came to blows between the regulatory state and the vested rights of commerce. Trader Jens Jensen obtained in 1872 "Commercial Citizenship" in the City of Stavanger, applying himself mostly to sale of finer groceries and foreign wines. In 1889, the bylaws of Stavanger in accordance with an 1884 statute provided that sale of less than 50 bottles of wine was dependent on council authorisation. The Magistrates Court found Jensen not guilty and the case appealed by leave to the Supreme Court, the State alleging error in law.[163]

First voting judge Motzfeldt opined that this was the "first Time that the Question in its Purity is presented before the Supreme Court, whether a later Law can make material Limitations or Changes [in those] prior to the Law's Promulgation issued and used Commercial Rights."[164] There could be no doubt that this had been "the Law's Meaning," by its "Words and its Preparatory Works." However, Motzfeldt could not "according to the Basic Law § 97 find the Legislation justified herein." Such rights could not be revoked when they were of considerable importance.

Judge Birkeland disagreed referring to *Lind*, *Marstrander*, and *Huun*, finding a conviction would "be most in Accordance with previous Decisions by the Supreme Court." The opinion found that another question was whether such legislation gave rise to compensation but the issue was not raised. In addition to hinting at compensation, the opinion favoured a lean sentence followed by pardon. Extraordinary judge Norbye agreed opining that "the Nature of the Incident" (Forholdents Natur) meant that some legislation was possible given "Development."[165]

Judge Hansteen agreed with Motzfeldt and undertook a detailed analysis of the three precedents. First, *Lind v. Heffermehl* "concerned one from this the present very different Object." Second, *Marstrander* concerned a residual

162. Smith (1993) from 163 and from 168.
163. *Jensen v. Norway* 455.
164. Ibid. 456.
165. Ibid. 457.

right that "prior to the Law of 1860 was commonly applicable to anyone." Thirdly, the licence in *Huun* contained "the Clause that [the trade] should be conducted in accordance with [statutory] Conditions." Hansteen, therefore, now found that here was the pure case, where continued exercise of trading rights granted could be neither criminalised nor restricted.[166] The Motzfeldt and Hansteen opinions held swayed five to two.

The case demonstrates the development of constitutional law through a series of cases. The *Jensen* case concludes the series of cases that considered the issue of previously acquired or granted rights in relation to the Retroactivity clause. The Norwegian Supreme Court by its published opinions and careful considerations, often treading a middle ground, was behaving according to the decision maker's calculus by not going too far in either direction, thereby convincing both sides that it would consider their arguments. We can see that the lower courts were keener still on established rights but that the Supreme Court walked a fine line, particularly as stated by justice Hansteen who became 'the swing Justice' of the late nineteenth century. The law developed dynamically case by case from the Officers' Clause cases to the Retroactivity clause cases.

One particular point that has to be made is that there is no evidence in the reported cases to suggest either any underlying aversion neither against the King nor against Parliament. The Court is much more concerned with its own precedent and the correct understanding of the Basic Law than it seems to be worried about either defending national, or class interests, or otherwise pursuing ostensible ideological causes. Of course, there may always be deeper reasons but none seems apparent in the published opinions and, therefore, none became part of Norwegian constitutional law as it was received through Supreme Court jurisprudence. The idea that the Court was fighting a rearguard action on behalf of the 'higher officials,' who gradually lost power to the broader masses and parliamentarism, appears to be myth and ill-founded rationalisation. Instead, the government's case is weakened by its bringing a criminal case, where the judges then as today expect the law to be sufficiently clear to convict, influencing their interpretation to the government's disfavour.

Another point however, is that although Norwegian constitutional law was being developed and, arguably, the norm structure was shifted and restated by jurisprudence, the level of sophistication in the suits is not too impressive. None of the series of cases from *Lind* to *Jensen* appears to have been ar-

---

166. Ibid. 458.

ranged as a test case, supported neither by any network of shared interests nor by political opposition initiative.

The view that Norway in the late nineteenth century got an aggressive version of judicial review epitomised by the *Jensen* case[167] with reactionary undertone seem completely misguided.[168] The case was only incidentally a judicial review case, foremost it was a criminal case adding the potential sting of conviction to recall of commercial licence. The case could obviously have been better framed by the civil authorities as a civil case perhaps offering compensation. In other words, just as *Lind* could have been decided otherwise, had the lawyers claimed compensation, *Jensen* could have been decided otherwise if the government had offered compensation and let the case be tested as a civil review of an administrative decision.

In summary, early Norwegian constitutional jurisprudence showed great potential and had a number of fascinating moments but still gives the impression that either the potential was lost on many of the possible parties or the issues were resolved elsewhere. Perhaps they were taken into account in legislative preparation or filtered out in legal education and by scholarly theory that ignored, denied or disapprove of constitutional review, test cases, case law and litigation as a way of changing the law.

Previous Practice

Economic Regulation Cases

Although the constitutionality of limiting trading rights had been dealt with in the 1880s and 1890s, it resurfaced again in the early 20th century. The case **Bakke v. Norway** (Rt. 1909-156) limited a statute that empowered municipalities to limit the sale of alcohol.[169] More importantly, **Thams v. Norway** (Rt. 1909-417) set aside a statute regulating the height of trees to be lumbered as a retroactive limitation of contractual rights.[170] This resurgence of protecting hitherto lawful activity against legislation, adding prospective force to the retroactive clause as it were, prompted much debate, with judge Hagerup Bull, for instance being a vocal critic both in the Supreme Court and in the Storthing; the discourse over review was rekindled.[171]

---

167. On these views Smith (1993) 164.
168. Smith (1993) 189.
169. Sandmo (2005) 117. Case not in file.
170. Ibid. 118. Case not in file.
171. Ibid. 121.

The case *Johansen v. Norway* (Rt. 1918-401) significantly changed both the property doctrine and the whole prominence of Norwegian constitutional judicial review. The case concerned a challenge to legislation on hydroelectric activity, according to which waterfalls could only be sold to the public authorities or private Norwegian entities that would depend on a concession from the State containing a clause making the hydropower plant property of the State after 60 to 80 years.[172]

Farmer Johansen claimed that his proceeds from the sale were reduced due to the legislation that partially expropriated his property. The Company Furuberg paid him 25,000 crowns in cash and 15,000 crowns as a mortgage, however, the payment of the mortgage was conditioned on Furuberg's unconditional proprietary rights; if the State claimed delayed property according to the Concession Act the mortgage would not be payable but Johansen could instead sue the State for the well-documented loss. Thus, a test case had been prepared to document the monetary loss suffered by proprietors selling land for hydropower according to the Concession Act. The trial case relied on § 105, the Property Clause, Johansen lost but with the three judges disagreeing as to the reasoning.[173]

In the Supreme Court, the first issue dealt with was the procedural question of disqualification of Extraordinary judge Stuevold-Hansen. The incident demonstrates just how much constitutional law is dependent on judicial appointments – and chance. Of the eight Justices, three were extraordinary members of the Court appointed as such by the King upon advice from his Government enjoying a majority in Parliament. One of them, lawyer Stuevold-Hansen was himself a member of the Storthing, when it in 1915 considered legislation relevant to the case but not the original Concession Act of 1909. Although the Court did not agree on his impartiality, the fact that Stuevold-Hansen wanted to recuse himself made disqualification a unanimous decision.[174]

First voting on the merits of the case was Associate judge Backer. He dealt with the issue of judicial review that was once again challenged by the State. In his opinion, "this question must be considered decided in both theory and practice, [the] constitution erects legal limits for the competency of the legislative power." The opinion cited both the constitutional casebook by Aschehoug, an article by professor Morgenstierne, and two recent cases. Furthermore, the opinion noted that the case following the trial verdict had

172. Ibid. 131.
173. Ibid. 131-32.
174. *Johansen v. Norway* 401-02.

"woken a scientific discussion."[175] The Backer opinion stated that he agreed with Aschehoug that "the courts should be especially careful in setting aside a law when the lawgiving authorities [considered the issue and found the law constitutional]." Backer found ownership to be "the right to control his property with the restrictions flowing from the law or the legal order ... in accordance with [society's development]." Furthermore, the Property clause should not be "extended beyond the area it directly concerns."[176] Then adding that the legislature had "meant or feared that the acquisition of waterfalls [entails] material dangers to the social and societal-economical development in the future," leading to a conclusion that the statute was not "in such conflict with the provision of the constitution § 105 that the law must be set aside."[177]

This rambling deference to the legislature and scholarly theory was dismissed by judge Mejdell, who opened his opinion with the words: "I do not think the questions arising in the present case can be solved on the basis of more or less metaphysically unclear natural law considerations. What apply are the positive commandments of the Basic Law."[178] Mejdell then went on to write what may be the longest West-Nordic opinion in a constitutional case, over thirteen pages he considered the issues.[179]

In the end, it was up to Chief judge Thinn. His opinion stated that he agreed with Backer in finding for the Government. However, extraordinarily, the Chief judge went on to discuss the "competence to disregard statute that they may find conflicting with the Basic Law or award compensation [regardless of what statute] provided or presupposed," claiming that none of the "Supreme Court cases cited in the process have answered the question in the affirmative."[180] Although some opinions could be said to support judicial review, Thinn "personally" found it to be contrary to the constitution to regard its provisions as anything but guidance but then conceded that this "is not the usual understanding of the law as it has developed and appears in legal-scientific literature and some court opinions."[181] On the merits of the case, he found no adverse effect on either vendor or emptor, "it is a voluntary case for this one if he wants to sell and for the other if he will be given the terms of the legislation." "Even material restrictions in the owner's exercise of his

---

175. Ibid. 404.
176. Ibid. 406.
177. Ibid. 407.
178. Ibid. 407.
179. Ibid. 407-20.
180. Ibid. 426.
181. Ibid. 426.

property rights" do not warrant claims or compensation on his behalf. Thinn further cited Aschehoug.[182]

The case is interesting to the point of astonishment. As Chief Justice Lasson had been the Norwegian Marshall, Chief Justice Thinn emerged as the Norwegian Anti-Marshall apparently renouncing judicial review and negating a full century of case law. Furthermore, although six of seven Justices rejected the government's claim that there was not right of review,[183] the entire Court seemed swayed by a disregard of case law, only briefly citing a few very recent cases of little distinction, not relating the issue to the great cases of the mid-nineteenth century. Instead, the Supreme Court seemed to have reached a state of *deference to legal science*, engaging in debates on Aschehoug's opinions rather than case law opinions. The Courts seems to have taken its case to a higher resolver, that of legal science.

As to the main contention of individual freedom versus utilitarianism, the case also showed the wafer thin majority in favour of the latter, wide economic regulation in the interest of the perceived dangers to the "social and societal-economical development." A few more test cases, not to mention a different bench, could have modified or even overturned *Johansen*. Nonetheless, the effect seems to have been that conventional wisdom accepted that economic regulation could limit property rights in all respects.

The case demonstrates the dynamics of constitutional law through West-Nordic judicial review. From regarding property rights as irrefutable and extending their reach, the Norwegian Supreme Court had swung in the opposite direction, limiting proprietary rights remarkably. The potential for reversed and restricting dynamics was now realised. Furthermore, the methodology of finding constitutional law in scholarly theory rather than in case law was now fully developed.

The new line was affirmed in cases such as **Vauvert v. Norway** (Rt. 1922-627), where the issue of alcohol licences was revisited. The late J.L.C. Vauvert was made Burgher in 1838 with a right to sell distilled alcohol that his widow continued until 1917 when new restrictions were enacted. In one year she had made the then enormous sum of 300,000 crowns, most of which was given to charity, demonstrating the, "meeting between the old and the new time. Here was stood the 19th century with its orientation towards the private, in the shape of rights and philanthropy, against the 20th century much stronger orientation towards the State and the public sector."[184] The Supreme Court

---

182. Ibid. 427.
183. Which was uncontested since "Dunker's campaign" Sandmo (2005) 133.
184. Sandmo (2005) 148.

found for the state, according to judge Lie reversing itself from previous practice that was both distorted by being mostly concerned with criminal cases and "undoubtedly wrong," thus denying any damages for revoked trading rights.[185]

This doctrine of utilitarian deference can be seen in later cases such as **Whalers v. Norway** (Rt. 1952-1089). The case concerned price regulation. The complainants were engaged in whale catching and were adversely affected by regulations that levied upon them heavy duties to the Price Fund and limited the way their products could be sold. They alleged that this violated an agreement with the government as well as being unconstitutional based on the non-delegation doctrine and the Retroactive laws clause.

The Supreme Court held that the price regulation fee was not a tax as it was intended for a limited purpose, held separately by the empowered entity, and was administered in accordance with the enabling statute, by which Parliament had delegated wide-ranging powers to the Price Directorate. Though this delegation of powers was exceptionally extensive, the assessment of the necessity for it made my Parliament could not be overturned by the courts, nor was this a retroactive law, nor in violation of the State's undertakings.

Judge Benediksby delivered the opinion that made extensive comparison between various other regimes as to which fees had be imposed, citing with approval several cases and learned writers that favoured such fees for specific purposes as constitutional and outside the ambits of § 75(a) of the Basic Law.

Judge Holmboe in a concurring opinion, in which a majority joined, stated that he could not in the Basic Law § 75 or any other constitutional provision basis for the understanding that delegation of taxation powers legally is in a different situation than delegation of legislative powers. Both kinds of power can be delegated and the courts have never overruled such delegation. It is clear, however, that there are limits. Parliament cannot arbitrarily give away its powers. First, the delegation must not go further than necessary. Second, Parliament must not substantially lose control over legislation and taxation.

The case shows how difficult it is to apply the 19th century constitutional clauses on enumerated powers, taxation, and retroactivity of laws on 20th century interventionism. Apart from that, the case demonstrates the dynamics of third party dispute resolution, as the case relies on Rt-1925-35, Rt-1928-353, Rt-1929-771, Rt-1933-1041, and Rt-1940-487 to explain why despite the words of the Basic Law, "It is rightly for the Storthing to ... impose Taxes," Parliament could nonetheless provide for an agency to be enabled to impose

---

185. *Vauvert v. Norway* 627.

feed of considerable redistributive effect, even determining the exact payments after the activity had actually occurred.

This doctrine was later affirmed by the landmark *Kløfta* Case, which although relying on the property clause to overrule a statute, upheld the deference to Parliament's margin of appreciation regarding the interpretation of the various provisions enumerating powers for the various branches of government. In other words, the *Whalers v. Norway* is an intermediate case, taking stock and restating the doctrine that within limits Parliaments can delegate and regulate its own powers.

War Cases

The so-called ***Klinge*** (Rt. 1946-198) case dealt with a Gestapo Officers' Condemned to death according to a provisional statute of 5 May 1945 as a foreign war criminal for having tortured "Norwegian patriots." The case was appealed claiming that the statute violated the Retroactive clause, that international law was not part of Norwegian law, and that the sentence was too harsh even if the provisional statute applied.[186]

First voting judge Skau opened by agreeing with the defence that § 97 "normally [was] an absolute bar" to retroactive laws and that not even "an extraordinary situation in itself could make it legitimate" to "criminalise earlier actions." However, Skau did not consider there to be a conflict with § 97. Torture was banned according to the Basic Law § 96 and the language of several international conventions. Skau further cited handbooks and textbooks on the laws of war. The Nulla Poena clause of BL § 96 was satisfied as the provisional statute of 1945 had "incorporated into Norwegian law" the international law principles proscribing torture. Turning to the Retroactive clause, Skau found that there was no retroactivity as the actions had been illegal as war crimes all along and that the 1945 law had merely authorised Norwegian courts to apply them "in contrast to the quislings of the individual allied nations."[187] The punishment of war crimes was foretold in declarations by the Allied Powers including Norway. Skau then discussed at some length why the law was not issued by the exiled Norwegian government and what importance to attach to the duress of war. Then he returned to his central point stating that the actions were crimes at international law and punishable by judgement issued by the Norwegian judiciary since the provisional act empowered the courts to apply this pre-existing law.[188]

186. *Klinge* 198.
187. Ibid. 200.
188. Ibid. 203.

Judge Holmbro for his part found that the State sought to apply a law retroactively. Holmbro found recourse to international law flimsy, referring to the Nulla Poena clause of § 96 of the Basic Law, "Norwegian courts cannot impose punishment [without] Norwegian formal statute." This could not be satisfied by reference to an "indeterminable international law sanction." Holmbro found that "international law [is not like in other systems of law] an integrated part of internal law, [it must be] implemented in Norwegian law."[189] The last sentence was a citation from the preparatory works of the provisional law. The opinion then pointed out that legislation pertaining to Norwegian nationals had been issued during the war for instance banning Nazi party membership that was not made retroactive. Further, cases against Norwegians were cited that seemed to support that both § 96 and § 97 required a pre-existing Norwegian statute. Holmbro then considered whether the extraordinary situation of war could justify breaking with § 97, opining that, "there has not during the occupation been any legal bar against updating the criminal code." Holmbro, finally, found that the acts could be punished by existing Norwegian law by 13 and a half years imprisonment.[190]

Judge Bonnevie agreed with Holmbro but for his part found that another provisional statute from 1941 was relevant and had not been considered at trial. In his opinion, the case should be remanded for a new trial.[191] Judge Skau was joined by eight Justices including Chief Justice Berg, Holmbro and Bonnevie each joined by one Justice, making it nine to four for upholding the conviction and death penalty.[192]

The case reveals how a legal system works under strain. The Scandinavians had not anticipated the need for making it a criminal offence to attack them and commit atrocities but this could be amended by reference to the law of war, indication of what appeal lies in grand principles of law and law common to a wider community. In its way, the *Klinge* case became a precursor to the use of wider common legal principles in Norwegian law.

There were other war cases but they again seemed only incidentally to be constitutional cases, mostly they were criminal cases dealing with a highly extraordinary situation that did not prompt a renewed interest in constitutional review but still opened the door to international law having immediate and direct effects in Norwegian law.

189. Ibid. 208.
190. Ibid. 209.
191. Ibid. 211.
192. Ibid. 213.

The Review Revival Cases

The Court's review activities picked up again in the 1970s. The *Haugen v. Norway* (Rt. 1970-67) case dealt with a familiar issue, expropriation without compensation. The disputed law restricted the use of property closer than 100 metres from the shore. The petitioner owned an islet that was in no place broader than 200 metres and, effectively, deprived him of almost all usage. The Court found for the government but the extensive reasoning of the case made clear that the powers of review was still there to used under the right circumstances.[193]

The modern breakthrough came in 1976 with the *Kløfta* (Rt. 1976-1) case. The case is widely regarded as having brought Norwegian judicial review back to life. The occasion was a statute authorising the expropriation of waterfalls and expressly only awarding the usage value as compensation, rather than the usual formula of the highest of the three, usage, rebuilding or market value. The Court set aside the formula in the law and returned to the old doctrine of allowing the statute to be applied but only as correctly understood by the Court in light of the Basic Law.

The case involved a huge number of parties disputing their compensation for land taken for a motorway. The issue was expropriation. A general statute on expropriation provided that compensation for land taken should be assessed with wide discretion, in some instances based on the value of usage rather than market value.[194]

The Court unanimously agreed that Parliament's view on constitutionality was important and that in doubt the courts had to apply the law as best fitting with the Basic Law.[195] The majority held that the statute gave too wide discretion to estimate a reasonable value for it to be compatible with the Basic Law provision on full compensation.[196]

Judge Blom wrote the majority opinion with several concurring and partly dissenting opinions written by other justices.[197] Judge Blom remanded most of the compensation suits back to the lower courts as either erring in its application of the law or too lacking in legal reasoning for the Supreme Court to perform its review.[198]

---

193. Smith (1993) 249.
194. *Kløfta.*
195. Ibid.
196. Ibid.
197. Ibid.
198. Ibid.

Part I of the opinion dealt with the constitutional issues. It is settled that if the application of statute leads to results incompatible with the Basic Law, the courts had to build their decision on a rule derived from the Basic Law, not the statutory provisions. This was clear from court practice and the Plenary Act (on review procedures) and not disputed by the parties. The disagreement was rather on how much it takes for the courts to set aside a statute as unconstitutional. Judge Blom opined that in case of constitutional provisions protecting the freedom or security of individuals "I assume the force of the Basic Law to be considerable."[199] Conversely, when dealing with provisions on the State Powers, Blom found that Parliament's views should be respected, citing with approval the *Whalers v. Norway* case.[200]

Constitutional provisions protecting economic rights form a middle group according to judge Blom. In these cases, Parliament's understanding must be given considerable weight. The question is whether the results are compatible with § 105 of the Basic Law, not if the result would be the same without statutory provisions. "I would, therefore, constrain myself in case of reasonable doubt. But if the right to perform judicial review shall have any real significance, the courts must use it when the results go beyond reasonable doubt as to constitutionality."[201]

Debating whether BL § 105 on 'full compensation' for takings was a legal standard was rather pointless, as it clearly contained a 'hard core' but at the same time gave the lawgiver a margin of appreciation.

The main question in this case, judge Blom held, is whether it is compatible with § 105 to generally assume the compensation to be lower than the market value that could legally be calculated. This would seriously disaffect one owner relative to another in a similar position whose property would not be taken. "I cannot accept such a result," citing *Opdahl v. Bergen*.

Parts II and III of the opinion dealt with interpretation of the statute itself, which was held to be very unclear, providing occasion for interpretation in light of the Basic Law § 105, referring to another case *Karmøy v. Kolbeinsen* (Rt. 1975-419) regarding potential usage of the land but finding it unnecessary to extend its doctrine. Judge Blom discussed a number of aspects of interpretation and application of the statute at hand and found he could not uphold the reasoning below regarding a number of aspects of interpretation.

199. Ibid.
200. Ibid.
201. Ibid.

In conclusion, judge Blom voted for remanding the case to the court below without reconstituting the bench. "In the new assessment, the court must apply the provisions as I have explained."

Judge Bølviken wrote a dissenting opinion, concurring in part; saying that he could not agree that the way expropriation compensation had been assessed in the past with emphasis on market value had become customary law. On the contrary, he felt that the vagueness of the wording "full compensation" and a development of the law, whereby more emphasis was placed on society's interests and a wide ranging regulation of property had taken place, led to a different understanding of the Basic Law § 105.

Three other Justices wrote partly concurring and/or dissenting opinions, including the justitiarius (Chief Justice) Ryssdal (later of the ECHR) stating that "in this area it has to be foremost the lawgiver's task to interpret the Basic Law."

The case is interesting for several reasons. Foremost, it reiterated that constitutional judicial review was part of Norwegian law. The Blom opinion dealt with many challenges of review. It set up the three categories of review cases, the least intense review of government's internal workings, reaffirming the Whalers' doctrine, more intense review of economics rights cases like expropriation, and most intense review when dealing with personal rights.

In the middle category, parliamentary considerations would have an impact in interpreting the constitutional standards, however, not beyond their core meaning.

As to method, the case focused on constitutional text, interpreting it by comparing different outcomes of the case at hand. Without citing the classical cases of the early period, this fits well with the early period doctrine of not declaring the statute invalid but by conditioning its application on the constitutionality of the results, construing the statute to include assumptions of constitutionality and the necessary means to achieve them.

Although review had lied dormant for some time, we see that the techniques were there to be used again. The Court is resolving the wider issues of law, not just dealing with the narrow controversy before it, discussing issues like 'extension of doctrine,' setting up constitutional categories to be applied by lower courts, explaining their application and providing carefully explained guidelines for a constitutionally compatible method of statutory interpretation, when cases fall into the said categories.

The lack of case law for a long while had created a presumption of constitutionality for statutory law[202] that was now being disproved. One might say that the burden of proof regarding constitutionality of statute was again clearly on the government, it has to show that cases falling within the language of the constitutional rights provisions lead to results compatible with the Basic Law.

The ***Traffic School Case*** (Rt. 2000-0279) indicates that the revival of review was at least in part influenced by the early Norwegian ECHR cases. The case revolved around the West-Nordic reluctance to 'name and shame' lawbreakers. Two traffic school teachers were stripped of their licences, one for two years, and the other for life. The paper Bergens Tidende reported on the matter, included the full identity of the errant traffic teachers as well as print excerpts from the administrative case. It summed up the matter with the headline "Unfit." This statement of the obvious was contended however by the teachers as being libellous under Norwegian law.[203] Judge Coward speaking for a unanimous five-member bench categorised the reporting as undoubtedly libellous per se and remarked that the paper had not raised truthfulness as a defence; instead, Bergens Tidende relied on the law. According to the opinion, the wide-ranging libel statute "must be interpreted restrictively [or] requires a violation of rights [in light of] both the Basic Law § 100 and international human rights instruments in particular the [ECHR] Article 10 and the [UN Covenant] Article 17. It must be clear that these limits can be changed according to the developments in our society and internationally."[204] The opinion went on to consider the three ECHR cases *Bladet Tromsø, Nilsen and Johnsen*, and *Bratholm* as well as textbooks and some preparatory works.[205] In conclusion, judge Cowards found that considering the importance attributed to the press as a 'public watch dog' and the permissibility of various reporting techniques, the reporting in question was lawful despite some inaccuracy and potential misinterpretation. He was emphasising the "release [of information] in accordance with the Freedom of Information Act, [previous reports from the trial case, and] a theme of common interest for the area of Nordfjord that forms part of the geographical area of Bergens Tidende."[206]

The case demonstrates the dynamic evolution of legal standards like freedom of expression. The Norwegian Supreme Court seems comfortable in tak-

---

202. Smith (1993) 104.
203. *Traffic School Case* 280.
204. Ibid. 285.
205. Ibid. 286-87.
206. Ibid. 288.

ing into account international law including case law of the ECHR Court. However, we see the ambiguity in reasoning when dealing the Basic Law, the purely Norwegian part of the reasoning seems mostly centred on deference to preparatory works and textbooks that lead to requiring reporting to be justified by some relevance to its readership.

There is a clear distinction in terms of methodology; on the one hand, probably because of the presumption developed by textbooks of international law compatibility, i.e. that national laws are always crafted to comply with conventions. International standards are used with great confidence and skilful reliance on case law, on the other the Basic Law is less comfortably used and is interpreted using very different sources to guide the construction. Saying there is schizophrenia in the reasoning is, of course, putting it too strongly but there are very clearly two distinct approaches in dealing with the two superior norms. Remarkably, although BL § 100 and ECHR Art 10 both deal with the same themes of freedom of expression, they have given rise to completely different schools of thought, a common law ECHR approach and a Nordic deference approach, which are both applied in same opinion. One might have expected that the Norwegian Court given its history would have combined the two, creating a hybrid approach or perhaps reviving its earlier case law based methodology. Instead it pursues two lines of though, restating and interpreting ECHR case law to check Art 10 compatibility, quoting and scrutinising textbooks and preparatory works to check § 100 compatibility, almost denying the Blom categorisation of *Kløfta*, still achieving the same result but apparently more due to international law than constitutional law.

An Excursion into EEA Review

Although, EEA and EFTA law fall outside our focus, they are other examples of the federalisation of West-Nordic review. An insurance case gives us a view of how the Norwegian Supreme Court views this kind of review.

In **Storebrand v. Trafikkskadde I** (Rt. 2000-1332), the Norwegian State claimed standing in a Supreme Court Plenum Case that centred on implementation of an EEA directive, where the Supreme Court might consider limiting or voiding statutory provisions due to incompatibility. Judge Oftedahl Broch wrote the opinion for a unanimous fifteen-member Court stating that, "a civilian case is according to the process code a process of the parties ... if others want to act in the case, it requires explicit statutory basis."[207] The opinion then considered the Plenary Statute that provides for the State to be notified,

---

207. *Storebrand v. Trafikkskadde I* (Rt. 2000-1332) 1334.

and that the State may have standing in a case where a statute may be found "in violation of the Basic Law."[208] This, the opinion states, "does not cover any constitutional question or any interpretation of the Basic Law ... In our case, it is not a question of violation of the Basic Law [but] violation of an EEA directive. In my opinion, we are then outside the scope of [§ 5] regardless of whether the case may raise questions of the content of or the application of constitutional rules such as [the Storthinget's] legislative powers."[209]

The case demonstrates that the Norwegian Supreme Court is aware of other constitutional issues than those relating to statute-Basic Law compatibility. In case of EEA law, it particularly considers the issue of legislative powers to be at stake when reviewing the compatibility of a Norwegian statute, potentially trumping it. Nonetheless, it seems obvious that the Court could have allowed the State to argue its points and have the issues of the case fully explored, including the obvious issue of the presumption of international law compatibility, whereby statutes would always be construed to comply with international law. Although the State was not allowed to intervene, the constitutional issues were addressed in the main case.

In the main case, **Storebrand v. Trafikkskadde II** (Rt. 2000-1811), the main question was the compatibility of a statutory provision with EEA law. The provision was on passenger's own fault in a car accident, where the passenger knew she was riding with a person driving under influence. All fifteen judges agreed on the incompatibility between Norwegian law and EEA law, on which the EFTA Court had issued an advisory opinion.[210] Nonetheless, judge Flock writing for the majority held that, "the situation is such that that the lawgiver, having considered the EEA directives [endorsed the provision]. The relevance of the EEA directive is thus not overlooked." Turning to the Norwegian doctrine of presumption of international law compatibility, the opinion found that there was no express will to violate the directive but "the wording of [the provision] limit, in my opinion, the use of the presumption principle." On the issue of transfer of powers, the opinion found that, "Setting aside the statute's provisions in favour of the non-implemented EEA directive, would approximate to giving directives direct effect with supremacy over formal law [contrary to] the basic preconditions for Norway' participation in the EEA treaty [of no] transfer of powers from national bodies to EEA bodies."[211]

---

208. Norwegian law-1926-06-25-2 § 5.
209. *Storebrand v. Trafikkskadde I* (Rt. 2000-1332) 1334-35.
210. EFTA Court 699EJ0001.
211. *Storebrand v. Trafikkskadde II* (Rt. 2000-1811) 1831.

The case seems to clarify the nuances of European federation and Norway's participation therein. Norway is effectively submitting to very far-reaching supranational cooperation that may lead to instruments that trump national law, a quasi-federation. However, the Supreme Court notes that the EEA is less integrated than the EU and reserves more scope for the national legislature; if the Storthing issues Norwegian law incompatible EEA law, it may be 'presumed' compatible but only within reason. Ultimately, the Storthing retains its legislative supremacy and must sort out any conflict on its own, actively legislating the necessary compatibility. Compared with ECHR law, EEA law thus seems less effective, which in turn seems perfectly consistent with the more economic and transient nature of EEA rights and regulations compared to the more enduring and personal nature of the ECHR liberties, thus confirming the Blum categories of *Kløfta*.

Recent Review

Freedom of Expression, Association and Religion Cases

In *Kjuus* (Rt. 1997-1821), "the development that our society has gone through," was used to define political expression.[212] We see how a dynamic style of interpretation is used.

The case *Islamsk Kultursenter v. A* (Rt. 2004-1613), dealt with the important issue of a balance between the Freedom of Association and Freedom of Religion as well as both statute law and case law on associations. Under Norwegian law people enjoy a right of membership and sue association to accept them as members, especially if already have been admitted or are fulfilling the ostensible criteria for membership, when the association in question provides the members with important services, social access, representation vis-à-vis the government and other essential services.

In this instance, a number of people either had obtained or applied for membership of an Islamic cultural centre and mosque organised as an association under Norwegian law. Ostensibly based on religious criteria, the Islamic association adopted bylaws and pursuant thereof excluded these members and pending applicants. The barred group sued to gain membership and specific access, lost at trial but won on appeal.

---

212. Eivind Smith "Grunnlovstolkning – opportunistisk eller lojal?" in *Grundlagens makt. Konstitutionen som politiskt redskap och som rättslig norm* SNS författningsprojekt (2002) 141.

The Supreme Court held that the Norwegian Basic Law § 2 and the ECHR Art. 9(1) prevented the courts from invalidating the exclusion as they cannot engage in religious evaluation but must defer to the autonomous religious communities. The leading opinion was written by judge Lund with whom all other participating Justices joined. Judge Lund noted that the association claimed that no other issues than religious had been raised but that the applicants for their part attached importance to gaining membership as relating to their general welfare.

Judge Lund then engaged the Appeal Court in a discourse by disagreeing with its summary of the law based on an analysis of case law. Rather than relying on the right to membership based on the importance thereof, the law presumes that the courts do not engage in religious assessment and the law gives priority to the autonomy of the religious organisations. The right to form autonomous religious societies follows from the freedom of religion as provided in the Basic Law § 2 and ECHR Art. 9 (1).[213]

Judge Lund cited ECHR case *Hasan & Chaush v. Bulgaria*, which states: "the autonomous existence of religious communities is indispensable for pluralism in a democratic society ..." The procedural consequence of religious autonomy is that cases based on religious assessment must be dismissed but the holding is limited in case of important loss of membership when the exclusion is proven to be based on other criteria. Judge Lund cited the textbook 'Woxholt Foreningsret' on the relative weight of Religious Freedom over general association law[214] and found for the association. As the case raised important issues, all costs were dismissed. The opinion chooses the reliable method of repairing the law through interpretation rather than outright setting aside.

The case illustrates several points. As to sources of law, national law is still interpreted through the medium of learned commentary, scholarly theory, whereas ECHR law is viewed in light of ECHR case law. As to methodology otherwise, both parties and lower courts are reported to have referred to case law but the opinion does not engage them in the specifics thereof. Again, the case law method is more confidently used on the ECHR aspects, whereas national law is assumed to be restated by textbooks. However, the result was clearly limiting the otherwise general right of membership in case of religious associations.

---

213. *Islamsk Kultursenter v. A.*
214. Ibid.

The case *TV Vest v. Norway* (Rt. 2004-1737) concerned freedom of expression in relation to political parties and their access to paid commercials in the media.

The political party "Rogaland Pensioners Party" paid for an advertisement aired on TV Vest. The Media Administration decided to impose an administrative charge on TV Vest for violating the Broadcasting Act, which limited political commercials. The fine NKR 5,000-35,000 – higher than the proceeds generated. TV Vest stipulated to the facts but claimed the charge violated constitutionally protected freedom of expression.

The Supreme Court majority held that neither the Basic Law § 100 nor ECHR Art 10 by their provisions on freedom of expression did hinder such a ban. judge Oftedal Broch wrote the majority opinion joined by Justices Lund, Øie, and Asland, which summarised BL § 100 as explicitly protecting printed expressions concerning the government, a protection that had been extended to other media and requires a balance between on the one hand the freedom of expression and on the other society's interests.

Judge Oftedal Broch then cited with approval the *Kløfta* case stating that it can be relevant if Parliament itself has considered the balance of these interests but to a varying degree pending the constitutional provisions at hand. Furthermore, the *Kjuus* case was cited with approval in particular that the review powers will be especially strong regarding BL § 100 where the lawgiver's findings regarding the constitutionality of penal limitations of expression are more likely to be disregarded.

Having thus summarised the standards of review, the opinion turned to broadcasting statute's ban on "commercials for beliefs or political message." The preparatory works stated that political commercials would "contribute to an unfortunate political debate form with groups strong on capital outspending weaker organisations; this can be viewed as an acceptable limitation of the freedom of expression." When amending the Basic Law Expression provision, the preparatory works expressly considered the ban on political advertising as consistent with the amended provision. Thus, the opinion concluded that no violation of Norwegian constitutional law had occurred.

Judge Oftedal Broch then considered the ECHR provision and cited *Handyside v. UK* that used the phrase "a pressing social need" in relation to the "necessary in a democratic society" requirement of Art 10(2). Furthermore, *Tierfabriken v. Switzerland* was cited indicating that prohibiting "clearly political" messages reduced the margin of appreciation, in that case the limitation was deemed disproportional; and *Murphy v. Ireland*, in which a ban on radio broadcasting of religious commercials was upheld as necessary in the Irish context and limited in its scope. Moreover, in the latter case, no European consensus was found to exist.

Judge Oftedal Broch analysed the cases very particularly but considered neither of the two ECHR cases to be directly in point but relied on the reference to lack of European consensus in concluding that there is wide margin of appreciation in this respect. He considered but dismissed taking the relative weakness of the political party in question into consideration as impossible to apply in general. In conclusion, it was held that banning political commercials is part of forming the boundaries of the political debate; that question is best left to the democratic institutions that have a wide margin of appreciation and no violation of Art 10 was found.

Judge Skoghøy dissented finding the total ban on political commercials on television to be disproportional under ECHR Art 10(2) and, therefore, the decisions impose a fine to be void. His opinion cited some ECHR cases and two textbooks on the ECHR, chiefly the Danish book by Lorentzen et al. He noted that a majority in Parliament now seemed to agree that the total ban was disproportional in relation to the Basic Law but found the question moot as the administrative decision was clearly invalid based on the ECHR in conjunction with the Human Rights Act.

The case shows sign of convergence of the two interpretive methods. The majority studied case law in determining Norwegian constitutional law, and the minority considered scholarly theory when dealing with ECHR law. However, we also see the result of the lacking realisation that ECHR law is quasi-federal and therefore is also constitutional in the sense that it trumps statutory law. The Plenary Act calls for a full bench to consider constitutional questions, if just one of the Justices wants to consider invalidating a statute based on the Basic Law. In this case, the dissenting judge considered the Basic Law point moot, as the decision was invalid 'already because' it violated the Human Rights Act, which enjoys a semi-constitutional status and will usually trump any other statute. So, although technically a matter of statutory interpretation, in reality it was a quasi-federal question centred on ECHR case law and just as much question of setting aside a statute because of a higher positive norm as if the higher norm was the Basic Law. In other words, it is interesting to notice that freedom of expression is found in two different higher laws, interpreted in different but increasingly converging ways, but only the one angle – the one less likely to lead to setting aside of a lower law – is considered a plenary question for the Supreme Court.

Frie Aktuell Rapport (Rt. 2005-1628) is an example of a judgement that uses the Basic Law as authority for dynamically interpreting and limiting statute. The case was a genuine test case that the editor of the magazine Aktuell Rapport had cunningly set up to test the limits of Norwegian pornography legislation. (Paradoxically, the publicity hungry editor is referred to as A in the case). A special edition of the magazine was made more lewd than usual and carefully distributed to MPs and adults on the streets of Oslo, who were not in the company of children and were informed of its content. Duly prosecuted, the editor was acquitted but an appeal by the prosecution service was allowed as to the law. The issue before the Supreme Court was whether the courts below had uses the term "obscene" correctly with the prosecution relying heavily on the legislative history indicating a strong Parliamentary intent on maintaining an effective ban on pornography.

The five-judge panel unanimously found for the defendant and upheld the case below. The first opinion stressed the use of § 96, the Nulla Poena Clause, and § 100, the Freedom of Expression Clause. The former created a presumption against too indeterminable standards in the penal code, the latter a presumption for allowing expressions. The Mykle case had interpreted the word 'lewdness' to mean a qualified degree of transgression given that the penal code had to be interpreted in the light of Basic Law clauses on nulla poena and freedom of expression, and that this case only produced pictures of consenting adults although more candidly than had previously been the publishing industry practice.

The case shows how the Basic Law in Norwegian jurisprudence is used dynamically to change legal standards, favouring constitutional principle over legislative intent and preparatory works. Furthermore, its shows the effective use of a carefully planned test case to further the dynamic evolution of constitutional law. Finally, as to the quasi-federal dimension, we see how an appeal as to law is allowed in the Norwegian justice system even though the defendant is acquitted. This may, of course, result in a case being retried burdening the defendant but at least it allows the Supreme Court to settle legal issues. The beneficial effect is that the law becomes more predictable by avoiding the courts below guessing the Supreme Courts attitude, over-interpreting precedent, or going in different directions. This does contrast with ECHR cases, where the Member State Supreme Courts' may over-interpret ECHR precedent resulting in acquittal but the State cannot challenge the judgement of the national court, because only a citizen may bring a case to the ECHR.

Property and Economic Rights Cases

Kvålen v. Norway (Rt. 2004-1985) dealt with balancing property rights and expansion of public access. In neighbouring Sweden, the idea of Everyman's Right, public access to property is very strong and codified in the Form of Government (Constitution) as a limitation property rights, or if you will a balance of general freedom and privacy of proprietors.[215] The Norwegian tradition is probably less strong yet important and to some extent regulated through statute. A new law provided that children under the age of 16 would gain access to free sweet water fishing by hand-held device within certain restriction that allowed for the most lucrative commercial rights to be retained by landowners.

Farmer Kvålen and others challenged the law. The opinion joined by a unanimous bench was written by Judge Flock, who gave a very engaged account of the contending legal views. The opinion noted that the issue was raised in Parliament with eminent scholars offering advice but the issued was apparently not dealt with directly in that forum. "On that background I see no reason to consider what importance must be attributed to the opinion of the Storthing," Flock opined and proceeded to consider the "Constitutional question in our case."[216] judge Flock then noted both the traditional protection and implications of property rights, of which fishing rights were an ancient part, and the gradual expansion of public access especially when the benefit to the public outweighed the nuisance to proprietors, comparing this new right to travel access, the right to pick flowers and berries, and the increasing regulation of outdoor activities. To some degree, such regulation has been codification, to some degree expansion without compensation.[217]

Judge Flock referred to leading case *Borthen*, restating that property rights constitute an intermediate class between "provisions protecting the individual peoples' freedom and safety and provisions on the procedures and competence of the branches of government." Thereby, an assumption for restrained review was created, leading to acceptance of "access to some adjustment in covenant with the time" of an area not previously encompassed by Everyman's Right, noting that "clear restrictions" were placed on this new right by "the lawgivers."[218] The opinion further notes that both sides attached great relevance to institutional writers, Castberg, Morgenstierne, and especially Aschehoug, however, "despite different means of expressions, they all assume a certain barrier before compensation is required." With the institutional writers thus inclined, the opinion proceeded to consider constitutionality based on "weighing different aspects."[219] A number of aspects were then considered leading to the conclusion that the law was only constitutional if

---

215. Ibid.
216. *Kvålen v. Norway* points 40 and 41.
217. Ibid. point 46.
218. Ibid. points 47, 49, and 51.
219. Ibid. point 55 and 57.

the said restrictions were faithfully policed and providing that "The courts must fully review the administrations decisions on this."[220]

Having thus rather extensively dealt with the Norwegian constitutional issue, noting but not expressly deferring to preparatory work and scholarly theory, the opinion then went on to consider the ECHR aspects of the case. This was done by quickly restating the principles of Protocol 1-1, noting that cases had been cited by the parties but finding that the "modest limitation" of the Norwegian property rights did not make it "necessary for me" to consider the principles of P 1-1.[221]

Finally, the opinion joined by four other Justices found the appeal to be "of principle interest not previously brought before the courts," thus not awarding the State any further cost.[222]

The case demonstrates a number of interesting aspects. As to the dynamics of constitutional law, the case clearly relies as much on the triadic rulemaking of the Supreme Court itself as on the constitutional text. As to deference, there is a very interesting point made, in effect telling the Storthing that if its opinion on constitutionality is to be weighed in, it has to be expressly made known; furthermore, the institutional writers seem to be respectfully mentioned but their scholarly theories considered to offer little concrete guidance on this new issue. Even the European dimension is rather played down; seemingly the Court finds that ECHR protection of property is at any rate vaguer than Norway's own. The point on review of administrative decisions clearly indicates that there will be little deference to agencies to expand this new right beyond the limited statutory intention. This promised strict review, the extensive reasons particularly on the 'real issues' and the lenience on cost clearly reflect a decision maker's calculus placing the result as close to the losing party's view as possible, indicating the potential success of further cases on the administration of the law as well as on other constitutional principles or untested statutory provisions. The case points to a Court confident in its mandate and an a gradually strengthening emphasis on its own case law.

A rather special freedom of religion case was that of *Norway v. KA* (Rt. 2010-535). The case revolved around the Norwegian concept of the "tomta" – a plot of land for building a house. The tradition is that people long-term lease these plots for their primary home or summer cottage. The very long periods involved create an uneasy relationship and raise many questions as to payment, sub-lease and other terms. This case concerned the Basic Law

220. Ibid. point 63.
221. Ibid. point 67, 68, and 69.
222. Ibid. point 71.

clause § 106 on State Church Estates, as a regulation sought to change the terms of the lease in favour of the lessee in the case of public lands. The Church Employers' Organisation and others challenged the instruction, alleging that the generous right-to-buy provision of the statute as interpreted by a statutory instrument depleted Church funds. The Supreme Court found that the Basic Law provision proscribed use of the land for other purposes than those mentioned in § 106. The Court gave an impressive survey of Basic Law and Church Estate history including previous cases on the subject and a painstaking dissection of the legislative history leading to the disputed regulation. Judge Støle ended the leading opinion by stating explicitly that in the event that the Storthing has considered the constitutionality of a potentially unconstitutional statute an pursuant instruments, "the courts must in difficult cases follow the view of the lawgiver," but adding that there "is not such a qualified doubt as to the understanding of the Basic Law that the view of the Storthing can be conclusive." The minority argued for a restrictively dynamic interpretation of the constitutional provision, arguing that it was now a political question, how the State Church should be funded and regulated, including how its house plots should be utilised.

The case further underscores the confidence of the Norwegian Supreme Court in review cases. The Court is not hiding behind easy assumptions or Delphic ambiguity in its reasoning. The case also indicates how broad the constitutional discourse in Norway is with even public officials such as the Lutheran State Church priests willing to challenge the hand that feeds them and revive a seemingly desuetude Basic Law provision.

Retroactivity revisited

Borthen v. Norway (Rt. 1996-1415) became a leading case, defining the present day approach to retroactivity. The issue was similar to cases in many other jurisdictions, namely a change of state pension rights due to weakened economies and populations getting older. Mr. Stig Borthen was a pensioner with a longstanding statutory entitlement to old age pension from the People's Welfare Fund (folketrygfonden). His pension included basic old age pension and an allowance for a dependant spouse. As cost was spiralling, the Storthing decided to make this latter allowance means tested, reducing it if the pensioner had other income above a certain level; however, a special allowance was created for those already receiving the old grant so that the amount hitherto received would be frozen, avoiding any loss in money terms. The actual loss suffered by Borthen was thus only the inflationary loss of the real value of his dependant spouse allowance.

Brothen initiated proceedings, first in the Pension Tribunal, where he narrowly lost, then in appeal court, where he unanimously won. The State appealed to the Supreme Court. The Court heard the case as a plenary case with judge Schei delivering the majority opinion, in which result 11 of the 17 Justices joined but with concurring opinions with substantially different reasoning.

The Schei opinion was rather long, extensively dealing with all aspects of the case. However, it all came down to "the authority of the courts to review constitutionality [that] must be seen as a general constitutional principle," not "limited to certain fields of the law. State pension law is therefore included."[223] Proceeding on this sweeping assumption, the opinion found that revoking statutory entitlements constitute "indirect retroactivity," which pending on the circumstances "clearly ... can clash with the Basic Law's § 97." The right to state pension had a "basis and character beyond ... statutory provisions ... giving them a strong position when it comes to constitutional protection," as people had relied on their pensions rights and the limitations provided by the Retroactivity Clause "considered as a given by lawgiver" in the preparatory works of the pension laws.[224] Having established that § 97 provided protection in principle, the exact nature of § 97 was considered to be a dynamic legal standard which supported "drawing legal consequences from the development of society and law," so that pension rights were protected.[225]

However, awarding unlimited protection by § 97 would "come into conflict with the considerations behind § 75 letters a and d," providing the Storthing with powers to levy taxes and manage expenses, citing the *Norwegian Gold Clause Case*.[226] Considering very extensively the economic need for restructuring the pension scheme and its effects, including the equal distribution of the inevitable reductions, judge Schei found that, "[the expectation to maintain the spouse allowance and the effect of the loss in relation to the ends pursued by the legislation did not constitute violation of § 97.]" In summary, the opinion found that pension rights were generally protected by the Retroactive Clause of the Basic Law but that these could be regulated to some degree without becoming unconstitutional, in this instance suffering inflationary depreciation.[227]

The main concurring opinion was written by judge Backer, who used a lot of effort to criticize the *Kløfta* doctrine on categorisation of constitutional

223. *Borthen v. Norway* 1424.
224. Ibid. 1424-25.
225. Ibid. 1427.
226. Ibid. 1428.
227. Ibid. 1433-34.

rights as well as the favouring of the legal standards theory discussed by much scholarly theory, treating individual rights as indeterminate and therefore open to authoritative regulation by legislation.[228] The Backer opinion focused in conclusion on the question of there being an individual right, which it found not to exist as "the expectations have no connection with his own effort in the form of payments related to the spouse allowance," making it unnecessary to consider the need for legislation that Schei had found so important. If there actually was a right to retain pensions, neither such need nor an equitable distribution of the increased cost of the pension scheme would have "had force to break through" such a right.[229]

The case portrays a divided bench. The Court agrees neither on methodology, constructive interpretation of constitutional language, deference to scholarly theory or preparatory works nor the relevance of case law and seemingly established doctrine. Not even the nature of the Retroactive Clause is agreed upon, whether it as an indeterminate standard for Parliament to ponder freely or a rights provision from which specific rights can be deduced of sufficiently clear content as be suited for the courts to uphold and protect. The case further underscores the need for increasing the plenary procedure as the developments in terms of method and doctrine in some chambers do not seem to be biding upon other Justices in future cases, meaning that all points can be revisited unless the Supreme Court somehow can meet in plenum with its entire membership reaching a collective decision. However, as the critique of *Kløfta* indicates, it is far from certain that even increased use of the plenum would settle these issues due to the schism between those who see constitutional law as something that case law can settle and those who either will revisit constitutional text or defer to Parliament, specialised agencies or scholarly theory.

For any individual with sufficient resources and even more so any organisation with a wider agenda for challenging or changing or just clarifying the law, the case provides a very clear imperative, provide the Norwegian Supreme Court with the relevant test cases and you develop the law, neglect to do so at your peril. For instance, if Mr Borthen had lost the spousal allowance altogether, he would have had a good chance of winning the case. Conversely, given the right circumstances, the government could apparently reverse much of *Kløfta* doctrine.

---

228. Ibid. 1437-39.
229. *Borthen v. Norway* (Rt. 1996-1415) 1439-40.

In *LO-Stat v. Statens Pensjonskasse* (HR-2006-00404), the issue of state pension rights was raised again. Norway has a sizeable public pension fund (People's Welfare Fund, folketrygfonden) and the pension entitlements established by statute are obviously economically valuable to its citizen. In this case the plaintiff supported by the national labour federation LO alleged that a change in the statute that reduced the pension awarded to an estranged spouse was unconstitutional as violating the Retroactivity Clause of the Basic Law as well as Protocol 1 ECHR.

The Supreme Court overwhelmingly held that the change in the law amending the status of divorcees was legitimate regulation due to changing attitudes. When dealing with the ECHR aspect, the Court were carefully considered a number of precedents.[230]

The case again shows the relative dynamics of the two human rights norm systems. The challenger of the law knows that retroactivity doctrine is relatively stronger in Norwegian jurisprudence whilst the property doctrine is the safer bet in ECHR context, indicating some sophistication in relation to the test case principle. The case seems to extend the *Borthen* doctrine but with a clearer division between the two approaches to method, with deference to statutory preparatory works and scholarly theory when dealing with the national issue, focusing more on case law when considering the ECHR issue.

Arves Trafikkskole v. Norway (HR-2006-00419) demonstrates the continued use of the Retroactivity Clause. The plaintiff was a private traffic school that was burdened with increased dues. The statute in question provided that it was to have legal force from the day that the preposition bill was submitted to Parliament. The majority found that the Storthing had not considered fully the retroactivity aspect of the case and that the way the statute was formulated and applied by the relevant municipal agency was too far reaching. The statute was limited through interpretation, making the assessment of dues in the particular case invalid but letting the statute remain on the books, restricted in its interpretation. The leading opinion made great use of case law ranging from a 1910 case to *Kløfta*.

The case demonstrates how retroactivity is refined through the dynamics case law, despite the uncertainties that mere mentioned in *Borthen*; as foreseen by the Schei opinion in that case, indirect retroactivity, where general future regulation may have some affect on earlier established rights, is only allowed if the Storthing explicitly considers this aspect and approves it and it is applied carefully. This refined approach gives the Retroactivity Clause

---

230. *LO-Stat v. Statens Pensjonskasse* (HR-2006-00404).

great relevance and emphasises a constitutional discourse, where Parliament may bend the legal standards of the constitutional rights provisions but must state so clearly and do it carefully; if not it becomes incumbent upon the courts to apply their understanding of BL § 97, narrowing the scope of the statutory law in question.

Revisited retroactivity doctrine as seen in *Borthen* and *Arves* is probably one of the finest examples of a balance between both the two ideal types of constitutional law and between the two methods of finding constitutional law. It will give way to parliamentary interpretation of constitutional law but only if carefully considered and it does view case law as explaining constitutional law and marking the limits of statutory law. To what extent the doctrine will be upheld or reversed by other Justices remain to be seen, however.

In ***Bergshav Tankers v. Norway*** (Rt. 2010-143) the issue was taxation in the context of retroactivity and potential ECHR review. Norwegian shipping industry had for a very long time been very important to the country with many special tax incentives designed to maintain an important industry in the context of a very competitive global marked. Essentially the regime was amended in 1996 to mean that taxes could – by opting into a special arrangement – be deferred indefinitely (if continuously reinvested) and would only be payable in the event of dividend payments or other de-capitalisation. This was changed in 2007 to require some taxation of all previously accrued income so that over a period of ten years it would either be taxed or used for environmental improvements, whereas in future the shipping companies would face a tonnage tax but no income tax. The shipping companies challenged the statute claiming it retroactively taxed income that they could have kept from taxation if reinvested in the business.

Judge Utgård gave the opinion of the Supreme Court with a well researched argument stressing the real effects of the changing tax regimes, summing up the effect of the disputed statute significantly increasing the taxation and depriving the companies of deferring taxation by refraining from paying out dividends. He then examined several earlier cases, including *Arves Trafikkskole* over several pages and a discussion of "an obiter dictum The opinion very neatly categorises various forms of retroactivity and technicalities in that respect, concluding that the Storthing has wide discretion in taxation but that "applies ahead in time [for earlier income] the Basic Law § 97 functions as a barrier." He found the new regime to be charging only those that had opted into the earlier special arrangement more heavily than the then latent taxation that could be deferred indefinitely. This was thus both retroactivity and discrimination. The judge expressly declined to explain what the Storthing could have done – "generally a case must be decided based on the laws actually on the table" – but also declined to decide the narrow criteria for the taxation of the affected companies, instead annulling the particular assessments and setting aside the new statute as unconstitutional.

The minority found neither problems with retroactivity nor ECHR protection of property and relied on *Kløfta* doctrine as to the intermediate class of cases concerning economic rights where "the courts to a wide extent must defer to the Storthing."

The case probably indicates the shift is happening from the uneasy double methodology, where ECHR questions are assessed through the case law method and Norwegian questions through the learned literature method, to a system where the case law method is used for the Norwegian questions as well and legal writings decline as the meta-source for constitutional law, although they still retain some relevance, and a very thorough examination of preparatory works also continuous.

In *A & A v. Norway* (R. 2010-1445) retroactivity came in the form of criminalisation of war crimes. The defendant was born in Bosnia and joined a creation paramilitary group and was later charged with having committed war crimes in attacks against Bosnian Serbs; the defendant had then lived for a while in Norway having obtained Norwegian citizenship. A majority joined judge Møse in finding that the Norwegian penal code of 1902 had no provisions on war crimes until 2005 – promulgated after the alleged crimes – so that a conviction of the defendant would have to rely on provisions already in the code such as homicide and rape and set aside the use of the later provisions. Both minority and majority discussed case law, not least *Klinge* which would indicate that activities contrary to international law can be criminalised and regulated by subsequent Norwegian law – and the defendant would anyway risk being more harshly dealt with by an international war crimes tribunal. However, the majority saw developments in international law that would indicate that a more developed international regime that did not need the same form of implementation that was called for in *Klinge* wherefore the normal barriers created by the retroactivity clause would apply.

The case further underscores the sophistication and development of constitutional case law in Norway.

Proportionality Cases

Proportionality could be another way applying a standard that judges feel comfortable using, like retroactivity it has potential to control the interpretation and application of statute in light of the way judges read or construct constitutional law. However, proportionality is not mentioned in the Norwegian Basic Law, making a standard difficult to access, unless the statute in question itself provides for a proportionality test or there is recourse to quasi-federal case law setting up a test of proportionality.

In *Utlendingsnemnda v. A* (Rt. 2005-0229) the Norwegian Supreme Court interpreted a recent statute in light of ECHR. The statute provide for deportation and periodic barring of legal aliens sentenced to relatively short imprisonment. The statute provided for a proportionality assessment of the severity of the adverse affect on the convicted and his close relatives. The question before the court was whether the proportionality test could be extended to the nature of the crime. A legal alien was convicted of battery and forgery when trying to claim that a nephew was his son and thus obtain residence permit. Consequently, the immigration service decided to deport him and bar re-entry for two years according to statute.

The Supreme Court held that the offensive acts were singular acts of the moment without risk of recurrence. The special circumstances meant that the burden on his children, who were Norwegian nationals, would be disproportional. Judge Bruzelius wrote the opinion in which all the other participating Justices joined. Judge Bruzelius stressed that the case was one of assessing proportionality. The alien statute expressly provided for deportation when someone "here in the Realm is convicted for an offence carrying more than three months imprisonment" and elsewhere that re-entry be denied for two years. However, the statute also provided against penalties disproportional to the alien or close relatives. The relevance of risk of re-offence was found supported by the preparatory works

Judge Bruzelius refers to an earlier case *A v. Norway*[231] where the majority held the statute to create a balancing test with full powers of review for the courts but that the lawgiver with open eyes had made deportation a legal sanction with a low threshold for deportation and severe burdens needed to prevent expulsion. Judge Bruzelius extended the proportionality assessment to the nature of the crime, noting that most deportations had involved conviction for possession of banned substances or committing sexual offences, the more serious the crime the stronger the link needed to hinder deportation. The opinion then cited the ECHR cases *Amrollahi v. Denmark* and *Boultif v. Switzerland* that referred to the nature and seriousness of the offence committed, the duration of stay, the nationalities of the various persons concerned and the applicant's family situation. In conclusion, finding the crime described under intense pressure and related to very specific events with the motive of helping

231. A v. Norway Rt. 2002-0509 at 599.

a relative and at the same time the potential averse results for the children severe, expulsion was found disproportionate.

The case is interesting for many reasons. As to method we still see the divide between national and ECHR law; case law is used when dealing with quasi-federal issues, preparatory works used nationally but coupled with extensive use of Norwegian precedent. As to the holding itself, it uses ECHR case law to legitimise extending the proportionality test to 'the seriousness of the offences' combined with preparatory support for including the risk of re-offence. The resulting doctrine is very eloquently put 'the more serious, the crime the stronger the link needed to hinder expulsion' – conversely, the less serious the crime, the weaker the link and adverse effects needed to hinder expulsion. The statute is effectively reviewed and repaired using flexible review techniques, here using an *interpretive* overruling of the result of the agency's reading of the statute, and a very persuasive and practical reading of the statute, in light of both sets of higher law, is formulated.

Presumption of Innocence Cases

We have seen that Norwegian constitutional law sometimes shows a development of the norm structure through a series of cases and the shift from a text-based norm structure, with many unanswered questions of interpretation, towards a norm structure modified by case law trough judicial triadic rule-making. There is still much doubt as to state of the law in many areas because of the lack of cases, and especially the intended test case with right facts for developing, distinguishing and sophisticating doctrine, the lack of consensus on the bench as methodology, especially on the relevance of case law to constitutional law. However, two classes of Norwegian cases seem to be litigated sufficiently to develop a clarified and very distinguished body of case law, the presumption of innocence cases and the double jeopardy cases.

The case that seems to have started or restarted the dynamics in the presumption of innocence cases was *Presumption of Innocence A* (Rt-2004-1275). The facts were as follows, a man aged 21 was at trial found to have had sexual relations with an underage girl of 13. The criminal code § 195(4) provided that punishment could be reduced if the two having sex were 'equal in age and development.' The appeal court, unlike the trial court, found this to be the case, as the man was very immature, the appeal court thus cancelled the sentence.

Judge Rieber-Mohn delivered the opinion of the unanimous Supreme Court overruling and remanding the appeal judgement, as the appeal court had wrongfully stated that §195(4) could be applied through an assessment of 'the totality of the circumstances;' these were two separate cumulating legal facts to be assessed separately. However, he also stated, citing precedent on criminal law, that the age difference was manifestly too wide to apply § 195(4).

Judge Rieber-Mohn then went on to discuss § 195(3) of the code, which had been raised by the defence, comparing it to the presumption of innocence in the ECHR. This section provides for an almost objective basis for conviction, even in case of careful good faith regarding the age of the victim. This deviated from the comparable § 196, which had a more traditional emphasis on criminal intent.

Judge Rieber-Mohn cited the ECHR presumption of innocence clause in English (sic!) and cited *Salabiaku v. France* that had been further developed in *Janosevic v. Sweden*. The former discussed the role of presumptions of facts, stating that states must "confine them within reasonable limits which take into account the importance of what is at stake and maintain the rights of the defence," the latter the need to "strike a balance between the importance of what is at stake and the rights of the defence."

Judge Rieber-Mohn opined that in this case – should it be further pursued – the proportionality between the need to protect young victims and the presumption of the innocence of accused would only become an issue "if the convicted is refused the opportunity to prove that he was in all respects in careful good faith regarding the age of the victim." Finally, adding that there would be no problem with the ECHR if § 195 had a similar approach to that in § 196.

The case demonstrates the many different elements of constitutional review dynamics. The reporting judge is aware of and very skilful in applying the ECHR law as it has evolved through triadic rulemaking, citing first the ECHR provision, then leading cases for the different relevant general aspects doctrine. The opinion deals directly with the issue that the courts below somehow had avoided; the lower courts had clear discomfort convicting, as the accused could not use lack of intent as a defence, but reduced the sentence rather than declaring the statutory provision contrary to higher law. The Supreme Court instead candidly explained that it would not apply a statute contrary to presumption of innocence doctrine. However, in its particularly flexible technique, it construed the criminal statute to presume innocence and allow the defence of lack intent, ordering the lower courts to find the facts accordingly. The Norwegian Supreme Court thus avoided ruling the law invalid for being quasi-federally unconstitutional, but nevertheless in effect overruled the law, sending clear signals to both lower courts, agencies and not Parliament on how such laws would and should be interpreted.

The second case, ***Presumption of Innocence B*** (Rt-2005-0833) had quite similar facts to that in *Presumption of Innocence A*. A man of 20 admitted to having sexual relations with a girl of 13 claiming ignorance of her age, as she claimed to be almost 16 years old. The penal code § 196 criminalised sexual relations with children under the age of 16 but allowed good faith ignorance as to age, whereas § 195 had the age limit of 14 without the ignorance defence. The trial court found that the immature adult had been flattered by the mature child and that the incident was not marked by abuse. The lay members of the court all voted for a suspend sentence. On appeal by the prosecution, the issue of presumption of innocence was raised on background of the judgement in *Presumption of Innocence A*. The appeal court quashed the conviction for not having assessed the careful good faith of the accused.

Judge Gjølstad delivered the leading opinion that was unanimously joined as to result but with dissent as to the reasoning. Judge Gjølstad considered the legislative history of the provisions, originally, the usual requirements as to intent and ignorance of facts had been included in the provision applied, however, in 1927 the law was changed to 'let the perpetrator seeking lewd conduct take the full risk of miscalculation.' Although this was criticised by many, including scholarly theory, the law was not changed on this point. As late as in 2002, the issue was considered in a criminal case but a 'clear will of the lawgiver' was found to be in favour of upholding the law.

Judge Gjølstad found, however, that the relationship between § 195(3) and ECHR Art 6(2) had not been considered when revising the code. This led him to remark that the Human Rights Act 1999 provided that ECHR were to take primacy over conflicting statutes. This was an equally 'clear expression of the will of the lawgiver.'

Judge Gjølstad then went on to consider the roles of Norwegian courts in relation to the ECHR Court in interpreting the ECHR. In this case, there were cases as to the general issues but no clearly controlling case, no case in point, as Norway seemed to be the only country with this particular criminal law provision. However, the general principles could be deduced from ECHR practice, and judge Gjølstad consequently went on to consider a number of ECHR cases and quoted from then extensively. The opinion relied mostly on *Salabiaku v. France* as the Court did in *Presumption of Innocence A* on the proportionality between penalising a simple or objective fact as such and the importance of the matter at stake and the right to a defence.

Judge Gjølstad also briefly considered some Norwegian and Danish textbooks and remarked that Norway seemed to be alone on this among the Nordic countries. Judge Gjølstad then concluded that to ensure compliance with the ECHR, § 195(3) could not be applied according to its language, on the contrary, the criminal statute must be interpreted to allow a careful assessment of intent, defence and proportionality of sentence similar to the reservations in § 196(3), the other provision criminalising sex with under aged persons.

Judge Mitsem joined by one other judge dissented as to the reasoning, relying more in scholarly theory, quoting Swedish writers, but all 17 Justices agreed as to the result.

The case demonstrates how quasi-federal principles of justice have taken hold especially in areas of 'lawyers' law' like criminal law where lawyers feel comfortable and not to be in conflict with the elected branches of government. Just like the American cases of *Griswold* and *Lawrence*, we see the legislation is rather old without recent popular mandate but being upheld by the prosecution service. Furthermore, case law comes natural to Norwegian lawyers and the defence in this latter case was able to rely effectively on *Presumption of Innocence A* as precedent even in the lower courts. The issue of legitimacy is then handled head on. Although it might be tempting to explain away the older legislation as being effectively amended by the Human Rights Act, the Court more explicitly states that the accession to the ECHR was an expression of the 'clear will of the lawgiver' and then proceeds to carefully consider the clash between the criminal law provision and ECHR doctrine. The Court clearly states that it will favour the case law doctrine that changes dynamically and follows indirectly from the human rights legislation over even very clearly expressed statutes and their preparatory works. At least this seems fair to say in fields of criminal law.

Another example of building case law in the Norwegian Supreme Court, using both Norwegian and ECHR precedent to interpret and correct statute is the **Promulgation Case B** (Rt. 2005-1401), in which the precedent of case **Promulgation Case A** (Rt. 2004-0357) is applied. The former effectively added a new quasi-federal constitutional requirement that criminal laws must be promulgated, officially published, prior to application. Norway has through its retroactive clause and nulla poena clause always had a strong tradition of requiring proper parliamentary procedures of enactment and then royal assent observed for new statutes. However, there was no constitutional provision on particular official publication of such statutory law. In his opinion, judge Coward held that Norwegian case law had established that the retroactive clause only referred to application prior to enactment, and "requiring that the law shall be promulgated cannot be deduced from the Basic Law

§ 97."[232] Summering the precedent established, judge Oftedal Broch stated that, "the judgement in Rt. 2004-0357 has held that Art. 7 ECHR hinders application of a law increasing sentencing; [if promulgated prior to the act ... the prior law must be applied]."[233] The guilty verdict was upheld as referring to relevant facts but the sentence was reduced, as the statute providing increased penalties was not officially published prior to the acts committed.

A similar situation can be seen in the **Wrongful Rape Case** (Rt. 2005-0246), in which citizen A had been cleared of a criminal rape charge but found at fault as to civil law, and the alleged victim awarded damages. A now turned the table and claimed damages from the State for wrongful prosecution. The Appeal Court ruled that verdict against A as to the facts barred him from suing for wrongful prosecution. The Supreme Court reversed citing *O v. Norway*[234] and *Hammern v. Norway*[235] and stating that the contested penal code provision "is in the Supreme Court's and the Appeal Chamber's practice given a changed content," a person found not guilty can claim damages "without proving it likely that he did not commit the act."[236]

Double Jeopardy Cases

A special bar to prosecution is known as the double jeopardy principle, meaning that the same sovereign cannot prosecute the same person twice for the same facts. The principle is well known in popular culture, and means that someone can turn out to have committed an act but is now free because the prosecution failed at first. Popular fiction notwithstanding, it is a generally useful principle to force the government to chose and to prosecute its cases carefully. However, the principle has not been elevated to constitutional law in the West-Nordic countries, nor is there any general statutory procedural bar to retrying the same facts or to the prosecution appealing a not guilty verdict. However, the general principle became part of ECHR law and therefore through mechanisms of quasi-federal law part of West-Nordic law.

Norwegian defence lawyers have used many opportunities to raise the point, trying to prevent prosecution against their clients. The prosecution service has likewise explored the exceptions and technicalities of this new constitutional principle. The issue of double jeopardy very complicated in today's regulatory state, where one factual situation may be relevant to several

---

232. *Promulgation Case A* (Rt. 2004-0357) points 12 and 13.
233. Ibid. points 13 and 14.
234. *O v. Norway* 29327/95 (2003).
235. *Hammern v. Norway* 30287/96 (2003).
236. *Wrongful Rape Case* (Rt. 2005-0246) point 21.

different statutes and several different administrative agencies may be enabled to dealt with the situation for various reasons. For instance, the import of some goods may be relevant as in terms of traffic, customs, taxation and criminal law at the same time with different agencies pursuing the various aspects. Norwegian lawyers and judges seem to have been very apt at exploring and settling the various issues through the dynamics of pursued case law.

The **Fishmonger Case** (Rt. 2004-1500) dealt with loss of privileges. A person had obtained registration as a "firsthand-buyer of fresh fish." Allegedly, his firm SFT had sold fish without registering the sale.[237] The misconduct was pursued by both the Fisheries Department, which revoked the licence for a period, and the prosecution service, which among other indictments included the same facts as the Fisheries Department.[238] The fishmonger was thus first stripped of his licence and later criminally prosecuted for the same factual misconduct.[239] The issue before the Supreme Court was whether the fishmonger could thus be prosecuted in a criminal trial for something that had already lead to his loss of licence.

Judge Støle writing for a unanimous five-member court found that the first issue was "whether temporary revocation of licence is ... part of penal prosecution," citing a Norwegian case in point discussing "the convention."[240] Secondly, he found the question to depend on "judging the totality of circumstances relating to national classification, the character of the offence, and the severity of the sanction." Referring to the *Engel* ECHR doctrine,[241] the opinion found that the decision on the licence "is not characterised as punishment according to Norwegian internal law."[242] However, when considering the latter elements of the *Engel* test, and applying further precedent, the sanction was considered so harsh, hindering both purchase of fish and the letting out the machinery, that this constituted criminal prosecution, leading to a bar against further prosecution and, consequently, a reversal of the conviction below for this factual element of the indictment.[243] The preparatory works were found to shed "only a limited degree of light on the purpose of the revocation rule."[244]

---

237. *Fishmonger Case* points 3 and 6.
238. Ibid. point 8.
239. Ibid. points 6 and 12.
240. Ibid. points 37.
241. *Engel case.*
242. *Fishmonger Case* points 38 and 39.
243. Ibid. points 44, 47, 52, and 54-56.
244. Ibid. point 43.

The case is interesting on several levels. As to the material issue itself, it resolves with very thorough arguments a clash between statutes, effectively baring the state from creating a regulatory prosecution or penalising system alongside the criminal prosecution system. The case suggests that many such instances may exist, where administrative consequences are harsh enough to be seen as equivalent to criminal prosecutions, thus hindering criminal proceedings as such, or perhaps the other way around. As to methodology, the doctrine of precedent is firmly used; the opinion is very impressive in its apt application, distinguishing between issues settled and issues pending, completely disregarding any deference to preparatory works or lawgiver – who either intended or at least accepted double sanctions. As constitutional status, the quasi-federal nature of ECHR could scarcely be stated clearer than referring to Norwegian law as "national classification" and "internal law." Norwegian case law is clearly finding its place in a new order that included the constitutionalization of human rights and the judicialization of wider constitutional law.

In another case, which we shall call the ***Motorcycle Case*** (Rt. 2005-1430), a man was convicted of traffic violations, speeding and criminally negligent driving on motorcycle. Apparently, the prosecution introduced evidence to the effect that he was also under influence of some amphetamine; the positive blood test was explained by the defence as resulting from medical doses of morphine. Trial court declined to rely on the evidence of influence but convicted the man for the other charges. Consequently, the prosecution indicted him a second time for driving under influence in violation of the traffic code as well as the general penal code.

The defendant claimed violation of the double jeopardy clause of the Human Rights Act and the ECHR. The trial court accordingly dismissed the case, which the appeal court reversed, ordering a trial. The appeal ruling was further appealed to the Supreme Court and handled by a five-member panel. The panel methodically restated that the ECHR protocol was valid as Norwegian law with supremacy in case of conflict. The Court further noted that a number of Supreme Court cases had dealt with the issue, finding a particularly relevant case in point, which had considered three ECHR cases, *Gradinger v. Austria*, *Oliveira v. Switzerland*, and *Fischer v. Austria*.[245] The Court found the most important test to be whether the charges included "the same essential elements," and concluded this not to be the case as negligent driving and speeding were "essentially dissimilar aspects of the driving." The Court,

---

245. Referring to an early jeopardy case (Rt. 2003-0394).

therefore, found that the appeal court had not erred in law. The Court added a distinction between the *Fisher* case and the present case as the Norwegian law did not contain several alternative provisions dealing with driving under influence. Finally, the Court explicitly found that no elements of the first indictment was included in the second, and that using intoxication as an aggravating fact in the first indictment did not prejudice the second case, but it regretted as "unfortunate" that the second case was not included in the first.

The case shows the level of sophistication of Norwegian review, confidently dealing with tests developed by Strasburg, distinguishing cases and dealing explicitly with all the issues raised. Although the case does not result in negation of statute, it clearly sends the signal that complementary criminal provisions may not be used in successive cases against the same defendant for the same facts. There is to be noted on the *unfortunate* double use of facts, trying to use some facts that could be prosecuted on their own as qualifiers of other facts separately pursued, probably sends the message that if relied on, such facts may not be allowed to be the basis for prosecution on their own. The issue is not settled by this case, in line with the common law principle that only facts actually material to the case at hand may create case law. However, at clear message is sent to tidy up both prosecution and future legislation.

End note on Norwegian Reasoning

Thus ends this survey of Norwegian reasoning. The Norwegian Supreme Court has shown itself remarkably able and subtle in forming case law, although there are several fits and starts, where issues are revisited, and we see periods of both expansive and restrictive dynamics, as well as periods of deference to different other authorities. We see periods of double methodology, as well as tendencies to distinguish between different areas of constitutional, including quasi-federal law, that will result in different standards of review. The cases surveyed could include many others, as hundreds of cases deal in some way with constitutional issues. However, most of them do so incidentally in the context of criminal cases or because parties seem to stumble upon them in controversies that otherwise centre on statutory interpretation or the effects of legislation. There is a clear impression that Norwegian judges know how to use the case law method and understand the implications of setting up judiciable supranational norms like the ECHR or EEA regimes. Yet they are not in agreement among themselves as to the full implications of this, and especially not certain whether to reclaim for themselves the influence deferred to scholarly theory and preparatory works, not to mention those rare instances where the elected lawgiver actually and wilfully challenges the principals of constitutional law.

Danish Review

Summary of Danish Review

Danish constitutional judicial review is historically very limited. The Basic Law of 1849 ended absolute rule by a monarchy in whose name the Supreme Court had functioned for ages. The Court and its judgements were for a long time extremely inaccessible. Due to its obscurity and complicity in repression during absolutism, most democratic and liberal forces viewed the Supreme Court with suspicion, their view apparently vindicate by the first cases where the liberal view of the Basic Law was trumped without any accompanying reasoning.

In Denmark, the legal issue of compatibility between statute and constitution surfaced late and only occasionally and played a very limited part in public discourse. Mostly, constitutional issues were raised only incidentally in court cases and no constitutional provision was effectively used to challenge laws much less to create tradition of dealing with constitutional controversies.

The legal basis for review was controversial even at the constitutional conference leading to the Basic Law. In court practice, it was firstly indirectly endorsed in a case concerning the highly technical dissolution of titled fiefs. The opinion seemed reluctantly to accept the Basic Law as positive law that could potentially trump statutory law. This doctrine led to some increase in review cases but the continued brevity and inscrutable style of the Court with little reference to precedent lessened the impact of the Court's endorsing judicial review in principle.

The Supreme Court was not instrumental in the constitutional developments from constitutional monarchy to parliamentarism and sided with the government in an important Court of the Realm case. The Supreme Court overall contributed little to developing the wider Danish constitution.

The rise of the administrative state brought with it some tension with the rights established in the Basic Law. Progressive legislation and new regulatory regimes were largely accepted by the Court's jurisprudence, which offered great deference to most administrative and regulatory initiatives. Danish law was also becoming receptive to views of law that stresses a limited interpretation of constitutional provisions, favouring the majority view as expressed by the elected "lawgiver." During World War II, the Danish Supreme Court took part in appeasement policy, upholding rather draconic measures of the wartime regime, lending it legitimacy, followed by its sanctioning of reprisals against overt collaborators after the war. Positive law was interpreted and applied.

The Supreme Court continued its role as dispassionate arbiter of the law with deference and restrained reasoning as its method. From the mid-1970s, however, Danish cases relating to EC (EU) law were judged by the European Court of Justice, exposing Danish law to transformative new legal methods, in effect establishing a quasi-federal legal system. Later, the European Convention on Human Rights began to have its impact but the Danish legal establishment was ill suited to handle issues of "just" or "necessary" treatment of the citizen, traditionally dismissed as non-legal value judgement better handled by parliamentarians or agencies. However, the effective supremacy of these supranational regimes based on higher positive law effectively gave Denmark judicial review and led to the first Basic Law cases explicitly setting aside statutory law and widening review.

Today's Danish constitutional judicial review is restrained but undergoing some development.

Review in Danish Constitutional Developments

The Danish Supreme Court has functioned since 1661. In many ways, however, it is a successor to the old King's Parliamentary Court and can thus trace its history back to the 11th century. Denmark has one of Europe's oldest continuous written constitutions, enacted in 1849 and modestly amended since. Nonetheless, the Supreme Court's tradition of deference to other institutions and its tradition of giving little to no public reasoning, means that the Danish constitutional case law is a challenge to analyse.

Constitutional judicial review has been a feature of Danish jurisprudence for a long time, though mostly in principle. Its development has been restrictively dynamic,[1] reducing the legal importance of the Basic Law, and limiting actual review to guarding the separate powers of the judiciary. Danish Supreme Court Justice and prolific writer Torben Jensen has characterised this by saying that the Danish Basic Law provisions suffered "reduced applicabil-

---

1.   Zahle (1997) 363.

ity" due to various "difficulties."[2] Judicial review has been considered in a number of cases but been decisive in few.

Constitutional Origins

Denmark proper has been a monarchy with an unbroken dynasty for a thousand years. Denmark is historically the amalgamation of three Norse lands.[3] Its rulers have through the ages rules various other realms and lands, most notably Norway, Sweden, and a number of German duchies, all recognised to be 'united in the King's sceptre', and not "in the language of law included under Denmark"[4] thus creating a federation of assorted dependencies.[5] Of all these 'Realms and Lands'[6] the realms Norway and Iceland and the lands Faroes and Greenland share as a common legacy the Danish legal tradition, what is here referred to as 'West-Nordic' law.

Danish constitutionalism before the middle ages was marked by traditional law, and a balance between the Things (parliaments), Lords, aspiring Monarchy, and the inroad of Christianity; the codes of the three Lands reflected this "time of upheaval between old and new."[7] Throughout the middle ages, the Kings consolidated their power, as did the nobility and the church, all to the detriment of traditional freedom and autonomy of the Things.[8] When ascending to the throne, the Danish Kings would sum up the constitution in a state-

---

2. Torben Jensen writes, *"Danish Courts' control of the adherence to those basic rules, which since the Basic Law of 1849 have had the purpose of limiting the exercise of public powers and are traditionally referred to as freedom rights or civic rights, have for almost 150 years been marked by difficulties that have reduced the practical applicability of the rules. The Basic Law has no provision on judicial review, which then can only be based on the distinction between the branches of government and a principle of protection of rights. A number of Basic Law provisions are statements of intention with reservations or deference to statute. Furthermore, it was crucial that in the 1800s, when the new state system was formed, only one reported case raised the issue of constitutionality and that both within legal science and among prominent politicians there have been opponents of, in any case, deeper review of the substantive constitutionality of statutory law."* Jensen (1995) 241.
3. Tamm (2005) 94, on their courts 176.
4. Phrase used by H. A. Ørsted, the distinguished Danish lawyer, see Jákup Thorsteinsson *Et Færø som Færø* SNAI (1990) 215.
5. For further references Kári á Rógvi "Land of Maybe" in *The Right to National Self-Determination. The Faroe Islands and Greenland* (2004).
6. See Grund-Lov om Indføds-Retten of 15 January 1770. The Danish words are "i Hans Majestæts Riger og Lande".
7. Tamm (2005) 96.
8. Tamm (2005) 96.

ment often referred to as a Hand-Tying. The conventional view is that, "the rights in the Basic Law of 1849 has historical predecessors in the hand-tying [issued by] the elected kings of the Middle Ages."[9]

Examples include the 1282 Hand-Tying of King Erik V 'Clipping.'[10] The document is comparable to the famous Magna Charta issued by King John I 'Lackland' of England in 1215.[11] This Danish Magna Charta included provisions on habeas corpus, nulla poena sine lege, local customs, taxation, property rights, procedural rights, and provisions on balance of power, rule of law, and judicial review, including a promise to hold Court at least ones a year, to respect the law-books, uphold promulgated statutes unless they were superseded with consent of the Court.[12] This Hand-Tying is often referred to as "Denmark's first constitution"[13] and was followed by similar documents until the advent of absolutism, creating a periodical restatement of the *monarchia mixta* constitution.[14]

The study of law in Denmark, even after the 1536 reformation, was that of Roman law and institutional writers in order to assess "the rationality of national laws."[15] Through the learned writings natural law was toughed to generations of Danish lawyers, as explained by one historian, "the Emperor's law is a law of its own, English, Polish law are of their own, our law is another, all to themselves, but in many elements the same for the sake of natural law that is in us all."[16]

After the middle ages, following the rise of traders and other rivals of the aristocracy and prolonged warfare, the King in 1661[17] proclaimed himself absolute in both Denmark and Norway,[18] in a sort of 'inverted glorious revolution,'[19] and issued intricate written, though initially secret,[20] constitutions for

---

9. Rytter (2006) 25.
10. Erik V of Denmark 1282.
11. Tamm (2005) 143.
12. See §§ 1-18, Tamm (2005) 144.
13. Tamm (2005) 143.
14. Tamm (2005) 152.
15. Tamm (2005) 164.
16. Tamm (2005) 164.
17. By the so-called Absolute Rule Act (Enevoldsakt) of 10 January 1661. The Lex Regia came in 1665.
18. Tamm (2005) 200.
19. The English Glorious Revolution in 1689 established constitutional monarchy and the Bill of Rights.
20. For a most riveting account these manoeuvrings see Wang (2005).

both these realms, called Lex Regia, a reference to Roman imperial tradition.[21]

The Supreme Court in Context

According to the new *lex fundamentalis*,[22] the King was the ultimate arbiter[23] and the judiciary was rearranged to include a Supreme Court with equal numbers of judges drawn from the bourgeois and the nobility, which had previously dominated the judicial council.[24] As the united Danish and Norwegian Supreme Court it was very much part of the move to centralisation and absolutism with the King being its Chair, single-handedly deciding Cases if he heard them.[25] The Court's obvious purpose was to serve as a centralising yet legitimising tool of imperial justice. The Lex Regia had establishing a new constitutional order with a common Supreme Court. The Court served to demonstrate just and orderly government by the King and its Justices were generally excellent lawyers.[26] As with decisions and laws, the King could reverse or exempt from any judgement,[27] even when he had heard the case himself.[28] Thus, review on whatever grounds was personified by the King and his *Iura Majestatis*.[29] The courts would judge according to the letter of the law but higher justice rested with the King.

Absolutism depended very much on the monarchs being personally strong and able; as the monarchs wakened, so did monarchy not long after the advent absolutism. In the Supreme Court, majority rule was established in 1670 and several specialised offices were established, including that of Secretaries and that of Justiarius (a title for Chief Justice continued in Norway, Danes now use 'President of the Supreme Court.')[30] This gave the Court some independence. However, in 1674, the Court was instructed in the writing of judgements to suspend with "eluding to previous Custom any Reason, why thusly or thusly is judged, but only [to write] that in that Case between such

---

21. Tamm (2005) 200, text at 202-03.
22. Tamm (2005) 200.
23. Ditlev Tamm "Domstolene som statsmagt – set med en retshistorikers øjne" *Ugeskrift for retsvæsen* (1997) B87 at 89.
24. The Danish "King's Parliamentary Court" (Kongens retterting) had functioned since the 12th century, as final court of appeal since the 16th century. Jensen (1999) 15.
25. Jensen (1999) 17.
26. Jensen (1999).
27. Lex Regia § III in fine.
28. Jensen (1999) 17. Tamm (2005) 184.
29. Lex Regia § VI.
30. Jensen (1999) 18.

Parties is decided thusly that this shall happen or not happen."[31] This ineloquent but effective *non exemplis sed legibus*[32] ordered by the rising administrative elite was for centuries to reduce the Danish Supreme Court's role as residual lawmaker and participator in constitutional discourse. Triadic rulemaking is not possible, when both 'custom, reason and why' are not allowed to be stated.

The Court avoided this 'gag order' to some extent in its official responses to government agencies, there even explaining controversial dissents but to the wider public the Court seemed mute on reason.[33] Furthermore, earlier judgements would actually form part of the Court's internal deliberations[34] but would not inform the wider public.

The secrecy of case law contrast with publicity of statutory law achieved with the two comprehensive codifications promulgated in the late 17th century, respectively the Danish Code of 1683 and the Norwegian Code of 1687. Together, these circumstances have probably contributed to the *sola scriptum*[35] approach to law in Denmark that was probably strengthened by the reformation of the church, which emphasised going back to basics, reading the bible text (translated into Danish), not relying on canonical tradition. Thus it seems fair to say that Danish legal culture and ideology for centuries has emphasised the reliance on published and comprehensive text, avoiding the dynamics of case law but still benefiting from a well-educated and informed elite.

The Justices were loyal members of the regime and any judgement could be overturned according to the King's prerogative. However, according to judge Torben Jensen, in 200 years, only one case was overturned explicitly against the Court's protests. The case was "a difficult constitutional question on the extent of the Supreme Court's right of review of civil servant dispositions."[36] A County Governor had imposed criminal sanctions on some fire fighters and revoked the licence of their lawyer, which the Supreme Court found "a judicial not administrative Act," but the King Christian VI annulled

31. Jensen (1999) 19.
32. Latin phrase from the Codex of Justinian meaning 'not by example but rather by legislation'.
33. Jensen (1999) 19.
34. Jensen (1999) 28.
35. Latin phrase used by early protestants meaning 'only according to scripture' – disregarding tradition and canon law, often without realising its importance filling gaps and providing interpretation Tamm (2005) 157.
36. Jensen (1999) 22.

the judgement over loud protest from Justiarius Sechman.[37] The distinction between judicial and administrative acts in relation to review was to resurface during the drafting of the Basic Law with a provision stating that it was for the courts to decide, which matters are judicial and which are administrative. The wider theme of the judicial province became visible again in the *Tvind* case when the Supreme Court in 1999 defended its turf, stating that it was not the power of Parliament to decide controversies, neither by implication the place of officials to promote their administrative acts by seeking parliamentary sanctions for revoking rights and privileges.

Absolutism was established and continued with the support of the educated and commercial elites, who appear to have favoured the orderly government it brought with it and they saw in it, the reigning in of aristocratic privilege. The regime sought legitimacy and continued support through enlightened and principled rule. Benign absolute rule was strengthened by the ideology of the Spirit of the Laws by Montesquieu, which had a profound impact on the regime spearheaded by the efforts of Attorney General Henrik Stampe, not least in formulating a new Instruction for the Court in 1753.[38]

The high point of internal constitutional review based on natural law and scholarly theory was probably witnessed under Attorney General Stampe, who issued numerous famed declarations running into several volumes, in which he pronounced on various aspects of government admonishing officials, correcting statutes based on "our constitution."[39] This probably gives to show that it is very difficult to hold back 'custom, reason and why.' The Danish jurisdiction needed like any other to ponder the interpretation of law, the filling in of the blanks where law is silent or scarce, as well avoiding the cost and inconsistency of revisiting the same issues repeatedly. The Danish tradition, however, became one where special offices like the Attorney General, later the Parliamentary Ombudsman, pronounced on the law, and where comments and scholarly theory restate, construe and expand the law much more than case law does.

---

37. Jensen (1999) 22 note 30.
38. Jensen (1999) 23 Stampe became a Supreme Court Justice the same year and remained on the bench until 1771, Jensen (1999) 23 note 32. It is interesting that both Stampe and Jensen wrote vastly more as writers of scholarly theory and various commentary than they did as Supreme Court Justices in published official reasoning of the Court. We can say that for over two centuries, there appear to have been many brilliant Danish judges sometimes making their learned views public but there have been few brilliant judicial opinions that have been made public.
39. Tamm (2005) 265, 287.

Constitutional Strife

At the end of the absolute era, the Court was faced with cases of political connotation, pitting the policing efforts of the ancient regime against ideals of freedom and benign rule. The later 'founding father' Orla Lehman, who was to add such poignant words as the Folkething, 'People's House,' to the Basic Law in 1848, was convicted to three months in gaol in 1842 for insulting "the system of government and the monarchy" by claiming that, "the Danish farmers had nothing to thank their Kings for." The Justices were highly divided, some wanting to uphold the fine at trial, others voting for up to two years imprisonment. Had the judicial differences become known, there might have been a broader understanding of how indeterminate law can be, and how it can be amended and improved. However, due to the repressed reasoning, the Court just seemed harsh and reactionary with "consequences for the Court's position ... sharp attacks in the opposition press and increased mistrust of the Supreme Court in leading national-liberal circles."[40] Consequently, the democratic era that was to follow was started with a distrust of the judiciary that can be distinguished from both the American and indeed the Norwegian experience. In the American colonies, the Declaration of Independence talks of the King's 'obstruction of justice' and much hope was placed in the courts upholding 'rights and immunities;' likewise in Norway we saw that the other West-Nordic Supreme Court became a pillar of the institutional independence of Norway and guardian of freedom and rights. It seems fair to say that little hope was placed in the judicial system from a democratic point of view, the courts were assumed to churn out the harsh judgements that followed from harsh laws; democracy and rights depended on new laws and a new constitutional arrangement.

Absolutism did not give way to democracy suddenly but responded gradually to the challenges including by forming participatory assemblies.[41] In the end, Danish absolute monarchy was swept away in the great European year of revolutions 1848. The King and his government felt forced to give in and allowed a constitutional assembly to draft a new written constitution with all the trimmings of separation of powers, individual rights, independent judiciary and jury trials.[42] This new Basic Law with its potent provisions could have triggered a rights revolution and constitutional judicial review but ambiguity in purpose, institutional inertia and later external events all proved to hinder such a development.

40. Jensen (1999) 28-29 with note 55.
41. Tamm (2005) 361.
42. Tamm (2005) from 361.

When considering the constitutional text, it seems clear that the inclusion of the judicial branch in the Danish Basic Law was as most of its provisions copied from contemporary constitutional language.[43] The threesome division of power was very much in vogue and the Danish version was straightforward. The judicial power was not defined but vested in the judiciary. The nature of the judiciary was described in the spirit of Montesquieu: "The courts shall only judge according to the law," adding that 'the courts shall determine the boundaries of administration.' Given that Montesquieu was really giving an idealised version of law that favoured clear rules over indeterminate standards and saw the judge as being more a fair administrator than a resolver of conflicting sources of law, a more thoroughly theorised Basic Law should have read quire differently. Providing that 'the agencies shall administer only according to law' and furthermore that 'the courts shall be empowered to review all administration and uphold constitutional rights' would have been the way to resolve the underlying conflicts. Instead of getting an administration free from interference in particular matters and independent courts to resolve the inherent conflicts between the purpose of particular laws and the principles of rights and proper procedures, Denmark got a system that distinguished between maters of administration and matters of justice, confining constitutional rights provision to parliamentary consideration and narrow adjudication in criminal cases.

The 'boilerplate' nature of the Basic Law's provisions notwithstanding, the lack of constitutional judicial review was to some degree a conscious decision, as the Constitutional Convention in 1848 actively discussed review and the delegates seem very knowledgeable of review elsewhere, they just disagreed on, one ventures to say not least because of the record of judiciary hitherto. Those opposing views included people like the liberal Tscherning who insisted that constitutional judicial review would be a "Seed for Division"[44] and that the judges would likely "commit Idolatry with the Past; they would be binding themselves to the Words and Letters of the Law that they have grown up with."[45] The conservative Anders Sandøe Ørsted, arguably one Denmark's greatest lawyers ever, opined that constitutional judicial review would entail that the judges would come to personify reason and the Constitution, it would create a conflict between the judges and the King and government appointing them, and, ultimately, lead to the appointment of Jus-

---

43. Tamm (2005) 363.
44. Christensen (2003) 11-12.
45. Christensen (2003) 11-12.

tices who would not overturn statutes.[46] On the other side, people like the na-tional-liberal C. C. Hall found constitutional review necessarily to follow from the whole idea of a Constitution. Likewise, people like T. Algreen-Ussing argued that judicial review would guard against tyranny by the major-ity.[47] In the end, a proposal was brought stating that, "All statutes and regula-tions contrary to the Basic Law shall be void." Tscherning moved for an amendment to limit this to legislation promulgated *prior* to the Basic Law.[48] The motion was carried but then the entire provision was defeated.

Thus, it seems that constitutional judicial review was left out because the question was framed in the wrong way, the rather categorical statement that old laws and regulations should be 'void' if unconstitutional was defeated but what if stated differently? What if the question was more centred on the re-view process that could be presumed to include the 'softer' options including ensuring constitutionality of the result, corrective interpretation of the law and other more discursive options like the Norwegian provision of judicial 'responses' to parliamentary questions? Of course, this is impossible to know but the general view seems to be that the Convention was inconclusive and judicial review viewed by 'the founders' as "not out of the question" but in all events supposed to be the subject to "restraint."[49]

The eventual provision (now Basic Law § 63) contained the ambiguous provisions on the "limits of the administrative authorities." Even the under-standing of this was divided at the Constitutional Convention. Some saw the judiciary and the administration (agencies and various tiers of government) as parallel institutions, and saw cases as falling either in the province of the one or the other. According to this view, the significance of § 63 was only that the courts could decide in which category a case fell, having decided that a case was administrative, the courts could not review it further but defer to the rel-evant administrative agency, tribunal or minister. Others saw it differently and considered judicial review to include the legality of administrative deci-sions but not assessments and the technical expertise of administrative deci-sions.[50]

The consequence in practice following the promulgation of the Basic Law in 1849 was that neither old laws, new statutes, nor administrative regulation and practice became the subject of judicial review. Thus, ambiguity lead to

46. Christensen (2003) 11-12.
47. Christensen (2003) 11-12.
48. Christensen (2003) 11-12.
49. Jensen (1999) 233 with note 1.
50. Christensen (2003) 33-34.

even less review than in all likelihood supported at the Convention. The former theory on BL § prevailing until completely until after 1870 and resonated up into the 20th century. Indeed, it this view of the administration dealing with public law and the judiciary dealing with private and criminal law can be seen in procedural law, as there is no particular procedure for administrative review, which is therefore conducted as civil cases, using the same procedures as when dealing with controversies between citizens. Furthermore, the theory, especially its deference to agencies in case of any assessment resulting from legal standards or technical jargon, seems to have been revitalised by statutory positivist views of the post war period. After around 1870 and ever since, however, the courts started to work on the presumption that there were certain 'unwritten requirements' for the administration to abide by that could be review by the judiciary. Among these discovered requirements were the doctrines on abuse of power, legal criteria for administrative assessment, equality and proportionality.[51]

Like in Norway, an impeachment case in the specially constituted Court of Realm became important in the development of constitutional law but to opposite effect. The case against a previous conservative cabinet ministers alleged unauthorised defence spending during the Crimean war. All the Supreme Court Justices, who made up half the Court of Realm, voted to acquit, creating great resentment amongst the national-liberal government and prompting it to use the Basic Law provision authorising the dismissal of all Justices over 65 years of age. The retired Justices were replaced by lawyers of dependently national-liberal persuasion, including an active politician as Chief Justice.[52] These developments contributed significantly to the fact that "court control of laws' constitutionality was not realised in the 19th century, when the new system of government was being constructed."[53] From 1871 to 1909, all Chief Justices came from active political background, probably disinclined to put checks on their own factions.[54] This could have resulted in the kind of momentum for review that was observed in France's Fifth Republic but apparently did not, probably because there was not the same back and forth alteration in power between left and right but even more so because of a distrust of the judiciary and a favouring of parliamentary means. In any case, full-fledged review whether in France, the US or the EU seem never deliber-

---

51. Christensen (2003) 34-35.
52. Jensen (1999) 31-31 with note 62.
53. Jensen (1999) 32.
54. Jensen (1999) 32 with note 68.

ately constructed but being the result of the several conditions, including the absence of hindering cultural filters, being met at the same time.

In Denmark, power in terms of electoral support gradually moved from right to left, with the right wing losing ground to liberals, losing to farmers' left, losing to social democrats, with a more complex situation in the post war period. For almost a century from the mid-1800s, Parliament was divided. The upper house Landsthing was elected by very limited suffrage in terms of age and property, even more so after the war of 1864, which lost the control of the duchies and resulted in a revised more conservative Basic Law of 1866. One might say that another unresolved constitutional issue the federal dimension so to speak, adversely affected the young Danish democracy. The difficult relationship with the German speakers, made worse by ambitions of larger German countries, resulted in war in 1848 and again in 1864, leading to the loss of even the Danish speaking part of the duchy of Schleswig. The result seems to have been that the establishment including the King lost confidence in participatory and direct democracy and used the turmoil to revise the Basic Law, restricting voting rights, especially to the upper Landsthing that became a bastion of conservative and even reactionary forces.[55]

During this time, despite the limited suffrage, the liberal forces of 'the left," often referred to as "the farmers' friends" gradually overtook both the conservative 'right' and national-liberal 'old left' forces in popularity, gaining the majority in the popularly elected Folkething. The old right and left increasingly joined forces and governed with the support from the King and the upper house. Like the absolute government before it, the rightwing minority regime used the court system to curtail the opposition. Judge Jensen counts "54 judgements with connection to political conflicts. Even though the Court sought a moderate course, this [caused an increased] critique against the Court's composition and several judgements."[56] Condemnation of the Supreme Court were probably somewhat unfair, given that the Justices had different views and seem to have shown professional integrity as lawyers. For instance, the active right-wing politician judge Klein was vehemently arguing against the criminal statutes that the King signed when Parliament was in recess, in Danish called the 'provisory laws.' Alas, such dissenting opines were concealed from the public, as all the cases were published without reasoning and without mention of dissent.[57]

55. Tamm (2005) from 369.
56. Jensen (1999) 33.
57. Jensen (1999) 33 with note 74.

Courts can at times solve constitutional issues or facilitate constitutional discourse that leads to balanced solutions. The Danish Supreme Court had opportunity to make its mark in this way in the 1880s. The reactionary right wing that gained power over government following the constitutional reconstruction in 1866 used all means to maintain power without compromising with the more popular forces. The mentioned 'provisory laws' included financial budgets as well as criminalising the opposition, which seems to be a trait of authoritative regimes. The mentioned 'political cases' included people being convicted for shouting insults at the prime minister. Had the Court followed the 'rule of law conservatism' of judge Klein, the laws that criminalised such expressions as well as budgets without support from the popularly elected chamber might have been restricted or annulled, forcing the opposing sides to compromise and balance their priorities. It would have been easy for the Court to give effect to the many phrases of the Basic Law stating that such and such must be done "by law" by explaining that absent a state of emergency 'law' in this context meant the sanction of both Houses of Parliament. This opportunity seems have been lost due to the 'filters' of legal culture.

Ultimately, the King gave in to the popular mandate of the opposition and in 1901 appointed the first prime minister who had the confidence of the Folkething, often referred to as the *change of system*.[58] The King would not have a peasant in his residence, however, so he appointed a law professor "to some degree" belonging to the liberal factions of "farmers' friends,"[59] incidentally a law professor who had argued in favour of judicial review in his book on civil procedure.[60] This event and subsequent developments have often been misrepresented as evolving *customary law*. The better view is that this event caused by a political standoff resulted in a *precedent* being created which was since was followed but not necessarily so. The King guarded his prerogative actually to choose the prime minster, and even in 1920 tried to appoint an administration completely of his own liking. This prime minister lasted only a month as increasing displays of discontent persuaded the king that monarchy itself faced a loss of confidence. The King still formally appoints the prime minister at his pleasure but any sitting prime minister advising the King to ig-

58. Henrik Zahle *Regering, forvaltning og dom. Dansk Forfatningsret* Christian Ejlers' Forlag (1989).
59. Jens Peter Christensen "Norm og praksis under grundloven som aldrig ændres" in *Grundlagens makt. Konstitutionen som politiskt redskap och som rättslig norm* SNS författningsprojekt (2002) 110.
60. Jensen (1999) 234 note 5.

nore the precedent is sure to face impeachment and the monarchy will be relegated to history.

With the system change, the need for and potential usefulness of constitutional judicial review was considerably reduced, not surfacing again before some of supporters of 'the ancient regime' were adversely affected by the new government of the left. Before looking at more recent developments, however, it may be prudent summarise that Danish constitutional judicial review was conspicuous by its absence and thus added to the confrontational nature of the political discourse that lead to a parliamentary system, where the same majority controlled by the legislative and executive branches, even more so after the inevitable abolition of bicameralism. Thus, constitutional judicial review seems to have very different short and long-term effects, it might improve things and provide for gradual developments but over time that may hinder or delay more radical change.

This introduction must not be read as simple message of 'they could have and should have.' Rather it should give an insight into the nature of constitutional (and so much other) law as the saying goes more the result of accident and force than reflection and choice. The only very clear conclusion is not to see constitutional judicial review as something that with inescapable logical necessity either is or is not part of Danish democracy. Review is an option, or mostly an invention, with its particular implications. For a very long time, however, review was not part of Danish democracy *because of institutional, cultural and theoretical filters and other hindrances.* The most notable of these is the lasting ban on reasoning that to this day makes case law very inaccessible. The renowned scholar Henrik Zahle was himself a Supreme Court Justice for a while. In his book on caring for Justice, Zahle writes: "I have seen advocates argue, who could have benefited from knowing *that* a precedent was decided under considerable doubt (according to the voting protocol) ... *that* the criteria that according to the official reasoning vas decisive and was accepted in literature did not command majority support at all ..."[61]

For constitutional cases in particular, the restrictive dynamics that commanded a small majority in court but appeared as enigmatic statements to the wider public, created a legal environment, where there were doubts as to the balance of power and doubts as to whether the Supreme Court would every apply the Basis Law. This doubt as the legal relevance of the Basic Law "had

---

61. Zahle (2003) 133.

a self-increasing effect, as an understanding developed in advocate circles that it was useless to base claims on constitutional provisions."[62]

The quiet way of the Højesteret, was such that in the old day dissenters would discretely indicate their dissent by not signing the judgement.[63] This subtlety, which started out as an outright ban in 1674 made in the interest of centralised absolutism to avoid 'custom, reason and why' being widely known, has probably been rationalised as the way judges should behave, "the Supreme Court is not an institution of learning," as Justice Cosmus Meyer once put it.[64] As law should be logical and predictable, is should be applied as if no other option existed. As Zahle indicates, this is not so, not even to Supreme Court Justices, and especially not so in the multi-dimensional world of constitutional review, where you simultaneously construe statutory law and higher norms, both in the abstract and the result, relying on precedent, procedure and juggling several multi-factored standards at the same time. Thus, many outsiders came to view the convoluted style as untenable.

Already in 1856, the Supreme Court was by a statute given the choice between 'public voting' i.e. making its deliberations known or publishing officially reasoned judgements. Højesteret was apparently fearful that official reasoning might affect its ability to adjudicate speedily but chose the latter. The reform was "a decisive step forward for the lawyers, who had risked arguing based on wrongful understanding of the reasoning behind a prior decision;" likewise, there were advantages for Danish academia, "that had felt abandoned by oracle answers," and the deliberating judges "hitherto forced to seek the meaning of precedents revealed by time-consuming examinations of the voting protocols."[65] To some degree, however, the scholarly theory was of the opposite opinion for a very long time, claiming for itself the province of restating and explaining the law and urging judicial restraint.

The Højesteret has become much more accessible, however. Recently its workload has been eased, as fewer cases reaching it as direct appeal. The stated objective of recent reforms has been to make sure that the Supreme Courts resources are used for the central tasks of 'ensure unity of law, issues

---

62. Jensen (1999) 233.
63. Jensen (1999) 18.
64. á Rógvi (2001) 253. For a better view Christopher L. Eisgruber "Is the Supreme Court an Educative Institution?" 67 *New York University Law Review* (2004) 961.
65. Jensen (1999) 30 with note 61. Justice Jensen wrote a spectacular article on failings of university teaching of practical interpretation in Jensen (1988) where he explained the reasoning behind a Faroese case, which we shall look into further in the Faroese section.

of general importance for the application and development of law or of wider importance to society.'[66] This has happened even after a number of cases, where the Court has widened the access to judicial review, expanded on reasoning, applied quasi-constitutional law using the case law approach of the ECJ and the ECHR courts, and where even one case outright declared a statute unconstitutional and void. Before we introduce the various periods and then survey the jurisprudence, it seems fair to say that the Danish Supreme Court has a deserved reputation as being impartial and has increased its relevance and credibility in the form of triadic rulemaking. Increased rulemaking through case law seems indeed explicitly endorsed by the latest reforms and seems likely to lead to increased constitutional judicial review but in all likelihood mostly using flexible, even subtle techniques.

Introduction to Previous Periods

After the 1901 system change, the popularly elected Folkething finally got the upper hand in the tug-of-war with the aristocracy and establishment figures of the Landsthing. The 1849 Basic Law provided that all privileges based on noble titles were revoked and that no feudal trusts could be established. The existing feudal trusts, however, had continued under the conservative minority government. Now time was ripe for overturning these baronies and feudal trusts. Noble families had in ancient times created trusts that included their castles and estates. The land could be used by the nobleman holding the title but could not be sold or otherwise transferred. The nobleman was protected from his creditors and each generation could enjoy the fruits of the holdings but could not dispose of the capital.[67] For many aristocrats, the prospect of changing the law and freeing up the assets was probably welcome but the progressive majority wanted something in exchange and provided for some redistribution of land, compensated the aristocrats with less than the market value of the taken land. This led to a number of cases, where constitutional judicial review was established in principle.

By now, cases were being reported, but still only in very incomplete form.[68] Most of the judgement consisted of a narrative of the facts and the opinion of the court appeared as a very short reasoning where the individual opinions of the judges were not devolved and dissents not made public.[69]

---

66. From homepage www.domstol.dk
67. Tamm (2005) 211 Jensen (1999) .Tamm (2005) 236.
68. Jensen (1999).
69. W. E. von Eyben Juridisk Grundbog 3. Dommen – sproget Jurist & Økonomforbundets Forlag (1989).

This may have hindered further review as seemed to a reserved power for extreme events, not a way of fine-tuning and developing the statutory law in light of higher principles. Few constitutional cases seem to have been brought in the period from 1901 until the Second World War. As we have seen in Norway and the US, constitutional review was on a restrictive trend and Denmark did not go against this trend.

By the 1930s, a new left wing had arisen with radicals and social democrats with a new redistributive agenda and apparently little faith in using the courts to implement their program. The amended 1915 Basic Law had introduced female suffrage and broadened the electorate of the Landsthing. By the late 1930s, the new left was strong enough to propose amending the constitution again, including electing the upper house in accordance with the principles of corporatism. Interestingly for our purposes, the proposal was also introducing an ombudsman who could listen to complaints from the public and would report to Parliament on how the courts interpreted the law. Apparently, there was an understanding that statutes might be subject to construction and rulemaking by the courts and Parliament now wanted to monitor these developments. This can indicate distrust but might also have led to a discourse and increased development of law through altering rounds of case law and statutory law. However, the proposal was not sanctioned by enough votes at a referendum.

I the post-war period, the Basic Law has been amended once, in 1953, abolishing the Landsthing altogether and introducing the present Parliamentary Ombudsman that does not monitor case law or judicial review. The 1953 Basic Law included an interesting provision on joining supra national entities and transferring constitutional powers to them. This was later to lead to EEC/EU membership that was to change judicial review profoundly. It is interesting to note that much of the 1849 language was retained but interpreted completely differently. Basic Law is its § 56 on MPs being 'bound only by their conscience' was originally a ban on political parties but Denmark today has very strong party discipline. Numerous Basic Law provisions still place executive government and other powers firmly in the hands of the King but parliamentarism means that most of these powers lie firmly with the prime minister or the executive government as a whole, whose members are most often MPs at the same time. In addition, devolution to the Faroe Islands and Greenland, EU and ECHR membership and other developments mean that the rather similar 1848 and 1953 language has very different meaning.

We shall survey a selected number of the published cases that deal with constitutional issues during little over a century from the 1870s to the 1990s, the grouping of cases of *previous practice*. Danish Supreme Court cases dealing with constitutionality are limited compared to Norway. However, a number of cases deal with constitutionality in various ways. The object is to gain an insight into the dynamics from the early democratic era until quasi-federal review begins to have its impact. We shall look at the *early cases*, when review was awkward and new, then the *economic regulation cases*, concerning the battle between rights provisions and progressive reconstituting of the economy. Then, the *war cases* provide an insight into legal reasoning under extreme circumstances. Finally, the *review reconsidered* section deals with a number of issues tackled by the Højesteret from the 1970s to the 1990s.

Introduction to Recent Period

The by far most profound constitutional developments since the advent of the Basic Law was Denmark's accession to the European Communities, now European Union, in 1973 and to the European Convention on Human Rights in 1953 with so-called incorporation in 1992. The full effects of these accessions were delayed, but for the Supreme Court it meant "changes in its position as supreme instance of law." The status of constitutional judicial review in Denmark had been such that the Højesteret had reserved its power to use it but had also developed a doctrine of restraint that meant that it very rarely did so, taking a century and a half to find a clear incident of a statute in breach of the constitution. However, now the "Supreme Court cut off from an independent interpretation of the content of union provisions and extent, and the system that is built through the ECHR causes the Supreme Court's decisions – both concerning traditional civil rights and those procedural and criminal principles etc. contained in the convention – not necessarily are final but under certain conditions can be reviewed by the ECHR in Strasbourg."[70]

With EU law came a renewed interest in case law. To the astonishment of Danish law, the EJC foregoes preparatory works, disregards (Danish) institutional writers, and develops its own interpretation through meticulously reasoned judgements forming an intermeshing constellation of precedent. This new methodology means that issues are now more systematically settled, meaning that the Danish Supreme Court must prejudicially ask the ECJ for its judgement on EU law under the "as delineation criterion established principle of acte claire."[71] Danish constitutional law became part of a dynamic process evolving what originally may have seemed like a regional trading block established by normal multinational treaties without much direct effect in na-

70. Jensen (1999) 51.
71. Ibid. 70.

tional law into a sui generis system of law. This new legal order ultimately adjudicated by a Court with supreme jurisdiction applying concepts that are unimaginable prior to accession, concepts like the supremacy of EU-law, direct effect and common basic rights.

With ECHR law came less of an interest at first. Denmark signed and ratified early; for years, the ECHR Court was scorned for being an "unemployed Court"[72] and no Danish cases were brought before it. However, after the Court practice picked up and Danes discovered that Denmark was not by definition observing all human rights, and that their content was debateable. In 1992, Denmark took the step of implementing the ECHR, which is formally a significant step in a nominally dualistic country. In the view of scholar Jens Elo Rytter, the ECHR "had already in prior court practice achieved a status as a significant source of law. The ECHR with accompanying ECHR Court practice has supremacy over conflicting Danish legislation, unless lawgiver has clearly made known a wish to diverge; [the] ECHR has not in itself constitutional rank but can indirectly [be given that if the courts] recognise the ECHR as unwritten constitutional law."[73]

Just how effective ECHR would turn out became clear with Denmark's first losses in the ECHR Court that came as great shock and surprise.[74] Jens Elo Rytter believes the first case to have been the "break-through," adding that just few years before "the Supreme Court [stated] the traditional dualistic perception that the ECHR is an international treaty inapplicable directly in Danish law."[75] This changed dramatically. "After Hauschildt the Supreme Court was suddenly more attentive to the ECHR as a source of law under Danish law. With three judgements in 1989 [it pursued] an active line [conforming Danish law] to ECHR law and ECHR Court practice."[76]

Whether the impact *unwritten constitutional law* and having the quasi-federal courts performing review of both Danish law and the jurisprudence of Højesteret is of course difficult to determine. However, in a period after the first setting aside of Danish law on the ECHR court, review based on the

---

72. Knud Waaben "Alf Ross 1899-1979" in *Politik og jura. Festskrift til Ole Espersen* (2004) 464. The article was never published, on another judge's request, exists "only in a limited number of private special editions."
73. Rytter (2006) 33.
74. Páll Hreinsson *Hæfisreglur stjórnsýslulaga* Codex (2005) 446-57 gives a very interesting and thorough account of the impact of *Hauscchildt* and contrast with earlier doctrine, especially in Iceland.
75. Rytter (2006) 35.
76. Ibid. 35.

Basic Law increased in force and the first case came that in effect invalidated an Act of Parliament.

Today, for all practical purposes, Denmark is committed to "continuous observance of the ECHR-complex either [through legislation or interpretation]."[77] The "ECHR's core should today be recognised as expressing unwritten Danish constitutional law" and legislation to the contrary will be set aside accordingly."[78] Thus, in practice, only in the substantive area of law outside 'the core' as perceived by the courts is it effectively still possible for Danish authorities act is if fully independent. This means that Danish constitutional law has changed dynamically without the Basic Law being amended. Denmark now has constitutional principles limiting the powers of her political bodies; these will be developed by quasi-federal institutions outside their reach and by increasingly assertive Danish courts. However, one challenge just like in Norway is that of methodology in finding and construing constitutional law. Højesteret seems at time like Høyesterett to use two methods, one centred on principles and case law, the other on preparatory work and scholarly theory.

Given the very long period of highly restrained review, and ideological commitment to parliamentary supremacy and distrust of the courts, a backlash might have been expected but review seems to have been accepted whether based on EU-law, ECHR-law, the Basic Law or principles found in the 'penumbra' of these. No adverse reaction like the earlier Norwegian of 'the last bastion of the reactionary forces' was heard.[79] This has meant that Danish courts now have to interpret 'the ECHR complex,' even in case of conflict that leads to overruling national law and even "with an eye to the dynamic development of the ECHR's protection."[80] Even the old tradition of distinguishing between administrative and judicial cases seems to be fading away with only very few statutory provisions remaining that limit general judicial review.[81]

Surveying later Danish cases, we shall divide them in sections according to their main subject. We begin with *reviewing Denmark's quasi-federal position*, cases that deal with the constitutionality of Danish quasi-federal membership. Second, we look at the *division of power cases* that dynamically deal with the relationship between the integrated legislative and executive branch-

77. Rytter (2006) 33.
78. Rytter (2006) 39.
79. Christensen (2003) 28-29.
80. Rytter (2000) 42.
81. Christensen (2003) 36.

es on the one side and the judicial branch on the other. Third, we shall look at *equal rights cases* dealing with Danish equal treatment especially of various minorities. Fourth, we shall look at *freedom of assembly and expression cases*. Fifth, we shall move into the *rights of the accused* focusing on presumption of innocence.

Previous Practice

The Early cases

The earliest reported case with the potential for constitutional review may be ***International Workers Union v. Denmark*** (UfR.1874.479H). The report does not mention constitutionality as an issue but the case was initiated pursuant the freedom of association clause of the Basic Law (§ 87 at the time), which provided that associations could be banned if formed for subversive purposes. Following the convictions of Louis Pio and other Danish union leaders on trumped-up charges,[82] their union was temporarily banned and now sought dissolved by court order.

The report notes that the named defendant, cigar-maker Peter Christian Johnsen, representing himself, argued for overturning the ban, presumably as being unconstitutional, but also claimed not to be the proper defendant, as he was only the chair of the Copenhagen chapter of the union. The reported reasoning only summarily decides the latter issue: "the plea of lacking competence to receive the suit is therefore of no importance." The report then summarises the reasoning as to the substance of the case to be that International Workers Union was "declared dissolved mainly by Cause of the Union's, by its Actions indicated, Perception of its Laws and Purpose."

The case shows many features of Danish case law. First, it illuminates the strange relationship between judgement and report, even to this day; the report often claims insight to the reasoning of the reported cases that is not confirmed by text directly quoted from the actual judgements. Second, although the substantive basis for the government's case was the Basic Law, the reported judgement does not consider the obvious issues of constitutionality, it just treats the provision banning associations as a straightforward law to be applied, not to be balanced with the freedom of association. Finally, we see that there was so little hope of succeeding with judicial review that a citizen in this situation could not obtain adequate representation. This was later ech-

---

82. Jensen (1999) 234 note 2.

oed in the Hauschildt case, where council would not allege violation of the ECHR.

The judgement seems to be a narrow decision. The case turned on simple interpretation of a sub-clause. Researching the actual votes of the Justices would be interesting and might show a deeper consideration of the freedom of association, was it seen as a substantive right or a procedural safeguard by any members of the Højesteret? For our purposes, however, the notable thing is that the case was reported as dealing with the Basic Law as any other statute, deferring to agency as to interpretation, proceeding to find facts supporting the result sought by the agency, given the deferred interpretation.

Another case to mention constitutionality was **Olsen v. Denmark** (UfR.1887.142H), where the issue was the constitutionality of provisory criminal legislation. The conservative minority government with the support of the King had promulgated the law while Parliament was in recess following an attempt on Prime Minister Estrup's life.[83] Sigvald Olsen, editor of the Social Democrat newspaper was consequently convicted at trial of defamation based on a temporary law not passed the Landsthing and Folkething.

As the case appears in the report, it seems that the Supreme Court upheld this temporary law, even though no pressing reason was shown why Parliament could not have deliberated on the matter when next in session. Højesteret seems to have endorsed the position that the best reading of the Basic Law was that the government could legislate on its own when Parliament was not sitting. The case probably contributed to the irrelevance of judicial review as part of the political process, as it seemed useless to bring cases on the constitutionality of the provisory laws. The Supreme Court, however, was split on the issue seven to five, with even rightwing Justices highly critical of the law.[84] The case was apparently hotly debated among the Justices: "the deliberation protocol reveals that the waves went high. In reality it there were only seven against five Justices of the Supreme Court that approved of the provisional criminal statute ... The dissenters opined, for instance: "Where would we end if provisional statutes could stand as valid for several years? It would be absolutism under false pretence.""[85] Apparently, the result had much to do with the way the case was framed by the defendant and no princi-

---

83. Ibid. 234 note 2.
84. Ibid. 33 with note 74.
85. Jørgen Mathiassen "Juridisk kalejdoskop" in *Juristen i Satirens og Humorens Streg* (1994) at 31.

ple stance against judicial review can be detected among the majority.[86] Thus judicial review was hindered by lack of reporting, a very effective filter.

Apparently, a number of cases dealt with the issue and could have stopped the practise of provisory laws but only *Olsen* was reported to be a case concerning constitutionality.[87] Had some doctrine evolved as to the use of provisory laws, the government would have had to seek compromise with especially the Folkething, it would not have benefitted so much from frequently dissolving Parliament, and ministers might even have faced impeachment for abusing provisory legislation. Just the knowledge if dissenting opinions would have triggered more cases to determine the limits of government powers. Instead, Denmark faced a long period of standoff, where the government issued provisory laws and the Folkething denied funding for the government.

Land Reform and Compensation

A few cases dealt with reforms somewhat similar to the Norwegian reforms in the officers' cases. However, Denmark did not have the same Officers' Clause so the issue was dealt with a few times as potential compensation according to the properties clause and the judges' clause. *Barfod v. Denmark* (UfR.1912.545H) considered the constitutionality of revoking the tithe, funding the state church priests directly instead. The Supreme Court noted the negotiations prior to the legislation and found against the lone plaintiff, "When it now cannot be doubted that the Lawgiving Power has acted rightly in establishing this new Order, especially when considering the fluctuating nature of the Income and previous regulation thereof." The Court let the reverend Barfod off easily regarding cost. The case seems to be a typical precursor to a 'Marbury moment.' The key phrase being that it is not enough for 'the lawgiver' to act – this must be done "rightly."

One judge wrote at the time that, "Whether or not it is assumed that the courts have the right to decide the question of the limits of legislative power it must be assumed that [the necessity of expropriation] is within the area of legislative power and is decided sovereignly by that [power]."[88] Thus, the ideology was clear, the judicial power was likely to focus on the constitutionality of the effects of legislation rather than testing all aspects of the law in light of constitutional provisions.

The Minister of Justice had apparently been informed that the Supreme Court "considered itself entitled to review constitutionality, though indica-

---

86. Jensen (1999) note 2.
87. Jensen (1995) 241 with note 2.
88. Jensen (1999) note 9.

tions to the contrary exist."[89] For the first time, constitutionality was openly debated, although to a very limited extent and longer explanation on the question of rightly exercise of legislative powers might have had greater impact.

In a 1934, in *Andersen v. Denmark* (UfR.1935.1H), the Supreme Court was faced with a number of judges who alleged unconstitutionality in their loss of tenure and full pay when the Civil Servants Pension Act was amended to force judges to retire at the age of 70. The Court concluded that the state could force the judges to retire: "when the Age-limit is provided so that Judges at that Age are no longer fully able to discharge their Offices." The Court found that no risk of arbitrary treatment or of loss of judges' independence or acquired pension rights. The Court referred to the preparatory works regarding the constitutional provision but no case law.

The case upheld the governments interpretation of the Basic Law clause on the independence of judges, now § 64, but did so conditioned on three specific criteria which may, emphasising the independence of the judiciary. The case may be similar to what we have seen in France, where laws are upheld only if construed according to principles explained by the Court. As to methodology we see emphasis on official of the Basic Law, which seems clearly to be considered as law, at least as a way of interpreting statute "The decision is a typical example of pragmatic interpretation in accordance with the real purposes, which carry the rules."[90]

Going back a few years, in a series of cases, the constitutionality progressive land reforms were tested. In *Sehested Juul v. Denmark* (UfR.1921.148H), the issue was whether the conversion of feudal land and feudal trust funds was violating the rights of the noble families in question. The law provided for the feudal land and trusts to be converted into free property, thus increasing the value for the holder who now became owner of the property. In return for this, some of the land would given others as smallholdings and a duty of up to 30 per of the value was levied. The duty increased, the longer the feudal holder delayed the conversion from feudal to free property.

The Supreme Court found the rights of the noble families to be a form of succession rights that was obviously within the powers of the legislature to amend. The report notes to the case give quite an interesting lesson in the history of succession right in Denmark. As to the duties, Højesteret found that it "must, rather, be admitted that the Rules on the Payment to the State and the Land-Relinquishing are very burdensome for the Holder ... and will function

---

89. Jensen (1999) 235.
90. Ibid. 238 note 14.

as a Coercion; but the Lawgiving Power is, nevertheless, not found by these provisions to have exceeded the Limits of its Authority." The Court then remarked that Basic Law § 91 specifically authorised the dismantling of feudal estates.

The holding concerning the rights of the successors to the feudal estates was affirmed as the sole issue in *Løvenskiold v. Denmark* (UfR.1921.153H). In *Lerche v. Sass* (UfR.1921.168H) and a companion case, the Supreme Court upheld the abolition of feudal rents. The Court remarked that the statute seemed to be within the limits of the *public good* as provided by the expropriation clause. Instead of his fluctuating return of rents, the holder would get a capitalised value, no less than "full Compensation."

Finally, in *de Neergaard v. Pedersen* (UfR.1921.644H), the Supreme Court was faced with land redistribution. The farm in question was part of the Fuglebjerg estate with Edvard de Neergaard as lord of the fee. The farm was held in tenure by tenant farmer Peder Pedersen, according to his succession right to tenure, for a succession fee of DKK 5,000 in 1884 and the annual rent of 50 barrels of two-rowed barley. The farm was valued in 1920 by the tenure relinquishment commission to DKK 35,000 (in addition to DKK 7,000 in value added by the tenant), based according to the law on conditions in 1916. The statute's formula gave farmer Pedersen a right to buy the farm for around DKK 28,000. However, the taxation commission in 1920 assessed the farm's value at DKK 52,000 and the lord of the fee claimed the market value of comparable farms to be around DKK 70,000.

Even though the fee lord's right to the fee was restricted, the payment was arguably somewhat slight and at odds with the full compensation provision of the Basic Law. However, the Supreme Court stated that "it cannot with the Certainty that is required for the Courts to set aside a constitutionally enacted Statute as unconstitutional be held that the Appellant has not [been adequately compensated]."

And there it was! The Danish Supreme Court had unequivocally stated that – with the necessary certainty present – the courts could set aside statutes as unconstitutional.[91] The underlying assumption of *Sehested Juul* as well as *Lerche* and *de Neergaard* was the same assumption that had prompted Marshall that it was *the province of the courts to determine constitutionality*. Cases on the feudal estate dissolution were not ideal for pushing a norm shift, as "it was a problem for several of the judges that the [law] was enacted unanimously in both Things ... it was therefore not he best suited case – for the first

---

91. Ibid. 236.

time – to declare a statutory provisions unconstitutional. The deliberation is a clear example on the conflict between law and politics ...""[92]

It seems that *de Neergaard v. Pedersen* could have gone the other way.[93] Again, the inadequate reporting and the strange silence of the minority Justices meant that the mentioning of review powers failed to register and reverberate, although now stated clearly, like in the *Olsen* case the power of constitutional review was stated very briefly and not explained. In Parliament, the reactions to the Supreme Court's general assertion of constitutional judicial review were largely divided along party lines with the conservatives and liberals in opposition in favour of it and the social democrats and radicals in government opposing it.[94] In the end, however, the land reform cases sparked no great constitutional discourse, the potential of review was not realised.

In 1952, a similar question had surfaced as a statute limited how much land could be inherited by or transferred to one heir in *Ahlefeldt-Laurvig v. Denmark* (UfR.1952.0797H). Fief-Count Ahlefeldt-Laurvig challenged the law that was upheld as legitimate regulation. The report note referred to *Sehested Juul* and its note on succession law, perhaps hinting at precedent.

War Cases

On 9 April 1940, Denmark acquiesced to being occupied by Nazi-Germany. Though warned beforehand, neither the Danish King nor Government nor Parliament decided to flee the country. They cooperated with the occupiers until late 1943, including supporting the formation of Danish battalions to fight on the eastern front. Unlike in Norway, the Supreme Court accepted the new allegiance and its implications.

In *N N I v. Denmark* (UfR.1941.1070-1H), three Justices of the Supreme Court affirmed two consecutive rulings by the Copenhagen trial court whereby a Communist Member of the Danish Parliament was first held pending sanction by Parliament and then, following a parliamentary resolution, to hold him indefinitely at the request of the Germans. The trial court had noted that there was no doubt as to the identity of the MP. The Supreme Court further noted that it only remained to assess if the conditions in the statute for release were satisfied, which they were not.

In *N N II v. Denmark* (UfR.1941.1070-2H), the second of the three Communists MPs alleged that the Communist Act that authorised their detention was invalid as the three Communist were barred from participating in the

---

92. Jensen (1999) 237 note 11.
93. Christensen (2003) 14-15.
94. Ibid. 15-16.

deliberations and as a violation of the freedom of association clause of the Basic Law. The trial court held that the statute was "enacted under the present extraordinary Circumstance and under adequate reliance on the Principle of Duress in a fully justified and constitutional Manner," further remarking that the identity of the defendant was certain. The Supreme Court added laconically that the argument on constitutionality "is found to lack Reason."

In *N N III v. Denmark* (UfR.1941.1071H), the pattern of *NN I* was followed with the trial court remarking that there was no doubt as to the defendants "hitherto Participation in communist Activity and Agitation."

The *N N* cases eerily affirmed *International Workers Union* and were so hastily prepared that no records exist of the deliberations.[95] The Højesteret may have taken the position that it was choosing the lesser of two evils, shielding the MPs by taking them into custody rather than having the Germans taking them to an even worse fate. The situation was of course extraordinary and akin to duress but the cases still leave the impression that the parliamentary statutes can, given the circumstances, control the interpretation of the Basic Law. Furthermore, the published reasoning is as limited as in the pre war cases, giving the impression that deference to others as to constitutional law was the normal state of affairs and that the courts would usually limit themselves to factual review.

Shortly after the *N N* cases, in **Wissing v. Denmark** (UfR.1941.1076H), grocer Willy Wissing challenged a statutory empowering of the administration to limit sales of certain goods. He was charged for having "continuously sold Milk and Cream regardless of the Fact that he at the shop was vending Coffee, Tea, Coco, and Conserves, and regardless of the Store not being open on all days of the Week," contrary to secondary legislation. His defence that both administration and Parliament were acting outside their constitutional powers in creating such laws was brushed aside. The trial court remarked, "When it cannot be accepted as claimed by the Defendant that the statute should be against the Basic Law ..." and promptly convicted him. The Eastern High Court is not reported to having said anything apart from affirming and thirteen unanimous Justices of the Supreme Court whilst noting the defendant claim for compensation if the law was upheld found that: "the Information in evidence is partly so unsure, partly in any Case not of such Character as to question the rules Validity."

The case begs the obvious question of when it is possible to question a law's validity. Furthermore, the case shows a reluctance to participate in any

---

95. Jensen (1999) 239 with note 15.

wider discourse, to explain legislative and executive powers, generally as well as under difficult circumstances, and the possible limits of these powers, substantively as well as procedurally.

Following the war, the Supreme Court upheld retroactive laws punishing certain acts of collaboration with the occupying forces. The Danish Basic Law did not contain any retroactive clause, and the courts found no occasion to apply or explain other provisions or principles in the collaboration cases. Readers may explore that issue in a number of works.[96]

Review Reconsidered

Like in Norway, no great constitutional cases arose in the post-war period. The profound change elsewhere in Western Europe with expanded civil rights and constitutional courts dedicated to their protection seemed not to extend to the West Nordic countries, probably because there was not complete breakdown in the faith in government institution. However, constitutional cases surfaced from time to time.

In *Arne Magnussens Legat v. Denmark* (UfR.1971.0299H), the issue was the return of ancient Icelandic manuscripts containing the celebrated sagas and other works to Iceland. By statute, the works were returned to Iceland free of charge. However, the independent Danish institution that kept the manuscripts claimed property rights and that the law was in effect expropriation without compensation. By this time, dissenting opinions were published and the several opinions in this case had rather different reasoning. However, this was "significant as the first example that a Danish court has declared a claimed effect of a passed legislation unconstitutional."[97]

The case is sometimes heralded a great review case. However, it only reviews the statute by construing its silence, holding that it had to be interpreted in light of Basic Law § 73 and in principle award compensation. "The law was silent on this issue ... no real "setting aside" can therefore be attributed."[98] Truly to set aside the law would have been to hold that the manuscripts could not be expropriated or awarding compensation contrary to explicit provisions of no compensation. Nonetheless, the case seems to have ignited a new interest in the questions of constitutionality and judicial review.

96. Tamm (2005) from 426.
97. Jensen (1999) 241.
98. Smith (1993) 82.

Recent Review

Reviewing Denmark's Quasi-Federal Position

Although there might have been some internal impetus for increased review, most momentum for review was external, following EU and ECHR accession. Most of the ensuing quasi-federal jurisprudence was completely unforeseen in terms of both content and methodology.[99] Concerning EU accession the 1953 Basic Law § 20 provided for constitutional powers to be transferred to a "determined extent." The initial accession was challenged as being indeterminate in extent. In the first such case, the Supreme Court held that Danish citizens did not even have legal standing to challenge the constitutionality of EU-accession in *Tegen v. Prime Minister* (UfR.1973.0694H). However, the case was not an impressive suit, appearing for himself a man of little means ineloquently alleged "illegal purpose" and an "illegal / unconstitutional referendum."[100] The Eastern High Court observed that the law was enacted by the Folkething and "signed by the Queen" and found there to be no "concrete and actual interest" in having the issue of constitutionality reviewed." The Supreme Court upheld for the reasons below.[101]

The case demonstrates how people raising legitimate constitutional issues lack the means to have them adequately adjudicated. Either through legal aid or pro bono representation, such cases should be heard, given the ECHR justice clause. The patronising treatment by the Eastern High Court especially, referring to his "claims"[102] seems rather distasteful, given that this was one the major event of constitutional history. This probably reiterated the futility of raising constitutional arguments in court.

As to the methodology, it is very interesting to see how 'a parliamentary vote and royal assent' seem to be all that is needed for a law to have the necessary constitutional legitimacy at this stage.

The doctrine of *Norup Carlsen v. Nyrup Rasmussen I* (UfR.1996.1300H) was later overruled. The suit this time was infinitely better prepared with distinguished lawyers joining and representing a number of eloquent plaintiffs. The Eastern High Court stuck to the old line of no individual interest but the Supreme Court overruled, finding that the individual interest was strong

---

99. For an early Danish account of how – and by whom – community law would be interpreted see Claus Gulmann "Nogle bemærkning om EF-Domstolens fortolkningsmetoder" *Ugeskrift for retsvæsen* (1978) B161.
100. *Tegen v. Prime Minister 695.*
101. Ibid. 695.
102. Ibid. 695.

enough for legal standing. Dealing with the merits of the case, in *Norup Carlsen v. Nyrup Rasmussen II* (UfR.1998.0800H), the Eastern High Court searched the preparatory works and found the EU membership "neither by the Basic Law's § 20 nor by its preparatory work"[103] could violate any requirement that would render the accession statute "voidable on constitutional preconditions."[104]

The Supreme Court found that at issue was Denmark's incorporation of the EC Treaty as amended by the Union Treaty and its compatibility with BL § 20, noting that if exceeding BL § 20 accession would require constitutional amendment according to the more cumbersome procedure in BL § 88.[105] The unanimous eleven-member court reasoned over an unprecedented three pages. The report's note on legal literature refers to all sorts of comparative material, including German Constitutional Court judgements.[106] The Court first explains that BL § 20 was enacted to make it possible to let "an international organisation to hold legislative, administrative or judicial authority with direct effect in this country [amounting to] wide frames for access to transfer of sovereignty [coupled with] sharpened requirements for passing of bills pursuant to the provisions."[107] Having established the scheme of BL § 20, the Court then found that such transfers cannot "violate provisions of the Basic Law, including the freedom rights. The authorities of the Realm do, actually, not hold such power."[108] As for the phrase "determined extent," the Court found it to be suitable for "spacey categories" that would in any case not be free of "assessment or doubts of interpretation." The Court then found that the "specific enabling provisions of the EC Treaty fulfil the requirement."[109] As for the then Article 235, the 'competence-to-competence' provision, the Court found according to Danish preparatory works and a plenary statement from the ECJ that it was only an auxiliary provisions that anyway "only can happen with unanimity [thus] the government can hinder" its use beyond the transferred powers.[110]

As for the powers of the European Court of Justice, the Supreme Court found it in "interpretation of the Treaty also emphasises other momentums of

103. *Norup Carlsen v. Nyrup Rasmussen II* 805.
104. Ibid. 806.
105. Ibid. 869.
106. Ibid. 871 note 1.
107. Ibid. 869.
108. Ibid.
109. Ibid.
110. Ibid. 870.

interpretation than the phrasing of the provisions [but this] is not in violation of the preconditions [of the] Accession Act [nor] irreconcilable with [§ 20]." The Court added that the "same applies for the ECJ's rulemaking undertaking within the bounds of the Treaty."[111]

As for its own powers, Højesteret found that it follows from "the determinate-requirement in the Basic Law's § 20(1) in connection with Danish courts' access to review the constitutionality of laws that the courts cannot be deprived of the access to review whether an EC instrument transgresses the limits of [the] transfer of sovereignty."[112]

As for the danger of transferral of power to a very wide extent, undermining independence and democracy, the Court found that such transfers could not happen "to such a degree that Denmark is no longer viewed as an independent state." However, assessing such limits "must to an overwhelming degree depend on considerations of a political character [and] it must be assumed left to the Folkething to decide [the need] for further democratic control."[113]

Thus, the Court found for the Government.[114]

The case is very important to the issue of Denmark's quasi-federal position. Although it is argued in this survey that, strictly speaking, sovereignty is not transferred but rather "powers" are, the Danish Supreme Court appears to see it otherwise – and the Court rules Danish law. Furthermore, the Court recognises the federal properties of all three traditional branches of government being attributable to the EC regime, even explicitly recognising the "rulemaking" powers of the ECJ as inherent part of the EC.

As for the more internally Danish aspects, the Court is very explicit in defending its own, and indeed all Danish courts', "access to review" as well as its supremacy in adjudicating the potential transgressions of EC instruments. Further to that, the Court's deference to the Folkething is explained as basically any power that Parliament itself wants to relinquish, providing it abides by the procedure in BL § 20 and not jeopardises democracy and independence entirely. Thus, the Court sets wide limits for what can be transferred – except for Danish constitutional judicial review that apparently cannot be transferred but has to co-exist with rulemaking ECJ review.

In *Hausgaard v. Prime Minister* (UfR.2011.0984H), the issue of legal standing to challenge amendments to the EU Treaty system was revisited. A

---

111. Ibid. 871.
112. Ibid.
113. Ibid.
114. Ibid.

number of people sued over the Lisbon Treaty and raised the familiar issues of the extent to which powers can be transferred according to the BL § 20 procedure as well as the proper procedures and lawful purposes of such transfer of powers. The Eastern High Court again found the question inadmissible and dismissed the case without considering its merits, as the Lisbon Treaty "created no new powers or tasks for the Union," it just amended those, including making the EU Charter of Fundamental Rights legally binding.

Højesteret on the other hand unanimously found there was a right to have the issue review and remanded the case. The Court explained its decision in *Norup Carlsen II* as establishing that it depends on disagreement on the treaty in question concerning questions of "profound importance to the Danish population in general." As the controversy was over legislative competence, concerning the division of power between EU Council and Parliament and more decision being made by qualified majority rather than by unanimity, there was the "necessary legal interest to have plea adjudicated."

The case shows a remarkable delay in the *Norup* doctrine filtering through but also limits of short reasoning. The Supreme Court had used abstract and general language in its earlier case, without the tests or examples or other kinds of expansive explanatory reasoning that other constitutional or supreme courts use to make sure that their ratio becomes applicable in later cases. Nonetheless, the case demonstrates that reasoning now increasingly takes recourse to Supreme Course case law rather than scholarly theory but this technique is somewhat in its infancy.

Division of Power Cases

Birk Keller v. Denmark (UfR.1993.0757H) considered the issue of taxation. The Basic Law had established that taxation could only be imposed by Parliament. However, after parliamentarism was well established and the administrative state had taken hold, a number of fees and payments were imposed by administrative regulation for various government services. Scholarly theory claimed that such payments were legally limited strictly to the cost of services rendered.[115] However, in this instance, the Ministry of Justice had imposed payments for issuing passports that were exceeding clearly strict cost and thus contributing to the general expenses of the ministry, which though had regularly informed Parliament of this practice. Due to the enduring criticism, a law was passed on prospective payment fixation the fee to the hitherto amount.

---

115. Jensen (1999) 247.

Birk Keller sued for the amount paid prior to the law. The Supreme Court in a nine to two decision sided with the ministry, finding that adding some of the general costs of running the passport services had happened with the knowledge of Parliament and been taken into account in the budgets. The case fully illustrates the "difficulties, which are connected to the interpretation of old legal standards [as] the payments were gradually moved into a grey zone of power [and] changes in parliamentary work and moderns relations [resulted in conclusions not expected] according to constitutional theory hitherto."[116]

The case is another example of negative dynamics, reducing the literal meaning of the Basic Law but doing so by respecting the norm shifting dynamics created by the political branches, the legislature had relinquished powers to the executive, the judiciary now acquiesced. The Supreme Court might have taken the view that this was a question of rights and that the people could not be subject to any indirect taxation without representation, meaning that the power of taxation was not one for the legislature to relinquish. Such a conclusion would have meant that rather large sums of money would have to be paid back. Perhaps using the flexible technique of *Defrenne* and making the ruling prospective might have made such ruling easier.

In any event, Højesteret used its powers of triadic rulemaking to decide that the constitutional taxation powers were to be construed as a *legal standard* and that there were grey zones of taxation where the actual fee exceeded the narrow cost and was used to finance the more general cost of the service and Parliament had known and accepted this. As judge Jensen points out in his comment, this conclusion was 'unexpected by scholarly theory,' which says a lot about Nordic theory of law. A better view of constitutional law would have observed that the taxation as a concept was not highly theorised or explained by the Basic Law. When the Danish constitution changed to allow for parliamentarism despite explicit provisions to the contrary, there was a high probability that other parts of the wider constitution would be skewed and Basic Law clauses would be even more open to interpretation, especially standards and otherwise ambiguous provisions. Furthermore, a realistic scholarly theory would have pointed out the obvious *grey zones* like administrative service fees, which are not mentioned in the Basic Law and whose underlying costs are difficult to determine. In addition, concerned citizens and especially interest groups would be wise to *test* such issues as soon as they appear, as the actual state of things will not change unless actively chal-

---

116. Jensen (1999) 248.

lenged. Thus, one might say that Danish scholarly theory lost the case being unable to predict all possible outcomes and unable to advice on the best course of action. Whether "constitutional theory hitherto" was seeking the only one possible and necessary solution out of 'Cartesian angst' or just lacking the tools for reflecting the several possible routes of unfolding dynamics, is difficult to say.

The case also demonstrates how unaffected Danish scholarly theory and legal teaching is by case law, insisting on a 'dictionary definition' of a particular phrase of the Basic Law when it was clearly predating current power balances and without any indication that the ultimate Danish legal authority was indicating this 'protestant' insistence on a particular definition of the word "tax."

In *T v. Denmark* (UfR.1994.0536H), the issue was the constitutionality of the Danish tradition of integrating the Ministry of Justice, police and judiciary. Judges started as junior judge trainees working part time as judges, part time in the Ministry and from time to time performing other duties in institution under the ministry such as the police.

Probably under the impression of the first ECHR cases to be lost by Denmark, especially the review of Danish judicial organisation in *Hauschildt*, the Supreme Court took a stand in a well-argued case, in setting aside by correcting a central statutory provision. Højesteret dealt with 'the complexity of ECHR law' by reinterpreting the procedural law in order to ensure the impartiality of the judiciary. The Court left remedying legislation generally to the Folkething but set in motion great changes in the administration of justice in Denmark.[117]

In *Tvind* (UfR.1999.841H),[118] the issue was that of singular legislation, which is often referred to in constitutional text and theory as a *bill of attainder*. The law was passed by Parliament on proposal from the Ministry of Education. The ministry had for a long time experienced difficulties dealing with a secretive co-operation of private schools referred to as the Tvind schools. The schools were eligible for public funding but were suspected of channelling some of the funds to other purposes, including foreign operations. The leaders of the Tvind movement were ideologically committed to international development but were also suspected of revolutionary tendencies and using funds for their own purposes. Lingering controversies and

---

117. Rytter (2006) 41.
118. Properly named *Veddinge Bakker v. Denmark* but *Tvind* is ovewhelmingly used.

opaque bookkeeping led the ministry to propose naming all the Tvind schools as legally disqualified to apply for further public funding.

The Supreme Court's result was narrowly worded, "§ 7 of [the Act] is invalid in relation to the appellant the Free School of Veddinge Bakker."[119] The reasons were given in a short opinion in which all eleven participating judges joined. The Court reasoned that, "In accordance with the general opinion of the constitutional literature it must be assumed that the Basic Law § 3, third sentence to some degree limits to which extent the legislative power can make decisions on the legal position of individual (singular legislation). This understanding is in accord with the security of rights criterion ("retssikkerhedshensyn") that is the primary behind the division of power in BL § 3." The Court then explained that the preparatory works indicated that the Folkething supported the minister of education who had lost confidence in the Tvind schools' proper use of public funds based on audit reports indicating widespread previous abuse but despite the schools' assurances that they would follow the law. The Court found that such "legislation – that consequently meant that the Tvind-schools were cut off from judicial review of their eligibility to funding – is in reality a final decision of a concrete legal controversy. According to the Basic Law § 3 such a decision does not belong under the legislative power but under judicial power with the ensuing guarantees of rights for the citizen. Højesteret therefore finds that [amendment act § 7] is invalid in relation to the Free School of Veddinge Bakker as contrary to the Basic Law's § 3."

The reasoning was based on a clash between legislation and the constitutional division of power clause, however the reasoning also emphasised that a division of power doctrine is necessary for all individual rights to be legally enforceable. This very much echoes the words of Marshall in *Marbury* that it is "emphatically the province of the courts to say what the law is." As Højesteret does not elaborate on the individual rights, are there individual rights that in themselves can invalidate legislation in case of direct clash? Are the rights protected constitutional rights, both enumerated n the Basic Law and otherwise? Is the Supreme Court thinking of administrative and procedural rights, or just rights that flow from the enabling statute that Parliament can take away but only though general legislation and proper procedures? These questions remain unanswered, as the Danish Court does not elaborate like Marshall did or like Lasson did or the ECJ and ECHR Courts do, although the reasons are by previous standards somewhat extensive and in the

---

119. *Tvind* (UfR.1999.841H) 851.

so-called literary note – which is a footnote to the judgement in the official case report – points to a number of sources, from which the Court's further inspiration may be inferred. The best reading is probably that the court defends 'regular review,' the right to have the individual *result* of a given legal status or controversy assessed through judicial review, whereas the right to constitutional judicial review is limited. There is still the presumption that the general will as expressed through legislation may produce almost any abstract rules but their individual result has to be subject to review. The only legislation that surely will be set aside as invalid are statutory provisions that themselves review individual controversies, in effect replace *judicial review* with *legislative review*.

Reading the case gives a clear impression that this was the proper 'Marbury moment' in Denmark, all the conditions were in place for constitutional judicial review but certain filters including the lack of case law reporting and the ideology of scholarly theory had delayed the 'moment' for a century and half. The *de Neergaard* case was in its way a Marbury case but he moment was so to speak lost through the filtering effect of scholarly theory. Preempting any criticism, the Supreme Courts starts out by quoting 'the general opinion of constitutional literature' rather than constitutional language or case law. Thus, the Court still defers to scholarly theory for restating and developing constitutional law.

The Court does not use the opportunity for instance to explain, reaffirm or distinguish its understating older cases such as *de Neergaard, Arne Magnussens Legat* or *Norup Carlsen II*. The first of these cases set a very high bar of unconstitutionality, the second only set aside the legislation by construing its silence in light of constitutionally provided individual results, and the last one promised to guard the courts' access to review the constitutionality of laws. Are we to draw a straight line and infer that Danish constitutional judicial review means that only in very clear cases of depriving individuals their particular right to regular judicial review of the concrete result of their legal position in a controversy with the government can a parliamentary law be set aside? Conversely, laws for instance limiting the freedom of the press, property rights, the autonomy municipalities or that of Greenland, or the rights of immigrants and asylum seekers will for various reasons not be constitutional voidable as long as review of the particular results for any individual is not specifically taken away?

Højesteret set aside one clause of the amending statute as invalid but not annulled erga omnes, the Court did not deal with the rest of the act or with the other twenty odd schools also named in the act, although the language may hint that the law is generally voidable. The Court just cannot pronounce on any matter not brought before it. Thus, the Court seems to be endorsing *compartmentalism* that is to say that all the constitutional institutions should stick to their own 'department' each taking the Basic Law into account in for their own purposes but not interfering with the other institutions. The legislature and the executive dealt with the matter in their way, and when one of the schools came forth, the judiciary dealt with the matter in its way – but only with the one school that sued, not the law in general, not explaining further the implications and perspectives of parliamentary legislation being voidable through constitutional judicial review. Even judge Jensen writes that it "could be argued that it follows from § 88 of the Basic Law on the procedure for constitutional amendment that legislation contrary to the Basic law in only valid when enacted according to § 88 and that the courts [therefore] can set aside laws." However, "more support is in the reference to the separation between the functions of the state power [in § 3]."[120] Thus, it seems that in the absence of litigation pushing the issue of clashes with or breaches of other provisions of the Basic Law especially using overlapping quasi-federal provisions and methodology as leverage, division of power doctrine is the only practical incident of clear judicial invalidation of parliamentary laws in Demark.

The case raises other issues that we shall look at later, not least the illusion that Parliament is considering and guarding the Basic Law in such a qualified way that the constitution is generally respected. However, it is interesting to note in relation to the discussion on the effects of constitutional judgements that the result of the case was reported in Lovtidende, the official gazette for promulgation of statutes and secondary legal instruments issued by the ministries. We can probably infer from this as an acknowledgement of triadic judicial rulemaking officially reported as we are informed that a particular provision of parliamentary law was amended by judicial case law. Lately, the web-based database – www.retsinfo.dk – has taken to include a number of decisions. Whether this is acknowledging triadic rulemaking or seeing courts' as stating the logically necessary interpretation that should have been obvious all along does not matter. The impact of cases like *Tvind* is probably not to increase *constitutional review*, which the legal culture is not quite ready for, but more to increase *general judicial review* as a way of restating, reconciling, developing, and explaining laws, including the filling in of the blanks by judges rather than bureaucrats or scholars. Thus, *Tvind* seems to the a catalyst of the trend to let supreme court judges deal with law as interpretation, con-

120. Jensen (1999) 236 note 10.

struction, and even rulemaking rather than as evidence and results. Subsequent reforms have increases the role of the Court in that respect, meaning that given the context Højesteret very successfully influenced Danish constitutional discourse.

A & C v. Denmark (UfR.2006.1149H) clarified some aspects of *Tvind*, as to the extent of the right of review. At issue was the right of asylum for a Liberian national that had lost contact to his parents who had received a right to live in Denmark on humanitarian grounds. The Danish agency claimed that the identity of the person was in doubt and that the decision not to allow "C" entry was an "assessment" not subject to judicial review according to the enabling statute.[121]

The Supreme Court severely admonished the agency's reading of the statute. Højesteret stated that it "is a legal question, within the scope of the judicial review according to the Basic Law § 63, what is to be understood by "near familiar [connection]" in the Foreigners Act [see] the Supreme Court's judgement [UfR.1996.529]. It is also within judicial review whether there is actually such a connection [see] the Supreme Court's judgement [UfR.2005.1780]."

The Court then found that factually C had "been treated as a child of A since birth" and that other circumstances related to the legal facts of the statute. This factual situation notwithstanding, from application in 1999, "the Ministry has not offered any concrete reasons for the decision" which was also found "unclear" in its result. The Supreme Court then remanded the case for new assessment.[122]

The case probably shows an extension of *Tvind* doctrine – and the extraordinary transformation of Danish law that may happen if the Supreme Court is supplied with the right cases and arguments. The Supreme Court is starting to refer explicitly to its own case law and is asserting its view that the Basic Law endorses judicial review. Furthermore, the Court is expanding from Basic Law § 3 to § 63, from its relationship vis-à-vis Parliament to its relationship to the administrative agencies. (Having in mind that previously BL § 63 has been interpreted both as hinder judicial review and later to limit it). This represents in itself a dynamic development from the old position of scholarly theory to the present one established by judicial case law. First, the review clause was seen as distinguishing between the two categories of 'judicial' and 'administrative' cases, then, there was a normative shift to full re-

---

121. *A & C v. Denmark* 1149.
122. Ibid. 1154.

view of administrative cases as to their results and assessment of facts but leaving *assessment* in the hands of the agencies. Now, there is even review of legislation, to ensure access to judicial review, including construing the statute to include as many questions of interpretation and evidence as possible, limiting severely the administrative assessment left to the agency.

As to methodology, Højesteret cites its own case law and is essentially though flexible techniques setting aside intended structure of the legislation by denying the wide unreviewable room for assessment, through which a very restrictive and arbitrary immigration practice could be implemented. The judgement forces Parliament to state its intentions as enforceable and reviewable statutory provisions not as delegation of the legislative to ministers and agencies. Effectively, the provision of the Foreigners Act that bars judicial review is set aside, however, not by declaring it invalid or by extending *Tvind* fully to mean that both singular and general bars to judicial review are unconstitutional. Nonetheless, the Supreme Court is still somewhat stuck in the conceptualist way of view that law is logically deducible from legal concepts, 'is a legal question whether such and such.' Having started to refer to case law, the Court might instead have explained and developed the doctrine rather than pointing out the cases as if they were just examples of the same inescapable logic as that of the present case. Compared with the quasi-federal courts or the Norwegian Court, the reasoning leaves rather a lot to be inferred and thus potentially deferred to either agency or scholarly interpretation instead of the Court's own authoritative interpretation. The question remains open as to whether the Supreme Court is concerned with the correct use of legal definitions or guarding its own powers or defending individual rights, procedural or substantive, and even un-enumerated rights like equality before the law, perhaps even guarding citizens against parliamentary attempts to avoid review.

Equal Rights Cases

In ***Ur Rab v. Denmark*** (UfR.2002.1789H), the issue was the constitutionality of Danish citizenship as a precondition for taxi licences. The Pakistani national Mahmood Ur Rab had lived in Denmark since 1970 and held taxi licences from 1977 and obtained Danish citizenship in 2000. In 1997, however, when Ur Rab held six licenses and applied for a seventh, the statutory requirement of citizenship was introduced. The change in the law meant that Ur Rab had until 2005 to obtain citizenship in order to keep his earlier licences and he was barred from applying for further ones.

Ur Rab claimed violation of ECHR Art 14 in conjunction with Protocol 1952 Art 1 as well as the UN conventions on racial discrimination and civil and political rights. The Western High Court heard the initial suit and held in an unusually long unanimous three-judge opinion that "there is no basis in the preparatory work or otherwise a basis for thinking that introduction of the citizenship requirement was intended as a contravention of Denmark's international obligations, including the ECHR. The High Court, therefore, finds that it can determine the question of statutory provisions' compatibility with the ECHR." The Court thus ruled out the intentional clash with international law that scholarly theory claims to be possible, and in its absence legislation will be interpreted in conformity with international law.

The Court then went on to point out the twenty years that Ur Rab legally had practised in the taxi business and found it unpersuasive that the requirement was already in force for bus drivers. Accordingly, it did not find that the law "would raise the standard in the industry, to be a sufficient rationale for such a discriminatory treatment." The High Court then noted that the State had not made its case that citizenship had any bearing on the transport sector and the requirement was anyway revoked two years later. Consequently, the High Court found that "applying the requirement to Mahmood Ur Rab was in violation" of the ECHR and Protocol and awarded damages and cost.

The Supreme Court then heard the case in a seven-judge panel. In its reasoning, the Court limited its arguments on Danish constitutionality to possible hints to the special equality clause and literary note references.[123] Højesteret found unanimously that "using Art. 14 ECHR requires that a discriminatory treatment concerns the rights and freedoms recognised by the convention." The Court then went on to cite six ECHR cases, not only in the literary note but by citing them specifically – not by number as West-Nordic cases are usually cited but by case name. Citations like "Hooffman v. Austria, premis 29," "Larkos v. Cyprus, premis 28," Andrews v. UK," "Saggio v. Italy, premis 24" are used. The Supreme Court even paraphrased its judgement, explaining that, "the possibility of obtaining a licence for commercial activity under such circumstances is not at right" under the First Protocol ECHR. The case "Gaygusuz v. Austria" that Ur Rab was relying on was distinguishes as concerning "the right to future social payments connected to payments made," and therefore clearly not a case in point. The Court found further support for legally barring Ur Rab from further licences in "Marckx v. Belgium, premis 50."[124]

---

123. *Ur Rab v. Denmark* 1797 with note 1and 2 on 1798.
124. Ibid. 1797.

The Court went on to consider two UN conventions that it found not to concern "such difference of treatment, which a State undertakes between its own nationals and foreigners." Two decisions by the relevant UN committees are cited in the case notes.[125] The Court found "the national requirement in the taxi law" to be enacted for "legal purposes" and the resulting "difference of treatment on the basis of nationality unintended [but comparable to common in requirements for] special functions [in many] countries in Europe." The opinion, stretching for almost half a page ended in stressing the room for "appreciation" of the Folkething in its "assessment of whether the requirement is purposeful."[126]

The case is very interesting for its apparent methodological schism. The Court is using case law to interpret the ECHR, using techniques associated with common law type courts. By contrast, the Supreme Court is not explaining Danish constitutional law at all. Further, the case shows the quasi-federal nature of the ECHR system as the Danish Court struggles to avoid grounds for an appeal, it has to explain and distinguish case law of the superior body. Again by contrast, the UN law is obviously seen as less of a threat, as it can be dismissed without considering case law. The case probably also shows the dynamic judicial discourse in Denmark. The Western High Court, based in Jutland, is generally more inclined towards civil rights. The Copenhagen based Eastern High Court, is more likely to side with the government and it did so in most of the review cases already mentioned. The Supreme Court is placed somewhere in middle but would clearly get somewhat different material to work with if more case came in from the west.

Compared to earlier methodology, there is a dramatic change towards recognition of the quasi-federal and indeed quasi-constitutional nature of the ECHR-regime. The implication is that when the Court is exposed to review by a citizen taking the case further to the ECHR Court in particular, there is a need for a case law based approach, including the refined common law techniques distinguishing cases. Quoting Danish legal textbooks and relying on 'the general opinion of constitutional literature' as in *Tvind*, which could not be appealed further, is not a viable method. The quasi-federal nature of ECHR law has in effect placed a 'giving reasons' requirement on the Danish Supreme Court that is one of the milestones in the gradual development form the ban on reasoning to the short official reasons to the longer reasons includ-

---

125. Ibid. 1798 note 3.
126. Ibid. (UfR.2002.1789H) 1797.

ing dissent to now finally lengthy justification through application of common ECHR case law.

Thule v. Denmark (UfR.2004.0382H) is perhaps difficult to categorise. The case concerned the constitutionality of the forced evacuation in 1953 of the Thule tribe of indigenous Inuits from the Uummannaq area to their present reservation of Qaanaaq. This happened just before the promulgation of the Danish Basic Law in Greenland and consequent Danish claim of integration of Greenland into the Realm. Following Home Rule in 1979, the natives started to assert themselves and the Thule tribe eventually sued the Danish State claiming rights to their old hunting and dwelling grounds and reparations for past transgressions.

The Supreme Court after an epic narrative of some 200 odd pages, relatively carefully considered the claims over two pages. First, it rejected claim based on the ILO Treaty of 1989, in force from 1997, as it found the Thule tribe "not to be a tribal people of indigenous population of its own" as there in Denmark is "only one indigenous people," the Inuit as a whole.[127] Following this technical dismissal of a rather comprehensive treaty, the Court turned to the grounds for dismissal of the case raised by the Government. The Court rejected those, stating that not being a tribe did not preclude the Thule from "filing suit according to the ordinary rules hereon."[128]

Turning then to the merits of claims based on domestic law, the Supreme Court found that handing over the area for the United States as a military base was sanctioned by Parliament according to the Basic Law and therefore legally binding and also "valid at international law." However, what had occurred was "an expropriation" but "that the substantive provisions of the then Basic Law, including the § 80 [Property clause] was not in force in Greenland." No equivalent law was found in either legislation or customary law.[129] As for reparations for what had occurred after the Basic Law came into force, the Supreme Court noted that they all at the time had received new houses and supplies and although the Government stipulated to "serious and unlawful treatment" endorsed smaller individual reparations, mainly for those that were aged 18 and over at the time the tribe was moved.[130]

The case is rather sad, as the Courts usually find some 'background law' to be valid when there is no formal law. For instance, the right of creditors to claw back assets in bankruptcy proceedings was found to exist in Greenland

---

127. *Thule v. Denmark* 605.
128. Ibid. 605.
129. Ibid. 605-06.
130. Ibid. 606-07.

without any formal statutory base.[131] Denmark was colonising Greenland and the Supreme Court could have held the government to the constitutional standard of compensating losses sustained by government coercion. Even though the Basic Law provision on expropriation was not formally promulgated in Greenland, it was a valid limit on the Danish government as was, presumably, the right to review that could have been extended to those being subjected to Danish government action abroad. Both *de Neergaard* and *Tvind* could have been extended and both the Basic Law and the ECHR seen as codifications of already existing and valid legal standards – subject to interpretation in light of relevant circumstances. However, this was not done.

The unanimous Supreme Court opinion with rather technical and uninspiring reasoning on the issue of being *in force* is largely void of any persuasive discussions or arguments but is largely a continuation of the narrative by other means. The gaps between the limited and careful constitutional case law so far and the stretch needed in methodology were probably too sizeable.

Freedom of Assembly and Expression Cases

In *TV-Stop v. Denmark* (UfR.1994.0988H), the Supreme Court overruled long-standing Danish libel law with reference to the ECHR. The case is interesting in showing the quasi-federal nature of ECHR-law, the possibility of law being restated in the *Defrenne* manner in light of hitherto neglected higher principles, and the relative ease of reasoning when there is no risk of further review, as the government cannot take its case to the ECHR Court.

In *Pehrson v. Denmark* (UfR.1999.1798H), the Danish Supreme Court considered the constitutionality of a statute forbidding the activities of 'rockere' – the bike gangs Bandidos and Hell's Angels. The gangs were at war with each other, even using rockets and automatic weapons not normally seen in use on the streets of Denmark. Therefore, The FolkThing, on the proposal by the Minister of Justice, enacted a statute whereby gang members could be forbidden from being present on properties associated with the gangs.

Leif Adler Pehrson was affiliated to the Hell's Angels gang and was served a police restraining order pursuant to the statute forbidding him to enter two premises in the towns of Roskilde and Snoldelev-Gadstrup respectively. Pehrson challenged the constitutionality of the statute. The issue of the constitutionality of the procedure whereby the police could issue the restraining order without a court sanction seems not to have been challenged.

---

131. Jeppe Wedel Nielsen "Dansk rets udfyldende karakter i Grønland" UfR.2011B.210 at 213.

The Court considered the Basic Law provisions on public assembly, free speech, and freedom of association relevant. However, the "provisions do not hinder statutory provisions that – without targeting the free speech of people assembled – limit the freedom of assembly ... within what is necessary, see also the ECHR Art 11."

The Court found the statute to be motivated by a concern for innocent by-standers and went on to interpret the statute in stating that: "These conditions must be understood so that a restraining order can only be issued if there is a real and actual – and not just abstract – risk of a dangerous attack." The decision is surely a sound one, and its test of 'real and actual' creates potential for a standard to be applied and extended in other constitutional cases. The case can definitely be read as using flexible technique to limit the scope of a statute, accepting it as constitutional 'only if' read in a certain way in light of the Basic Law and the ECHR.

As to method, the case is underwhelming, however, as it fails to explain Danish and ECHR case law and integrate the decision into a wider development of doctrines.

In ***Editor-in-chief A v. B*** (UfR.2004.1773H), the issue was freedom of speech in the context of verdict of 'not guilty' on charges of paedophile behaviour. A Danish paper, for some strange reason in the report only referred to as C with its equally anonymous editor-in-chief A, published the reaction of the alleged victim's mother. She said she wanted the indicted B to be "braded a paedophile" as she claimed that B only avoided conviction as crucial video evidence was ruled inadmissible. The Article gave some details of the case but did not mention the acquitted person's name.[132]

The trial court cited three Supreme Court cases and explained that the assessment of the B's claim of criminal libel had to be based on: "concrete assessment ... an assessment of the totality of the circumstances" based on the criminal code and the ECHR. After mentioning some abstract criteria and briefly recouping that the mother had criticised the law that led to the inadmissibility of the evidence and the paper only relayed that criticism, the trial court acquitted.[133]

On appeal, however, The Eastern High Court found that the article "appeared in the context as the independent opinion of the defendant." Stating the circumstances so that they appear to claim that someone acquitted was nevertheless guilty is libellous, the Court held, and briefly dismissed both

---

132. *Editor-in-chief A v. B* 1773.
133. Ibid. 1781.

ECHR and code provisions, explaining its judgement as "totality-assessment." The Eastern High Court then found A guilty of defamation and liable to pay a fine as well as civil damages.[134]

On further appeal, The Supreme Court found that B's anonymity was intact and that the "mentioning and of the case and [the mother's] reaction was reasonable as part of a public debate on problems relating to evidence and procedural rights in the context of child abuse cases. In conclusion: "After a total assessment the Supreme Court finds itself reluctant to hold that A is guilty in violating the criminal code §267(1) as it must be understood in the light of the ECHR Art. 10."[135]

The case note refers to a number of Danish cases, including 97/259 99/122 99/560 99/1572 02/2398 03/624, as well as *Jersild v. Denmark*, *Bergens Tidende v. Norway* and *Thoma v. Luxembourg*, in addition to a number of text books and articles.[136]

The case shows the difficulty of a methodology in transition. First, the trial court reveals how lawyers of course use case law to guide them in cases relating to balancing the open-ended provisions of libel and free speech. Unfortunately, this only leads to the mysterious transcendental consideration of the 'totality of circumstances' rather than a careful consideration of legal facts and concrete criteria for weighed and expressed assessment. Second, we revisit the old guard in the Eastern High Court finding any hint of critique of its previous judgements inherently slanderous, only mentioning the ECHR with distain, and ignoring the Basic Law as well as case law altogether. Finally, we find the Supreme Court balancing the need for debate against defamation provisions, effectively overriding statutory law with an 'only if' interpretation. In contrast with *Ur Rab v. Denmark*, the Court finds no reason to explain its understanding of ECHR case law, which is unsurprising given that the State has no appeal in the ECHR system.

---

134. Ibid. 1782-83.
135. Ibid.
136. Ibid. 1784 note 1.

Icelandic Review

Summary of Icelandic Review

Icelandic constitutional judicial review has a short history. Iceland got its Constitution in 1874 whilst still associated to Denmark. The Constitution has been an important symbol of Icelandic self-determination more so than of individual freedom; Icelanders emphasises limitation of government 'by law,' more than 'from law.' The main contention in Icelandic constitutional developments from 1874 until 1944 was the struggle to have power transferred to Icelandic institutions.

In Iceland, the issue of compatibility between statute and constitution surfaced early but never became a significant element in the wider constitutional discourse. Mostly, review cases dealt briefly with narrow issues that did not lead to much development of constitutional case law.

The legal basis for judicial review seems not to have been disputed but appears rather to have followed developments in Denmark of being recognised in principle but seldom used in practice. The first momentous case of explicitly setting aside statutory law came during World War II when Iceland was enduring protective occupation by allied forces. The judgement reveals a legalistic application rather than a principled and fully theorised position on constitutionality.

The Icelandic Supreme Court was established in 1920 according to the 1918 Union Act that recognised Iceland as an independent Kingdom in personal union with Denmark. Iceland had achieved parliamentarism years before, requiring the Government in Iceland to have the confidence of the Icelandic Parliament. The Supreme Court, however, never played any significant part in constitutional discourse, neither internally nor vis-à-vis the Danes.

The rise of the administrative state and interventionist regimes in Iceland caused a number of constitutional contentions. The Supreme Court mostly accepted parliamentary supremacy and showed great deference to government and agencies in interpretation of constitutional rights, though in some instances constitutional principles came to influence statutory application. Iceland was affected very differently by World War II than the other West-

Nordics. Iceland chose to use its opt-out clause in the Union Act to gain complete independence and establish the Republic of Iceland. The Constitution, however, essentially remained the same.

Judicial review was fundamentally revitalised at the end of the 20th century. The impact of accession to the European Convention on Human Rights caused the Supreme Court to amend doctrine, as the Icelandic tradition of deference to legislative judgment and the Court's legalistic approach to review fit ill with the dynamic and purpose-driven method of the ECHR Court. In response, the Icelandic Constitution was amended to include a revised chapter of basic rights. This created a new basis and impetuous for judicial review and a number of high profile cases followed. Further quasi-federal developments including case law resulting from membership of the European Economic Area and European Free Trade Agreement.

Icelandic constitutional judicial review today is restrained substantively and in terms of reasoning but becoming more intense. The economic crises has both raised a number of constitutional issues and created pressure to re-thinking the Constitution; a popularly elected convention has proposed a new Constitution to include a Law Council that is to perform constitutional review.

Review in Icelandic Constitutional Developments

The Icelandic Supreme Court has functioned since 1920. Prior to that Iceland had its own court system but with appeal to the Danish Supreme Court. The Icelandic judiciary can trace its history back to the judicial function of the Althing; records exist of its judgements back to the 16th century but some form of judicial function has been exercised since Iceland was united in the year 930. However, the percent judicial and constitutional system owes much more to Danish influence than older Icelandic tradition. The Icelandic written Constitution is very much a product of Danish influence, being first issued by the King of Denmark who at the time in 1874 had lost all his other dependencies save the Faroe Islands and Greenland and finally gave in to Icelandic pressure but without substantive consultation.

The Icelandic tradition of reported case law, though existing for an impressively long time, is very limited in terms of reasoning. The Icelandic Supreme Court is probably one of the most restrained and legalistic courts of final constitutional jurisdiction in the Western World.

Constitutional review has been a component of Icelandic jurisprudence for a long time. Its development has been restrained by short and enigmatic reasoning and, possibly, from a limited number of suitable cases, though hundreds of cases have considered constitutional issues.[1] Review has increased because of predictable circumstances, notably revision and re-enactment of the constitutional basic rights and becoming part of quasi-federal regimes with constitutional properties.

Constitutional Origins

Iceland is an ancient Norse Land, settled from the late 800s by people of Scandinavian decent, mainly from Norway. Iceland can trace its formal formation as a constitutional polity to the year 930. The country was united by the establishment of a constitutional order with powers being shared between the local Priest-Chiefs, the four regional Parliaments, and the national Parliament, the Althing, the latter with both legislative and judicial functions, in which ultimate powers were vested.

In the Middle Ages, the Scandinavian region consisted of a number of Lands loosely organised around the Things. They were by various strongmen united into larger kingdoms. The Kings of Norway tried to extend their influence to include the kindred Norse settlements out West. The process of Norwegian dominance lasted from the early 11th century through the late 13th century, probably indicating both the remoteness of Iceland and weakness of the Crown. In 1262-64, Iceland's Chiefs finally signed the 'Old Treaty.' It recognised the crowned King and the Icelander's duty to pay taxes and remain loyal in exchange for maintaining the authority of the Chiefs, implicitly other elements of autonomy, and six ships sent every year to maintain trading and communications. The Old Treaty contained a clause on termination in case of breach found by "best men."[2] This may be one of the rare examples of an actual written social contract between people and sovereign.[3]

The short but well written old document and its implied recognition of Iceland as a separate polity has been the basis of Icelandic self-understanding ever since. Icelanders perceive the Old Treaty to provide for a personal union

---

1. Professor Gunnar Schram cites a number of cases on the inapplicability of constitutional laws Gunnar Schram *Stjórnskipunarréttur* Háskólaútgáfan (1999) 438 with note 1 and his case book Gunnar Schram *Dómar úr stjórnskipunarrétti* Bókaútgáva Orators (1991) lists some 500 constitutional cases (though many reoccur under several headings) and most are either more administrative, procedural, or just relating to wider constitutional issues without considering the constitutionality of laws much less setting them aside.
2. The Old Treaty is reproduced in many publications.
3. Guðmundur Hálfdanarson "Gamli sáttmáli – frumsamningur íslenskt ríkisvalds?" in *Líndæla* Hið íslenska bókmenntafélag (2001) 194.

and association of free entities, not integration.[4] Alas, the significance of the treaty-based origins of the wider Realm has mostly been lost on Danish lawyers of the conceptual persuasion. For instance, Danish expert on the constitutional status of the dependencies Frederik Harhoff does not mention the central Icelandic figure Jón Sigurðsson and his remarkable ability to unite Icelandic opinion around the *old treaty theory*. Harhoff dismisses the theory by laconically noting that by the loyal oath of the Althing to the King in 1662 "absolutism was also implemented in Iceland. Hereby was the "Old Treaty" of 1262 replaced as the legal basis for Iceland's government under Norway."[5] This seems unpersuasive per se, as a Treaty can hardly be superseded in such an informal way, especially if intended to set aside the *best men* clause and implied right to self-determination. Secondly, the Icelandic view of constitutional association was ultimately successful and it therefore cannot be dismissed in favour of a theory of a unitary absolutist state that just happened to devolve a lot of power.

Nonetheless, Iceland's formal constitutional status was the subject of much debate and disagreement for a number of years especially from 1814 when it was separated from its original principal,[6] as the by then Norwegian-Danish King ceded the mainland part of his Norwegian Realm to the King of Sweden (see Norwegian chapter). This led to continued constitutional disputes over the nature of Iceland's association to the King and his principal Realm of Denmark. Icelanders took part in the 1849 Constitutional Convention but insisted on their own Constitution. They had secured the King's support for Icelandic self-determination prior to the convention.[7] When Danish officials wanted to promulgate the Danish Basic Law in Iceland, an Icelandic National Convention was called that rejected the Danish Basic Law while affirming allegiance to the King.[8] Their weakness in number and armour notwithstanding, the Icelanders managed to gain crucial concessions and Icelandic government bodies, including its courts, were manned by Icelanders throughout the Danish period. In 1874, Iceland got its own written Constitu-

---

4. Ragnar Lundborg *Þjóðarréttarstaða Íslands* Þjóðræknisfélag Íslendinga í Vesturheimi (1939) 95.
5. Frederik Harhoff *Rigsfællesskabet* Klim (1993) 185. Generally on Iceland from 183.
6. Treaty of Kiel 1814 point 4. Andenæs (2001) 112.
7. Thorsteinsson (1990).
8. The Icelanders famously refused to accept the Danish Basic Law at a national convention called in 1851 that ended with the words: "Then most [of them] said in one sound, We all oppose," adding when the Danish officials had left in protest, "Long live our King, Frederik VII."

tion, when the standoff over the Danish Basic Law finally paid off when the King Christian IX visited Iceland for the 1000-year anniversary of Norse settlement – and handed over an Icelandic Constitution. The official Danish position seems to have been that Iceland and its Constitution were subordinate to the Danish Basis Law. Simultaneously, the Icelanders were able to maintain the old treaty theory and see their own Constitution as the highest legal document and the King as being the monarch of two independent nations, Iceland's powers limited only by the powers rightfully vested in the monarchy.

The Icelandic Constitution was gradually amended, most importantly to include a wide-ranging autonomy in 1903 with a Minister for Iceland being appointed to serve independently of the Danish Government. This created the basis for further developments. Denmark finally recognised Icelandic sovereignty and Union of Crowns in the 1918 Association Act. This provided for a common Supreme Court but Iceland could choose to establish its own Supreme Court. This opportunity was taken almost immediately, so that effective from 1920 Iceland had its own Supreme Court.

The struggle for independence seems to have overshadowed or at least intertwined with the struggle for individual rights. Neither the 1874 Constitution, nor the realignments in 1903 and 1918, nor full independence seems to have provided the impetus to provide for enforceable basic rights or a scheme of effective remedies. Judicial review to assess individual, group, or opposition rights seems to have been neglected in favour of national empowerment and parliamentary powers

Furthermore, the phrase most often used to denote judicial review "*endur-skoðanarvald dómstóla*" literally means 'the power of the courts to review.' This angle to the issue probably signifies that judicial review was seen as a question of the powers of the judiciary vis-à-vis the legislature, rather than a question of the people's right to have the instruments and actions of the legislature or its agencies reviewed.

Icelandic constitutional principles relating substantive restraints on legislation and review thereof seem remarkably little effected by the gradual change of Iceland's relationship with the King and Denmark. From unrepresented dominion to gradually increasing internal self-rule, to sovereign state in association, to fully independent republic, Iceland seemed to rely on the same omnipotence of the lawgiver and residual powers of the executive, the main contention being who was to hold said positions.

The most interesting development for our purposes, therefore, has been Iceland's accession to the ECHR in 1953 and later to the EFTA and the EEA (though we shall focus on the former). Iceland assumed that it like the other

Nordic countries was fulfilling its commitments and would continue to do so.[9] However, loosing cases before the ECHR Court resulted in "the voices becoming louder who recommended that the ECHR became law."[10] This pressure led to incorporation of the ECHR in 1994 and new human rights chapter in the Constitution in 1995.

In his chapter on "positive law,"[11] famed Icelandic scholar Sigurður Líndal discusses a part called "constitutional laws," the first heading under which is the "European Convention on Human Rights," preceding headings on "status of constitutional laws" and the effect of "unconstitutional statutory laws."[12] His book cites no ECHR case but explains that after coming into force, the ECHR was binding on the Icelandic Realm at international law with "laws of the land ranking before the provisions of the convention in case of inconsistency." It was "assumed that [no such] inconsistency was between the convention and Icelandic law without [any supportive research]. The experience was, by contrast, somewhat different."[13]

Iceland could maintain its cherished dualist conceptualist outlook on the ECHR but the irony is that by amending its own Constitution to resemble the ECHR it is now potentially the country most affected by the quasi-federal status of the ECHR and the ECHR Court. Iceland has conveniently provided litigants and courts with an excellent basis on which to challenge the substantive legislative powers of the Icelandic State by means of the Constitution used in conjuncture with ECHR case law. This has given rise to case law becoming evident as "now there are examples of the Supreme Court referring to reasoning in cases as precedent or rejects them as precedents."[14]

Whatever the potential of ECHR case law, the revisions of the Constitution strengthened human rights in Iceland and created the basis for a number of cases on constitutional grounds and presumably had even more of an effect on the preparation and application of laws in light of the increased constitutional status.[15]

Iceland is today the largest European country apart from Norway and Switzerland from West of the old Iron Curtain to have remained outside the

9. Líndal (2002) 83 with note 5.
10. Ágúst Þór Árnason *Mannréttindi* Rauði Kross Íslands (1994) 31.
11. Líndal (2002) from 79.
12. Líndal (2002) 80, 82, 83 and 85 respectively.
13. Líndal (2002) 83.
14. Líndal (2002) 239.
15. On the link between the Constitution and international human rights Schram (1999) 461-62.

European Union. Iceland's relations with the EU are likely to provide for yet another leap in constitutional terms.

Apart from all else, the democratic paradigm might evolve to put greater emphasis on individual and group freedom, procedural fairness, opposition challenges to government legislation, public access and participation in governance, all of which are likely to increase to call for judicial review.

The Supreme Court in Context

Even though Iceland has struggled for independence and the independence of law has been at the centre of that effort, Icelandic law is very much influenced by the Danish legal tradition, even more so than Norwegian law. This is especially apparent in the emulation of the early enigmatic Danish style of judicial reasoning. In the words of Ragnar Aðalsteinsson: "the ideas that really have influenced the conclusion should appear in the reasoning of judgements, and the judges should carefully state by which method the conclusion as been reached. In our country, the courts, for historic reasons, have taken hold of the Danish path on the composition of judgements. They are short and say as little as possible or even less."[16]

The Icelandic Supreme Court is in many ways a successor to earlier courts. The judicial functions of the Althing go a long way back and were succeeded by the Land's Appeal Court, from which appeals went to the Supreme Court in Copenhagen. Following the Icelandic Constitution of 1874 and the Home Government in 1903, Højesteret in Copenhagen was the Supreme Court of two different realms with each their own Constitution. This could have provided the setting for interesting constitutional controversies to be solved by the Court. Political developments could have gone in different directions and individual rights raised in different ways. Not least, the federal arrangement itself could have meant clashes between the two countries.

However, few such cases appear to have materialised. The struggles may have been there but were probably resolved elsewhere. However, some cases exist that indicate that judicial review had its potential in the context of Icelandic association to Denmark. The Supreme Court in Copenhagen applied the Icelandic Constitution to cases on basic rights and it does appear to have accepted what in fact was the creation of a federalisation of Denmark's relationship with one of its dominions. The Danish Basic Law certainly could have been read to exclusive legislative powers other than the Danish Parliament. Instead, a legalistic approach was taken and both Icelandic and Danish

---

16.   Ragnar Aðalsteinsson "... "einungs eftir lögunum"" 53 *Úlfljótur* (2000) 569 at 598

instances "assumed they could not apply laws contrary to the [Icelandic] Constitution."[17]

When Iceland was recognised as an independent Kingdom in 1918, the Supreme Court remained the common highest court but Iceland could opt out and establish its own Supreme Court. This was done almost immediately and Iceland established its own Supreme Court, maintaining the Court of Appeal as the intermediate between district courts and the Hæstiréttur. For a small nation to establish its own judiciary speaks volumes to the resolve of the Icelanders. Compared to a number of British Commonwealth countries that for a long while retained the Privy Council Judiciary Committee as their supreme court, Iceland undertook quite a challenge in establishing its own Supreme Court in the context of a small community.

After a while, the challenges became too cumbersome and the Court of Appeal was abolished, leaving Iceland with a two-tier court system. This appears a good idea given that the number of cases warranting three levels of scrutiny is probably limited. However, Iceland was relying on Danish tradition, especially with appeals not being on the record but entire new trials within certain procedural restraints. The Icelandic Supreme Court is thus burdened with an enormous number of cases that are purely matters of evidence and simple reassessment of the case results. The judges do not hear all cases together, never sit in plenum but are drawn randomly to form panels for each case.

The Icelandic Supreme Court has roughly the same ambiguous constitutional provisions on the Court's role to work from as the other West-Nordic Courts. The constitutional language suggest a co-equal branch of government, presumably guarding over a number of human rights and organisational provisions that could be interpreted as substantive limits on the other branches of government. However, the Court has not assumed much of a position in real terms, preferring to adjudicate in a terse matter of fact style even in constitutional review cases.[18]

Iceland's Supreme Court seemed content to lead the life of restrained interpreter but two circumstances seem to have changed this. First, the shock of suddenly finding themselves in effect in a new relationship with federal qualities, having to accept that the methodology of deference to preparatory works and academic comment was not flying in Strasbourg. Second, as a related de-

---

17. Schram (1999) 438.
18. As can be seen in *Hrafnkatla* (Hrd. 1943.237) at 239, translated in Ragnhildur Helga-dóttir *Judicial Activism and Restraint in the U.S. and in Iceland. LL.M. dissertation University of Virginia* (1998) 8.

velopment, a new human rights chapter of the Constitution was provided with potential for reviewing cases. The difference between the Icelandic constitutional and ECHR texts creates a potential for clashes and differing applications, however, the ECHR is likely to prevail as "even though it is not expressly provided for [ECHR rights] in the constitution, they in reality enjoy constitutional protection."[19]

As in the other West-Nordic countries, the ECHR had little impact at first, seen as international law that had to be incorporated to any direct effect and was anyway thought to be of little relevance as full compliance was assumed. From around 1990 its influence, however, has been substantial.[20] Icelandic courts are "[in] light of this evident connection between the convention and the constitution" Icelandic court's look increasingly to the ECHR and ECHR case law.[21]

EFTA membership and the EEA agreement has led to the principle of *Francovic* been transplanted into Icelandic law. Those trade regimes contain fewer opportunities for individuals to claim economic and especially social rights[22] and it will be interesting to see how far these dynamics will go and to what extent they will follow EU developments.

Generally, when it comes to judicial review, Iceland lies somewhere closer to Denmark compared to Norway. Though Iceland was long the last stronghold of traditional Norse law, today it is very close to the Danish tradition of law in many ways, especially in terms of court system, legal education, and legal philosophy. Like their Danish counterparts, Icelandic courts were reluctant to trump legislative choice and deference to '*the lawgiver*' looms very large in judicial consciousness. Judicial review has been exercised on occasions, however, and certainly took an upwards surge when the Icelandic Constitution was revised, replacing the human rights provisions that were largely inherited from Denmark with another version modelled more on the ECHR.

19. Eríkur Tómasson "Réttur til réttlátrar málsmeðferðar" in *Mannréttindasáttmáli Evrópu* Mannréttindastofnun (2005) 197.
20. Thorarensen Bjørg "Áhrif Mannréttindasáttmála Evrópu á vernd tjáningarfrelsis að íslenskum rétti" 53 *Tímarit Lögfræðinga* (2003) 373 from 415.
21. Bjørg Thorarensen "Áhrif meðalhófsreglu við skýringu stjórnarskrárákvæða" *Rit Lagastofnunar Háskola Íslands* (2003) 51 at 102.
22. Hans Petter Graver "Welfare State and Constitutionalism under the EEA Agreement" in *The Welfare State and Constitutionalism in the Nordic Countries* (2001) 107.

Introduction to Previous Practice

With its Constitution in 1874, Iceland had the kind of super norm that may bring about constitutional judicial review. That the country was still associated to Denmark and according to the Danes was still subject to Danish sovereignty and the Danish Basic Law added a federal element that could have provided the legal basis for further contention.

However, Icelanders only took this opportunity to a very limited extent. The Constitution itself is largely copied from the Danish Basic Law and remained so largely until the 1990s, half a century after the final break-up of the Danish-Icelandic Union. There seems to be a parallel for many countries where the struggle for rights becomes second priority relative to the struggle for independence the potential for review was largely not realised and the principle of legislative supremacy was quietly disseminated into Icelandic deep structure law as without further controversy. There is just no record of them reappearing in case law.

The Icelandic rights provisions were the same as the Danish equivalents. This probably reflects a general attitude to constitutional law that the constitution must reflect the obvious rights of the people that the government will then respect. There is little reflection and choice to be discerned in the Icelandic approach. This 'Old West' approach is a great contrast to the 'New West' with the American Declaration of Independence that is more rooted in human rights and principles of justice, subsidiarity, and participation than in centralised control of national self-determination.

The change from associated kingdom, to disassociated dominion during the War, to sovereign Republic in 1943/4 could have initiated a new formative period but Iceland had essentially the same Constitution from 1874 onwards and no appeal to federal jurisdiction was possible after 1920. No great revival of constitutionalism and judicial review occurred after full independence.

For our purposes, then, judicial review, though established in principle at the beginning of the 20th century,[23] begins in Iceland in earnest with two cases in 1943.

For more than twenty years, no cases seem to raise individual rights issues. There seems to have been a wide-ranging consensus that Iceland had high standards of individual protection and that any issues pertaining thereto would be settled by Parliament. Indeed, the focus in Iceland seems to be on the phrase "by statute" in several of the constitutional provisions, the gov-

23. Helgadóttir (1998) 7.

ernment can only ban, hinder or force the citizens if so authorised by law enacted by Parliament. This probably happened for two reasons. Partly, it was a remnant of the Danish era when the struggle was for Icelandic parliamentary jurisdiction to ensure basic rights. Partly, it was due to later ideological conceptualist influence, stressing that the indeterminate nature of human rights meant that they could only be settled by the elected parliament.

The consensus in Iceland seems to have been that the translated clauses of rights provision provided the sufficient and necessary protection of basic rights. This conventional understanding seems particularly evident when the question arose whether to sign and adopt the ECHR. The Icelandic view was that the ECHR added nothing new to the corpus of Icelandic law. The attitude was very well summed up by the Minister of Judicial Matters, Bjarni Benediktsson in his speech in Parliament regarding the ECHR, claiming that the Convention would be "no innovation, because they are already included in the rights that the citizens have enjoyed and recognised as self-evident elements of [Icelandic law.]"[24]

The next batch of cases was also testing the fidelity of Courts, should they favour privilege over nation when latter was in dire difficulties? The cases all dealt with rather draconian taxation of the wealthiest Icelanders, who over a span of seven years twice had to pay some twenty per cent of their assets in tax in an effort to stabilise economy and government of the island. Naturally, this led to litigation with matters of principle raised including aspects of constitutionality and deep structure issues such equality and retroactivity. The cases caused relatively much reasoning on part of the Supreme Court but most of it was on a technical issue dealing with shareholding.

The notion that the ECHR was 'no innovation' because the rights "are already included in rights enjoyed and are recognised as self-evident' was probably universally received by the legal community in Iceland. Similarly, the attitude seems to reflect the perception that the rights were respected be-

---

24. Summed up by the Minister of Justice in 1951: "About the rights that are mentioned here it can briefly be said that in all matters of any importance, all those rights are already directly provided to the citizen in plain words in Icelandic legislation in some instances in the Constitution itself, or they are such basic rights that are regarded as main rules of Icelandic law even though they may not be stated in plain words. Therefore, it must be said that the first chapter of this Convention will be no innovation, because they are already included in the rights that the citizen have enjoyed and recognised as self-evident elements of the protection of the Icelandic citizen against the powers of the government or injustice from others." Bjarni Benediksson "Evrópuráðssamningur" *Alþingstíðindi* (1951) D. 239-240, referred to as relevant preparatory work in *Ægisson v. Iceland* (Hrd.1990.2) 4.

cause they were on the statute books and therefore law. There seems to have been little inclination to test the balance between principles, the attitude of judges, or the dynamics of law.

The earlier cases included in this study can be divided into three periods. First, the property rights cases, decided from late 19th century to the early 20th century. Second, the cases decided between the Second World War and early 1960s, mostly around the issues of expression, expropriation, and regulations. Thirdly, the intermediate cases, decided until the mid-1990s, when very few issues were raised but when Iceland was finally awoken to the fact that rights in Iceland were not self-evident and even so that the what mattered in the end was their obvious character in the eyes of the Strasbourg Justices.

Introduction to Recent Period

Icelandic review in recent years has been marked by a number of cases and new impetus from both an increased reliance on the ECHR as well as a new chapter on human rights in the Constitution of the Republic.

The situation of having a somewhat anachronistic constitution, that in large parts was handed-down from country to country (the Belgian 1830 Constitution translated into Danish in 1848 and then Icelandic in 1874), was always likely to cause a more reflected document to be drafted. The review process was undertaken in the 1990s and led to the chapter on human rights being revised in 1995, which caused an increase in court cases relating to rights issues. Since then, a number of cases have explicitly dealt with these issues and have created a situation of constitutional discourse and growing case law.[25]

For Iceland, the law has very much been a medium for independence and development. Icelanders were able to pursue their political agenda through legal means and the legal education has been instrumental in developing the country for a remote agrarian economy to today's achievements. However, much of the process of development included adopting elements of foreign legal systems, most notably the Danish. The Icelandic review cases, therefore, often reflect the conventional wisdom of Danish constitutional law, for instance in seeing Freedom of Speech as a formal freedom from prior constraint rather than a substantive protection of political and expressional speech.[26]

---

25. Thorarensen (2003) 74 note 43.
26. In *Hrafnkatla* (Hrd. 1943.237) at 239, the Icelandic Supreme Court held: "The Act has prescribed a prior obstacle to the publishing, which must be viewed as incompatible with article 67 of the constitution. No punishment will therefore be inflicted for violation of the Act's article 2." As translated in Helgadóttir (1998) 8.

Since the *"kreppa,"* the economic crises, a number of cases have raised issues very similar to the old cases of

Previous Practice

In Icelandic case, the reasoning by the court of last resort is most often contained on one or two pages. Therefore, no report page numbers will be indicated as the relevant section is easily found in the short section immediately preceding the conclusion of the judgement. Later on-line reports do not indicate by page numbers. As is the case with Danish judgements, the *'head resume'* given to the case in the report is not issued by the court itself. The report is often lengthy on the narrative including the claims and positions of the parties but usually neither facts nor contentions are explicitly commented, nor the reasons of the courts below. Those elements external to the official and explicit reasoning by the court is only used occasionally as contrast to the reasoning, as it is never clear what of the resume and narrative has been material to the ratio.

Early Cases

The earliest reported case that regarded judicial review in the wider sense was *Eyjólfur Jónsson v. Iceland* (1 L&H 249), decided in 1877, just three years after the sudden promulgation of the Icelandic Constitution. The facts of case are scarce; we only know that Eyjólfur Jónsson was convicted at Gullbringusýsla police court for minor offences. The Appeal Court then apparently heard the matter exclusively as a matter of jurisdiction, noting that the judge Jón Jónsson secretary to the Governor "has based his power to try and judge said matter on a royal mandate to him." The mandate gave the latter Jónsson exclusive jurisdiction in all matters of a certain type as judge, administrator, and executor throughout Iceland.

On this, the Court remarked that, "the Appeal Court cannot see it otherwise than here is such an alteration made of the organisation of the judiciary that according to the 42nd article of the Constitution cannot be provided except by statute." The Court likewise found that the 13th article did not provide for such wide-ranging exemptions from valid statutes. To qualify the extraordinary situation, the Court explained that even though individual cases were referred to particular judges, at least since 1718 when Norwegian law was incorporated in Iceland, no commission was given to individual men granting jurisdiction over "a whole flock of matters." The judgement below was consequently reversed "as judged by a man that was not correctly empowered to sit on the judge's bench."

The case may be a good example of how federations give rise to judicial review. The Icelandic Appeal Court quite effectively guarded Icelandic self-determination and the limits of the federal powers vested in the Crown by setting aside a regulation of jurisdiction and procedure. The extraordinary jurisdiction given to one particular judge did exceed the powers of the King for administrative and provisional rulemaking and should have followed the more cumbersome procedure involving the Icelandic Parliament. Likewise, this can be read as an example of judicial review under semi-autocratic regimes where the reviewing Court relies on procedural remedies rather than striking the disputed instrument down per se.

The case may have given rise to the Icelandic insistence on statutory law as essential – and sufficient – to guard human rights. Apart from that, the case could have offered a wider use of judicial challenge to the King and his Icelandic administration but no dynamic tradition seems to have been initiated by *Eyjólfur Jónsson*. This may be because of the subtlety of the reasoning, because the Danish-Icelandic power struggle was settled elsewhere, or because of few opportunities for litigators to explore such matters of jurisdiction.

A fascinating case of the horizontal effect of the human rights provided by the new Constitution was provided by **Halldórsson v. Simonarson** (2 L&H 455). The priest Daníel Halldórsson had obtained and executed an attachment against local farmer Jónas Simonarson for priest and church dues. Simonarson, however, won his suit in district court for the annulment of the attachment and a full refund of the dues. The District Court based its reasoning on the freedom of religion clause of the new Constitution. The priest launched a ferocious appeal even alleging gross misconduct on part of the district judge and claiming cost from him personally.

In its judgement, the Appeal Court noted that it "could not at all approve" the view of the district court. The Icelandic Constitution provided that everyone could establish their own community to worship God according to their beliefs, "but it does not at all give them the right to evade paying the ordained parish priest and church all statutory dues." The Appeal Court insisted that there was nothing in the Constitution providing otherwise and even offered the analogy that those who opted for another priest within the National Church, as was allowed by statute, were still liable to pay their dues locally. The court issued a stern reprimand to the district judge but found insufficient grounds for damages; instead, it awarded the priest more costs from Simonarson than actually claimed against him.

The case shows at least some degree of reasoning by analogy that could have given rise to further cases by pursuing various analogies and ambiguities but the condemnation of the district judge and the righteous confidence in tone probably discouraged further litigation and further trial judgements on constitutional points. The methodology is very clearly that of finding 'the right and logically necessary solution' in no way accepting that law is developed or refined. The opportunity to consider the relationship between constitution and legislation, the implications of religious freedom and the discouraging effect of imposing high costs on future legitimate litigation are all completely lost on the Appeal Court.

In *Zoëga v. Reykjavík* (6 L&H 176), the merchant Einar Zoëga claimed that a fee of 300 crowns executed by the bailiff of Reykjavík was unconstitutional as it was levied according to statute only on wine merchants selling alcoholic beverages. The Appeal Court briefly noted that the Constitution did not preclude legislation levying annual fees as in the case at hand. Furthermore, as the appellant had not used the procedure in section 9 of the statute to claim earlier licence rights, he was rightly required to pay said amount. The short opinion may be read to recognise the power of the Court to review the constitutionality of legislation implicitly.[27]

As a procedural issue, the question was raised whether appeal judges Jónsson and Jensson should be excused and replaced by other judges because they had both been members of Parliament when the law was enacted the year before. Though both had voted in favour of the act, the Court found that they had not expressed any particular opinion in that context relevant to the judicial procedure. The case was probably not a very carefully chosen test case for establishing constitutional judicial review.

The merchant Benedikt S. Þórarinsson raised the issue of vested property rights in *Þórarinsson v. Iceland I* (9 L&H 809) and on appeal to the Danish Supreme Court in *Þórarinsson v. Iceland II* (10 L&H 601). In the first case, the narrative part of the reported judgement was quite extensive for the time. Over five pages of carefully explained circumstances and arguments are reported. Þórarinsson was issued with a merchant's licence in 1894 that included the right to sell alcoholic drinks. In 1899 a new statute was enacted that required wine merchants to pay 500 crowns annually for the continued licence; the statute apparently did not contain provisions on the duration of the licence, though certain incorporated licence holders were limited to 15 years. In 1909, another statute provided for revoking wine licences by 1915. Þóra-

---

27. Helgadóttir (2006) 1 note 2.

rinsson tried to renew his licence in 1915 by paying the 500 crowns but he was denied renewal. He then claimed damages of 5,000 crowns annually for his own and his wife's lifetime or 50,000 in lump, alleging that the licence could not be thus revoked without compensation.

The actual holding of the Appeal Court was predictably minimalist. The Court conceded that: "it can be concluded that the words property right and property in this provision of the Constitution do not only mean property right in the word's narrower sense, rather also other valuable claims, such as right to use, obligation claim, author's right, monopoly right." However, even though the abstract interpretation of the Constitution led to a wide concept of property: "it is though on the other hand not concluded that the right of commerce, which is here concerned, falls within the scope of the said constitutional provision." Remarkably, the Court added that, "neither are there sufficient grounds for referring said right per analogiam under the ambit of the provision."[28]

The Supreme Court was brief in its judgement; it concluded that the licence according to the original statute was a limited right. The Court held that the recent statute's provisions, "was not intended to interfere especially with the commerce right of the appellate nor has it done so as the said provision is only an application of the empowerment that the legislator has to provide general rules regarding commerce matters."

The *Þórarinsson* cases show the deference of the West-Nordic Courts in constitutional matters. The Icelandic Appeal Court does not elaborate on its finding that the trading right 'is not concluded, not even by analogy.' *Þórarinsson* provided ample facts to limit and explain the judgement, not least because the licence was quite recently issued per statute and very gradually limited and after ample warning finally revoked. This situation could obviously be distinguished from older rights, rights established by other means than statute, rights revoked without warning; licences withdraw from some but not from others. Furthermore, the balance between legislative regulation and reliance on government statements and practice could surely be explained extensively.

Margrét Zoëga, widow of Einar Zoëga, likewise claimed damages for a license to sell alcohol issued in 1883 that was revoked according to the mentioned legislation of 1909 in *Zoëga v. Iceland I* (10 L&H 20) and *Zoëga v. Iceland II* (10 L&H 603). The Appeal Court extensively summarised the arguments presented by Zoëga and briefly commented that although the origi-

---

28. See also Helgadóttir (2006) 63 note 259.

nal legislation stated that older licences were not revoked this did not "tie the hands of the legislator to limit or ban" the activity without compensation. The Supreme Court used almost the exact phrase as in *Þórarinsson v. Iceland II* and stated that, "this ban is only an application of the power or empowerment that the legislator has to provide general rules regarding commerce matters, and the appellant cannot build claims for damages on the 50th article of the Constitution of 5 January 1874."[29] There was little to indicate any circumstances under which the Court would award damages much less declare legislation invalid.

The two licence cases were the last cases for a while that even raised the issue of constitutionality. That the issue was not raised again is consistent with the theory that completely one-sided reasoning according to the dispute resolver's calculus tends to be wholly unacceptable to one side and it, therefore, does not seek the judgement of that particular dispute resolver any more but pursues its agenda by other means or resigns the issue. The challenged statute itself seemed to recognise some sort of limits to the 'provide general rules of commerce' by giving the traders several years' notice. Had the judgements discussed this aspect and explained whether freedom of commerce placed any restrictions on legislation at least in form of implementation, an entirely different dynamic might have unfolded. As it turned out, the 1974 Constitution did not give rise to judicial review of Icelandic legislation pursuant to it.

Intermediate Cases

The most famous of the intermediate cases was ***Hrafnkatla*** (Hrd. 1943.237). Finding parliamentary legislation inapplicable as contrary to the Constitution, this was arguably a judicial review breakthrough, Iceland's Marbury moment. The fascinating facts set it apart from most other Marbury incidents as it deals with freedom of expression. A statute forbade publishing of ancient sagas without prior permission, which was only given if they publication stayed in line with original spelling, etc.

Icelandic law adopted the Danish view that the Constitution provides only formal freedom from prior constraint rather than a substantive protection of political and expressional speech. However, the Icelandic Supreme Court held that, "The Act has prescribed a prior obstacle to the publishing, which

---

29. See comments and slightly differing translation in Helgadóttir (2006) at 95 note 385.

must be viewed as incompatible with article 67 of the constitution. No punishment will therefore be inflicted for violation of the Act's article 2."[30]

The majority, judges Eyjólsson and Árnason, described factually how the saga at hand, written around the year 1300 and printed in 1847, was now republished with modern spelling in apparent violation of the statute. The opinion then discusses the rights of authors, and the state's statutory monopoly over writings predating the year 1400. The opinion then notes that freedom of printing is established by the Constitution, publications may be subject to liability but not censorship, which is clearly forbidden and may not be provided by statute. The Act's creation of a prior obstacle to publishing was therefore in violation of the Constitution's article 67. In conclusion, no punishment could therefore be inflicted for violation of section 2 of the statute.

However, judge Bergsteinsson in the minority was not satisfied that there was a clear violation of the Constitution. He found that; "there is no power in article 67 given to the courts to invalidate law number 127/1941, and the courts can not set aside laws that the general lawgiver has provided unless the constitution itself gives unambiguous powers to do so." Bergsteinsson writes one of the longest reasoning on constitutionality seen in Icelandic cases, fully two A5 pages, but does not cite any case, scholar, tradition or any other source except statutes and preparatory work, notably on the comparable point of required prior permission by the owners of copyright and libel law. His approach begs the obvious questions of what the point and legal relevance of a Constitution is, and just how, in the great scheme of the sources of law, the Icelandic Constitution can be trumped by preparatory materials to statutes.

The majority provided a very neat result but it in turn raises the question why not the entire statute or at least some of its provisions are held to be invalid? Furthermore, why ignore the points raised by Bergsteinsson rather than taking them head on and explaining them? The applied constitutional provision was a clear rule and a sub-clause of the broader standard of freedom of expression. The majority fails particularly to explain this context and say whether there are any limits to content-specific bans that are applied *after* publication and thus do not qualify as censorship *prior* to publication.

The difference in reasoning is interesting. The majority chooses a formal reading whereby anything can be proscribed but not censored prior to publication by the authorities. The minority seeks certain enabling of courts and, presumably unambiguous unconstitutionality before using such powers. Both factions take a minimalist approach, the majority by simply considering the

---

30. As translated in Helgadóttir (1998) 8.

prior issue, the minority by assuming *the lawgiver* will provide laws that have considered any constitutional aspect.

The contrast between the opinions and the failure to take on the issue of constitutionality was noted by retired judge Arnórsson in a scholarly article.[31] As he was a government minister at the time and only semi-retired, judge Arnórsson might well have sent Icelandic judicial review on a different course had he sat on the bench on any constitutional case. Elected politicians turned Supreme Court judges are often more inclined to overrule unconstitutional legislation than judges who never have held elected office, especially promoted civil servants, consider Chief Justice Warren.[32]

The case was of course significant in establishing review but the two limits of, first, just setting aside the result of the particular controversy not invalidating *erga omnes* and, second, only setting the legislation aside because there was an unambiguous constitutional rule, whereas most constitutional provisions clearly belong to the category of standards.

The case ***Reykjavík v. Knudsen*** (Hrd.1943.154) went further in expressly limiting the applicability of a statute that revoked a tax exemption. The case seems not to have had much wider impact, possibly because its ultra short reasoning appears clear-cut and because the case refers to the property clause and may at the time have appeared in line with vested-interest theory and practice in the other West-Nordic countries.[33]

The lower court explains the facts rather well. Mr. Knudsen and a partner had benefited from a statute that sought to diversify the Icelandic economy by granting a three-year tax exemption for one company in each new line of business. The exemption was conditioned on approval and the retention of most profits in the business. In accordance with the statute, Knudsen was granted the tax exemption in October 1938 and complied with its terms. By another Act, however, Parliament revoked the said law in 1941 when Knudsen still had some months to go. The trial court decided that the legislature was not empowered to rescind the exemption without compensation, especially given the individual nature of exemption, the reliance thereon, and the taxpayer's compliance with its terms.

The Supreme Court limited itself to stating that it; "Must be stated that it is not possible with the revoking of laws no. 57/1935 to deprive of the tax ex-

---

31. Einar Arnórsson "Stjórnarskráin og Hrafnköktlumálið" 3 *Tímarit Lögfræðinga* (1953) 14 at 26.
32. Schwartz (1995) 263-85.
33. Helgadóttir (2006).

emption those companies that had been granted it according to statute, according to article 62 of the constitution no. 9/1920."

The case shows how extremely short the reasoning gets. By upholding the judgement below, the Supreme Court may – or may not – have agreed with that slightly more elaborate reasoning. The Court clearly admits the Constitution into the realm of legally relevant texts but there is no reverence of that document in the laconic mentioning of name and number. Citing the year and number of the Constitution in Icelandic cases is somewhat puzzling, as there is but one Constitution, it certainly indicates that there is no special veneration of a 'living document' – it is a law with year and number, as any other.

The relevant constitutional clause on property is used without considering that this might be more of a retroactivity case and there is a valid interpretive question whether a licence or other beneficial administrative decision are protected against retroactivity or subject to sufficient notice given, especially considering the *Þórarinsson* and *Zoëga* cases that apparently went the other way. An interpretation of the property protection standard as well as distinguishing this from previous cases seems to have been called for. There seems to be an underlying *vested rights* or *reliance* doctrine that just is not explained. On the other hand, the minimalist approach of the Court should given rise to a number of cases testing the protection of reliance and vested rights as property in various settings. Either the 'filters' function to have lawyers advice against or fail to advice in favour of testing the matter, or else political powers took notice and avoided such situations.

The case **Svarfaðardalshreppur v. Jónsson** (Hrd.1945.345) was closer to the core of the property clause but similarly faced with a statute that changed the status of rights without considering compensation. The court had heard the initial case in 1944 but remanded it for procedural reasons to the lower court that had upheld the law that authorised an uncompensated expropriation by the municipality, as "the legislature must be allowed to make decisions concerning land necessary in order to guarantee that socially useful things like a harbour get built."[34] The second time around the law was struck down both at trial and in the Supreme Court, the latter holding that it was, "Not possible with section. 10 of laws nr.66/1931 to rescind without compensation the property right to seafront land in the harbour area."

The case demonstrates how expropriation can easily be explained away depending on the bench. Furthermore, it is interesting for resisting any further explaining of the various issues raised. Nonetheless the case falls in line with

---

34. Translation per Helgadóttir (2004) 209 note 580.

Hrafnkatla way of using flexible review techniques in dealing with unconstitutionality, construing the result of the case so that the legislation complies with the Constitution rather than explicitly setting aside the law wholly or in part.

Following the war a number of cases dealt with difficult economic regulations in troubled times. **Kampmann v. Strandgata** (Hrd.1951.268) concerned currency clauses in contracts affected by Icelandic revaluation as part of restructuring the economy in the post war era. The problem was familiar to the situation in other countries in times of economic trouble. The law was upheld as general measure within the appropriate powers of the political branches. The case compares well to the doctrine in Norway and Denmark.

The basic fact were that Kampmann a Danish national had sold property in Iceland and the buyer had agreed to pay the remainder of the payment due in successive instalments to be paid in Danish currency. An Icelandic statute devalued the Icelandic currency by around half and provided that contract debts in foreign currency should be capped at the equivalent value in Icelandic crowns prior to the legislation. The buyer sued Kampmann for a discount and he in turn claimed violation of the property clause.

Hæstiréttur remarked that the debts originated in Iceland and they were thus governed by Icelandic law. Following some factual description, citing of statute, and calculation, the Court found that it; "Is not considered that the 67th article of the constitution hinders the general lawgiver in organising currency matters in the context of the devaluation in the way it is done."

The case demonstrates again the use of passive and formal language to state the inevitability of the chosen interpretation. No further consideration as to the criteria and conditions implicit in "the way it is done." The reasoning sounds like that of the trial court in *Svarfaðardalshreppur*, stating that 'the legislature must be allowed to make decisions' without explaining any conditions or limits on this power to decide. Furthermore, it reveals the uncertainty that minimalism creates; there is no explanation as to the distinction between *Kampmann* and *Knudsen* or any of the other cases that had limited legislative power by construing the result of the case in light of the Court's understanding of the Constitution.

In **Víðir v. Iceland** (Hrd.1952.142) and **Guðmundsson v. Iceland** (Hrd.1952.434), very draconic taxation of financial instruments were disposed of without much recourse to higher principles. Professor Ármann Snævarr, who joined the bench as an ad hoc judge, with judge Eyjólfsson dissented and would have exempted the securities in question from the regulation but did so purely for reasons of statutory interpretation. Both minority and majority ignored the constitutional question entirely.

Thus the constitutional question broached in *Kampmann* was not revisited, developed or distinguished.

In *Alfons Jónsson v. Iceland* (Hrd.1954.073) and **Hamar v. Iceland** (Hrd.1954.093), the constitutional aspects, however, were tackled more directly although were briefly. The trial court briefly held in the former that the statute was passed in a constitutional manner, further, that the constitutional provision on taxation only required that tax was levied by statute and, finally, that "The general legislator appears to have very free hands regarding expropriation."[35] The Supreme Court chose not to pronounce on the issue and upheld the judgement with only a few lines of reasoning.

In the latter, the majority of Hæstiréttur addressed the point by simply stating that the alleged unconstitutionality could not be substantiated, as the lawgiver had not singled out any particular undertakings. The statute, therefore, did not violate the property clause.[36] Professor Ármann Snævarr joined by judge Eyjólfsson did not consider the constitutional issue but again focused on certain technicalities of the statute.

These cases of (absolutely) minimalist constitutional consideration seem to give an insight into the filters created by scholarly ideology. There is a clear cultural opposition to judicial review and development of doctrine through precedence and dispute resolution. The lower courts seem to think that they at least have to address the issue but the Supreme Court either ignores it or deals with it in an abstract and self-explanatory way. Most notably the learned professor's views of constitutionality are conspicuous by their absence, Snævarr neither takes the opportunity address constitutionality nor to extend reasoning in general.

The issue resurfaced regarding the second property taxation statute in **Guðmundsson & Víðir v. Iceland** (Hrd.1958.753), when the parties from the first two cases joined forces to challenge the second statute to tax and regulate certain securities. The Supreme Court judgement is remarkable for its relative length with extensive reference to the parties' arguments and otherwise to the narrative. However, regarding constitutionality and interpretation of the property clause, the reasoning was short and dismissive. The obvious issue to be tackled were those of whether very high taxation amounts to expropriation and, furthermore, whether there is any implied standard of equal treatment prohibiting singling out certain assets for draconic taxation.

---

35. *Alfons Jónsson v. Iceland* 76.
36. *Hamar v. Iceland* 95.

The Rise of Human Rights Cases

Following a very long hiatus, review cases resurfaced in the 1980s. As so often in watershed cases, the initial controversy appears marginal and petty and yet raised profound constitutional issues. In *Kristinsson v. Iceland* (Hrd.1985.1290), Jón Kristinsson was convicted at trial for speeding and failing to stop his car. He appealed the case based on Article 61 of the Icelandic Constitution and on the ECHR Fair Trial Clause, alleging that the case had not been heard by an impartial judge. Outside Reykjavík, offices of bailiff (bæjarfógeti) and sheriff (sýslumaður) held both police and judiciary powers.

The Supreme Court found that no specific allegations of impropriety had been made against the assistant bailiff who had appeared as prosecutor in the case. Furthermore, both the court case and the police investigation were conducted according the statutes, the Court cited "3rd main section of 73rd section of laws no. 74/1974, conferred with 11th section of laws no. 107/1976." Finally, the accused had represented himself at trial, admitting to speeding whilst denying the other charge but alleging wrongdoing by the police, and was refused the opportunity to question the chief of police.

For these reasons, the conviction for speeding was upheld and the other conviction quashed.

The case was referred to the ECHR system as we shall later see.

The case gives an interesting insight into Icelandic judicial reasoning prior to the 1995 Bill of Rights. First, both constitutional and ECHR claims are completely ignored in the reasoning and judgement of the Court; no reference is made to these instruments at all. Second, the propriety and lawfulness of the proceedings are demonstrated by characteristic Icelandic reference to chapter and verse of statute, thereby dispensing of all constitutional and interpretive issues without further analysis.

In *Sverrisson v. Iceland* (Hrd.1987.0356), the issue of propriety in prosecution resurfaced. Farmer Sverrisson was at trial court convicted of having removed a fence that was erected by the local council, but hindered his access to some of his land. The trial judges, who sat without a jury, was the local sheriff who functioned both as chief of police and magistrate. On appeal, Sverrisson alleged that this arrangement was contrary to the balance of power provided by the Constitution as well as the fair trial provisions of the Icelandic Constitution and the ECHR. The Supreme Court categorically refused the balance of power argument, noting that the 1874 Constitution in Icelandic Matters, the 1920 Constitution of the Kingdom of Iceland, as well as the 1944 Constitution of the Republic of Iceland had all been in force whilst sheriffs and bailiffs had exercised both police and judicial powers. Furthermore, judges were explicitly allowed to hold other offices by article 61 of the Constitution. The ECHR argument was dispensed with by observing that it had not been incorporated as law "here on land." The suspended sentence was upheld, though one justice dissented on another point.

The case shows how unwelcome constitutional issues were in the Icelandic jurisdiction. Although *Eyjólfur Jónsson* had concerned constitutionality of jurisdiction some 110 years earlier, this was not a very developed concept in Icelandic case law. The Supreme Court refused to consider the issue in light of ECHR case law that would otherwise seem obvious since Iceland had ratified ECHR in 1951 and was obligated to follow its provisions as interpreted by Strasbourg.

The case *Ægisson v. Iceland* (Hrd.1990.2) was heard by seven Justices indicating the importance of the case, including one of the Justices who heard *Sverrisson*. Guðmund B. Ægisson was convicted of a number of counts of fraud by assuming a false alias. The trial judges was a Deputy of the Sheriff and thus at the same time a functionary of the police, prosecution and judiciary. For the third time since 1985, it was claimed on appeal that this arrangement was contrary to the ECHR.

Whilst the case was heard, the *Kristinsson* case heard by the ECHR Committee that unanimously held that the said procedure was a violation of Art. 6(1) ECHR as the criminal court of Akureyri was found not to have been an impartial court when it found the defendant guilty and sentenced him to punishment. Alas for academia, the Government of Iceland settled the matter and initiated legislation to ensure separation of powers in criminal matters, disassociating police and prosecution from judicial functions.

The Supreme Court then issued a short opinion in stark contrast to its holding in *Kristinsson* and *Sverrisson*, noting that the "the constitution of the republic is built on the principle that the powers of the realm are divided into three branches and that independent judges hold judicial power." However, the Court explained, "special historic and geographical circumstances," led to some officials outside of Reykjavík holding both administrative and judicial office, though this practice "is of less importance now." In short, succinct sentences the Court then noted the new statute on the judiciary, carefully citing the numbers Iceland had committed itself to the ECHR, and then the unanimous holding of the ECHR Committee.

The Court then went on to explain the procedural statutory provisions that obliged a judge to recuse himself when he could not hear the case impartially. Though explicitly finding that "nothing has been revealed that the assistant judge, who read the judgement, has viewed the case subjectively." Nonetheless, it "shall be agreed with the ECHR Committee that in general it is not sufficiently securing the impartiality in judicial offices when the same man functions in both those and the police offices." The Supreme Court then concluded that the assistant sheriff should have recused himself and then remanded the case to the court below for a new trial.

The case is quite extraordinary in so many respects. First, the case clearly demonstrates how Iceland had in effect contrary to official and scholarly understanding, committed itself to a quasi-federal system where its courts could effectively be overruled. Second, that the mechanism whereby the federal review worked was open to individual complaint, not just abstract review of the general obligations of the signing state at international law. Third, that the Icelandic Supreme Court decided to abandoned its quite recent doctrine of mixed powers "here on land" without explicitly overruling or distinguishing its previous case law. Fourth, that the Court found it necessary to find statutory provisions as an ostensible legal basis for achieving the result, which it could ill escape, claiming that domestic law could lead to the same result. Fifth, that the law was left unclear on many issues, most notably what would be the case if Iceland lost in Strasbourg but no national statutory procedure or remedy was available in order to construe Icelandic law in concurrence with the Strasbourg ruling? Sixth, the utterly unpersuasive nature of the legal reasoning that can lead to diametrically opposite results – the same terse citation of chapter and verse leads to one categorical result in *Kristinsson* and negates it in *Ægisson*.

Arguably, this new reality could have led to a number of cases challenging Icelandic law on various points of law that potentially violated the ECHR in light of Strasbourg case law, test cases on the justiciability of Justice. However, this quasi-federal constitutional situation did not seem apparent to Icelandic litigators but *Ægisson* may have contributed nonetheless to the revival in review practice a few years later.

Then in **Gunnarsson v. Iceland** (Hrd.1992.0174), the Court ruled that it followed from the ECHR that a criminally convicted should not be forced to pay for the translation costs of the trial.

Recent Review

Freedom of Association and Freedom of Expression Cases

In *Ólafsson v. Iceland* (H. 1999-065) Ólafur Högni Ólafsson and other had been demonstrating in a publicly accessible place when an American TV crew was filming, protesting against various American policies, chanting slogans etc., Icelandic police arrested the demonstrators.

The Supreme Court awarded damages for wrongful arrest; it held that the activities were undoubtedly activities covered by Freedom of Expression and Assembly Clauses and that, also, the arrest had to comply with the provisions of the Constitution on limitations of these freedoms. Therefore, clear statutory powers had to be on the books to enable such arrests. Nonetheless, the reasoning mostly centred on whether sufficient statutory powers were in force at the time to comply with the constitutional protection of freedom of assembly. The five-judge panel was unanimous in its result but one judge dissented as to reasoning.

The case is in its way interesting. First, because the potential for judicial review based on constitutional and ECHR provisions presents itself. Second, because the Supreme Court seems to indicate that human rights are to be taken seriously and will trump government action. Third, however, the Court clearly tows the old conceptualist line in indicating that the constitutional freedoms are formal constraints on government, not substantive limits to legislative powers. Implicitly, anything can warrant an arrest of a person conducting expressive demonstrations, just as long as the necessary statutory provisions say so explicitly.

In the case *Alþýðusamband v. Iceland* (H. 2002-167), the Court upheld a district court ruling on a statute ordering the end to a strike subject to arbitration as to the terms of employment for a certain prospective period.

A strike was called by some of the trade unions in the Icelandic fishing industry. Parliament decided to end the strike through legislation that obliged the negotiating parties to submit to arbitration that was to settle the terms of employment for a given period. The legislation was challenged on grounds of freedom of association including freedom of trade unions to negotiate their own terms.

The trial court dealt relatively lengthily with the constitutional issues. A three-judge panel opined unanimously that according to the statute on civil cases the courts are empowered to adjudicate all issues pertaining to the law of the land. The Constitution does not pronounce on the powers of the courts to review the constitutional validity of statutes but the courts have, nonetheless, exercised review and this has become an accepted rule of Icelandic constitutional tradition that the courts can assess whether or not comply with the Constitution. However, pleas regarding constitutionality have to comply with the procedural rules and demonstrate a current controversy where the interests of the parties are at stake.

The reasoning regarding the constitutional and ECHR issues were limited to Icelandic preparatory works and reasoning from the wordings of the instruments, the only other source external to the instruments themselves being reference to ILO conventions.

The trial court then went on to assess constitutionality and compliance with the ECHR, concluding that neither prevented Parliament from enacting laws that dealt with individual conflicts of interests between employer and employee organisations but that Articles 74 and 75 of the Icelandic Constitution and Art. 11 of the ECHR limited the way in which the State could regulate trade unions, including that it must be done by statute and be proportional to the public interest at state. Consequently, the legislation was upheld generally but held inapplicable in respect of three local unions who were sufficiently linked to the original controversy.

The Supreme Court held unanimously that the judgement by the trial court should be upheld. The case was heard as an important case with seven judges sitting rather than the usual five. However, the judgement deals with the issue in a single line of text, deferring to the judgement below; "With reference to the reasoning of the district court, the judgement is upheld."

This is probably telling of the ambitions of Nordic courts. Faced with an occasion for stating the law and pronouncing on both dogma and method and an opportunity to opine on the parameters of judicial review itself, the Supreme Court goes mute. Given the chance to clarify the new method needed to deal with that amorphous supreme instrument that is dynamically interpreted by the ECHR Court, the Icelandic Supreme Court settles with a one-liner upholding the judgement for the reasons given.

The lack of initiative on part of the Court to state its own reasoning is probably revealing on the perception of the importance of case law as a source of law relative to statutory law, preparatory works, and textbooks. Secondly, Icelandic formalism reveals itself again; apparently, anything depends on statute, the power to review statutes is itself linked and conditioned on statute. Further, prima facie contestable actions, say limitations on the right to form associations, can "only be limited by statutory law;" this is not too reassuring as it overlooks that with Parliamentarism, the same majority rules both executive and legislative branches.

Vigfússon v. Iceland (H. 2001-461) also known as *White Iceland* dealt with the balance between freedom of expression and the defence against hate crimes.

The case probably demonstrates how the cybernetic communication of the ECHR network of national Supreme Courts is not fully functional yet and how the precedents provided by the ECHR Court are misinterpreted. Comparative capability and case law analysis is becoming relevant but is yet to develop full sophistication in jurisprudence.

The newspaper DV ran an article under the headline "White Iceland." The piece was an interview with the chair of the Icelandic Nationalist Association stating amongst other things, "You don't have to be a genius or a genetic scientist to demonstrate the differences between an African Negro with a stick in his hand and an Icelander. Western nations feel very sorry for the African people but they live there in the most fertile continent in the world and could produce six times the amount of food that they need if they cared. We live here on a piece of rock, have nothing but fish and ice and we are doing just fine while they don't bother fighting off the flies." Vígfússon was convicted of violating section 233a of the General penal code in the district court. The Icelandic Supreme Court held that the criminal proscriptions of section 233a satisfied the tests in the Icelandic Constitution and in the European Convention on Human Rights as a legitimate limitation of expression; the conviction was upheld and the sentence increased.

Now, there can be little doubt that both prosecution service and the *Vigfússon* Court had *Jersild v. Denmark* (ECHR 1994)" in their thoughts. The prosecution service probably decided not to indict the DV journalist because of the simple rationale that he was a journalist disseminating racism and the Jersild Court had discharged a journalist disseminating racism, apparently use of case in point. However, this is far from certain; *Jersild v. Denmark* does not give free range for racist dissemination. Actually, the holding is worryingly narrow, stating that "Jersild was not sharing the view, balanced the program, did not exaggerate or emphasise the racist views." Conversely, the ECHR would have accepted a conviction of a journalist sharing the view or exaggerating and emphasising the view, as was clearly the case in of the "White Iceland" article.

A reading of the DV article as relayed in the case shows quite to the contrary that the DV journalist with the headline "White Iceland" and other editing gave the impression that the country was about to be ethically purified if Vigfússon and his lot had their way. Quite on the contrary, Mr. Vigfússon seems just to make a rather unsophisticated economical argument that seems very much open to rebuttal and the racist part of his statement "Negro with a stick" is in any event much less provocative that the equivalent remarks by the Green Jackets of *Jersild v. Denmark*.

Therefore, it seems that the Icelandic Supreme Court likewise misread *Jersild v. Denmark* in reasoning that it authorised convicting the interviewee whilst compelling letting of the interviewer.

If the proposition is correct that *Jersild v. Denmark* was considered a controlling case by both prosecution, defence and court – and it properly should as law and facts were essentially similar – it shows how much the Nordic practitioners have yet to learn on the practical comparative approach. The prosecution should have brought charges against the journalist that distorted the views of Mr. Vigfússon and made them appear more racist and provocative. The defence should have pointed out that Mr. Vigfússon was indicted, essentially, for being a silly and bad at economics and his conviction would deny others the chance to defeat him at the marketplace of ideas. The court should have explained the ECHR practice and if necessary scolded the prosecution for misunderstanding precedent.

In ***Mathiesen v. Hafsteinsson*** (H. 2003-36), The Supreme Court similarly chose to ignore the potential ECHR aspects of the case.

The fisheries expert and writer Magnus Þ. Hafsteinsson, who later turned to politics, made some TV news segments on the throwing away of small fish in the Icelandic fishing industry. The fisheries Minister Árni M. Mathiesen reacted angrily to the news reports, accused Hafsteinsson of hurting Icelandic interests with outrageous allegations that he compared to other incidents of blemished reporting. Trial court convicted Mathiesen of libel for some of the statements.

The Supreme Court held in a unanimous three-judge opinion that even a Minister of State was free to express himself and that his statements had not exceeded the boundaries of his freedom of expression.

Neither trial court nor Supreme Court used any reference to, let alone analysis of, ECHR provisions or ECHR case law, though the parties mentioned it.

The case demonstrates, first, the preference for deciding appeal cases on a narrow factual basis. Second, that the Court deliberately disregards the opportunity to provide guidance as to how far legislation or judge-made case law based on open-ended libel standards can go relative to freedom of expression.

In ***Shelton v. Þórláksson*** (H. 2005-181), the Supreme Court again dealt enigmatically with Freedom of Expression. The highest placed Icelandic tax official wrote an article in his newsletter that was later repeated in the country's main daily newspaper. In it he commented on 'tax-dodging,' especially the possibility of transferring funds out of the country scot free, and mentioned an article giving specific advice on how to do this that was co-written by "the known expert in tax dodging," referring to E. G. Shelton. The latter brought a libel suit in Iceland. The trial court narrated the issue at length, and repeated the provisions of the Constitution and acquitted in a verdict based on 'the totality of the circumstances.'

The Supreme Court held that the word 'tax-dodging' does not have an unequivocal meaning but entails, of course, a way not to pay taxes. When asked, the defendant had stated that he was not referring to actual lawbreaking acts. The Supreme Court then endorsed the 'totality of circumstances' reasoning of the lower court.

The case is mainly interesting for dodging the issue of Freedom of Expression. Though it could have been used to clarify free speech in the context of public debate involving public officials, difficult legal issues and professional reputations, the case got a flat landing with a very specific focus on the meaning of a single phrases coupled with a lofty reference to the indeterminate whole.

Equality and Social Rights

In *Social Security Case* (H. 2000-125), a panel of five Judges heard a potentially wide-ranging issue of social security legislation. The national league of pensioners alleged that from 1994 to 1999, the relevant agency had acted ultra vires in issuing regulations that calculated half of the spouse's income when determining social security benefits for invalids (certain disabled people). Furthermore, the suit alleged that the statute in force after 1999 was unconstitutional as violating the Welfare Clause and the Equality Clause of the Constitution.

The Supreme Court split with Judges Erlendsdóttir, Henrysson, and Bragason forming the majority finding for the pensioners on both counts. In its opinion, the majority found that Icelandic law should be interpreted in conformity with international obligations, including the United Nations Rights, the ECHR, and the European Social Rights Convention. Taking the issue of legislative supremacy head-on, the majority stated that, "even though the general lawgiver has a margin of appreciation in determining which minimum rights should be provided the courts cannot avoid deciding whether that determination is compatible with the principles of the constitution." The majority then cited all the relevant documents 'chapter and verse' and concluded that the agency was generally at fault though "the conclusion in this matter cannot lead to any inference as to the rights of the individual beneficiary."

The partially dissenting Judges Gíslason and Hafstein cited earlier constitutional texts and their general meaning as well as preparatory work for the new rights provisions. They found that, "the lawgiver is empowered to decide whether the income of the spouse shall be counted."

The case is interesting for its potentially wide effects, though the caveat of the majority made it burdensome for social security recipients to claim retroactive benefits. The central holding may give actionable cause for several suits in the future and put a substantive limitation on legislative powers. Furthermore, the development of an ultra vires (proper powers) doctrine, perhaps not clearly seen since *Eyjólfur Jónsson,* is very significant. Finally, however, the case shows how extremely opaque Icelandic legal reasoning remains, there is a quantum leap between the textual references that both majority and minority make to constitutional and treaty provisions and the conclusions they make as to compatibility or non-compatibility of the contested law. The reasoning of the majority could equally well have led to the conclusion of the minority by adding the word "not."

Shortly after the above case, the pensioner organisation wanted access under freedom of information law to a memo that the government had issued on the implications of *Social Security Case*. The case, **Öryrkjabandalag v. Iceland** (H. 2001-397), was heard by the same panel. The majority of four found that the pensioners' league had a right of access to the document under statutory law but also referred to constitutional sources: "compare also the 73rd article of the constitution the 10th article of the ECHR, which was provided with legal force in Iceland by the laws no. 62/1994, but said provision has for instance been explained so that it shall ensure that statutory provisions that give the public access to information shall only be limited in such a way that is found necessary in a democratic nation to guard the lawful public and private interest."

In his dissent, judge Gíslason claimed that the correct interpretation of the freedom information statute was such that the document could be legally withheld thus voting to affirm the decision below, "and neither the 73rd article of the constitution nor the 10th article of the ECHR stands in its way."

The case demonstrates several interesting features of Icelandic judicial review. First, how important the composition of the bench is. Second, it shows that the increased reliance on human rights provision in the Constitution and the ECHR means that Icelandic statutes interpreted in light of these human rights. Third, we see how the technique used is claiming that the ECHR is valid because of statutory implementation but, even though this would only mean that ECHR was on par with the freedom of information statute, the former clearly governs the latter. Forth, the implication of letting the ECHR govern interpretation of the Icelandic statute is that a special Iceland ECHR case law doctrine is forming, as there is no reference to ECHR Court case law. Fifth, the reasoning by both majority and minority are so summary in quality that neither seems persuasive nor principled, the majority mentions the numbers and quotes the text, the minority just numbers. Ultimately, this means that that Icelandic constitutional law is unpredictable as the judgements provide little guidance to the solution of other similar matters, because this recourse to self-evident and understanding unexplained but for the gut feeling of judges serves essentially to make Icelandic law unpredictable.

The case **M v. K** (H. 2000-419) provides the clearest example in recent years of activist judicial review. A man believing he was the father of a child born out of wedlock filed a paternity suit against the mother. The district court dismissed the case, as the Paternity Act did not allow for the action.

The Justices Gíslason, Kolbeinsson, Erlendsdóttir, Claessen, and Hafstein unanimously remanded the case to the district court, as they found this to be in violation of sections 65 and 70 of the Constitution on Equality and Judicial Recourse as well as ECHR Art. 6. Further, they found the child had a right to be 'rightly fathered.' The right to challenge the legal status in a court of law was limited by insufficient reasons and the paternity law treated men and women differently.

The reasoning also took a close look at the preparatory work that indicated that the purpose of the statute included serving the best interest of the child in question. This suggests that the whole issue might have been resolved by discovering internal conflicts in the instrument itself, without constitutional or quasi-federal references.

The case is interesting for several reasons. First, the Court endorses equal rights and access to the courts as basis for review, indicating a widening access to review. Second, it uses correcting interpretation, a flexible technique, even when an easier, less controversial route was available. However, the statutory interpretation, indicates that some sign of the lawgiver's preference for the outcome must guide such a correcting interpretation.

In **Guðmundsson v. Iceland** (H. 2002-499), the Supreme Court took up the old issue of retroactive taxation.

Icelandic Taxpayer Jónas Guðmundsson had invested in stocks and carried forward the cost to be deducted in his tax statements in following years in accordance with the tax code. Parliament then amended the tax code to reduce from five to three the number of years the expenses could be carried; the tax authorities whose decision was confirmed by the tax tribunal, accordingly, overruled the taxpayer's carried expenses. The district court overruled the tribunal on grounds of constitutionality.

The Supreme Court held in a 3-2 decision that this was a breach of the Icelandic Constitution Article 77 (2) stating that taxation requires that statutory taxation powers were in force when the taxable activity occurred, this amounts to a ban on retroactive taxation laws.

The majority, Erlendsdóttir, Claessen, and Henrysson found that the ability to deduct and carry forward losses formed part of the circumstances of the taxable activities and held the State liable to pay damages – the princely sum of ISK 21,460 with interests and ISK 400,000 in cost at first instance, ISK 350,000 on appeal.

The dissenting judges, Gíslason and Bragason, argued against tying the hands of the lawgiver and found that amending the tax code in this way was general prospective tax legislation that citizens could always expect. The focus of all judges was on language and preparatory works and the dissent was only to the issue of reliance on prospective deductibility.

The case is raises several issues. First, we see how closely decided the Icelandic constitutional cases are; had the bench consisted of seven judges or just different judges, the outcome might be different. Second, we see that judicial review does not lead the Court to invalidate the statute erga omnes in question but to award individual damages. Third, accessibility for regular Icelanders is probably rather limited when the legal costs awarded exceed the claim by a factor of thirty-five, and they amounts may not even cover the full costs incurred. Fourth, the sources of law are limited to legislative language and preparatory works.

The case *SÍ v. LÍÚ* (H. 2003-046) concerned a labour dispute. An extraordinary mediation panel ended the dispute; among other issues, the panel provided a new formula and a special procedure for amending the sharing of the catch in individual ships in the event of technological changes. The case challenging the said procedure was heard by Justices Sigurbjörnsson, Gíslason, Claessen, Bragason, and Hafstein. The majority found that the mediation according to statutory law was correct in its treatment of the case and left open individual challenges but barred further action by the seamen's union.

Dissenting, judge Bragason provided an unusual reasoning. Considering the Association Clauses of the ECHR and of the Constitution of Iceland, the dissent found the law authoring the panel to be excessive and referred to precedent (H. 2002-167) as supporting "strong conditions on such legislation."

The case may be indicative of a change in reasoning to come. Having opened the door to scrutiny of statutory laws and giving reasons for its holding on constitutionality, the Supreme Court is also creating the normative basis for the next cases, as the younger associate judge demonstrates in invoking precedent.

Sveinsdóttir v. Áshreppur (H. 2005-051) dealt with the right to free schooling. Sveindsdóttir alleged that her local council was in breach of statute as well as constitutional and ECHR provisions on free schooling for paying boarding for her children. Case decided on interpretation of statute and regulations.

Probably an easy case, but nonetheless a rather summary dismissal of the constitutional and human rights issues, sending the opposite signal of *Öryrkjabandalag v. Iceland* (H. 2001-397),

Criminal Procedure and Fair Trial

In *Óskarsson v. Iceland* (H. 2002-156), a taxpayer alleged that a statutory provision barring court challenges to taxation six months after the tax assessment by the administrative authority infringed his Fair Trial rights. The taxpayer Jens Valgeir Óskarsson alleged that the time limit was a violation of his rights under the Fair Trial Clauses of the Icelandic Constitution and the ECHR.

The Supreme Court set down a panel of three, already thereby indicating that the case was of relatively limited importance. The Court unanimously held that the statute was clear and unambiguous and, furthermore, that this was not violating neither Constitution nor ECHR, "When it is neither concluded that the provision of 5th main section of the 29th section of the statute are so unclear nor that the time limit so short that it is violating against the 1st clause of the 70th article of the constitution, as it was amended by the 8th section of the constitutional act no. 97/1995 or the 1st clause of the 6th article of the European Human Rights Convention."

The case demonstrates that the method of legal reasoning that led to the *Kristinsson* doctrine and was overruled by *Ægisson* is still the dominant backbone method of the Icelandic Supreme Court. The above quote is the total reasoning devoted to the ECHR issue in the case. There is neither any reasoning by way of deduction from principle, nor apparently any research into or comparison with ECHR Court practice or comparative Scandinavian case law – just 'it is concluded.'.

The case *H. I. Guðmundsson v. Iceland* (H. 2002-338) involved a customs officer, who had been wrongfully accused, suspended, and arrested on suspicion of involvement in the smuggling of alcohol. The Supreme Court relied on both Constitution and ECHR in holding that the relevant statutes had been exceeded or breach creating liability on part of the state.

The case demonstrates how the twin norm structures, the Constitution of Iceland and the ECHR, have become legally relevant, and may affect both interpretation of statute as well as the outcome of the case in terms of remedy awarded.

In *Júliusson v. Iceland* (Hrd. 2003-112), Pétur Júliusson was convicted and fined of offences according to the VAT and accounting laws. However, the relatively straightforward investigation had been drawn out to such an extent that it was found to be contrary to the Constitution Article 70 and the ECHR Art. 6(1). Therefore, half the fine was deferred for three years.

The case shows how human rights provisions can be used as procedural hurdles, constraining and compelling government agencies in their activities.

In *X v. Iceland* (H. 2004-460), X was indicted for attempted murder, seven counts of violent offences, as well as other crimes. The trial court decided that X was to leave the courtroom when some witnesses were to be heard in the interest of their safety.

The Supreme Court reversed the decision. The unanimous three-judge court held that when interpreting the relevant procedural provisions, section 70 of Icelandic constitution had to be taken into account. The Court gave a relatively long narration, and then found that this entailed active participation in one's own defence by being present at trial to listen to testimony, consider evidence and occasion questions. The Court, however, gave no citations for these insights.

The opinion then added that it would also "look at the provision of ECHR Art. 6(1) and 6(3)(d) in conjunction with Act 62/194 on the ECHR." In conclusion, the Court found that in this case genuine fear for the safety of the witnesses was not proven and the conditions for excluding the defendant, therefore, were not satisfied.

The case raises several issues. First, the Court takes on the issue of constitutional review only to decide the issue on a, seemingly, narrow factual holding. Second, even if the Constitution or the ECHR did guide the Court as to the interpretation of the statute, it is unclear just how that happens. Third, what little guidance is given as to the right of participation of the accused at his trial is untraceable to any systematic logical reasoning from the Constitution or other authoritative constructions of it. Fourth, the reference to the ECHR seems, anyway, to be added as cross between an afterthought and a 'tick box' formality.

In *Reykjavík v. Jónsdóttur* (Hrd. 2005-248), Kristine K. Jónsdóttir, who was disabled with low income, was ordered to pay fines and costs in criminal proceedings. She paid the fine but not the costs. The Chief of Police in Reykjavík obtained court ordered security in her property for the costs but this was later overturned by a district court.

The Supreme Court held that the lower court had acted rightly in interpreting statutory law in light of Art. 6(3)(c) ECHR. The unanimous Supreme Court opined that; "Although the judgements of the ECHR Court are not binding in Icelandic national law, see Act 62/1994 section 2, it is nonetheless appropriate to look at its interpretation of [the ECHR]." As Jónsdóttur was without property and means to pay back her legal aid, the district court judgement was upheld "referring to its reasons to interpret [the criminal procedure statute] in light of the relevant provisions of the ECHR."

Neither the district court nor the Supreme Court mention any ECHR cases nor any other references such as text books that can identify the supposedly convincing readings of the ECHR by the ECHR Court. As most often, the Court's interpretation of the relevant provision is eluded to as self-explanatory.

The case is interesting for several reasons. First, the Court exercises judicial review and refuses to defer to the controlling agency. Second, review is applied through the 'interpretation in light of' method. Third, the Supreme Court of Iceland tries to deal with the quasi-federal nature of the ECHR regime by claiming to be 'persuaded rather than bound by the ECHR Court.' Fourth, in doing so it opens Icelandic law to a whole host of issues pertaining to precedent, including when a case can be identified as being sufficiently to-the-point to be potentially persuasive or otherwise dismissed as not binding. Furthermore, of course, the case fails to grapple with the issue of what would happen if it did go against relevant – but not binding – ECHR case law. In sum, those practising law in Iceland are left unguided as to the method of interpretation when faced with a potential clash between human rights and statutory provisions.

Alþýðusamband Íslands v. Iceland (H. 2002-167) dealt with the freedom of association and the principle of proportionality. The Icelandic Constitution provides ... and likewise the ECHR ... This poses the question to what length trade unions can go in strike or lockout action in pursuit of their interests thereby detrimentally affecting the interests of others including the general economy and public policy.

A strike was called by some of the trade unions in the Icelandic fishing industry. Parliament decided to end the strike through legislation that obliged the negotiating parties to submit to arbitration that was to settle the terms of employment for a given period. The legislation was challenged on grounds of freedom of association including freedom of trade unions to negotiate their own terms.

The Court held Articles 74 and 75 of the Icelandic Constitution and the ECHR Art. 11 limited the way in which the State could regulate trade unions, including that it must be done by statute and be proportional; consequently the legislation was upheld generally but held inapplicable in respect of three unions not sufficiently related to the original disagreement.

The case was expected to have important ramifications and was at trial level handled by a three-judge panel that gave very extensive reasons by Icelandic standards. Interestingly, the issue of judicial review was expressly addressed: "The Constitution says nothing on the powers of the courts to decide the constitutional validity of statutes but the courts have nonetheless done so and it has already become an accepted rule in Icelandic constitutional law that the courts can assess whether provisions of statute measure up to the provisions of the Constitution."

However, the court also attaches great importance to controversy requirement stating that the review powers to decide 'constitutional validity' can only be applied in conjunction with fulfilling the duties according to "the 1st main section of the 25th section of statute number 91 of 1991" dealing with adjudication in civil matters according to the law of the land.

In the Supreme Court, seven judges sat in – indicating an important case – but they only issued a summary opinion vindicating the trial court judgement referring to its reasons.

This is confusing. Why gather seven of the best jurists of the land if only commend the reasoning of the trial court? Surely, there must be some reasons that can be clarified and explained, quite apart from the need to consider ECHR case law or its own practice?

Jónas Guðmundsson v. Iceland (H. 2002-499) concerned the twin aspects of legal basis for taxation and retroactive laws. The Icelandic Constitution requires a substantive legal basis for taxation as well as a budgetary basis. This is considered to entail that taxation has to be prospective, tax laws must be known to the taxpayer before she undertakes a given activity. The obvious issue to raise, then, is when a change in the law is impermissibly taxing in a retroactive manner, for instance if something was made deductible and no longer is but the taxpayer has not yet be able to deduce the amount against other taxable earnings.

Icelandic Taxpayer Jónas Guðmundsson had invested stocks and carried forward the cost to be deducted in his tax statements in following years in accordance with the tax code. Parliament then amended the tax code to reduce from five to three the number of years the expenses could be carried; the tax authorities whose decision was confirmed by the tax tribunal, accordingly, overruled the taxpayer's carried expenses. The district court overruled the tribunal on grounds of constitutionality.

The Icelandic Supreme Court held in a 3-2 decision that this was a breach of the Icelandic Constitution § 77 (2) on legal basis for taxation and the principle of retroactive laws, consequently, the tax tribunal's ruling was overturned and the State held liable to pay damages. The dissenting judges argued against tying the hands of the lawgiver and found that amending the tax code in this way was general prospective tax legislation that citizens could always expect.

It is interesting to observe how the different views clash in this case. On the one hand, is an extension of the constitutional language by analogy. If retroactive taxation is forbidden then so is retroactive withdrawal of tax deductions, holds the majority opinion. On the other, is the well-known deference to the lawgiver. Legislative omnipotence and the necessity of changed circumstances appeal more to the dissenting minority. All judges agreed, however, on the narrative parts of the judgement, including a rather extensive recounting of parties' arguments and the use of preparatory works as the main external source of interpretation. Neither Icelandic nor other Nordic case law is referred to as persuasive or otherwise.

Furthermore, the Supreme Court limited itself to uphold the trial court verdict of invalidating the taxation tribunal holding and awarding damages with interests and costs. The offending provisions of the code were not held to be invalid themselves and the wider implications, including how the carrying of losses could be validly reduced were not discussed.

Much has happened in Iceland since the defence of this thesis following the financial meltdown on much national soul-searching, notably the President's use of his veto and the following 'popular review' as well as moves towards a new constitution. Neither these developments nor new cases are reflected in this edition – but could be the subject of much further research.

Greenlandic and Faroese Review

Summary of Greenlandic and Faroese Review

Faroese and Greenlandic review have a very short and less than remarkable history.

The Faroe Islands have been associated to first Denmark and then by a Union of Crows to Denmark, increasingly so after 1814, following the Treaty of Kiel, when Norway proper was ceded to Sweden. The Faroese were able to influence their own affairs and gained increasing autonomy as Absolutism gave way to democracy, especially so after the ancient Lawthing Parliament was reconvened in 1856 after 40 years of recess.

The Faroese, however, were not as conscious as the Icelanders when it came to the formal framework for autonomy. When Iceland got its Constitution in 1874, the Faroese were jubilant over the royal visit when the King landed in the Faroes on his return voyage from Iceland. No constitutional battle over the Basic Law, its scope and application ensued. Likewise, when Iceland gained increased autonomy in 1903, the Faroese rejected a similar offer from the Danish Government because of internal conflicts rather than as a rejection of its merits. Gradually though, the independence movement achieved more autonomy and Lawthing Act of 1923 was a first step towards a Constitution. The Second World War with occupation of both lands led to an Interim Constitution that awarded the Lawthing legislative powers. Following a referendum favouring independence, at deal was struck with Denmark that built on this and provided a framework for increased autonomy, including internal constitutional issues. A Faroese Government Act of 1948, revised in 1993, became the Faroese Constitution, though lacking rights provisions and other limitations of government powers.

Very few Faroese cases challenged government powers throughout this period. It seems that the prevailing view after ages of submission to a distant metropolitan power was that the government was the law and, whereas factual challenges were frequent, the Faroese did not seek and did not get constitutional judicial review. Change may be on the way, as a Constitutional Committee established in 1999 has suggested a revised Constitution with provisions on self-determination, human rights, other restrictions of powers, as well as clear authorisation of judicial review and default judicial rulemaking.

Greenland was colonised by Denmark under the pretext of regaining the lost Norse settlement of South West Greenland. Denmark sought to integrate Greenland in 1953 and has since granted increased autonomy through arrangements similar to the Faroese model. A new Self Rule Act is enacted but without rights and review provisions.

Both arrangements contain provisions on a special review body with politicians from Realm (Denmark) and Land (Greenland or Faroes) and Supreme Court Justices to review breaches of the Home Rule Convents. This could have provided opportunity for dynamic triadic rulemaking but has never been used.

Today's Faroese and Greenlandic constitutional judicial review is restrained substantively and in terms of reasoning and shows only limited signs of becoming more intense. However, a new dynamic may come from the formation of appeal courts for Greenland and the Faroe Islands.

Review in Faroese and Greenlandic Constitutional Developments

Regrettably, the Faroe Islands and Greenland have been largely excluded for lack of material; although the constitutional status of those polities associated to Denmark could have been developed through judicial review, the relevant cases are too few for a full analysis.

An early case that according to anecdotal evidence has had profound impact on legislative and administrative discipline is ***Klaksvík Fishermen v. Faroes*** (UfR. 1958.170H). The fishermen did not refer to any constitutional provision but still raised some profound constitutional issues pertaining to what Danish theory would refer to as basic principles of law, "retsgrundsætninger."

The Faroese Parliament had enacted several fiscal bills to provide for trouble treasury. Among these was a levy on petrol of DKK 0.20/litre. To offset the impact on small-scale fisheries, a subsidy was provided in another bill, calculated relative to amount of landed fish, roughly offsetting the impact of the levy but favouring boats that landed a bigger catch. The language of the actual provision referred to "útróður" – a Faroese word meaning 'rowing out (to fish),' a term of art gradually extended to even larger motor boats, though not trawlers and other relatively larger ships. However, the administration, which turned out to have the support of parliamentarians, saw the provision as intended to benefit only smaller boast, thus construing the term 'rowing out' more narrowly in this particular context than what was agreed in the case to be the usual wider meaning. Larger boats driven by heavier fuel and landing bigger catches wanted part of the subsidy. Their industry federation sued claiming that the language of the statute referred to an established term that could not be narrowly construed because of intent or other circumstances.

The Faroese trial court found for the government with the Eastern High Court and the Danish Supreme Court finding for the fishermen. Although the case is foremost a case on statutory interpretation, it apparently marked a great shift in Faroese tradition with the possibility of review of the administrative authority's interpretation. The Faroese polity was very much a parliamentary system, where the same ruling coalition controlled both the legislative and executive branches with the latter in most cases formulating the bills proposing new laws. Thus, it was perhaps inevitable that their work would become sloppy and based on an understanding of 'we know what we mean by this.' The government actually brought a Member of Parliament as a witness, stating that 'all of us' meant to restrict the subsidy of smaller boats. However, as the government accepted the wider sense of the word as the usual meaning, the Supreme Court found no basis in the law or preparatory work for the "limiting interpretation" of what was seen as a "claim at law" i.e. a precisely worded provision not open for interpretation, at least when this term of art was agreed upon. The fame of the case among Faroese lawyers is perhaps over-rated, as apparently the government would have won if it only had disputed the meaning of 'rowing out' and the review was almost akin to interpretation of contracts.[1] Nonetheless, the case served to discipline the drafting of statutes, a much-needed feature in a parliamentary system where the draftsman more often than not is the same as the administrator of the law.

Few cases have dealt with the obvious federal issues in the Home Rule arrangement. The Faroese Home Rule Act § 6(2) provided for a special arbitration procedure, involving Danish and Faroese politicians and Supreme Court judges, however it has never been used. Thus, disputes as to the limits of the powers of the Faroese government were probably mostly dealt with informally, or left unresolved. However, some issues found their way into court cases like **Werner Larsen v. Faroe Islands** (UfR.1983.986Ø) on equal treatment of Danes according to the Home Rule arrangement. A Danish doctor residing in the Faroe Islands, who had gone native and was very much integrated into the local community, felt discriminated for not getting a tax credit that was only

---

1. Kári á Rógvi & Bárður Larsen in "Dansk rets udfyldende karakter på Færøerne" UfR 2013B.25 at 27.

awarded to those with 'strong links' to the Faroe Islands, belonging to the community.

The Eastern High Court unsurprisingly remanded the case to the tax authorities, referring to the Home Rule Act § 10(2) that provides for a non-discrimination principle except for Faroese elections. The case had the impact on legislation that the Lawthing started to use defined terms of residence as a criteria rather than nationality or belonging, which seems to have been subsequently upheld, although cases are hard to find. This is probably confirming the normative shift of the TDR process, with the non-discrimination clause of the Home Rule Act first being ignored, then affirmed in case law, then modified again to mean that long term residents could be favoured in legislation without barring other citizen of the federation (Danish citizen) entry into this group.

The case *FAG v. FA* (UfR.1986.314H) on Faroese pre-emption of Danish legislation was in a way a case of statutory interpretation but had profound constitutional and practical impact. The Faroese had taken over the policy area of labour law at the start of the Home Rule era in 1948. However, the less than prolific legislature did not provide for a labour law tribunal to replace the Permanent Tribunal (later called the Danish Labour Court) in Copenhagen, which subsequently dealt with at least one Faroese case, a large-scale strike action in 1954. That case probably had an adverse affect on the development of Faroese labour law, as the unions came to see labour tribunals as unjust and draconian in their sanctions.[2] However, the result was not a comprehensive Faroese solution but a negative answer, when the Copenhagen government asked whether a new Act on the Labour Court should be extended to the Faroes. This meant that the old statute was still in force in the Faroes, the new statute only in Denmark. The question before the Supreme Court was thus, how to resolve a situation, where the parties of the collective labour agreement had agreed on an ad hoc tribunal for matters of interpretation but not matters of breach, and the court competent to deal with breaches of collective agreements no longer existed but another somewhat different court existed, albeit without jurisdiction over the Faroes. The Supreme Court decided to endorse the Faroese *sorinskrivari* (trial judge), sending the case to the ad hoc tribunal (thus increasing its clout) and declining both the majority of the appeal, which held the case should be sent to the Labour Court, and the minority, which found the case should be remanded to the general courts.

---

2. Kári á Rógvi: "Arbejdskonflikter på Færøerne" Arbejdsretligt Tidsskrift [2006].

In legal positivist Denmark, the Supreme Court had thus in effect invalidated a promulgated law, causing much scholarly debate.[3] The debate was settled by the eminent Supreme Court Judge Torben Jensen, who explained[4] that the case was a very particular ruling, based on the idea of *lex imperfecta* that it was absurd to enforce a law that referred to an institution no longer in existence. However, the case was not to be seen as a *leading case* in setting aside otherwise valid laws. The language used in Jensen's comment clearly indicates an understanding of common law and triadic rulemaking.[5] The case ultimately led to at Faroese Permanent Labour Tribunal being set up.[6] No further reported case law seem to have built on *FAK v. FA* to clarify other issues created by the gradual transfer of policy areas, although the judiciary certainly seems to have been ready to do its part.

It is noteworthy that the substantive issue in the case was essentially settled in Denmark proper in 1913[7] in case law by the Permanent Labour Tribunal that was very active in judicial rulemaking but substantive labour law did not filter trough from Denmark and was not created though a triadic process in the Faroe Islands (nor legislation). The substantive questions were essentially adopted by accepting the Danish practice as persuasive precedent in the eventual ad hoc tribunal but it took four instances and fourteen judges to square the federal circle.[8] The case should have initiated triadic rulemaking on a large scale, given that both the issues of jurisdiction in this federal situation and vast sways of substantive law needed to be addresses, at least in the patent absence of legislation. However, this has only happened to at limited extent and only in unreported cases.[9]

---

3. Blume, Harhoff, Wang.
4. Commented in Torben Jensen "Kompetencen til at afgøre arbejdskonflikter på Færøerne" *UfR* (1988) B31.
5. Kári á Rógvi & Bárður Larsen in "Dansk rets udfyldende karakter på Færøerne" upcoming in Ugeskrift for retsvæsen.
6. Kári á Rógvi "Fasti Gerðarrættur" 5 *Faroese Law Review* (2006).
7. Niels Waage Arbejdsretten i 100 år, bind I 39-40, referring to Danish Permanent Labour Tribunal Case 106 of 25 October 1913. Commented in á Rógvi and Larsen (2013) 30 with note 23.
8. á Rógvi and Larsen (2013) 27.
9. Faroese labour law cases can now be found at the web site www.fg.fo of the Faroese Labour Law Tribunal that is an indirect result of both the *FAG v. FA* case and this thesis (as there was a need to supplement the sponsor money) and it provided a way of applying the theories on the importance of triadic rulemaking as the project was underway.

One unreported case dealt with substantive labour law. *Faroe Islands v. Starvsmannafelagið* (Unreported)[10] raised an issue that was likewise settled long ago in Denmark proper, namely that supporting industrial action 'sympathy conflicts' were allowed as an exception to the duty of peace that forbid strike action whilst collective labour agreements are in force. The issue as so often in Faroese law was not settled in written sources, neither collective agreements nor legislation. At trial, the employers claimed that the institution of sympathy conflicts was not part of Faroese law but lost this point. The same *sorinskrivari* as in *FAG v. FA* held that the institution was part of Faroese law but added in a rare example of an obiter dictum by a Danish educated judge that 'the conflict could be illegal for other reasons, such as to short notice give.' The employers subsequently appealed and won on this very point. However, the reasoning by the High Court was so convoluted and brief that it created a massive reaction among the unions and the question has been revisited a number of times in the newly created Faroese Permanent Labour Tribunal.[11] The Eastern High Court created a still raging conflict, as several unions vehemently deny the legitimacy of the longer notice. This occurred by just referring to 'basic principles of labour law' rather than acknowledging that it was creating a leading case by adopting a balanced point of substantive law, including rights and duties incumbent on both sides of the argument, and was doing this through persuasive precedent, cited and explained. The final ruling on the law should, of course, have given the parties ample opportunity to argue the state of Faroese substantive party practice and case law to avoid the semblance of simple application of Danish law that might appear as lacking legitimacy.

The case demonstrates that triadic rulemaking is essential in a jurisdiction with inactive legislators, be they parliament or other empowered institutions. However, when dealing with an under-theorised federation like the Faroese association to Denmark, it is necessary not to appear to imposing metropolitan law on the associated entity but rather carefully filling a role as a *Faroese court* in special policy matters (those transferred to Faroese control only) and a *common federal court* in common policy matters.

Another unreported case *Elektron v. Faroe Islands* (Unreported)[12] highlights the many constitutional or interpretative issues caused by the federalisation of the Danish Realm, in this case the double federalisation, where Denmark concedes powers to the EU on the one side, and the Home Gov-

10. Case of Eastern High Court 5th division AS 109/1991.
11. á Rógvi and Larsen (2013) 29.
12. Case of Eastern High Court, 5th division AS B 205/2001.

ernments on the other. The case concerned the relevance of Danish and EU case law in Faroese law[13]

The case ***Perorsaasut v. Paamiut (UfR.2002.2591Ø)*** on the constitutional status of Greenland laws, clarified the issue of whether Greenlandic and Faroese statutes are proper 'laws' according to Danish theory, thus satisfying the many constitutional clauses requiring, for instance, expropriation to happen according to "law." The case held this to be the case, unsurprisingly perhaps, but the result would probably have been different immediately after the establishment of Home Rule government. Thus, case law can help clarify constitutional developments that occur indirectly or discretely elsewhere in the discourse between metropolitan government, associated government and citizen.

Thule v. Denmark (UfR.2004.0382H) is referred to in the Danish section.

The reported case most explicitly dealing with constitutional rights provisions is the ***Confiscation case*** (UfR.2005.261Ø). The case dealt with confiscation of illegal fishing gear. The Eastern High Court demonstrated an impressive dexterity using flexible constitutional review techniques, by which courts instead of saying 'we override this law as being contrary to higher law' say 'we interpret this law in accordance with the background legal principles that we know that we share with the honourable legislators.'

The Lawthing had adopted mandatory confiscation of the entire catch and gear in case of illegal fishing. This could ultimately lead to a mixed catch, following a long voyage and large amounts of legal fishing, one might happen to commit some illegal fishing as well. The question was whether such a mixed catch could be confiscated in its entirety. The Faroese fisheries inspection considered this to be the case, and the fishermen lost also the otherwise lawful early catch. The High Court explained that forfeiture is a "supplementary criminal sanction of a criminal offense" and requires an offense and a certain connection between the offense and what is desired confiscated, typically dividends or tools that have been used by the offense. By contrast, confiscation of property acquired in a legitimate manner would expropriation of property subject to compensation. The court found the mandatory confiscation clause to be motivated by a desire for a stronger protection of fisheries, it must "never pay to fish illegally." The court then cunningly applied triadic rulemaking by stating that '*it cannot be assumed that the Lawthing intended*' to introduce a compulsory expropriation-like confiscation of assets from an accused in cases where the evidence is certain that there was no link between

---

13. Commented in Kári á Rógvi "Um fordømi og fordómar" 1 *Faroese Law Review* (2001) 241 at 244, 263.

the legal acquisition and illegal fishing in Faroese fishing territory. As it was not disputed that 75 % of the catch was made in a lawful manner, the value of it was thus released.

The case indicates a quite creative approach. However, it does not explain the higher constitutional principle applied. The principle may be assumed to be that parliament provide for confiscation of illegal catches and may also enact expropriative provisions, but since the latter must be both specifically justified and is subject to compensation equal to the value of what is taken, it makes more sense to bend the statutory text and construe it not to include expropriation. The creativity is perhaps a bit rich, given that the court finds nothing to support the notion why the intention 'it must be assumed' to be such and such. What would happen if parliament reiterated the language of confiscation of the entire catch? Would that mean that parliament had ruled on the constitutionality of the wider taking without compensation? Alternatively, would the court then partly annul the compensation, or award simultaneous compensation for the legal part of the catch?

The case masquerades as a statutory interpretation but is, despite the High Court's choice of words, more of a deliberate corrective interpretation in accordance with higher principles of positive law than a correct reading of the legislature's intentions. Faroese autonomy should more correctly be interpreted to include the limitations of power, which also the Lawthing expressly has supported by positively resolving to adopt the ECHR and its implementation. Human rights and the presumption of liberty should be seen as forming part of the common basic principles of law, and corrective triadic rulemaking in light thereof be explicitly stated.

Some reported Greenlandic cases like **Greenland Bankruptcy case** (UfR.2012.2360/2H) have adopted principles of law or solved other issues of jurisdiction. The particular case dealt with the advent of the new Greenland High Court, a new appeal instance for Greenland. A question arose of cases appealed to the Eastern High Court before the new arrangement. The Supreme Court held that the Eastern High Court could admit trial cases decided before the new arrangement. This case and others[14] unreported seem to have added substantively to Greenland law in cases of legislative inactivity or similar quirks as seen in the Faroese cases mentioned.

This section has somewhat little to offer, and the examples are admittedly hard pressed to demonstrate *constitutional* judicial review. However, consti-

---

14. Jeppe Wedel Nielsen "Dansk rets udfyldende karakter i Grønland" UfR.2011B.210 at 213.

tutional judicial review is conspicuous by its absence in the 'Community of the Realm' as the Danes like to refer to the autonomy arrangements for Greenland and the Faroe Islands. The lack of reported cases, the convoluted reasoning, and the lack of further dynamic development through triadic rule-making all indicated the need for restructuring the Faroese judiciary.[15] A reform could include case reports, an appeal court, and expressed authority to use review more actively both to clarify the law and to evolve the autonomy and by evolving legal principles including constitutional and rights issues that pertain to these particular jurisdictions. The reform of the Greenland judiciary to include its own appeal court may have unleashed such a process that will be interesting to follow.

15. Kári á Rógvi "Færøernes retspleje frem fra glemslen" 12 *Lov & Ret* (2002) 22

Quasi-Federal Review

Summary of Quasi-Federal West-Nordic Review

Quasi-federal West-Nordic constitutional judicial review has a short but profound history. Quasi-federal European review has developed dynamically and expansively since the EEC (EU) and ECHR were established in the 1950s. Compared to Nordic review, quasi-federal European review has been astonishingly open and accessible with legal reasoning in cases concerning Nordic parties dwarfing reasoning in national Nordic case law. Legitimacy of such review has been disputed and its case law even ignored at national level. However, in the wider context, Nordic opposition (by judges and legal scholars) has not mattered much.

In the West-Nordic countries, questions of compatibility between national law and EEC Treaty or ECHR Convention took a long while emerging and have still to become part of the political discourse the way that its is in more properly constructed and self-conscious federations. Many cases seem brought by people decidedly on the fringes of mainstream discourse but gradually the interest for and use of quasi-federal review has widened.

The legal basis for quasi-federal review was long neglected. Though there was no denying that the ECJ and the ECHR Court had judicial authority, conventional wisdom steadily maintained that these were systems of international law not directly relevant and legally not relevant to individuals in the Nordic countries. Loosing several cases has taught the Nordic citizen that their governments in practice cannot escape the review authority of the European Courts and even their own courts.

The European Courts have lead a revolution of Nordic constitutional law as they have created a horizontal division of power between nation-state and quasi-federation and a vertical division between what a government can do and what is the exclusive sphere of the citizenry as well as ensuring formal restraints on government when it acts within its allowed sphere of influence. As the focus is still on nation-state law, the full potential of this new constitutionalism will gradually be realised.

The rise of the administrative state had largely eliminated Nordic judicial review but combined with the un-intended effects of the ombudsman institutions European review countered the freedom to regulate and even compelled other types of regulations like equal economic opportunities and horizontal freedom from impositions from others. The Nordic opposition to judicial review and judicial legislation has apparently not resulted in any discernable effort to reign in the European judges through strategic appointments or amendment of constituent documents.

As a result, Nordic judicial review has been revitalised because of increased quasi-federal review. In particular, the Norwegian Supreme Court has changed its activism and increasingly its methodology but the others are showing signs of following the same path.

Today's quasi-federal West-Nordic constitutional judicial review is activist and dynamic though still far from its full impact, being restrained by the reluctance of parties and lawyers actively to pursue legal and political aims through review lawsuits and the generational lag among judges educated in the tradition of unconditional parliamentary supremacy. Quasi-federal review is likely to increase in both European and Nordic forums.

Review in Quasi-Federal Quasi-Constitutional Developments

The European Court of Human Rights (the ECHR Court) has functioned since the 1950s with the Nordics joining the ECHR and in principle the ECHR Court's jurisdiction early on. To some degree it may be said to be the continuation of earlier efforts to create common standards and common institutions to guard shared values such as democracy, rule of law, and individual rights. The Second World War had finally made it apparent that things could go awfully wrong and that unrestrained democracy and legalistic traditions could lead to both horrible internal mistreatments of minorities and destructive external aggression.

The ECHR's contemporaries, the Coal and Steel Community leading to the European Economic Communities and the United Nations both had the two dimensions of ensuring domestic respect and prosperity and preventing international conflict. The Treaty of Rome and the Universal Declaration both have become important legal and political documents.

The European Convention on Human Rights (the ECHR) is by now one of the oldest constitutional documents in Europe, much older than the post-communist Eastern European Constitutions and a number of revised Western European Constitutions say for instance those of Sweden and, Finland of

2000 and even Iceland's Human Rights Chapter of 1995 or Norway's constitutional commitment to European rights or Denmark's implementation on.

With an enormous body of case law and jurisdiction over hundreds of millions of people and an authority based on persuasiveness rather than executive power, the ECHR Court is arguably one of the most impressive courts of all time. The ECHR is a functional federation without enormous powers, although it has little legislative activity and almost no executive apparatus, the Convention, the ECHR Court and other bodies effectively rule great sways of law. Seemingly, legitimacy means more than legions (Stalin famously asked how many legions the Pope had).

Judicial review based on the ECHR has been a feature of West-Nordic jurisprudence for half a decade now. Its development has been dynamic and exponentially so, rising with the dawning realisation of the ECHRs potential and its influence on national constitutional doctrine. Review based on the ECHR has expanded to being performed by the West-Nordic national courts as well as the ECHR Court and other ECHR institutions. Review of West-Nordic cases has been exercised in dozens of cases.

Constitutional Origins

The Court's inception is likely explained by the European experience in the preceding decades, culminating in the atrocities of the Second World War. The ideas of unlimited and unchecked national sovereignty were fundamentally discredited and a consensus developed to commit to preventing relapses and developing understanding of and respect for universal legal rights.

Unlike the EURATOM Treaty or the EEC Treaty, the ECHR was not constructed as a fully-fledged polity. Formally, the ECHR appeared as any international treaty subject to usual modes of interpretation and options for the signatories to honour their commitment to varying degree, especially in case of conflicting national law. Yet, the difference was the institutional structure. The Council of Europe was empowered to function proactively, including proposing amendments to the ECHR and producing various other Acts. The ECHR Commission could hear complaints and ultimately a judicial body would render decisions on alleged infringements.

Viewed as a federal formation, the ECHR regime has a constitution of great scope that provides for effective procedural and substantive rights. Furthermore it has active bodies proposing amendments in the form of additional protocols and performing oversight. More importantly, it has an activist judiciary that explains and expands the written norms. Crucially, the member polities respect the ECHR including its case law; when both political bodies and law courts largely respect a common regime as legally superior, there is effectively a federation, given its limitations a quasi-federation, if you will.

What the ECHR lacks, of course, are general legislative, executive, fiscal and foreign policy branches and other usual trimmings of a federated polity. However, these deficiencies do only limit its substantive scope and procedural ramifications. As a matter of law, a federation does not have to be over-ambitious; economic federalism was left to the other structures of EEC (EU) and EFTA. The success of the ECHR regime is its commitment to its defined substantive scope and its methods of oversight and jurisprudence that together have, the lack of other branches notwithstanding, proven more effective than most comparable national human rights schemes within its jurisdiction.

Even thought the Member States can leave both the ECHR and the EU, European law is effectively legally supreme in the short to intermediate term. European federal law is respected as superior law within its subject matter, although the nation-states may still be sovereign, constitutionally superior and thus legally superior in the long term because of their ultimate right of withdrawing their allegiance and their principled reservation of ultimate loyalty. This may give added reasons to use the phrase *quasi-federal*.

Constitutional Strife
We shall not pursue the EU dimension in this study except for some comparative points. That the EU is effectively federal (or supranational, or quasi-federal, pending terminology preferences) is fairly generally accepted by now. However, the present day EU 'small-c constitution' is the result of constitutional strife and the judicial legislation through the dynamics of dispute resolution performed by the European Court of Justice. (Furthermore, comparative points complicated by only Denmark of the West-Nordics being a full EU Member and Norway and Iceland forming part of the kindred structures).

Our focus now will be on the ECHR dimension Therefore, the quasi-federal aspect is probably better observed in ECHR case law. Furthermore, the ECHR Court unlike the ECJ allows dissenting opinions and ensures a respondent State one of its nationals on the bench; this means that in ECHR jurisprudence we can always observe directly the battle of ideas between Nordic and Continental judges.

The constitutional strife leading to the present state of things has been strangely absent from public debate. Because the ECHR was viewed as international treaty and its provisions legal standards, the conventional wisdom was that nothing was changing, legal rights were still only directives to politicians to consider the various rights catalogues when legislating. The attitude is summed up by the first Danish judge on the ECHR Court who saw it as an "unemployed Court."[1]

With the legal profession initially in denial, ECHR review arrived by stealth and was then rationalised as inherently Nordic, which it was not, as human rights lost their statues as effective legal trumps through the process of restrictive dynamics as demonstrated above. To the Nordics this is often a confusing new reality. In the words of the East-Nordic scholar Husa: "When both EU membership and the ECHR, and their influences on Danish jurisprudence are taken into account, a change in the legal culture towards a more active judicial review of the constitutionality of the laws in the courts could turn out to be a continuous development trend. ECHR requires [national] courts to review the conformity of national [instruments] in their relation to rules of the Convention. This is *de facto* a kind of (selective) judicial review."[2]

As is evident from the quotation above, the Scandinavian mind is not entirely at ease with this new state of affairs. Calling this a *de facto* as opposed to *de jure* and *selective* (in brackets) rather than *general* judicial review reveals a certain discomfort with the result of the analysis. What Husa is observing is more accurately described as a *de jure diffuse judicial review within the subject matter of the treaties*. The ECHR regime as seen from the point of view of the Scandinavian citizens is a matter of law (de jure) that can be relied upon in all courts of law (diffuse) where statute laws can be trumped or corrected (judicial review). However, this can only be done to the extent that question at hand is deemed to fall within the ambit of the higher norm relied upon (review within the subject matter of the treaties).

The "change in the legal culture" that Husa observes is the gradual change from national to federal legal culture. From the point of view of the man on the street with his grievance against the government, or from the point of view of the legal practitioner when she is asked for advice and representation, there are now the twin options, which are *culturally federal*:

1. of referring to quasi-federal norms and case law before national courts or agencies;
2. of appealing the case to quasi-federal courts or agencies.

The difference is quite startling and profoundly different from the dualistic nation-state view of law that has been prevalent in the West-Nordic countries

1.   Waaben (2004) 464.
2.   Husa (2002) 138 with note 64.

– and is still evidently the preference of scholars like Husa. The idea that statutes could be contrary to "international obligations" has been a staple of Nordic law for years and has undoubtedly had an impact especially in the drafting of new statutory legislation and secondary legislation and determination of agency policy. However, it is difficult enough to find a West-Nordic case where the complaint is based on international law, let alone a judgement that explicitly overrules a statute based on international law.

That is why the change is so profound – the ECHR-kind of international law is applicable, functional, and can be executed; the grieved citizens can challenge a national law, find a definite resolution to his controversy, and have it respected by the government, national, local, or otherwise.

Increasingly, the quasi-federal and judicialized aspects of Europe's constitutional structure today become apparent to scholars as well as to the courts. Estonian scholar Uno Lõhmus points this out in the case of Estonia, "... principles and rules in international law are an inseparable part of the Estonian legal system. In a judgement the Supreme Court wrote: In creating the general principles of law for Estonia the general principles of law developed by the institutions of the Council of Europe and the European Union should be considered."[3]

The point has been put even more bluntly by Lithuanian scholar Toma Birmontiene, "... try to assess whether the decisions of Constitutional Court could become the object of investigation by the European Court of Human Rights. At first sight, this might look impossible ... we can nevertheless assume that in cases where interpretation denied one of the rights protected by the Convention, the jurisprudence of the Constitutional Court could be a subject for investigation. This is exemplified by several cases ..."[4]

However, one of the rather sweetly innocent features of Scandinavian conceptualists is to insist on formal distinctions. That may be very well for purposes of history and explanation but even people like Husa, who above observes '*de facto* a kind of (selective) judicial review,' insists elsewhere that: "ECHR is used in all of the Nordic countries as an instrument of interpretation. Since the ECHR system is, by its nature, a classical construction of public international law it, nonetheless, is not as challenging to the national constitutional system as the supranational EU law."[5] So, the ECHR forms

---

3. Uno Lõhmus ""Strict" or "Liberal" Interpretation? Comments on Estonia" in *The Constitution as an Instrument of Change* (2003) 217.
4. Toma Birmontiene ""Strict" or "Liberal" Interpretation? Comments on Lithuania" in *The Constitution as an Instrument of Change* (2003) at 239.
5. Husa (2002) 166.

part of constitutional law in the Baltics but not in the Nordics, according to the Scandinavian conceptualist.

Now, it is all very well to note the distinction between supranational law and classical international law but seen more perspicaciously, we are dealing with federal formations. Husa notes as much in the following footnote: "Formally the situation in the Nordic countries is such that laws or other regulations cannot be promulgated if they are contrary to ECHR's Articles, although there is a margin of appreciation ..."[6] So, this 'classical construction of international' law hinders promulgation in national law. Well, this constitutional denial is altogether unpersuasive.

In the final analysis, when you are not allowed to legislate contrary to a superior document and there is an institution showing both "courtness" (in Husa's phrase)[7] and superiority, we sure do have, to coin a Finish-formalistic phrase, clear case of 'federalness.'

This folly of confusing conceptualised reality with actual reality comes clear when Husa deals with Norway in relation to the EU: "Since Norway is not an EU member, it is partly excluded from the discussion below."[8] Actually, Norway is associated to the EU in a more complicated relationship through EEA and EFTA that has distinct elements of 'federalness,' including a symbiotic relationship between the ECJ and the EFTA Court.

To get the full picture of judicial review in the West-Nordic countries it is necessary to take a closer look at the judicial review that has occurred in the context of supra-national quasi-federal arrangements. For whatever reasons, even in periods of relative activism the impact of judicial review was limited in the West-Nordic countries and did not lead to fully formed nuanced case law covering and developing countless points of constitutional law. This is very different from the ECHR that has a very detailed and developed case law. However, the Nordic cases are still relatively few, which is perhaps to be expected given the relative tranquillity of the region but the respect for ECHR judgements should prompt relatively more legal challenges than in say Turkey.

We have seen that the West-Nordic courts seem mostly to have allowed the ruling factions to hold their sway. The respect for the 'lawgiver' has for more than a century been overpowering. The courts failed to rise to the occasion and corrected neither the excesses of pre-Parliamentarism, the progressive cancellation of property rights, the prevalent oppression of free speech, nor even the collaboration with Nazis, in the case of Denmark. This is the

6. Husa (2002) 166, note 158.
7. Husa (2002) 116.
8. Husa (2002) 181.

paradox of democracy that it can ostracise its minorities. As American scholar Ely wrote, "A regime this horrible is imaginable in a democracy only because it is so quintessentially involved the victimization of a discrete and insular minority."[9]

The change following accession to the ECHR, EU, and associated regimes is not to be 'misunderestimated.' Suddenly, the court of final instance is not responsive to the arguments pertaining to the superior legitimacy of the lawgiver. The supra-national bench with it multi-national background is not in the same way impressed with the national assembly's or the national specialists' or special interests' views of the compatibility between their actions and the higher norms.

Accepting that it should be legally, enforcedly, and quasi-federally prohibited to deny citizens certain enumerated rights, and much less to persecute them, has now led Scandinavian law through a new dynamic formative period.[10] Now disputes involving claims that higher legal principles are trumping legislative instruments are being adjudicated by the European Court of Human Rights.

At first, this leads to the question of whether the practice of the ECHR is persuasive or binding in nature.[11] Then the realisation hits that the latter is the case, as the Swedish judge Johan Much put it: "the judgement would not be upheld by the ECHR." Just the language says it all; after centuries as an independent and even neutral state, Sweden is in a directly subordinated relationship within the subject matter of the ECHR, where the Supreme Court(s)[12] is no longer. When judgements will or will not be 'upheld' by external judicial bodies, there is a quasi-federal legal arrangement.

To use an example, imagine yourself in Iceland around 1980, you are driving in the less than dense traffic and suddenly a police officers stops you and claims that you were speeding and failing a full stop. You find these accusations unfounded. The police officer takes you to the local Sheriff's Office. As it turns out, the police and the prosecution are both answerable to the Sheriff. Having in vain argued your case before the integrated police and prosecution,

---

9.   Ely (1980) at 182.
10. Torben Jensen "Anmeldelse – Grundrettigheder. Domstolenes fortolkning og kontrol med lovgivningsmagten" 83 *Juristen* (2001) 374.
11. Jens Garde and Jensen "Den Europiske menneskerettighedsdomstols praksis – et tungtvejende fortolkningselement eller en ubetinget bindende retskilde?" 84 *Juristen* (2002) 76.
12. Sweden has a Supreme Court, Høgsta Domstolen, and a Supreme Administrative Court, Regeringsratten.

you would probably startle to find the trial judge, sitting without a jury, an employee of the Sheriff as well. The petty nature of the crime aside, the process has a certain Kafkaesque feeling to it. Unsurprisingly convicted, you appeal but face a Supreme Court that has consistently held that Icelandic rights provisions mainly consist of the guarantee that those rights will only be limited by law enacted by Parliament and that such lofty notions as rights and justice are anyway so indeterminable that only Parliament can decide on them (duly advised by experts). When you in desperation refer to the ratification of pan-European document guaranteeing justice and fair trial – you get only the brief highbrow patronising of the elders of a legal tradition centred on the infallibility of statute and preparatory works. Then unexpectedly you find a way out of the maze by appealing to a foreign body that sees things your way.

Such was the situation of Icelander Jón Kristinsson whose case we contemplated above in the section on Icelandic review. However, Jón Kristinsson prevailed in the ECHR forum. The case only went as far as the Commission as Iceland reached an agreement with the applicant based on the Commission report. In matters of procedural law at least, Iceland was (once again) associated to a larger polity, a polity with all the aspects associated with a federal appellate jurisdiction, superior norms, forums, and case law. The two *Kristinsson* cases have the exact opposite result, unanimously so in both instances, although the law is arguably the same, the difference being more a matter of people and attitudes than sources.

The trivial offence aside, the manifestly unjust criminal procedure should have come up in earlier cases and should have seemed at odds with the penumbra of procedural rights already established in the 1849 Danish Basic Law and the 1874 Icelandic Constitution.

Other cases indicate that a number of serious human rights violations have occurred regularly in the West-Nordic countries, not least the cases concerning freedom of expression, freedom of the press and fair trial.

This observation seems admittedly counter-intuitive – why would these Nordic beacons of human rights, these international missionaries of democracy be violating their own citizens rights? The full answer is probably very complicated but the institutional answer is fairly simple, they could get away with it through compliant courts that were integrated into the bureaucracy, produced inaccessible case law, and were ideologically committed to the supremacy of statutes.

That said, we must hasten to add that the Nordic countries are still among the safest countries to live in with fairly benign governments that seem to harbour little desire to single out any groups or individuals for ill-treatment (in Scandinavia, it seems any government inflicted misery is equally distributed). However, when governments do abridge or limit freedom, the West-Nordic judicial systems provide only limited checks and no balances. The procedural check and, indeed, constitutional balance provided by the ECHR changes the situation – a Nordic government must now give reasons for its interpretation of human rights and may fail to persuade the ultimate arbiters as to the merits of its argument.

This does, of course, pave the way for judicial legislation, for repudiation of parliamentary supremacy, and for expert rule from the bench rather than draft committee. Such is the nature of the review paradox; if you do not review, you invite tyranny; if you do review, you end up legislating through case law, in the former case people may suffer as individuals or groups, in the latter they may suffer collectively as the electorate.

The ECHR rights-revolution becomes complete with the teaching of human rights law as substantive restraints on the legislature and as (nearly) directly applicable law.

To sum up, the ECHR adjudication provides for a number of the factors that lead to constitutional judicial review – a new constitutional text in the form the ECHR Convention, a new forum in form of the ECHR Court, a federal dimension through its autonomy and effective (subject matter specific) superiority, and increasingly a renewed teaching of law that emphasises formal and even substantive rights over the omnipotence of the elected legislators. This new dimension of West-Nordic constitutional law was unintended and is still not recognised for what it is, a new dimension of constitutional law.

Introduction to Previous Practice
We shall now examine the formative period of West-Nordic law's alignment to the new quasi-federal supremacy. The ECHR cases are selected from the cases involving the three respondent states Norway, Denmark, and Iceland. Mainly cases where the Court found a violation of the ECHR are considered, as they give the best picture of judicial review being exercised and the contrast between West-Nordic and Continental judicial views.

All the initial cases seem rather incidental and haphazardly prepared. No great defence funds or political movements with coherent strategies like the ACLU or NAACP in the United States are identifying test cases and pursuing succinct strategies. Rather, the cases seem to depend on the nagging single-mindedness of certain irrepressible litigants.

Following the initial somewhat stumbling cases, gradually more interest seems to have been building, probably not least due to the expanding case law of the ECHR, only a fraction which was dealing with Nordic cases.

Freedom of Expression was inevitably going to come up in ECHR review. Scandinavian theory from its pragmatic inception in the 19th century to the conceptualist in the mid to late 20th century seems to have emphasised the formal character of the Expression clauses. The theory was that the 'responsibility before the courts' could encompass any expression, meaning that any utterance could be made illegal but it had to be proscribed by parliamentary law and only be prosecuted after the fact as censorship was banned. This line of thought was evident in *Hrafnkatla* and we earlier look at Danish theory, according to which even broadcasting football events can be criminalised.

The Freedom of Expression clause ECHR is differently worded, providing for freedom of expression unless the State can demonstrate a public interest in constraining the expression and can justify that the actual extent of a particular restraint was particularly necessary and consistent with democratic values. More importantly, ECHR theory and practise has emphasised both the formal and substantive side of the freedom. (Sports broadcasts will have to be endured for some time to come).

Early Cases

Initial Cases

In *Kjeldsen v. Denmark* (ECHR 1976), a number of Danish parents took the step to appeal to the Strasbourg Court the newly introduced sex education in Danish schools alleging breach of their religious freedom. There were three separate applicants with differing views; the first named Kjeldsen even withdrew his complaint due to disagreement with the others but the Commission maintained the case.

The Commission requested the Court to decide whether the facts of the case disclosed a breach by the Respondent State of its obligations under Article 2 of Protocol no. 1 to the ECHR and Articles 8, 9 and 14 of the ECHR. The Case was heard by a seven-judge bench including the elected judge of Danish nationality. Denmark disputed the jurisdiction of the Court, claiming that the compulsory jurisdiction of the ECHR Court was limited to suits brought by another "declarant State." However, following a debate in the Danish Parliament, the Danish Government had "decided to withdraw with immediate effect [their] preliminary objection, thus accepting ad hoc the jurisdiction of the Court." The Court "Chamber noted that its jurisdiction was henceforth established for the case at issue, whether on the basis of the special consent expressed in that message or by virtue of the general declaration made by the Kingdom of Denmark on 7 April 1972 under Article 46 (art. 46) of the Convention, as the delegates of the Commission contended." Thus, albeit under a dispute as to its general scope, the ECHR Court had jurisdiction to hear the case.

The applicants, who had initiated the proceedings, all objected to the integrated and compulsory sex education in Danish schools. Sex education had been introduced gradually first being only used locally then being recommended as part of biology. The Government "anxious to reduce the disconcerting increase in the frequency of unwanted pregnancies, instructed a committee in 1961 to examine the problem of sex education." The expert committee issued a report arguing for compulsory sex education that led to legislation and various other instruments with the intent of "avoiding insecurity, promote understanding, and stress the importance of responsibility and consideration in matters of sex." An amendment to allow parents to have their children exempt from the subject was defeated.

The applicants maintained that support for compulsory sex education was very limited, that it did not result in the desired reduction in the number of unwanted pregnancies, and that the State had failed to "respect the right of parents to ensure such education and teaching in conformity with their own religious and philosophical convictions."

The Court examined the "travaux préparatoires" and found that the ECHR text finally adopted was not very specific on the rights to private schooling and respect in State teaching "for parents' religious and philosophical convictions." The standard was found to be that of "safeguarding the possibility of pluralism in education which possibility is essential for the preservation of the "democratic society" as conceived by the Convention. In view of the power of the modern State, it is above all through State teaching that this aim must be realised." The Court then found unanimously "that the Danish State schools do not fall outside the province of Protocol No. 1."

Applying this standard, the Court found that the sex education "is aimed less at instilling knowledge they do not have or cannot acquire by other means than at giving them such knowledge more correctly, precisely, objectively and scientifically." Even done carefully the instruction would be "capable of encroaching on the religious or philosophical sphere." However, "by providing children in good time with explanations it considers useful... indeed of a moral order, but they are very general in character and do not entail overstepping the bounds of what a democratic State may regard as the public interest." The Court, therefore, found that the "[legislation] in no way amounts to an attempt at indoctrination aimed at advocating a specific kind of sexual behaviour [or] exalting sex [Further], it does not affect the right of parents to enlighten and advise their children ... in line with the parents' own religious or philosophical convictions." Any abuses could be dealt with by "the competent authorities."

The case is interesting in many ways. First, it had taken a great many years for Danish nationals to consider using the ECHR Court and appealing to the ECHR substantive rights. Secondly, when it finally happened the parties seemed somewhat unsophisticated in their framing of the challenge. Thirdly, though the challenge was unsuccessful, its reasoning should have reverberated throughout the legal hills of Denmark due to phrases like *the bounds of what a democratic State may regard as the public interest*, and *encroaching on the religious or philosophical sphere*, and conditioning the finding for the State on abuses being *dealt with*.

Especially the idea of the public interest in legislation having to outweigh in a balancing test the substantive rights being potentially infringe appears not to have registered at all with the Danish legal community because almost no cases seem to have resulted from this revolutionising idea that public interest bounds could be overstepped.

Rasmussen v. Denmark (ECHR 1984) concerned Mr. Per Krohn Rasmussen who alleged violation of the Discrimination clause of the ECHR as he was barred from challenging the paternity of the younger child born when he was married to his estranged wife. Rasmussen had delayed bringing suit as he struggled to save the marriage and later to settle the divorce. Ultimately, he was barred from suing whilst his wife retained the right to challenge paternity.

Denmark this time recognised the compulsory jurisdiction of the Court and a seven-judge bench was appointed to hear the claim endorsed by the Commission.

The Court first found that the ECHR Discrimination clause was complementing the "other substantive provisions of the Convention and the Protocols ... there can be no room for its application unless the facts at issue fall within the ambit of one or more of the latter," citing case law.

The Court then considered the Fair Trial clause the Family and Private Life clause. Both clauses were found to be applicable to the case as it concerned "litigation which, by its very nature, is "civil" in character ... an action contesting paternity is a matter of family law ... [Article 8] protects not only "family" but also "private" life ... the determination of [the legal relations undoubtedly concerned private life]."

The Court established that statutory constraint were in force on part of the husband's access to paternity suits whereas the mother's access was determined on a case-by case basis by the courts. Thus, there was a difference of treatment and the Court set out to determine "whether the difference of treatment was justified. It will proceed on the assumption that the difference was made between persons placed in analogous situations."

The Danish State then had to demonstrate a legitimate State aim and proportionality between that aim and the means employed in its pursuit. Denmark contended that the interest of husband and mother differed and that the mother's "coincided with those of the child." Furthermore, Denmark considered it "natural that, in weighing the interests [the legislature should let] the weaker party ... prevail." In addition, Denmark found it necessary to use time limits to ward against threats "in order to escape maintenance obligations."

The Court was persuaded by the 'natural law' argument and found that the Danish "authorities were entitled to think that as regards the husband the aim sought to be realised would be most satisfactorily achieved by [the statutory rule,] whereas as regards the mother it was sufficient to leave the matter to be decided by the courts on a case-by-case basis. Accordingly, having regard to their margin of appreciation, the authorities also did not transgress the principle of proportionality." Consequently, the difference of treatment complained of was not discriminatory, within the meaning of Article 14." The Court throughout its reasoning cited numerous cases and found case law to illuminate most issues raised.

The elected Danish judge, however, dissented as the applicability of Family and Private Life clause based the preparatory work that to the Danish judge appeared only to guard against "arbitrary interference in private life." Although granting that already some thirty years had passed with "social and cultural developments [that] justify a broader understanding," there simply was a gap "so great that it seems doubtful whether one can ignore the preparatory work completely in this case."

The case shows, first, the development in ECHR case law that still had not been received into the deep structure of Danish law. Second, the Court unlike the Danes found there was a complete sphere of private law that was potentially substantially protected and not just formally protected against *arbitrary* incursion. Third, though the Danish State won the case, it was only saved by the margin of appreciation, which shows a clear substantive difference between Danish and ECHR law, as the Danish Courts would not even accept a case challenging the law based on discrimination or lack of equal treatment.

Fair Trial Cases
Hauschildt v. Denmark (ECHR 1989) concerned the Fair Trial clause of the ECHR. The precious metal dealer and broker Mr. Mogens Hauschildt was repeatedly retained by the trial court and alleged that the Judge was then not fit to preside over the eventual trial.

Faced with an investigation for breach of the tax code and the penal code, Hauschildt was brought before the City Court in Copenhagen, charged with fraud and tax evasion. The Court directed that he should be kept under arrest for three consecutive periods of twenty-four hours; apparently, his council did not even raise an objection. Following that, the Court found the charges "not ill-founded" and remanded him in custody in solitary confinement. Repeatedly, at least at four week intervals, Mr. Hauschildt was brought before the court, mostly with Judge Claus Larsen presiding, who prolonged the detention for over fourteen months, eight of which in solitary confinement, until the trial finally began, some three months after he was presented with the 86 page indictment. Judge Larsen said that there had to be a flight risk and a risk of continuous offences and even remanded the defendant's wife on suspicion of being an accomplice. The legal basis was later extended to referring to a section of the procedural code that required a finding of "particularly confirmed suspicion," for which detention was required "in respect for the public interest." Judge Larsen, furthermore, ruled on a number of issues pertaining to the defendant's contacts, correspondence, and particular confinement.

At trial, the same Judge Larsen appeared with two lay judges to decide both matters of law and fact. Hauschildt objected to the same judge hearing his case who had already found the suspicion strong enough to remand him continually for a considerable period. The ECHR Court, however, noted that, "At the trial he was advised by his lawyers that section 60(2) of the Act debarred any challenge of the judge on the basis of the pre-trial decisions that he had made."

The trial took nineteen months before the verdict was handed down. The trial involved hundreds of documents, witnesses, and court sittings. Furthermore, the accused was continuously detained for the duration of the trial. The trial court returned a guilty verdict and a sentence of seven years imprisonment. The case was heard on appeal by the Eastern Appeal Court that was composed of three career judges, who had already heard numerous appeals as to the retention, and three law judges. In accordance with Danish tradition, they heard the case de novo.

Hauschildt raised an objection against one of the judges, as that judge had served on the City Court and had been involved with authorising seizure of documents at pre-trial proceedings. Again, the ECHR Court record notes that "counsel for the defence refused to argue this point on the basis of section 60(2) of the Act, and Mr Hauschildt withdrew the objection."

The appeal trial lasted for months and the appeal verdict was handed over four years and one month after the defendant was first detained. The Appeal Court sentence was for five years imprisonment and the judgement explicitly considered the detention harsher than usual imprisonment and, consequently, released him on the same day and reduced the sentence to time served.

The Supreme Court had heard appeals on the issue of detention twice during said four-year period and eventually, by majority verdict, overruled the "the particularly confirmed suspicion" but still accepted risk of evasion and re-offence.

Danish law provides that a judge can be challenged for various reasons. However, a particular section prescribed that a judge who had previously "had to deal with a case" would not be disqualified "when there is no ground, in the circumstances of the case, to presume that he has any special interest in the outcome of the case." Lawyers in most jurisdictions would assume that this section would lead to cases like that of Hauschildt being reviewed and explained and thus a doctrine evolving as to when the *circumstances* and *special interest in the outcome* would lead to a judge being or not being *disqualified.* The widespread use of detention on remand notwithstanding, the Danish Government submitted that at the time, "no case-law on section 60(2) had been established by the Supreme Court at the time."

A later Supreme Court ruling had just restated the open-ended nature of said clause, stating that, "if a judge has directed [custody] of a person charged with a criminal offence, this shall not in itself be deemed to disqualify the judge from taking part in the subsequent trial and delivery of judgment." Subsequently to code was amended to provide that judges having ordered detention solely based on "particularly confirmed suspicion," would now disqualify as trial judge unless the defendant confessed to the charges.

At the ECHR Court, the Danish Government objected to the case being heard on grounds of non-exhaustion of domestic remedies. The Government claimed that Hauschildt could have challenged the judge based on the aforementioned section 60(2) and that the said Supreme Court judgement confirmed that having decided pre-trial detention could lead to disqualification. That the defence lawyers had advised that the objection could not be raised was according to the Government "a quite obvious misinterpretation."

The ECHR Court answered this by saying that it could not "share the Government's view that the [interpretation by counsel] for the defence was quite obviously wrong." Furthermore, "The Government have not alleged ascertainable facts – such as previous case-law or doctrine – which should have caused counsel for the defence to have doubts concerning his interpretation." On the contrary, "for several years nobody had ever challenged a trial judge on the ground of his having made pre-trial decisions." The ECHR opinion then added that this "suggests general acceptance of the system, or at least of the interpretation." Neither Judge Larsen nor the Appeal Court had on their own accord addressed the concern that they knew the defendant harboured. Consequently, the preliminary objection was dismissed.

Hauschildt alleged that his case was not heard by an impartial tribunal. In particular, he criticised that the very same judge is expected to conduct the trial after at the pre-trial stage having assessed the strength of the evidence or as appeal-court judges having already decided matters pending appeal. The Danish Government and the majority of the ECHR Commission found no violation per se. The Court observed that it was not to decide "to review the relevant law and practice in abstracto, but to determine [if they] gave rise to a violation of Article 6." For this purpose, the Court had devised a two-pronged test consisting of one subjective and one objective element. The court cited ECHR case law as authority for the test. When performing the test, the Court compared the present case to others and distinguished the cases.

The subjective test was readily dealt with, as the applicant alleged no personal bias on part of the Danish judges. As to the objective test, the Court explained that at issue were "ascertainable facts which may raise doubts as to [impartiality, even appearances, because what] is at stake is the confidence which the courts in a democratic society must inspire in the public [and] in the accused." The Court found that the Danish trial and appeal judges "had already had to deal with the case." In particular, the Court found that "the Court cannot but attach particular importance to the fact that in nine of the decisions continuing Mr Hauschildt's detention on remand, Judge Larsen [and appeal judges] relied specifically on section 762(2) ... satisfied that there is a "particularly confirmed suspicion." The ECHR Court therefore concluded that the "applicant's fears in this respect can be considered objectively justified." Denmark was found to have breached Article 6 ECHR.

The case was decided twelve to five. Several separate and concurring opinions were filed. The Danish judge, Mr. Bernhard Gomard author of many textbooks on procedural law and commercial law, and Icelandic judge, Mr. Þór Vilhjálmsson, joined another judge in writing a dissenting opinion. In it, they explained regarding the Danish code sections on disqualification of judges that "the original proposal, dated March 1875 [said] that normally a judge in a criminal case is not disqualified because he has had to deal with the case in another capacity before trial, but that disqualification may ensue because of special circumstances." They found that this should have been dealt with on direct appeal as the "only information available now [is] a simple list of the number and contents of decisions made by various judges." In their opinion faith should be taken in "the strong traditions of the judiciary and the ability of the judges, deriving from their education and training, provide the necessary effective and visible guarantee of impartiality." The two West-

Nordic judges added that there "is no indication whatsoever of any lack of impartiality ... no objective or reasonable subjective ground to fear ... improper motive."

The Norwegian judge filed a short concurring opinion. Other judges filed dissenting opinions mostly dealing with the difference between criminal law procedure with and without investigating judges.

The British barrister at law, Mr. Robertson, was able to persuade the Court and was probably instrumental in presenting the subtleties of the case, in particular the notion that the defendant had a right to feel confident that the court was a fair-minded tribunal.[13]

The case is obviously interesting on so many levels. First, the case clearly demonstrates the quasi-federal regime that Denmark has joined; the Danish Supreme Court is no longer the final arbiter of human rights applicable to Danish citizens. Secondly, the normative shift resulting from third-party dispute resolution and reliance on the ECHR forum's own case law is quite apparent; Danish and ECHR law together have to be read through the perspectives of case law. Thirdly, Danish legal reasoning has taken a thorough beating. This is evident in the attitude of the Danish defence lawyers, who are held back from even raising an objection because of their overpowering legal training. This is also clear from the fact that no case law had arisen in the State of Denmark on the issue based on neither domestic statute, nor constitution, nor ECHR law. It is further evident from the attitude of Professor Gomard; as the leading professor in this field in a jurisdiction heavily reliant on 'theory,' he should have suggested the outcome or at least the potential conflict in his books.

The case seems to have had a great impact on Danish law but largely the impact seems focused on the particulars of the case rather than to the general issues of fairness and justice generally. Efforts were made to reconstitute the Danish judiciary to avoid the exact Hauschildt situation occurring again but there seem not to have many cases concerning other potential injustices.

The Hauschildt case is also interesting in the less noticed aspect of cost and remedy. The ECHR Court awarded less than what was claimed as actual expenses the verdict did not remand the case nor lead to any rehabilitation. The lessons seems to be that although a judgement against a national government may cause huge embarrassment and lead to changes in the future ap-

13. At lectures at the University of Copenhagen (and elsewhere) I remember Professor and ECHR judge Isi Foighel quoting Mr. Robertson arguing that, "the procedure must be just and appear to be just." The 'appear to be just' maxim is now readily part of Danish legal tradition.

plication of the law, it takes a wealthy and determined convict to pursue the matter that 'hath in it no profit but the name.'[14]

Kristinsson v. Iceland (ECHR 1989) was concerned with a criminal conviction with the defendant alleging violation of the ECHR Fair Trial clause due to the integration of police, prosecution, and judiciary in the Sheriff's office.

The case is discussed further in the Icelandic section.

A v. Denmark (ECHR 1996), concerned a number of haemophiliac Danish citizens who had contracted HIV due to negligent treatment when receiving blood transfusions at Danish hospitals. A number of the victims had developed AIDS, leading to severe illness and, for many, death.

Since 1982 it was known that the HIV virus could be transmitted through blood products and that screening of donor blood was necessary to protect against infections. However, it took a number of years for the procedure to be prescribed and implemented, at least some ninety people received contaminated blood as a result. In 1987, a scheme of compensation ex gratia was introduced but the terms were repeatedly amended and issues like the amount to be awarded and whether dependants could be compensated were not settled for several years. Various inquiries led to the criminal conviction of producers of unscreened or untreated blood products.

Late in 1987, the Danish Association of Haemophiliacs brought a civil suit against government agencies and a private company claiming compensation for negligence. The matter quickly became entangled in procedural issues, in particular whether the Association could proceed without named plaintiffs and whether the procedural issues should be dealt with prior to the trial on the main issue. Two years later, in late 1989, the Association provided named victims on the condition of their anonymity. From late 1990 and well into 1992, the case was embroiled in issues pertaining to the appointment and commissioning of medical experts to advice the court. In Danish procedure, parties are usually barred from presenting their own expert opinions, consequently the parties and court have to find suitable neutral experts and formulate the questions for their examination.

By late 1992, the presiding judge had become impatient and ruled that although all requests for adjourning the proceedings had been joint motions, from now on any more submissions to the medical expert "should first be presented in court." Following this, the expert opinion was presented in court but it took until mid-1993 to agree on additional questions to be submitted.

---

14.   Shakespeare's Hamlet, Act IV, Scene IV.

These questions were answered in late 1993. By now, a number of named plaintiffs either had lapsed into worse stages of their illness or had actually died from their afflictions.

In March 1994, the final preliminary hearings were held, the trial scheduled for November but by acceptance from the plaintiffs moved to December 1994 through January 1995. The judgement was handed down in February 1995 – more than six years after the suit was filed. The Eastern High Court found a Ministry and another agency negligent during a certain period resulting in a very limited award of money to one of the plaintiffs.

Following the judgement, the Government and Parliament responded to provide added compensation and help, regretting what had occurred. The Haemophiliac Association was satisfied with the proposed scheme and did not wish to pursue the matter further in the courts. However, three of the eight plaintiffs decided to appeal the case to the Danish Supreme Court where a trail was scheduled for September 1996.

Meanwhile, the Haemophiliac Association still considered the time lapsed to be an injustice and complained to the ECHR Commission that found a violation of the Fair Trial clause and the case was presented to the ECHR Court that issued its judgement in January 1996 – before the Danish Supreme Court even scheduled its trial.

The ECHR Court found "that the applicants contributed significantly to the length of the proceedings," furthermore it was "mindful [that] the proceedings in issue were not inquisitorial but were subject to the principle that it was for the parties to take the initiative." These difficulties that the national authorities were faced with, however, "did not dispense them from ensuring compliance with the requirement of reasonable time in Article 6 para. 1," citing a number of ECHR cases as authority. In particular, the "judicial authorities" failed because "when the first seven applicants joined the case, it had already been pending for approximately two years before the High Court." This meant that by "that time the High Court was presumably familiar with a number of the issues involved and would have been able to take on an active role in conducting the proceedings before it. Despite this, the High Court granted all of the parties' numerous requests for adjournments, hardly ever using its powers to require them to specify their claims, clarify their arguments, adduce relevant evidence or decide on who should be appointed as experts."

On the point of the medical opinion, the ECHR Court noted that the Danish High Court allowed almost two years to lapse on the appointment of the experts, "without ever intervening." In addition, the periods between the end of pre-trial preparations and the actual trials in both High Court and Supreme

Court were found excessive. The Court found there to be an "exceptional diligence required by Article 6 of the Convention in cases of this nature," and "even having regard to the delays caused by the applicants," the Court concluded that the competent authorities had not acted in accordance with the diligence required by the ECHR. The applicants were awarded 100,000 Danish crowns each in non-pecuniary damages and some cost.

In two instances, however, in case of the plaintiffs Feldskov and Lykkeskov Jacobsen, the Court reached the conclusion that they were not victims of a violation. The two, respectively a widow and parent of victims that died of contamination, probably suffered no loss in money terms.

Three judges dissented, among them the Danish judge Isi Foighel and the Norwegian Rolf Rysdal, President of the Court, who had previously been the Norwegian Chief Justice. The two West-Nordics found "no delays attributable to the State which may justify the finding that a reasonable time has been exceeded in the present case." They cited no case law or other authority but pointed out the role of applicants' own counsel, and that in the appeal case, the plaintiffs were not alleging delay at trial.

The case speaks volumes as to the state of West-Nordic justice. At this stage, the provisions of the ECHR and Fair Trial case law have still not penetrated the deep structure of the law. Neither government agencies, nor plaintiff association, nor judiciary, nor trial lawyers seem to have considered the issues in relation to the ECHR fair trial doctrine.

On the level of reasoning, the West-Nordics seem to agree on a dichotomy dividing law into rules and assessment, the former can be review whilst the latter is to be left to the appropriate agency or court. As far as possible, law is to be reduced to certain rules that can be easily applied to facts. When the law occasionally prescribes a legal standard or otherwise lacks the clarity expected of rules, the assessment of facts according to the available standard is to be conducted as some kind of internal intellectual contemplation process that cannot be made concrete in words or systemised as a series of arguments – the 'totality of circumstances' approach. When an assessment is made by agency or lower court, review by (higher) court should only take place in exceptional circumstances. The law-assessment dichotomy is particularly evident in the pursuit of neutral experts to provide the court with but one expert assessment (here medical assessment), rather than having both sides providing legal testimony, making it possible for the court to assess the methodology of the experts, and reducing the time needed to agree on relevant questions for the neutral experts in advance.

The majority in the ECHR Court, on the contrary, develops the law, building on case law. It identifies different categories of cases, requires different levels of diligence accordingly, and identifies a number of relevant factors pertaining to the applicants, the courts, and particular elements of the process.

After the case, Danish courts have seemingly made an effort to reduce trial time measured from filing to judgement.[15] However, the more nuanced distinctions of the ECHR Court seem not to have been taken to heart, nor is the 'neutral expert' system abolished. This reveals another aspect of West-Nordic law. When a case is decided, its implications may be taken to extremes and rationalised as the understanding that everyone should have had all along.

Freedom of Expression Cases

Thorgeirson v. Iceland (ECHR 1992) concerned two separate issues of criminal procedure and of freedom of expression. Þórgeir Þórgeirsson was a writer who wrote a controversial newspaper article in the 'I accuse' tradition.[16]

His claim was that the Reykjavík police had a special task force that would rough handle misbehaving people in the local nightlife. Referring to earlier reports, Þórgeirsson wrote that the real problem was much bigger than previously alleged. To prove his point, he wrote about a young man he had met in a hospital, who was "a promising and charming young person, but he was paralysed ... his chance of recovery was minimal." Allegedly, the "young man's room-mates told [that] his injuries had been inflicted by bouncers [and] policemen ... a victim of the Reykjavik night-squad." Even after this devastating treatment, Þórgeirsson opined that "suing a policeman in such a case would be hopeless. The investigation would be undertaken by [the] elite group who see it as their duty to wash all policemen clean of any accusations." Central to the critique was that "the real problem lies with a system where policemen investigate other policemen's violations of correct professional conduct." Þórgeirsson argued for the formation of a committee of trustworthy people to investigate the allegedly widespread allegations of police brutality and clean up the system.[17]

Following these allegations, police officers, including the chair of the police association, had appeared on radio and had answered these allegations apparently with personal critique of Mr. Þórgeirsson, who in turn wrote an-

---

15. When I practices law as an advocate trainee in the Faroe Islands, the Sorenskrivarari (Faroese Preceding Trial Judge) was extremely focused on moving cases along, however, there was no discernable effort to ensure that the cases were well prepared, and the system of 'neutral experts' persisted. Emphasis was on '*not delaying* justice' rather than 'not delaying *justice.*' As Faroese cases are not reported, I regrettably cannot cite cases.

16. *Thorgeirson v. Iceland.*

17. Ibid.

other article. This was led to by criminal investigations when the Reykjavik Police Association called for the public prosecutor to investigate the allegations. The State Criminal Investigation Police undertook to examine whether the publications constituted defamation. Following the investigation, the public prosecutor indicted Þórgeirsson charging him with defamation of unspecified members of the Reykjavik police. The prosecutor considered defamatory passages such as "beasts in uniform," the above allegations concerning the young man, and allegations of use of excessive force, bullying, forgery, unlawful actions, superstitions, rashness, and ineptitude.

During the pre-trial meetings, counsel for the defence challenged the judge on the grounds that he was appearing for the prosecution absent any counsel for the prosecutor. Judge Guðgeirsson dismissed the motion as unfounded. During trial, Þórgeirsson refused to identify the alleged paralysed man, claiming that he was just one of so many people that he had seen and it was impossible to do so. In his defence, Þórgeirsson claimed that his writing "was intended to raise a lawful, urgent question."

In his judgement, Judge Guðgeirsson found the specific allegations concerning the paralysed victim unfounded and the general accusations against the police defamatory. Citing Icelandic Supreme Court case law, the judge found that defamation could be made against a group of civil servants. Þórgeirsson was fined 10,000 Icelandic crowns, in default to eight days imprisonment; he was also ordered to pay all the costs of the case, including his own counsel's fees.

Both parties appealed to the Supreme Court that upheld the judgement and dismissed the arguments concerning the non-appearance of prosecution. Freedom of Expression was apparently not raised as a particular issue but features as part of the majority construction of the penal code. However, a lone dissenting judge voted to acquit and wrote that, "the conditions for punishment [for] violation of [defamation] which is to be construed in the light of the fundamental principle of Icelandic constitutional law relating to freedom of expression in speech and writing, have not been fulfilled."

Þórgeirsson mainly alleged not having received a hearing by an impartial tribunal according to ECHR Article 6. Apparently, this was the main contention of the applicant. The ECHR Court dismisses this argument as unfounded. As to the subjective test devised by case law, there was no evidence submitted; as to the objective test, this particular Icelandic procedure was found acceptable, as the prosecution had only been absent during meetings when evidence was presented and the judge was not in any way presenting the prosecutor's case.

Þórgeirsson further alleged violation of Article 10 ECHR. The ECHR Court considered "that the applicant's conviction and sentence ... as upheld by the Supreme Court constituted an interference with his right to freedom of expression." This was not disputed by the Government. The question was then whether this interference was prescribed by law under legitimate aims and necessary in democratic society.

The Court found that manner in which the defamation provision was construed was "not excluded by its wording [and was] supported by precedent." Thus, the *prescribed by law* terms was complied with.

When dealing with the application of Article 10 to the matter at hand, the Court recalled that it was "applicable not only to "information" or "ideas" that are favourably received or regarded as inoffensive or as a matter of indifference, but also to those that offend, shock or disturb." Although the applicant himself was not a member of the press and not acting on part of any media,[18] the Court referred to Freedom of the Press that must not "overstep the bounds [inter alia for the] protection of the reputation [of others]. Nevertheless, the Court found that not "only does [the press] have the task of imparting such information and ideas: the public also has a right to receive them. Were it otherwise, the press would be unable to play its vital role of "public watchdog.""

The Court referred to case law and in particular took issue with "the questions of general principle raised by the Government ... there is no warrant in its case-law for distinguishing [between] political discussion and discussion of other matters of public concern." As to the story of the paralysed man, it was not shown to be "altogether untrue and merely invented ... the applicant was essentially reporting what was being said by others about police brutality ... his criticisms could not be taken as an attack against all the members, or any specific member, of the Reykjavik police force." Particularly disturbing was that, "the conviction and sentence were capable of discouraging open discussion of matters of public concern." Consequently, though the aims pursued had been legitimate, the means had not been proportional.

The Court then found by eight votes to one that there had been a violation of article 10.

Dissenting was ad hoc Judge Gíslason, who is a notable conceptualist of the Icelandic Bench. Gíslason has championed deference to Parliament and administration, restrictive construction of the Icelandic Constitution, and minimalist reasoning in some cases, tried to apply a certain burden of proof to the journalist reporting on alleged wrongdoing on part of the police.

---

18. Kjølbro (2005).

In this case, Judge Gíslason found that "Allegations that crimes have been committed are either true or falsed" This burden of proof was not lifted, the "applicant did nothing to substantiate this story, [there] is no indication that the young man [was] ill-treated." Gíslason further found that he was rightfully "convicted not only for vituperation and insults but also [for] imputation to policemen of serious crimes." On the issue of freedom of expression, Gíslason found it "certainly "necessary" to restrain false allegations of serious crime in order to protect the reputation or rights of others."

The case further demonstrates how restrictive the West-Nordic view of freedom of speech is different from the view expounded by ECHR case law. To the West-Nordic lawyer, freedom of speech is the freedom to express anything that can be substantiated and is not proscribed by law; to the ECHR Court, a public discussion of issues is important in itself. It is notable that neither on appeal nor in the ECHR process did counsel rely much on freedom of expression but rather on the strange procedural issue of challenging the judge. Challenging the judge could presumably only have lead to the case being remanded for a new trial whereas the issue of expression was substantively governing the case and could lead to acquittal.

The case demonstrates effectively the third-party dispute resolution rule making of the ECHR Court. This resolved the conflict of norms between the substantive protection and efficacious proportionality standard of Article 10 ECHR, as construed by case law, and the formalistic minimal protection in the West-Nordic constitutions, as construed by case law. Though the Constitutions remained unchanged as documents, the constitutional law was effectively changed.

Jersild v. Denmark (ECHR 1994) probably provided one of the greater cultural shocks to be delivered by the quasi-federal European judicial review on the West-Nordic legal community.

The dispute arose over a particular provision of the Danish criminal code that proscribes dissemination of racial and other viciously offensive statements. The obvious issue here is the scope of this provision and its compatibility with the right to freedom of expression. It is noteworthy that the provision itself does not seem to require any particularly offensive nature, nor any victim, nor any actual harm to the victim. It is what Danish law refers to as an abstract (criminal) delict; like all delicts of the criminal code it also covers attempts and collaboration in the crime.

It does not take a particularly twisted legal mind to imagine the possible clashes with freedom of expression. This wide-ranging criminalisation is certainly not in the spirit of the "..." Clause of the Basic Law, though it arguably fits the positivist reading of the "Responsibility" Clause. For instance, a simple debate on race issues or reporting on racism in Denmark may ...

Just such an instance came to pass in the *Jersild v. Denmark* case. In Denmark, a number of groups of disgruntled youngsters formed and became known as 'the green jackets' due to the items of clothing that they took to wearing. These adolescents were generally discontent and took a particularly aggressive disliking to immigrants with foreign racial appearance whom they blamed for all of society's ills. The TV-reporter Jens Olaf Jersild took an interest in this grass-root movement and wanted to produce a program about them. For this purpose he made interviews spanning several hours and with commentary and other interviews these green jacket conversations were fitted into a program that lasted an hour.

This insight into the racist milieu of Denmark naturally provoked stark reactions. Many were appalled that such views were held by people, others took offence at their being aired on television. The program included remarks by the green jackets that the immigrants to who they referred in derogatory terms "breed like rats" and more in similar veins. The participating green jackets were prosecuted according to the Racism Clause and no issue of their freedom of expression seems to have been raised.

The prosecution went further, however. Acting on a complaint from a Lutheran bishop, the prosecution service decided to indict Mr. Jersild for his furtherance and distribution of the racist slurs. Mr. Jersild was duly convicted at trial court and the conviction upheld by the Supreme Court. As is evident from the Supreme Court judgement, it is difficult to defer to several authorities at the same time. The instinct of the Danish courts is to defer to legislation and especially the agencies policing the legislation but it is also defer to international documents. In this case, the Danish Supreme Court was satisfied that the prosecution service had interpreted both the criminal code and the human rights convention correctly and it seems likely that the issue of the convention influenced the sentencing.

The Danish Supreme Court reduced the fine to DKK 1,000, a relatively small amount as crimes go, but, nonetheless, Jens Olaf Jersild was convicted of racism for making a program on racist in Denmark. Mr. Jersild was not happy with this state of affairs and appealed to Strasbourg ... The judgement of the Court of Human Rights was clear. With this judgement, the Danish legal community was finally faced with a substantive set of human rights. It could no longer be said that anything – even "broadcasting a football match" could be banned and people made "responsible" for them.

What is perhaps most surprising to outsiders is the fact that this came about at all. Mr. Jersild is one of the most respected investigative journalists in Denmark, who was making a sober documentary on racism and racist groups. The totalitarian ring of criminalising such reporting should not have escaped the judges as their own constitution for a century and a half had been guaranteeing that "censorship can never be implemented." Instead, the reductio ad absurdum of the constitution had been allowed to explain it as merely as stating formal guidelines for oppression, not a bulwark against it.

Also, even the Danish tradition of deference is taken to extremes in this case. As shown above, The Folk Thing (Parliament) had not wanted the freedom of the press restricted and Parliamentary debate did not seem to focus on either the best reading of the constitution, nor the Necessary Standard of the European Convention.

Indeed, the Supreme Court could have retained its reputation, had it stated that: 'prosecuting incidental furtherance of racist slurs is not clearly shown to be inherent in the best reading of the provision and the Folk Thing has not clearly expressed that it has considered it to be necessary in a ... society to ban these types of 'second hand' or collaborative transgressions by the press.'

Thereby, the Court could have in real terms deferred to the elected lawmakers. However, as explained earlier, the drafting of legislation by agencies and experts, the 'instant review' performed by the secretariat to the Speaker of Parliament, and subsequent agency interpretation all work to hinder the legislators in performing this role, but so much more reason for the Supreme Court to assume a democracy enhancing role and insist on proper democratic procedures to be followed before even considering the curbing of any freedom.

Instead, the Danish Supreme Court had to be lectured by Judges from the old Soviet Bloc on how important the freedom of the press is and how criminalising of incidental furtherance of unlawful slurs is not "necessary ..."

Bladet Tromsø v. Norway (ECHR 1999) concerned another restriction of the press. The local paper in the city of Tromsø, Bladet Tromsø, decided to investigate the seal hunt off the coast of Norway. For this purpose it printed stories from Odd F. Lindberg, a free lance reporter, who had not previously been critical of the seal hunt, had applied to become a seal hunt inspector issuing a report and had also used this position to conduct a number of interviews. The paper printed several anonymous interviews that suggested that although basically a sound industry its practice "provided Greenpeace with good argument" as many hunters apparently caused "unnecessary suffering" that gave cause more inspections to ensure compliance with regulations. Defamation cases were brought against the paper, and a district court found several statements to be defamatory, unlawful and not proven to be true.

The ECHR Court found that there was an overall balance of reporting as the paper "published almost on a daily basis the different points of view, including the newspaper's own comments, those of the Ministry of Fisheries, the Norwegian Sailors' Federation, Greenpeace and, above all, the seal hunters." The Court recounted *Jersild* and the need for each country to find its own way "depending among other things on the medium in question." However, this is subject to scrutiny by the ECHR Court and the "most careful scrutiny on the part of the Court is called for when, as in the present case, the measures taken or sanctions imposed by the national authority are capable of discouraging the participation of the press in debates over matters of legitimate public concern." The Court found the paper to act in good faith and that the paper "could reasonably rely on the official Lindberg report, without being required to carry out its own research into the accuracy of the facts reported." The crew members' conducting the hunt had an "undoubted interest in protecting their reputation" but this could not "outweigh the vital public interest in ensuring an informed public debate over a matter of local, national as well as international interest." Thus the interference by libel law was protecting 'the rights of others' according to Art. 10(2) but as applied the restrictions on the press were not "necessary in a democratic society."

The case shows the difficulty the West Nordics have in dealing with the balancing tests of the ECHR provisions, rather lopsidedly applying the letter of law when it comes to libel and other restrictions of the press and not counterweighing the right to report and receive information that in some cases may override the generally legitimate restrictions. The case probably demonstrates the filters that have hindered Scandinavian lawyers in implementing and using the substantive freedom of the press.

The case **Bergens Tidende v. Norway** (ECHR 2000) is analysed in the Mechanics section. The case emphasises the perhaps surprising restraint that the Nordic countries have laid on the freedom of the press. May people, not least those in public office or administration, might find themselves scrutinised, but if you as a private citizen hint that other people's behaviour borders on criminal behaviour, the West-Nordic justice system will make sure the messenger is killed unless he has cast-iron proof. In this case the reporting of genuine suffering by plastic urgent patients was judged libellous as being hurtful to his business.

The ECHR Court unanimously held that there had been a violation of Art. 10, as "the Court cannot find that the undoubted interest of Dr R. in protecting his professional reputation was sufficient to outweigh the important public interest in the freedom of the press to impart information on matters of legitimate public concern. In short, the reasons relied on by the respondent State, although relevant, are not sufficient to show that the interference complained of was "necessary in a democratic society." The Court considers that there was no reasonable relationship of proportionality between the restrictions placed by the measures applied by the Supreme Court on the applicants' right to freedom of expression and the legitimate aim pursued.

Recent Review

Fair Trial Cases

Siglfirðingur v. Iceland (ECHR 2000) concerned the Icelandic Labour Court, an arrangement similar to that of the other Scandinavian countries where certain questions of labour law are the exclusive province of a Labour Court than ensures fast and specialised adjudication. However, this procedure involves only one instance with no appeal and the company in question alleged this to be a violation of fair trial.

Before the case could be decided, Iceland had settled the case, paying compensation for legal costs and loss of opportunity, in addition to promising to pursue an amendment to the law "which provides for the possibility to have decisions of the Labour Court concerning fines reviewed by the Supreme Court."

The case shows the impact of ECHR law as quasi-federal; the Member States amend their laws not a result of national discourse but in anticipation of being pre-empted from above. However, the case appears not to have impeached the other West-Nordic countries, so the question remains whether the special Nordic labour law tribunal procedures would be set-aside by the ECHR court.

Orr v. Norway (ECHR 2008) concerned the kind of double jeopardy cases that Norway has seen so many of and have been analysed to impressive levels of detail and sophistication. The applicant was a pilot who was alleged to have raped a fellow crew member on a required stop-over in Oslo. The facts were difficult to assess and ultimately Orr was acquitted by jury verdict on appeal but the professional judges found against him in the concurrent civil case. Orr found this to violate his presumption of innocence as he was criminally acquitted but still judged liable on the same facts.

The ECHR Court found in line with precedent that the issue of compensation could rightfully be pursued in the same proceedings as the criminal case, even using different burdens of proof. However, the Court found that the Norwegian High Court had based its findings on "a description of the facts giving details of such matters as the nature of the sexual contact, the applicant's awareness of the absence of consent... the degree of "violence" ("*vold*") used by him to accomplish the act and his intent in this respect. In other words, it covered practically all those constitutive elements, objective as well as subjective, that would normally amount to the criminal offence of rape." Thus the ruling by the professional judges effectively did "set aside" and "cast doubt on the correctness of the acquittal." Accordingly the rights to fair trial were violated.

The case demonstrates how the finer points of the fair trial provision are being sorted out by case law. Far from being what Nordic lawyers at first saw as a 'directive to legislator' to consider fairness in procedure provisions, Art. 6 ECHR has very specific meaning, including a ban on the professional judges impeaching the jury verdict by stating that all the elements of crime were present, when the jury found otherwise. Likewise, the case shows how the Norwegians are more likely to raise issues thus 'fine tuning' case law both because of the longer and more extensive experience with case law and also because the Norwegian opinions are more extensive and thus leave themselves more open to scrutiny.

A. and E Riis v. Norway (ECHR 2008), which had been dismissed earlier, dealt with prolonged bankruptcy proceedings. Certain companies had declared insolvency in 1975 and from 1990 the applicants had tried to sue the State for damages for allegedly caused by the Ministry of Finance hindering the proceedings. The complicated matter lingered until 2006 when it was dismissed.

The ECHR Court explained its case law as to reasonable time "with reference to the following criteria: the complexity of the case, the conduct of the applicants and the relevant authorities and what was at stake for the applicants in the dispute." The Court found itself in chartered territory, stating that it had "frequently found violations [in cases similar to this one]." The Court further found that the Government had not put forward arguments that could persuade it differently, emphasising culpable circumstance especially several periods of inactivity due to lack of diligence on part of the national courts as well as the total duration of sixteen years. The Court added that the first applicants contribution to the length of proceedings "could not absolve the authorities of the respondent State from their oblgation under Article 6 § 1 to ensure that the proceedings be concluded within a reasonable time."

The case probably indicates a common feature of Nordic law, namely allowing the parties to drag out their own case if they want to. The ECHR Court has just decided differently, namely that there is a duty to move cases along independently of obstruction, incompetence or idiosyncracies of the parties themselves. The most interesting aspect is probably that the ECHR Court found the case so straightforward and the point of law so settled in practice, and yet that information had not seeped through to the national courts. Thus this probably indicates the kind of filters that hinder the realisation of applicable quasi-federal norms.

Haslund v. Denmark (ECHR 2009) and *Moesgaard Petersen v. Denmark* (ECHR 2009) both similarly considered very complicated proceedings in some of the many so-called 'tax asset stripping cases.' These cases involved a very complex series of transactions that ultimately defrauded the revenue service of due taxes. In these particular cases, proceedings ran from 1994 until 2006 when Supreme Court review was finally denied.

The points of ECHR law were largely similar as in the previous cases mentioned. However, the ECHR Court particularly noticed that "after more than nine years of criminal proceedings, it took the Leave to Appeal Board approximately one year and eight months to decide [whether to grant appeal, the main reason being that the case lay dormant by mistake for eight months."

The case probably did not settle any great points of law but reached rather predictable conclusions. The case pointed to later cases on the lack of national remedies required by the 'effective remedy clause' in Art. 13 to deal with obvious instances of violations of the ECHR.

Nielsen v. Denmark (ECHR 2009) was likewise one of the complex tax fraud cases by way of tax asset stripping. The ECHR Court particularly pointed out that the case was pending before the High Court from 1997 to 2008, which "does appear excessive" with particular reference to the very lengthy periods used to try finding settlements and the time lost due to re-scheduling. The Court emphasised that the High Court "had authority and the obligation to monitor the progress of the proceedings and to ensure that they were not delayed."

The case may fine tune some points of law – as to settlement negotiations and re-scheduling – but mostly it shows the inability of Danish courts to absorb and apply ECHR case law.

The case *Valentin v. Denmark* (ECHR 2009) dealt with this issue of national remedies directly. The applicant had significant assets tied up in companies that entered bankruptcy proceedings in 1988 and lasted until 2005 when it was concluded that all creditors had been satisfied, handing over the rest to the applicant minus costs. Valentine alleged this violated his rights under Art. 6 and 13.

The Court found that proceedings lasting over seventeen years were excessive – even though they were "complex and time-consuming" and even that "it does not appear that unjustified delays as such occurred." The Court used more space to deal with the issue of remedies, noting that at the relevant time no Danish provisions were "specifically designed or developed to provide a remedy in respect of complaints of length of bankruptcy court proceedings." It thus found violations of both fair trial and effective remedy clauses of the ECHR provisions as well as the property clause of Protocol 1.

The case demonstrated how the ECHR includes a duty to find and follow case law and implement it either by statute or domestic case law – law *designed or developed* to fit.

Christensen v. Denmark (ECHR 2009) revisited the issue raised in *A v. Denmark* (ECHR 1996), the haemophiliac case, namely the long time factual discovery takes in some Danish cases. The alleged malpractice happened in 1992, administrative appeals took from 1993 to 2000, and court cases from 1995 to 2006, with substantial time being used by Christensen to formulate questions and frequent changes of council, finally the Supreme Court upheld the lower courts' and boards decisions against Christensen.

The Court noticed that the case had been pending in both national High Court and Supreme Court for periods of seven and three years respectively and although the Medico-Legal Board was quick to respond to the many questions and much delay was caused by the applicant, the overall time used was "excessive for two judicial instances in such a case." Thus Art. 6 was breached and the Court examined Art. 13, reminding that it "guarantees the availability at national level of a remedy to enforce the substance of the Convention rights and freedoms in whatever form they may happen to be secured in the domestic legal order." The Court then found Danish procedures for reviewing and compensation people for breach of the reasonable time requirement to be lacking, for instance the High Court could only take into account the time "until the passing og its judgement, as opposed to the total length of the proceedings in the present case, " adding that "the Government has not submitted any domestic case law or in any other way proved that the applicant in such circumstances had an effective remedy before the Supreme Court." Thus it followed that there had been also a violation of Art. 13.

The case shows the friction between the 'letter of the law' and one-dimensional approach of the Nordic lawyers and the 'spirit of the law' multi-dimensional method of the European lawyers. The Danish system sticks to applying the individual provisions and does not implement overarching ECHR provisions on length of proceedings and available remedies through case law as the ECHR Courts expects it. The phrase "domestic case law" sums up the difference, as the usual Danish phrase would be 'court practice' indicating usage of law already prescribed by parliament, whereas case law implies the more infrequently used Danish phrase 'judge made law' ("dommerskabt ret" as opposed to "retspraksis"). Likewise the many references to "national" and "domestic" issues in the case are reminders that we are dealing with an effectively quasi-federal system where it falls upon all layers of government to implement the federal principles, not awaiting implementation by parliament.

Freedom of Expression and Association Cases

In *Sørensen v. Denmark* (ECHR 2006), the peculiar West-Nordic labour law system again came under review, this time the aspect of freedom of association.

The two cases of Morten Sørensen and Ove Rasmussen were joined. The former applicant was a young man just about to embark on his university studies when he applied for a temporary job with the Danish co-operative movement as shop assistant. He was informed when applying that he would be required to join SID, one of the unions forming the Danish National Labour Federation know by the acronym LO. The Latter was employed in the gardening sector and resigned the Union SID (member of LO) as he disagreed with its political views and support of certain political causes. Both men were terminated without notice and without pay as they respectively refused to join and (again) resigned union membership. Both men wanted to join other unions than the

Both cases were pursued in national courts. Sørensen alleged that the relevant Danish statute, which provided that an employer could condition employment on union membership, violated Article 11 ECHR in a suit against his employer.

The Western High Court heard the case and found that Sørensen was aware that SID membership was a condition for his employment and that when he did not comply with this, "the conditions for dismissing him are fulfilled in accordance with [the Protection against Dismissal due to Association Membership statute]." Domestic law was thus clear, Sørensen could be dismissed; no Basic Law provision or Danish case law was even considered by the High Court.

The Court then addressed "the pertinent question [whether the Act is] at variance with Article 11 [ECHR] in the light of the interpretation this Article has been given by the Court of Human Rights in its recent case-law." The High Court then cited "the British Rail judgment (*Young, James and Webster v. the United Kingdom*, Series A no. 44)" (this citation includes 'nickname' and report number as West-Nordic lawyers traditionally dislike party names and traditionally prefer report page numbers or 'nicknames'). The High court read *Young v. UK* as establishing that "in certain circumstances Article 11 also secured the negative right to freedom of association." When finding out these circumstances, the High Court opined that "the starting point must be taken from the Act of 1992 incorporating the [ECHR]. According to the preparatory notes, incorporation of the Convention was not intended to change the existing balance between the Danish Parliament and the Danish courts." From this starting point, the Court deduced that "Parliament still has considerable discretion when laying down Danish law," adding ominously that "abolishing or limiting [the closed-shop] will have far-reaching consequences" for the Danish labour market. Though its attitude was already clear, the High Court further considered *Sigurjónsson v. Iceland* and *Gustafsson v. Sweden* relied on by Sørensen. Though the said cases had detailed reasoning on comparative points, "in the view of the High Court an interpretation of these judgments does not establish with the necessary certainty that [section 2 (2) of the Act] is at variance with Article 11 of the Convention."

On appeal, the Danish Supreme Court upheld the judgement and opined that the said statute "was passed notably in order to comply with the negative right to freedom of association to the extent that such an obligation could be established according to the interpretation of Article 11 of the Convention given by the Court of Human Rights in the *Young, James and Webster v. the UK* judgment, Series A no. 44 (British Rail)." The Supreme Court then restated this doctrine by citing its own resent case noting that "the latest judgments of the [ECHR Court] provide no grounds for a different assessment of the lawfulness of closed-shop agreements from that appearing in the British Rail judgment."

As to the second applicant Rasmussen, his case and that of his co-plaintiff Jensen was decided by the Supreme Court that found for Jensen but against Rasmussen. In that judgement, the Supreme Court tried to distinguish the suit at issue from ECHR case law by opining that, "[*Young v. UK*] did not decide on closed-shop agreements as such, but only on its effect on the three applicants. [In *Sigurjónsson v. Iceland*,] there was no duty to join the association when Sigurjónsson obtained his taxi licence as the original requirement to do so lacked a legal basis."

Sørensen v. Denmark provides great insight into the changing constitution of Denmark and the imminent paradigm shift in legal reasoning. The very particular statute on Protection against Dismissal due to Association Membership in issue in the case is itself the reaction of a statutory system of law to the higher norms emanating from a case law based system. Like its reaction to EU case law, Denmark's reaction to ECHR case law is to enact statutory law rather than simply letting the Danish courts rely on ECHR case law. This could be seen as a sign of sophistication as the Danes try to react to ECHR case law and distinguish the judgments; likewise, the loss at the ECHR Court may be viewed as somewhat deliberate given the Government's efforts to achieve greater 'negative freedom' by statute. However, the sophistication seems lacking when these issues reach the High and Supreme Courts as their opinions do to reveal a very perspicacious or discerning approach.

Rather than assessing the distinctions made by the Government and considering central reasoning from the obviously relevant ECHR cases, the Danish Courts refer to national preparatory works both on the general implementation of the ECHR into national law and the statute in issue. Without any written reasoning at all, the courts simply present their 'assessment,' the statute is compatible with the ECHR because it says so and because a 'consideration of the totality of the circumstances' leads to the same conclusion. Unlike its Norwegian counterparts, the Danish courts try to fit the ECHR case law into Danish reasoning were assessment is transcendental. The ECHR cases are quoted by a given nickname and by report page and, seemingly, only reluctantly by party names, their limitations emphasised and their reasoning left un-discussed and undistinguished.

To wit, the Danish courts could have shielded Denmark from the wrath of the ECHR Court by deciding that termination for 'known prior union requirement' was lawful but only by given notice and paying redundancy pay for a normal period of discretionary termination. Alternatively, the Danish courts could have said that in light of the ECHR, any union membership would satisfy the employer's requirement. Furthermore, the Danish Courts could have anticipated the ECHR ruling themselves and given a verdict stating that Denmark was in probable violation and either decide to find for the plaintiffs or still find for their employers but indicating that the plaintiffs had cause for action to obtain damages from the government for its breach. At the same time, the courts could have hinted the need for amendment of the 'protection statute.'

Vörður Ólafsson v. Iceland (ECHR 2010) concerned again the negative aspect of freedom of association as Iceland forced all industries in Iceland to contribute to the activities of the Federation of Icelandic Industries through an Industry Charge. Ólafsson was a member of the builders' association but not of the federation and alleged that he and other non-members were left with too little influence as to the use of the charge, in effect forcing him to contribute to an association that he wished not to joined thus infringing his right not to join a particular organization.

The State argued that there was "a fundamental difference between the situation at issue in the present case and that in previous judgements of the Court concerning the *negative* aspects of the freedom of association, notably [*Young, Sigurjónsson* and *Sørensen*, a refusal to pay would not have led to his loosing employment or livelihood. What was involved was only a tax, not a membership fee."

The Court found that "in the present case the applicant was obliged by statute financially to support a private law organisation that was not one of his choosing." Although the contribution was "modest from an individual point of view, the systematic, extensive and continuous character of the Industry Charge scheme gave it a considerable impact" as no fewer than 10,000 entities were obliged to support an organisation with little more than 1,100 members, providing "the greater part of its funds." The Court also read the relevant ILO conventions differently than the Government and concluded "that the statutory obligation on the applicant to pay the Industry Charge impinged on the applicant's freedom of choice in his pursuit of his occupational interest as a trade union member." Thus Iceland had again breeched Art. 11.

The case highlights the rather crude an one-dimensional Icelandic approach to assessment that Icelandic law has more in common with the Danish than with the Norwegian tradition. The need to balance the negative and positive urges to associate should have been clear from ECHR case law on West-Nordic instances of forced association from *Sigurjónsson* to *Sørensen* as well as cases like the Swedish *Gustafsson* case that showed a much more nuanced understanding of the balancing act of the freedoms of various actors.

TV Vest AS & Rogaland Pensjonistparti v. Norway (ECHR 2008) tested the case that we analysed in the Norwegian section, where the facts and judgements below can be seen. The Pensioners' Party of the Rogaland region of Norway had paid for a short portrayal of the party on local TV to make its case as an alternative to the incumbent political parties. This fell contravened a blanket ban on political content in television advertising in Norway.

The ECHR court summed up its case law, including *Jersild* yet again and then applied its principles to the case. The Court noted that the "prohibition was permanent and absolute and applied only to television, whilst political advertising through all other media was permitted." Further, the Court found that "the content of the speech in question was indisputably of a political nature [and] the impugned advertisement obviously fell outside the commercial context of product marketing, an area in which States traditionally have enjoyed a wide margin of appreciation." Added to that "there is nothing to suggest that the advertisements included any content that might be liable to offend intimate personal convictions within the sphere of morals or religion." Having establishes that this was non-offensive political material that could have been spread through other media, the Court was "unable to share the opinion held by the Supreme Court's majority that the present case was more akin to *Murphy* [powerful effects of audio-visual media] than *Vgt* [strict margin of appreciation in case of political parties]... as the case under consideration is distinguishable from that of Murphy" Thus the Court decided which case was more to the point, because in a system of dynamic case law finding the case-in-point is crucial. Consequently, the ECHR Court "[agreed] with the minority (see paragraphs 80-81 of the Supreme Court's judgment, cited at paragraph 21 above) that the political nature of the advertisements that were prohibited calls for strict scrutiny on the part of the Court and a correspondingly circumscribed national margin of appreciation with regard to the necessity of the restrictions." There was a basis for guidelines to be found as "regulation of the right to vote and the right to stand for election may justify [rules.] However, while it is true that the broadcasts at issue had been aired [in the run-up to the local and regional elections that year, it should be noted that the advertising ban [was absolute and permanent and did not apply specifically to elections]." As the State had made no proportional intervention, no balancing of speech and justification for regulation, the Court found a violation of Art. 10. Norway and several intervening parties had urged that there was no alternative to a general ban but the Court found that "there was not, in the Court's view, a reasonable relationship of proportionality between the legitimate aim pursued by the prohibition on political advertising and the means deployed to achieve that aim. The restriction which the prohibition and the imposition of the fine entailed on the applicants' exercise of their freedom of expression cannot therefore be regarded as having been necessary in a democratic society."

The case further underscores the dynamic case law of the ECHR – complete with the language of the common law tradition of finding 'cases-in-point' and 'distinguishing' earlier cases. The blanket ban seems rather inexplicable given that political parties using enormous amounts on advertising in newspapers, posters, direct mail etc., alternatively allowing local political TV ads but limiting them around election time would rather obviously have been a more proportional approach but the balancing tests derived from ECHR case law have some time sinking in to the West-Nordic consciousness.

The two cases of *Erla Hlynsdóttir v. Iceland* (ECHR 2012) and *Björk Eiðsdóttir v. Iceland* (ECHR 2012) demonstrated again the particular West-Nordic approach to libel law. The stubborn idea is that there is no "material" or substantive freedom of expression that people can be "answerable to the courts" for anything they say if outlawed and further that there is a general assumption that general libel includes all public suggestion that someone has done something wrongful in the course of their profession that might adversely affect them.

Thus the two journalists Erla and Björk were both charged for exploring the red light district of Reykjavík, reporting allegations that the so-called champagne gentleman's clubs, which supposedly sold champagne and entirely innocent interaction with scantily clad ladies, were hiding illicit gangster activities such as human trafficking, prostitution and coercion. The less than robust attitude to public discourse on such matters is seen from the fact that the two journalists were mentioned by name whereas the two putative gangsters supposedly feuding in the "Strip Kings Battle" were 'anonymised' to A and Y. Mr. B was able to bring proceedings for general "defamation" and having certain remarks declared "null and void." The district court found that referenced in the reporting to the Lithuanian mafia were defamatory innuendo and should be declared null and void, as well as fining her heavily. Appeal to the Supreme Court was denied as the matter was of too insignificant monetary value and no special circumstances warranting an exception.

The ECHR Court found occasion to lecture on ECHR case law, quoting rather extensively and citing numerous cases. Among those cases cited was Bergens Tidende as to the issue of "their common sting" i.e. that the main point of the article was not alleging mafia activity but reporting on the general issue of the champagne clubs, including the allegations may be credible sources that organised crime was involved in crimes committed in this context, although not specifically concluding on Mr. A's role in this. The Court particularly was "not persuaded by the Government's argument that the "subject-matter" of the applicant's article and the impugned statements did not concern an important social issue [and contribution to the ongoing debate]. Likewise, the Court cited Jersild on the importance of interview as "one of the most important means whereby the press is able to play its vital role of "public watchdog."" In this case, the Court said, "the applicant journalist cannot be criticised for having failed to ascertain the truth of the disputed allegations [as she] acted in good faith, consistently with the diligence expected of a responsible journalist reporting on a matter of public interest." Thus the Court found both that the reason relied on were insufficient "even assuming that they were relevant" and that "there was no relationship of proportionality between measures applied [and the aim pursued]."

The Cases demonstrate the function of the filters created by legal writings. The preparatory works of the Icelandic accession law notwithstanding, Iceland has subscribed to a regime that requires all restriction on expression to be manifestly necessary with the assumption created in case law that the press has particular freedom to raise issues and even with impunity report on allegations by third parties that in of themselves would be wrongful it the issue raised is of public concern and the reporting as balanced and fair. The effect of the prevailing legal ideology even hindered an appeal of this case that obviously raises ECHR issues.

Property Rights Cases

The above mentioned *Valentin v. Denmark* (ECHR 2009) also dealt with property rights, as the issue was raised that the prolonged proceedings hindered the peaceful enjoyment of the assets involved. The Court found that the long procedure to have violated the free enjoyment of property.

The Case demonstrates that national lawyers need to adjust their own traditional view and reading of constitutional clauses to ECHR points of view. Protection of property clauses may be viewed as mostly dealing with expropriation but the ECHR protection in Protocol 1is wider, even including at right not to be hindered by excessive government procedures.

Lindheim and others v. Norway (ECHR 2012) dealt with other aspects of the Norwegian plot or ground lease statute than those that we saw challenged as to church land in the Norwegian section. The rights of the lessees were strengthened by an amendment, enacted with overwhelming majority, which granted a right to extend leases on the same conditions as previously and without limitation in time. This was challenged based on the retroactivity and property clauses (§§ 97 and 100) of the Norwegian Basic Law. The Norwegian Supreme Court upheld the law and also held as to the ECHR property clause (Protocol 1, Art. 1) that there was precedent in an earlier case *James and others v. UK* (ECHR 1986) that granted certain rights to the detriment of the landowner that were upheld as being in pursuance of legitimate social, economic or other policies.

The ECHR Court, on the other hand, found that no "specific assessment was made of whether the [amendment] regulating the extension of the type of ground lease contract [at issue] achieved a "fair balance" between the interests of the lessor [and] those of the lessee." This lopsided approach to the rights of the two groups was so stark that the court was "struck by the particularly low level of rent... bearing no relation to the actual value of the land." Although to some extent there was hardship that warranted protection of lessees, there seemed to be "no general interest" that was "sufficiently strong to justify such low level of rent" and the amendment anyway "had a much wider reach than merely addressing situations of potential financial hardship and social injustice." Moreover, the Court added, there would be no "possibility of upward adjustment in the light of factors other than the consumer price index [excluding] value of land as a relevant factor." Indeed, the lessee could sell his house and increase in the value of the lessor's land would only "accrue to the lessee." By contrast, if the lessor were to sell, "the price would reflect the low rent that would be kept at a low level indefinitely." The Court concluded that there was not a "fair distribution of the social and financial burden involved but, rather, that the burden was placed solely on the [lessor]."

The ECHR Court directly responded to the Norwegian Supreme Court's assessment of ECHR law, stating that "it is unable to share [the] starting point for this assessment," namely whether the inability of the lessor to regulate the rent upwards to reflect "the actual land value" contravened the Convention. This was a plainly wrongful reading of the provision that did more than diverge from actual value, it "in effect prohibited any rent increase" beyond the consumer price index. As to the case of James *and others v. UK* the Court corrected the Norwegians by finding that "that judgement dealt with a situation which in many respects was different from that at issue in the instant case," and the ECHR Court itself had "regard also to several more recent rulings referred to from its case-law, representing jurisprudential developments in the direction of a stronger protection under Article 1 of Protocol No. 1." Thus, the ECHR Court found a violation of the property clause.

However, the Court did more than find an individual violation. The Court added that Art. 46 ECHR was applicable as "the problem underlying the violation [of property] concerns the legislation itself and that its findings extend beyond the sole interest [in] the instant case." The Court added that "This is a case where the Court considers that the respondent State should take appropriate legislative and/or other general measures to secure in its domestic legal order a mechanism which will ensure a fair balance between the interests of lessors on the one hand, and the general interests of the community on the other hand, in accordance with the principles of protection of property rights under the Convention. It is not for the Court to specify how lessors' interests should be balanced against the other interests at stake. The Court has already identified the main shortcomings in the current legislation [the State remains free to choose the means by which it will discharge its obligations arising from the execution of the Court's judgment]."

The case shows the first West-Nordic instance of a clear striking down of an entire law, remanding the question to the national legislature for 'executing the Court's judgement.' This, of course, reflects what Kelsen and others foretold that a court with constitutional review powers logically would turn into a quasi-legislative body, very much 'changing the existing balance between parliaments and courts.' Some will deplore this development, even deny its existence, others will rejoice in the protection of rights. The most important observation in terms of legal science and methodology is to ask why the West-Nordic lawyers did not see this one coming and what took them so long to effectively make use of the normative constitutional properties of the ECHR and the powers of the ECHR Court to decide the interpretation of the

Convention through 'jurisprudential developments in the direction of a stronger protection' – a development that requires cases and controversies placed before it and the operative tools of the case law method.

The ECHR Court turned out to be all but unemployed.

Legal Reasoning
and West-Nordic Review

The dividing line in Western Law is often said to be that of the Continental *civil law* tradition and the Anglo-American *common law* tradition. The principle differences are certainly there but there is no clear dichotomy dividing all law into two neat categories. As we have seen, the civil law jurisdictions deal with statutory law, codifications, Roman law maxims and other features supposedly hallmarks of civil law. Likewise, the precedent used in French constitutional law, restrictive dynamics of Scandinavian constitutional law and vast areas of law still not codified but covered by *judgemade law* and *legal principles*, all suggested as properties of common law. The two great quasi-federal creations of the last half century, EU law and ECHT law both necessarily amalgamate the two traditions and bridge the gap anyhow. In this context, Nordic law and its way of reasoning in hard or complex cases may be difficult to categorise as either civil or common. Perhaps it was for a long time closer to the codifying tradition of the continent but developed its own third-way tradition that became a "legal thinking that is more *pragmatic*,"[1] a "*way of thinking* [that combines] a cautious form of judicial review and constitutionalism with popular sovereignty and (limited) supremacy of Parliament."[2] This might have been so but at times Nordic law has had its share of formalism[3] especially through the statutory positivists and conceptualist thinking.

However, the pragmatism for West-Nordic law in particular may stem from its nature as an academic study of law actually enacted and practised in the region. This was established by Anders Sandø Ørsted who in addition to academia served as cabinet minister, member of constitutional conference, civil servant, and Supreme Court judge. His works written in Danish on Danish commonwealth law were intended for teaching the law as it stood. This was a change from studying Roman law, Natural Law, and, earlier, Canon

1. Husa (2002) 174.
2. Ibid. at 185.
3. See Blandhol (2002).

law; now Danish law was seen as something worth studying as such. The elite would still be taught Latin and Roman law for their valued academic properties but it became possible to graduate as "Danish layer" only studying Danish sources. In time the purely national teaching of law took over and in my own time at Copenhagen University, the study consisted mostly of 'dogmatic courses' determining 'valid law' from Danish sources.

Using a phrase coined by notable Icelandic jurist Sigurður Líndal, perhaps Nordic university law became too much the teaching of *lögtækni* rather than *lögfræði* – the teaching of legal technique rather than legal wisdom, churning out too many lawyers and too few jurists. Not to say that legal techniques, the trade school aspect if you will, is not important but rather that analysis and adaptation hinge on reflection and realism that in turn require the wisdom, philosophy and comparative outlook that flows from studying more than the black letter law simply restated.

What this survey reveals is a perhaps most of all the result of missing contemplation, namely a lack of self-awareness of conflicting dynamics, of the rise and fall and rise of *rights* as trumps on legislation, of the rise and fall and rise of *justice* as an ideal that means that judges openly state that the legal system has to make sense, refuting the 'tongue of the law' approach of statutory positivism whether as a ideal of clarity or the ideology of the 20th century technocrat, clearing the way for all assessment to be made by specialist agencies and mandated central administration, not generalist judges or representative juries. This lack of self-awareness has made West-Nordic law miss out on opportunities, reflected responses – as well as the proper teaching of the techniques of the trade, given that your jurisdiction is now a part of a human rights quasi-federation, given that your jurisdiction is now part of a quasi-federal trade block, given that rights and other trumping concepts are in play domestically.

It seems that studying law the way we do, we pick up the narrow dogmatic state of the contracts, administrative law, etc., etc. Including rather early on in the five year studies a rather un-reflected view of constitutional law as 'the three branches of government, the freedom-rights provided, and a number of strange legalistic points, like whether the present calendar can be amended as the Danish Basic Law mentions days of the week. Such questions have certain analytic qualities but writings of Henrik Zahle on restrictive dynamics, peaceful pluralism, polycentric sources of law, legal philosophy and legal research should have been taught rather than his musings on the calendar and much more narrow chapters on issues like judicial review in his standard text book on Danish Constitutional law.[4]

Legal reasoning in the West-Nordic countries has been so restrained that much needed reinterpretation and fresh inquiries into valid sources of law have been frowned upon and sometimes appear as *'retspolitiske betragtninger'* – literally legal-political considerations when they should be framed as critical analysis. Pointing out for instance that Nordic courts are ignoring ECHR law should not be framed as 'legal-political' urging for the legalistic solution of bringing legislation in line with ECHR law, it should be the basis for bringing your suit to Strassbourg or arguing your case better in Copenhagen, Oslo or Reykjavík.

The teaching of constitutional law as national, harmonious, legalistic and current practice described as deducible from the original documents is neither well serving as *legal technique* nor adequate or indeed fulfilling as *legal wisdom*. The result is that most Scandinavian lawyers are utterly unaware of the fact that their constitutional law has changed and is changing continuously. They lack the concepts, methods and encouragement to make the observations and resulting arguments, counterarguments, adjudications or judgements that take this into account. We do not have the separation of power in Scandinavia that they have in the US or other presidential systems – but this is *despite our constitutional language* – any reasonable reader without preconception (from Mars or just legally naive) would guess that Norway and America had very similar constitutional systems, the former with a strong King, the latter with strong President. They are not similar for reasons of constitutional dynamics, including judicial. The Former has weaker judges and individual rights relative to the latter that has weaker agencies. However, the judges and rights of the former have strengthened considerably of late as the country that officially is 'free, independent' has become bound by common quasi-federal constitutional rights provisions and judges lacking the deference that were instilled into Nordic lawyers for a couple of generations.

Is this good or bad? That is mostly for another book. For now, we are where the scientific community was when Columbus set sails. Just appreciating the roundness of the world is a big step, appreciating that you do not fall off but rather travel in circles around the globe opens up your mind to a wholly different paradigm. We need to appreciate the properties of constitutional dynamics, triadic lawmaking, flexible review techniques and all the rest of

---

4. See the various sources by Zahle.

multi-dimensional *new constitutionalism* before more making the choice to forsake it on reflection or perhaps conclude that it is unavoidable.

The old quotation on "Extreme American Teaching"[5] indicated lacking ability to fully understand the great systems of foreign law for the purpose of academic comparative study and gaining the fruits of such comparison.[6] There is greater understanding that West-Nordic constitutional judicial review could have gone either way as indicated by judge Jensen.[7] This appreciation of the indeterminate state has spawned courses on *the reasoning of courts*[8] that did in their way prompt this study as did teaching of law as practical, pragmatic, polycentric and outward looking.[9] However, the teaching of new constitutionalism still faces opposition from those schooled in the old tradition, as Zahle remarked, "anyone basing a claim on the Basic Law, generally, will not be taken seriously"[10] – a truism that will be waning with time.

Reducing important legal tools to nothing has meant that Nordic theory has to insist on various quantum leaps of faith. Most notably, the constitutional reference to 'the King' in the Danish Basic Law is explained as, 'it should be read as 'the Prime Minister.' This is, of course, nonsense; what has happened is that through a constitutional tug-of-war various other bodies and institutions have, based on their sense of justice, purpose and self-interest, usurped the powers of the King. With such important precedents as the appointments of Prime Minister in 1901 and 1920 and the various non-confidence motions, and the devolution to associated lands, the constitutional struggle has lead to new constitutional conventions that act as amendments of the constitution bypassing the formal amendment procedure and not over-ruled by case law. However, without concepts such as *precedent, purpose, justice, constitutional struggle, case law, and convention,* the only available method is the un-historic *'it must be presumed/read.'* Law must include expe-

---

5. Quoted in Koch (2002) 24.
6. Jaako Husa writes *"To my surprise the comparative study of constitutional doctrines appears to be showing more similarities than differences ... there are some common key questions which do seem to puzzle, in constitutional matters, lawyers' and scholars' minds, regardless of national boundaries. The remaining differences, which do exist, seem to be deeply rooted in cultural matters."* Husa (2002) 6.
7. Jensen (1999).
8. The Works of Ole Due and for instance Hjalte Rasmussen *European Community Case Law. Summaries of Leading EC Court Cases* Handelshøjskolens Forlag (1993).
9. Zahle (2005) 331.
10. Zahle (1997) 374.

rience and ways of analysing practise to qualify as a tool of academic and practical relevance.[11]

Among the great errors of constitutional law for a long while has been the proposition that Parliament is 'the supreme Authority in Constitution-Interpretation-Questions.' At best, this is aspirational; it would have been great if the will of the people was distilled in its fine representatives and every generation moulded the constitution for the common good, that constitutional issues were settled by the parliamentary decisions of the lay element. In reality, Parliament does little business in pondering constitutional issues.

Likewise, the immensely important European methodology has been subject to almost off-hand dismissal in leading textbooks on legal method. Professor Stuer Lauridsen called the ECJ's method "a rather unique example of a method, which to an extreme degree interprets [wording based on a wish of effective implementation and is] to an unusual degree political. For instance, it does not use preparatory works ... Seen from a more nuanced viewpoint of interpretation, this is a simplified and free, yes almost primitive form of legal application."[12] Admittedly, the observation is partly accurate but this 'Scandinavian unrealism' fails in pointing out that the European Courts are unaffected by this criticism, that they churn out hundreds of judgements and that the law of land in Denmark, realistically, will be determined by this 'rather unique method' regardless of the supposedly 'nuanced viewpoint' offered by Danish law. This being especially so when Parliaments do not engage in constitutional issues.

Even Norway with its relatively frequent use of constitutional judicial review and reasoned accessible cases has found constitutional debate within the politics conspicuous by its absence. There, "constitutional arguments in daily political work are surprisingly rare and few;" the parliamentary constitutional office is mostly concerned with "the time space between the first and second readings of a Bill;" even the straightforward procedure in the Norwegian Constitution allowing Parliament to submit questions for its opinion is almost never used as "it is assumed that the Supreme Courts would prefer not."[13]

The Danish Member of Parliament Birthe Rønn Hornbech has given an account of what she terms "The Political Madhouse, Tvind."[14] When the law to quash "[basic principle in our rechtstaat on the divisions of power]" was

---

11. Zahle (2005) 11 and from 28.
12. Stuer Lauridsen (1994) 153.
13. Tom Thoresen "Constitutional Arguments in Political Decision-Making: Norway" in *The Constitution as an Instrument of Change* (2003) 75 and 76.
14. Birthe Rønn Hornbech *Så gik der politik i det ...* (1997) from 76.

enacted, 68 of 179 Members of the Folkethinget were not present and of which none of the spokespeople on legal policy of four of the major parties. There was no principled debate in the Folkethinget, everything "was decided beforehand and behind closed doors between [the Minister and spokespeople controlling a majority]."[15] The ministry had failed to prove fraud on part of the Tvind schools and feared that administrative action would result in a number of cases, thus a "legislative solution" was preferable.[16] Several legal experts reacted to the blatant Bill of Attainder; the Speaker, charged with ruling on constitutionality declared himself "generally safe" in relying on the assurances from the Ministry of Justice of constitutionality. The Speaker admitted that "something wrong in hearing [those] proposing the Bill if it's alright" but since the Ministry had issued its opinion, he "could not set aside a Bill." As an alternative procedure, the Speaker favoured a "law council" of yet more experts to ponder constitutionality.[17]

The result, as we know, was that one of the schools won its case to have the Act set aside by the courts in the *Tvind judgement* and the shock of this first example of (almost) ultimate review lead to the conclusion of the case being promulgated in the official legal gazette.[18] Otherwise, only statutes and regulations are promulgated, judgements are the province of private reporting.

The 'Tvind Mad-House' reveals that, regrettably, the choice is not between elected and unelected officials ruling on constitutionality but rather on which bunch of officials and experts and by which procedures. Neither in *Tvind* nor in *Jersild* was it the clear intention of the Folkethinget to take a judicial decision or restrict the press respectively. It was the opinion of unelected lawyers that condemning Tvind and Jersild was called for and permissible; Parliament at best supported orderly school funding and combating racism, at worst was not paying attention. Judicial review may lead to the Supreme Court functioning as a (third) chamber of Parliament[19] but the alternative may be letting the ministries and secretariats function as constitutional courts and legislators.

We have seen that the Danish courts reduced their public reasoning to the near enigmatic for reasons originally relating to the needs of absolutism,[20] later rationalised by tradition and reinforced by legal ideology. Norwegian Courts first followed but were forced to go public with their reasoning and

---

15. Ibid. 76-77.
16. Ibid. 79.
17. Ibid. 80-81.
18. Bkg. nr. 137 of 15 March 1999. Lovtidende.
19. Shapiro and Stone Sweet (2002a) 207.
20. Jensen (1999).

then developed a clear alternative to the Danish way. Iceland stayed much closer to the Danish role model of stating what is "absolutely necessary."[21] However, they all appear to have shared an ideology of deference to the political branches that is slowly being replaced by increased scrutiny and reasoning on issues relating to their own constitutional position, to some rights, and especially to the quasi-federal constitutional formations.

Still, we are some way away from judgements explaining the law with "principle and clarity."[22] Even Danish cases like Tvind are presented as extensive narrative and terse logic for legal reasoning. Norwegian cases may have longer reasoning but much narrative is mixed up in it with likewise terse and deferring reasoning. The main source of change in reasoning is unlikely to be the change in academia, as the impact of Smith, Zahle or Høilund is probably somewhat delayed by the time it takes their students to reach the Supreme Court. The main impetuous is quasi-federal; the prospect of being reviewed by the European courts is controlling aspects of jurisprudence in Nordic courts.[23] The "State has a duty to ensure and protect these rights. Lawgiver has in particular a duty to protect the individual's freedom against intrusion from a third party."[24] For all practical purposes, federalism is upon us. We may qualify it as quasi-federal or insist on it being international but for the time being serious resistance to the European courts is limited to "rather theoretical situations."[25] We are seeing "certain deep transformations in

---

21. Ragnhildur Helgadóttir writes, "*Icelandic Supreme Court decisions are, like their Danish counterparts, extremely brief, often less than a page. The majority of arguments are often omitted and the court states only that which it considers absolutely necessary to reach a conclusion. The very fact that [something is] mentioned is therefore significant.*" Helgadóttir (2006) 144, note 581.

22. Preben Stuer Lauridsen writes, "*[Danish judgements] are to be found on a level where the typical is that the judgement's narrative is considerable, but the legal reasoning is scarce and short, and, although perhaps precise in phrasing, apparently written without the ambition to explain the state of the law in terms of principles and clarity.*" Stuer Lauridsen (1994) 145.

23. Boesen, Steffen "*Højesteret frikender svensk præst for homohetz*" Politiken 29 Nov. 2005, Swedish Justice Johan Munch quoted saying: "We consider it likely that the judgement against reverend Green would not be upheld by the European Court of Human Rights."

24. Rytter (2001) 121.

25. Christensen writes, "*In my opinion there is the necessary basis for surmising that Danish courts are not bound by any future practise of the ECHRC. Such a censorship of the ECHRC's practise will, probably, only be conceivable in very special – an at least for now – rather theoretical situations.*" Christensen (2003)

governance that have resulted from the establishment of enforceable constitutions"[26] in the West-Nordic countries.

Nordic legalism is challenged by European dynamics;[27] Parliament as well as Supreme Court must now convince the ECHR Court that restrictions of freedom are necessary. There are now several 'authorities on constitutional interpretative questions.'

These authorities leave a paper trail of precedent. Tough precedent is a feature of all legal orders;[28] precedent sits awkwardly with Nordic law.[29] When precedents are discussed, the focus always seems to be on the result of the case, the central holding rather than on the reasoning[30] and the law presented as following from text and preparatory works. Because the Nordics are clinging on the formally non-binding nature of precedent, "there is no formal doctrine of *stare decisis* familiar to common law, however, in each of the examined this form of control is practiced, and it occupies a central position within constitutional doctrines and debate."[31]

By contrast, European law today is openly built on the jurisprudence of the ECJ and the ECHR Court as the most impressive modern creation of truly common law. The establishment in precedent of judicial review, supremacy, enforceable rights, and numerous other legal principles have created in short order amazing legal systems.[32] The difference between traditional Nordic law and European common law is similar to the difference between the English and American traditions. The English tradition is very much an oral one whereas the American developed more reliant a written legal arguments and written court opinions that have caused developments in legal reasoning, not only elaboration of facts.[33] The Nordic Courts that focus on the case at hand, deciding it shortly after hearing oral arguments explains the overly narrative style.

---

26. Stone Sweet (2000) vii.
27. Zahle (1997) 362.
28. Shapiro and Stone Sweet (2002c).
29. Stuer Lauridsen (1994) from 143; á Rógvi (2001) from 251.
30. Preben Stuer Lauridsen (in what was at the time the standard text book on legal theory at the university of Copenhagen) writes, "*It is applicable, in usual circumstances, seemingly, to many judges that decisions, which are more than 5-10 years old, under any circumstances, and regardless of the fact that the legal situation has not been changed in legislative sense, will be considered as only slightly usable as precedents.*" Stuer Lauridsen (1994) 146. (vagueness of the text is deliberately maintained).
31. Husa (2002) 22.
32. Stone Sweet and Brunell (2002).
33. Suzanne Ehrenberg "Embracing the Writing-Centered Legal Process" 89 *Iowa Law Review* (2004) 1159.

Danish Court have apparently focused on delivering the judgement expeditiously in ancient times. According to judge Torben Jensen, "Already before 1661 the procedures were marked by elements known today: ... including as quickly as possible judgement by reading aloud the result in a public court meeting."[34] This was further strengthened under the auspices of Attorney General Stampe, the Instruction of 1753 required quick and continuous deliberations and proscribed "influencing" of colleagues. It banned "taking to Adjudication immediate or announced Cases to [Conversation] ... or making Agreements on the Judgement and Outcome of the Case, or if the most Experienced would guide the Younger to bring them into the same Opinion." Astonishingly, "Even until the 1990s, it has been respected that the Justices neither under the preparations nor procedure should discuss the result of the case."[35] Danish Justices are still duty bound not to reveal deliberations, except to the extent that they are allowed to comment on cases in learned articles.[36] In Denmark, appeals are not on the record and not checking and revising the lower judgement.[37]

The European courts are much more reliant on the record of the inferior courts and focused on the legal issues. The Norwegian Supreme Court forms a kind of middle ground. Like the American tradition, the European experience became a writing-centred legal process, probably accidental rather than by design. In typical European style, it was determined that the opinions of individual justices would not be revealed. Thus, the whole court has to agree or at least a majority has to agree sufficiently to agree on the entire reasoning. This might have lead to short opinions but seems instead to have lead to more extensive reasoning than in most European courts. The office of the Advocate General seems also to have helped.[38] He plays in some way the role of the trial court, summing up the facts, and suggesting the legal reasoning as well as result. The interplay between Advocates General and Court has become quite stimulating for the reasoning; deliberation in the Court is starting with an entire written proposal for judgement on the table and thus the discussion can centre on reasoning rather than on summarising facts.

The prejudicial nature of the procedure before the European Court of Justice also helps. Whereas in most courts the prejudicial nature of the abstract reasoning of the court is incidental in nature, the legal reasoning is always of a general

34. Jensen (1999) 16.
35. Ibid. 24 with note 34.
36. Ibid. 25 note 37.
37. Judge Ziegler in Lov & Ret.
38. Stone Sweet and Brunell (2002).

nature in the ECJ. Indeed, the court has pointedly refused to decide the actual outcome of cases. This created a clear distinction of law and fact. The facts of the national case will be neatly summarised by the questioning court, as it wants to get as good an answer as possible, as will the national law applicable, which in relation to EU law in the case before the ECJ is to be regarded as fact as well. The act clear doctrine[39] has further underlined this. Courts are not obliged to seek prejudicial judgement when the abstract reasoning of one prior case can be easily applied to the factual situation of another. Docket control increases the impetuous to write principal judgements, as they will potentially reduce the number of future cases, especially trivial ones.

So, what should the Nordic Courts do? Should we leave the oft-quoted maxim of Cosmus Meyer that "the Supreme Court is not an institution of learning"?[40] Should our courts instead explain the law in wider sense?[41]

Is it then also time to abandon or lessen restrain in review? As pointed out by Eivind Smith, "one part of the electorate votes according to its preferences in certain matters, e.g. abortion, taxation, or EU-membership," and the entire election may be swayed by dramatic or important single issues."[42] Consequently, it is a false argument to say that any statute should trump the Basic Law, most statutes are either passed by prior to the sitting Parliament or enacted by the majority of the present one but outside the core electoral platform, on which it was elected. This further supported by the fact that very often, parliamentary governments are not supported by a majority of the voters.[43] Very rarely do our Supreme Courts face issues that have actually been contested in elections and decided by Parliament accordingly.[44] As unlikely is it that a changing majority will compensate the disproportionately oppressed minority during the last Parliament, as hanging laws of uncompensated expropriation or draconic limitation of the press does not repair the damage done.[45]

The lesson from cases like *Tvind* is that, "the actual "lawgiver" rarely is to be found outside the constitutionally responsible organs. Anyway, when the matter does not have strong political overtones, [the lawgiver is more likely

---

39. Stone Sweet and Brunell (2002).
40. á Rógvi (2001) 253. For a better view Christopher L. Eisgruber "Is the Supreme Court an Educative Institution?" 67 *New York University Law Review* (2004) 961.
41. Eisgruber (2004).
42. Smith (1993) 317.
43. Smith (1993) 320.
44. For an example see Smith (1993) 318.
45. Smith (1993) 317.

found] in the administration or the bigger special interest groups." This does not undermine correctly enacted instruments their status as law, but "gives another reason against attributing political ratifications with a holiness that not even the majority seems to claim."[46] Furthermore, when constitutional review leads to results that a persistent majority wants overturned, the majority may as in *Johansen* try persistently for a 'switch in time' or use the constitutional amendment as "not the courts but the constituting authority has the last word on constitutionality."[47]

The answer is not easy, however. The courts may be equally likely to fall for the temptation to strike down laws to their personal disliking rather than just being "guardians of game rules of democracy."[48] The lessons from our inquiries into the dynamics of judicial review is that the courts are '*damned if they do and damned if they don't*' – there is no easy middle ground.

However, on way would be for the Nordic courts to reverse their aversion to re-interpret the Basic Law provisions in light of their own application of corresponding ECHR provisions.[49] A change in methodology to more openly common law or at least persuasively comparative approach might be ventured.[50] See constitutional review as a process and a discourse[51] and constitutionality as a matter of degree might do the trick with courts, parliaments, citizens, academia, and others refining both constitutions and statutes. Skilfully put, by a judgement, the "ball, one might say, [would be] tossed by the Justices back into the legislators' court, where the political forces of the day

---

46. Ibid. 321.
47. Ibid. 322.
48. Ibid. 327.
49. Christensen (2003) 24.
50. Donald E. III Childress "Using Comparative Constitutional Law to resolve Domestic Federal Questions" 53 *Duke Law Journal* (2003) 193 at 210 writes: "The common law approach to constitutional interpretation produces a flexible approach to decisionmaking. Under this approach, the judge is not constrained by simple text or structure, but has to take into account, as a scientist would, the totally of the evidence in order to render a decision. In this mold, comparative constitutional analysis is appropriate, for it affords the judge an opportunity the law as never definitively given and always to be sought, in the endlessly original process of resolution of individual disputes through law."
51. Tom Ginsburg writes, "*When political conflict becomes too severe, democracy can be trampled by political institutions run amok. By transforming political conflicts into constitutional dialogues, courts can reduce the threat to democracy and allow it to grow. To play this important role of contributing to democratic stability and deliberation, courts must develop their own power over time.*" Ginsburg (2003).

could operate."[52] In the words of Eivind Smith, "alternative ways to solve conflicts has great principled importance in well functioning societies."[53]

However, this survey was from the outset meant to avoid making normative statements as to how the law should be rather than what it is. As one last reminder of the dangers of normative theory, consider the development of Danish theory on judicial review. As we saw, the constitutional convention of 1848 could not agree on the issue. In 1869, the national-liberal professor of constitutional law, C. G. Holck, wrote in his textbook that the courts had no power to perform constitutional judicial review. When the conservative H. Matzen took the chair, he explained that constitutional judicial review followed from "the whole constitutional system" and "the principle the rechtstaat." Based on this, J. P. Christensen opines that: "with all due respect – it must be assumed that Matzen's style of interpretation was also born by his undoubtedly well developed political eye for the conservative guarantees provided by judicial review against the all too advancing forces of reform."[54]

Since then, Nordic legal writings for a long while claimed to be a peculiar brand of realism that may have been convenient as favourable to the Welfare State.[55] Today, the Welfare State is arguably as strong as ever and a common denominator for all political parties. Therefore, opposition to legally enforceable constitutions may be practised by 'rump-realists' that continue to apply rigorous realist analysis "without clear intentions to be legal realists."[56]

A return to legal pragmatism may, therefore, be the best advice. Legal pragmatism does not "lend itself to simple answers to hard constitutional questions. The pragmatist's answers may be less elegant, but in the end I believe they are more satisfying than those that any grand theory could provide."[57] Anyway, the alternative is much worse, as Stone Sweet notes: "(In fact, most students of constitutional law in German, Italian or Spanish universities do not read any case law for their courses, but rather a treatise – a 'synthesis' of the law written by a constitutional scholar.) In France, scholars have even produced a Code Constitutionnel that combines exegesis of the

---

52. Ruth Bader Ginsburg "Speaking in a Judicial Voice" 67 *New York University Law Review* (1992) 1185 at 1204.
53. Smith (1993).
54. Christensen (2003) 13.
55. Stig Strömholm "Uppsalaskolan och konstitutionens normativitet" in *Grundlagens makt. Konstitutionen som politiskt redskap och som rättslig norm* SNS författningsprojekt (2002) 41.
56. Blandhol (2002) 67.
57. Daniel A. Farber "Legal Pragmatism and the Constitution" 72 *Minnesota Law Review* (1988) 1331 at 1378.

constitution, provision by provision, with discussion of how relevant decisions have clarified the meaning of constitutional text. In constructing a 'pure' system of constitutional law, scholars enhance the court's authority, to the extent that constitutional rule-making is portrayed as the by-product of purely normative reasoning."[58]

The best way for West-Nordic lawyers is to understand those 'extreme foreign theories' and use them to understand the concepts, conditions, dynamics and mechanics of constitutional law as it is formed in the discourse of constitutional judicial review. As the respected professor W. E. von Eyben noted years ago, having concluded from research that precedent was vastly more applied than recognised, "There is, therefore, all occasion to recommend a further development in the direction of explicitly in the judicial reasoning to include direct citation of precedent. Rather than there being made more or less correct deductions from citations in case report notes or the narrative of arguments."[59] We who teach constitutional law must stop portraying constitutional law as a purely normative phenomenon that easily deals with cases and instead teach that cases make constitutional law[60] and how to analyse, argue and decide such cases self-aware of the moving dynamics.

The alternative is more unrealism, more of the same insulated teaching immune to critical perspectives and incapable of participating in the development of new constitutionalism.[61]

---

58. Stone Sweet (2000) 148.
59. W. E. von Eyben *Juridisk Grundbog. 1. Retskilderne* DJØF (1991) 116.
60. *Stone Sweet (2000) 147 writes: "scholars extract from the case law those purely normative elements that can be incorporated into the rule system they are building, all but ignoring other elements ... most standard [European] texts on constitutional law make little or no mention of who litigates and why, what kind of legal arguments were made and rejected or even how the constitutional court reasons through rules."*
61. *Stone Sweet (2000) 147 writes: "In Europe, the social power of public law scholars has depended critically on their capacity to insulate the law from the social world, and especially from 'politics': the world of political parties, ideology, interests, and 'non-legal' values. This way of doing things – the maintenance of the law/politics distinction as an article of disciplinary faith – has reproduced itself over many generations. That Continental legal scholarship is highly formalist, relatively immune to critical perspectives of law, largely disinterested in questions of legal interpretation, but none the less committed to enhancing the prestige and legitimacy of doctrinal and judicial power are tendencies that have been widely commented upon."*

A Note on Alternative Forms of Review

Whatever the future of West-Nordic constitutional judicial review, there is clearly unease with courts pronouncing on constitutionality. Many reviewed statutes have, furthermore, passed through the legislative process without the constitutional issues being properly raised and debated.

Thus, when suggesting alternatives to judicial review, the obvious place to start is parliamentary procedure. The West-Nordic Parliaments can set the agenda themselves and tackle the issues to some degree. This can happen by several means. Among the most obvious are parliamentary constitutional committees charged with scrutinising from constitutional point of view legislation that other committees view from a more substantive angel.[1] The Parliamentary committee can makes its own assessments[2] or facilitate a wider discourse through parliamentary hearings where affected parties, academics, parliamentarians and others can publicly air their views on the constitutional issues, ultimately ensuring that the parliaments actually debate and decide their views on the constitutional issues. The advisory functions can also be institutionalised creating a formal system of review at the legislative stage, the Swedish Law Council (Lagrådet) has for instance effectively blocked singular laws[3] and defended the ban on retroactive taxes.[4]

A more formal way that can become a middle way between judicial and parliamentary review is the French way of establishing a Constitutional Council to review legislation in the abstract before it is promulgated. This solution holds the advantage of being more accessible for the parliamentary opposition, it provides a focused discourse, and can immediately provide a dif-

---

1. Koch (2002).
2. Bull (2002) 144.
3. Thomas Bull "Konstitutionella snedsteg – en studie av svensk trohet mot grundlag" in *Konstitutionell demokrati* (2004) 80.
4. Fredrik Sterzel "Finansmakten – i konstitutionens centrum och periferi" in *Konstitutionell demokrati* (2004) 99.

ferent, more specialised bench.[5] Drawbacks include more judicialization of politics than many may perceive as desirable.[6]

Another way of devising constitutional review in more comforting settings is to let the ombudsmen focus more on constitutional issues. Arguably, they already have a reviewing function based on semi-constitutional norms and a clear shifts in the norm structure can be seen based on the third-party dispute resolution function of the ombudsmen. Charging them more explicitly with constitutional, including quasi-federal monitoring may be a very equitable way of promoting suitable review.

Many of the constitutional issues, however, come down to value judgement in (often criminal) cases that may not be easily framed in abstract debate but need the raw facts of actual controversies to be adequately decided. This may prompt increased use of the jury as representing the people in making these value judgements. We could propose a system where the jury was asked separately whether the accused was guilty of breaking the law and, secondly, whether conviction should nonetheless be set-aside because the State was bared or the defendant constitutionally justified (e.g. as an exercise of human rights). In cases like *Jersild, Kristinsson,* and *Bergens Tidende* this might give an indication of the support of the law without the statute as such being invalidated. The more such concrete overruling, the more reason for tidying up the statute, allowing for exceptions, or for the courts to generally interpret the law narrowly. Such a procedure could be enacted as a general right for defendants to ask for a jury trial and for a supplementary constitutional question. The defendant would still, especially under ECHR law, retain the right to an appeal. The discursive value of more jury cases would presumably be immense and give real meaning to the margin of appreciation. Fewer cases of constitutional potential would go unnoticed or unheard.

Speaking of unnoticed cases and constitutional discourse, the origin of the Danish Parliamentary Ombudsman is an aborted attempt to have an interlocutor with the courts. The Danish constitutional Bill of 1939 envisaged a legal office that was to inform Parliament on court practice. Establishing such an office might be another way of alerting Parliament of constitutional and other

---

5. Stone Sweet (2000) 40 writes : "The normative logic of a constitutionalism that limits legislative sovereignty by recognising the rights of the individuals and the prerogatives of the sub-national government all but necessitates the establishment of a means of enforcing these rules ... Kelseninan constitutional review provides a means of defending constitutional law as higher law while retaining the general prohibition on judicial review."
6. Bell (2001) from 19 and from 227.

issues pertaining to the interpretation of its statutes. In the West-Nordic countries, it would, of course, be just as relevant to survey the interpretations by administrative tribunals and leading agencies.

Reforms on the judicial side may also include expressly giving powers to the courts to use other techniques in review. The West-Nordic courts already use interpretative override as an alternative to setting-aside. Many other forms of judgements are possible, with one of the most promising being prospective judgements, previous unconstitutional practice notwithstanding laying down the law for future instances as in *Defrenne.* Increased use of clearly articulated calls for further legislation or even time limits for such legislation with the courts filling out legal voids in the alternative would also increase discourse.

Furthermore, increased legal aid or recovery of cost when raising constitutional issues in cases of little economic value and the reintroducing into West-Nordic law of substantial non-pecuniary damages would be ways of increasing the focus on other types of constitutional issues. Today, the ECHR provides both more opportunity to gain costs and monetary remedies as well as winning in the court of public opinion.[7]

Courts that "get into character [as they can] match the ECHR Court in legal [scholarly] strength [and if they chose] to play an active role as well argued as those of the ECHR Court, [surely they would influence the interpenetration of the human rights and] Strasbourg would listen.]"[8]

However, in the meantime, the most realistic alternative for practicing lawyers and public alike is to grasp judicial review as it is. This entails seeing "[litigation naturally] as one mode of activating government, and courts as one set of arenas for achieving policy goals [taking] the courts out of the realm of independence and neutrality, and down into the day-to-day politics depicted by pluralist theory."[9]

The judgement this summer against Iceland, questioning the statute for review of medical mistakes illustrates the reality of new constitutionalism and its still very limited impact on legal behaviour. The law in question was older than the Icelandic Republic, it was defunct in naming ex officio members from agencies no longer in existence. The unfairness of having an allegedly negligent doctor judged by several of his own colleagues, should be obvious. Presumably there are patient organisations, ideological fractions, and re-

---

7.   Caroline Taube "Regeringsformen: positiv rätt eller redskap för rättshaverister?" in *Konstitutionell demokrati* (2004) 67.
8.   Smith (2001) 58.
9.   Shapiro and Stone Sweet (2002b) 7.

sourceful individuals, who could have figured it out, found a suitable test case and brought down the legislation years ago. Why did it take the tragic case of a mistreated newborn to get the issue raised? At least since *Ægisson*, it should be clear that the ECHR insists on real separation of powers and functions.

The answer lies in legal culture and its reliance on the lawgiver to correct inequities. *Ægisson* for its part would not have happened without *Kristinsson*. Professor Eiríkur Tómasson writes that "Ever since I was appointed defence counsel in the prosecution case against Jón Kristinsson before the Supreme Court in 1985 [the ECHR Fair Trial Provision] has been present in my mind."[10] The Icelandic statute was arguably unfair, however, it was left on the books until Eiríkur advanced the argument, and until the case had reached a forum that accepted the argument.

Again, determined rights activists, concerned trial lawyers, political opposition, or individuals unfairly treated could all have raised the issues of fairness much earlier and in a much more prepared and persuasive way that the resources of a public defender allow. The bakers of Oslo figured out this method a century and half ago, why not contemporary Icelanders, Danes, or Norwegians?

A 'real realism' would include the realisation that legal and political goals can be achieved through judicial review, which as a real alternative to winning elections, lobbying, or stirring public debate to have the law changed. Cases from the United States, the home of mature and restrained review, show us that many laws are 'uncommonly silly' – as in case of both *Griswold* and *Lawrence* – but legislators will neglect them if not in the press, the agencies will ignore them if not hindering their work, but zealous individual officials may execute them. Not even reverence of parliamentary sovereignty should make people refrain from this because in effect it treats overbearing unelected officials to their own treatment. Whether doctors, police chiefs, prosecutors, or supreme court justices, they can all benefit from eating humble pie in Strasbourg. After all, neither *Kristinsson* nor *Eggertsdóttir* prescribe a particular new law, they just deem the effects of present law unacceptable. This should give both public and Parliament its opportunity (though a group of us experts, lawyers, and special interests will likely draft something) to engage in a debate on what the law then should be.

Finally, it may be suggested that more of the existing procedures are opened up. The Norwegian Plenary Act may be amended so that all quasi-federal questions are submitted to plenary procedures. The ECHR procedures

---

10. Tómasson (1999) 5.

may be amended so that Member States may appeal cases that they lose a national level. The logic of the federal element means that there must be some access for a state to have its own independent courts review by the central and ultimate authority, just like in US or EU cases where a State can (within limits) access the US Supreme Court or the ECJ – and those courts can develop the law by pronouncing on cases brought by States as well as citizens.

Conclusion Summary

At the outset of this thesis, we set out to find the answer to a number of questions pertaining to West-Nordic constitutional judicial review in particular but also to judicial review in a wider context and to the dynamics of case law.

The survey has revealed that constitutional judicial review and thereby by implication, also the constitutions are remarkably dynamic. However, giving this state of affairs there is equally surprisingly few cases – hundreds rather than thousands – in the West-Nordic jurisdictions. Of the cases that have resulted in normative shifts very few seem deliberately tried as test cases with the explicit purpose of changing or at least tilting the state of constitutional law.

This probably reveals a disquieting lack of understanding and teaching of the dynamic, historic, and comparative developments that can explain both how the law got to its present state and where to it might advance. Seeing that Norwegian case law was arguably more advanced in the 1870s than in the 1970s indicates that skills needed to perform or follow active judicial review are not alien to Nordic lawyers, they have just been repressed or denied for a long while.

Those who benefited from making the constitutions subordinate to legislation and case law secondary to textbooks may sigh for the constitutional middle ages. However, commitment to the quasi-federations of Europe mean that constitutional judicial review is back and case law heading for a revival in the polycentric competition of legal sources.

The legal cultures of the West-Nordic countries appear amazingly sheltered, not to say that they are isolated in absolute terms but rather that they feel highly autonomous and do not cite each other's case law in judgements. This is particularly strange given the influence that European case law now has; comparing and pooling their own case law would presumably be a way of responding to external pressure and finding regional solutions, especially so in case of human rights where the Nordics assume to be the vanguard anyway and where the famed margin of appreciation allows for particular developments.

The West-Nordics may also preserve their autonomy and democratic traditions in other ways. There is hardly a case involving freedom of expression or other political rights where the legislation was explicitly intended to go so far as to stifle all debate. All such cases depend upon either a particular interpretation ventured by unelected officials such as prosecutors, or trial and appeal judges, all of whom may read more restrictions of freedom into statute than the politicians themselves.

The constitutions may be assumed to be representative of what the people want as their superior legal norm, in particular that the Nordics do not want their politicians to take away certain freedoms. If so, then the people should be allowed to decide some of these issues through either referenda or jury trials – does this law go too far either in general or particular? Yes or no.

In any event, new constitutionalism is increasingly influential in the West-Nordic countries with its repudiations of legislative supremacy, rights as substantive conditions, and a quasi-federal legal system with increased relevance – and potential – for judicial relevance.

Answers to Thesis Questions

Initially, we posed the following questions that shall now be answered short and to the point.

What is the most relevant definition of constitutional judicial review for legal practitioners?

Constitutional Judicial Review is the control that any institution exercises over legislative instruments based on legally superior norms if potentially leading to disapplication of the legislation. This includes review performed by international courts or specialised national institutions, review of instruments of general application regardless of their formal status, review based on any written or unwritten norm as long as it trumps, and any kind of disapplication whether invalidation, correction in light of higher norm, or other form of disregard.

Is constitutional judicial review a general phenomenon common to the several legal cultures?

Constitutional Judicial Review appears common to human culture. The hierarchical arrangement of legal norms seems instinctively common to all legal cultures, at least those surveyed. The difference seems more to be which legal norms are placed highest. Choosing to proscribe review as the French Constitution does in principle and as Danish theory has done in practice is in itself establishing a hierarchy with parliamentary statute placed highest, reducing the constitution to a set of procedural rules for the legislative process. The historical perspective demonstrates how affording superior legal status to basic rights and letting independent institutions guard them, is something that can be both received, later disregarded, and then rediscovered by legal cultures. Given certain conditions, constitutional judicial review seems possible in all legal cultures.

What are the key concepts of constitutional judicial review?

Key concepts of constitutional judicial review include the superior norm structure, the federal element, the review forum, the adversaries and their access, and the effects and techniques, including methodology, of review. Identifying a norm structure that is potentially higher than a given instrument is crucial. Many lawyers have for instance overlooked the superior norm potential of the ECHR but also notions of justice or other theory may prove effectively superior, the disregard for the legal properties of West-Nordic constitutions is effectively a product of controlling theory. The federal element is likewise important, especially as it may control other factors, say, reduce the effect of nationally prevalent theory, shift the methodology and forum. The review forum and the access to it is similarly important, as recruitment, organisation, and procedure may determine the outcome of reviewed cases. The effects, techniques, and methodology of a given forum or norm structure may counter-intuitively vary of great importance for a case.

What are the conditions that trigger or hinder constitutional judicial review?

The conditions are certainly both the obvious and the more deeply imbedded. Obviously, there is a need for a hierarchy of norms; the most obvious super norm is the written constitution, less understood are informal norms (such as justice, natural law, human rights) and quasi-federal norms (such as EU, EFTA, EEA, WTO treaties, and the celebrated ECHR). Their effectiveness as superior norms all depend on the presence of a forum with jurisdiction which might be termed effective legal respect. Individual rights are particularly apt at facilitating judicial review because they may vastly expand the potential number of adversaries. Scholarly theory and teaching is remarkable for the fact that it can for long periods hold back both judges and strongly even lawyers from applying or asking for review.

How do the dynamics of constitutional judicial review work and affect a given legal order?

The dynamics of judicial review work to mould the given norm in practice. The dynamics are inevitable in all but the easiest of cases, as reviewing bodies can hardly escape restating the norm, resolving conflicts and questions. Dynamics can be both restrictive and expansive of the constitutional norm. When the former occurs, the constitutional norm becomes neglected and less relevant, making room for, in effect, constitutional amendment through legislation or administration. When the former happens, the body thus correcting the law will, in effect, legislate through its decisions, shifting the norm and creating a new basis for further controversies. However, dynamics have more impact the more cases are brought, depending on a number of factors such as the accessibility of case law, of the relevant process, knowledge, and acceptance of the constitutional norm and dynamics among the legal community, and resources and costs of the potential adversaries in using this form of discourse. Historically, West-Nordic review has displayed various dynamics, both restrictive and expansive, both partial and prolonged processes.

How do the mechanics of constitutional judicial review typically function?

The mechanics of judicial review are the procedural framework that works to facilitate or hinder the deeper conditions and dynamics. The most important distinctions pertain to when constitutional controversies may be brought, on what level of abstraction or concreteness they are reviewed, who has access to review, which bodies may perform review, and the level of the independence of a given reviewing body. These mechanics can be varied immensely but are crucial for anyone trying to observe, analyse, or practise constitutional law, as it determines whether the underlying conditions can lead to the reviewing process whose dynamics ultimately mould constitutional law.

To what extent are these factors present in the West Nordic countries?

The West-Nordic countries are influenced by a number or relevant factors, though many have opposite effects. There are a number of superior written norms that potentially clash with legislation, there are competent reviewing bodies and potential parties and expansive dynamic developments. However, there is also opposition in scholarly theory and teaching, there are restrictive dynamics, and there are hindering mechanics, especially less than independent review performed by agencies close to the legislators. The most interesting factors at work today are the quasi-federal norms and the increased use of the case law method and its increased potential for dynamic developments. Future developments may include more independent and reflective review before promulgation of laws and increased review activity within the framework of the national constitutions and the margins of appreciation afforded by quasi-federal law.

How is quasi-federal constitutional judicial review presenting itself in this context?

Quasi-federal review (or review based on directly applicable international or supranational superior norms) has significantly influenced West-Nordic review. In the relevant fields, especially economic regulation and legislation effecting human rights, the state of constitutional law can effectively be determined either by quasi-federal courts of final instance or by national courts applying quasi-federal superior norms, with a very wide access for potentially aggrieved citizens to challenge national laws. This has already had profound impact by greatly increasing the number of statutory laws that have in one way or another been set-aside in the region, and indirectly influencing the enactment of new instruments. However, the full potential is probably vastly larger, as the federal factors gradually influence national constitutions (best example Iceland), judicial methodology (best example Norway), and the width of reviewed issues (best example Denmark).

What are the effects of these developments on West-Nordic judicial reasoning?

West-Nordic judicial reasoning shows signs of schizophrenia and transitions. The former is evident in cases where the national courts decide that no breach of quasi-federal (or corresponding national) norms has occurred. The potential for overruling review by the effectively supreme quasi-federal courts forces national courts to use case law as the meta-source of constitutional law, using previously unknown or unneeded analysis and persuasiveness directed externally. However, even cases that do find violation show a tendency of emphasising the wide and substantive content of quasi-federal rights whereas national rights are neglected or more summarily dealt with, relying more on deference to preparatory works and legal theory. The implications are profound for lawyers in the West-Nordic region as a dual methodology is needed, probably leading to increasing alignment of methods with a case law oriented method, aware of the dynamics of review, spreading to national constitutional law (in Norway's case reappearing) and gradually dissemination of other parts of the legal system where principled legal issues are being raised in the context of litigations.

Are there indications of shifts in the constitutional norm structures in this context?

Normative shifts are widely apparent. The most apparent shift is the Icelandic incorporation of human rights provisions that replace the Danish inspired rights with ECHR influence. The shift appears as formally conform constitutional amendment but is in reality preceded by unexpected quasi-federal review and followed by continued external as well as increased internal review. Norway follows a similar pattern but with less formal amendment and more explicit recognition of the superiority of the quasi-federal norms that are placed more on the intermediate level between statutory and national constitutional law. Even Denmark, however, reluctantly implementing the ECHR with reservations against judicial activism, is just as bound by the European Courts, arguably even more so as full member of the EU.

What use do comparative approaches to constitutional judicial review offer in this context?

Comparative studies are likely to be both the easiest and most persuasive way of arguing West-Nordic constitutional law when national law is unsettled. Ultimate control by European Courts of certain issues makes it arguable that this is a more straightforward observation of a dependant system than a comparative analysis. However, with the countries being sovereign States, the quasi-federations substantively restricted, with the wide margins of appreciation, with the overflowing dockets of the quasi-federal courts, most issues are dealt with nationally meriting the persuasive techniques of comparative law. With the shift in methodology, the comparison of statutes gives way to comparison of cases and the dynamically determined constitutional law of the other West-Nordic countries becomes a potentially effective argument for practitioner, academic, and judge alike.

Which alternatives can be suggested to strictly judicial constitutional review?

Alternatives to judicial or similar review can be highly recommended. Most effectively reviewed statutes seem enacted with a clear presumption of constitutionality, making it arguable that a better deliberative regime might have considered the issue more carefully initially or reacted and supplemented review more pertinently. Discursive review by parliaments and remand to deliberation are the best suggestions for alternative supplements to judicial review.

What is the likely future of West-Nordic constitutional judicial review?

Future indicators point to increased review that can take West-Nordic constitutional law in different directions to varying extent. Understanding the concepts and conditions, dynamics and mechanics of constitutional judicial review will prepare lawyers, politicians, and the broader public for following – and influencing – that future.

Tables of Cases

All Cases

Table of all cases referred to by the author in the thesis, sorted by party names indicating page number of reference.

Cases by Jurisdiction

The next tables are sorted by year and report. For page references, see table of all cases.

Case Name or Parties indicate party names as explained below.

Case no. indicates docket number of court.

Report indicates report, year, and page. For sorting reasons, page numbers may be preceded with zeroes.

Year indicates year of decision.

Norwegian Cases by Year

Case names are shortened, as they very often are quite long in the case reports, party names are usually shortened to just one surname. In civil cases (including all administrative cases), the Norwegian State, and most state entities are just referred to as Norway with the other party cited as the first party. In criminal cases, the State may be referred to as Norwegian Prosecution. Some cases are referred to by a widely used name such as Kløfta. In an annoying number of cases, the defendant and sometimes both or all parties are known only by letters, most often "A". Such cases are cited by the other party's name first but sometimes by a cunningly invented title.

When a case appears in the text for the first time, the report citation is given, usually in the mode of Rt.1841-274, indicating the report Retstidende, year and page number. The on-line report of is only available by subscription through www.jus.no. Other reports include, SmH, Samling af mærkelige Højesteretsdomme i Tidsrummet 1815-1835, UfL, Ugeskrift for Lovkyndighed.

Case Name or Parties	Case no.	Report no.	Year
Blom v. Aars		SmH.132	1822
Peterson v. Aars		Unreported	1823
Allum v. Bjerregaard		Unreported	1824
Frederiks Universitet v. Gjerdrum		Unreported	1831
Morgenstjerne v. Petersen		SmH.504	1833
Zeier v. Stang		SmH.626	1835
Young v. Norway		Rt. 1841-274	1841
Rolfsen v. Petersen		Rt. 1845-513	1844
Dahl v. Norway		Rt. 1854-093	1854
Lützow v. Norway		2 UfL (1862-3) 200	1862
Wedel-Jarlsberg v. Norway		6 UfL (1866-7) 165	1866
Hansson v. Norway		8 UfL (1868) 393	1868
Kristiania v. Jensen		Rt. 1880-278	1880
Lind v. Heffermehl		Rt. 1882-229	1882
Marstrander v. Nikolaysen		Rt. 1887-793	1887
Huun v. Nikolaysen		Rt. 1888-200	1887
Jensen v. Norway		Rt. 1890-455	1890
Bakke v. Norway		Rt. 1909-156	1909
Thams v. Norway		Rt. 1909-417	1909
Johansen v. Norway		Rt. 1918-401	1918
Vauvert v. Norway		Rt. 1922-627	1922
Klinge		Rt. 1946-198	1946
Mortvedt v. Norway		Rt. 1951-019	1951
Opdahl v. Bergen		Rt. 1951-087	1951
Whalers v. Norway		Rt. 1952-1089	1952
Mykle		Rt. 1958-479	1958
Norwegian Gold Clause Case		Rt. 1962-369	1962

Danish Cases by Year

Case names are shortened; party names are usually shortened to just one surname. In civil cases (including all administrative cases), the Danish State, and most state entities are just referred to as Denmark with the other party cited as the first party. In criminal cases, the State is referred to as Denmark. Names are usually shortened to just one surname. When a case appears in the text for the first time, the report citation is given, usually in the mode of UfR.1943.154H, indicating the report Ugeskrift for Retsvæsen, year, and page number and a letter indicating Court (H for Højesteret – Supreme Court – V and Ø respectively for the Western and Eastern High Courts).

The on-line report is only available by subscription through www.thomson.dk.

Case Name or Parties	Report no.	Year
International Workers Union v. Denmark	UfR.1874.479H	1874
Olsen v. Denmark	UfR.1887.142H	1887
Barfod v. Denmark	UfR.1912.545H	1912
Sehested Juul v. Denmark	UfR.1921.148H	1920
Løvenskiold v. Denmark	UfR.1921.153H	1920
Lerche v. Sass	UfR.1921.168H	1920
de Neergaard v. Pedersen	UfR.1921.644H	1921
Andersen v. Denmark	UfR.1935.0001H	1934
N N I v. Denmark	UfR.1941.1070-1H	1941
N N II v. Denmark	UfR.1941.1070-2H	1941
N N III v. Denmark	UfR.1941.1071H	1941
Wissing v. Denmark	UfR.1941.1076H	1941
Ahlefeldt-Laurvig v. Denmark	UfR.1952.0797H	1952
Arne Magnussens Legat v. Denmark	UfR.1971.0299H	1971
Tegen v. Prime Minister	UfR.1973.0694H	1973
Radio Search	UfR.1976.0184H	1976
Military MD	UfR.1976.0395-2V	1976
Jersild v. Denmark	UfR.1989.0399H	1989
Birk Keller v. Denmark	UfR.1993.0757H	1993
Denkavit v. Denmark	UfR.1994.0430H	1994
T v. Denmark	UfR.1994.0536H	1994
TV-Stop v. Denmark	UfR.1994.0988H	1994
Norup Carlsen v. Nyrup Rasmussen I	UfR.1996.1300H	1996
Norup Carlsen v. Nyrup Rasmussen II	UfR.1998.0800H	1998
Tvind	UfR.1999.0841H	1999
Sørensen v. FDB	UfR.1999.1496H	1999

Pehrson v. Denmark (UfR.2002.1789H)	UfR.1999.1798H	1999
Ur Rab v. Denmark	UfR.2002.1789H	2002
Thule v. Denmark	UfR.2004.0382H	2004
Editor-in-chief A v. B	UfR.2004.1773H	2004
A & C v. Denmark	UfR.2006.1149H	2006

Icelandic Cases by Year

Case names are shortened; party names are usually shortened to just one surname. In civil cases (including all administrative cases), the State, and most state entities are just referred to as Iceland with the other party cited as the first party. In criminal cases, the State is referred to as Iceland. Names are usually shortened to just one surname.

When a case appears in the text for the first time, the report citation is given, before 1999 usually in the mode of Hrd.1943.154, indicating the report Dómar Hæstaréttar, year and page number. From 1999, only the on-line report of www.haestirettur.is used, the reference H.1999-065 indicates year and docket number. On the web page, the mode 65/1999 is used; in this table, the said mode is used for sorting purposes. Older cases are from the report Landsyviréttardómar og hæstaréttardómar í íslenzkum málum, cited as 1 L&H 246, indicating volume, report and page number.

Case Name or Parties	Case no.	Report no.	Year
Eyjólfur Jónsson v. Iceland	H. 1877-24	1 L&H 249	1877
Halldórsson v. Simonarson	H. 1885-8	2 L&H 455	1885
Zoëga v. Reykjavík	H. 1900-6	6 L&H 176	1900
Þórarinsson v. Iceland I	L. 1916-22	9 L&H 809	1916
Zoëga v. Iceland I	L. 1916-53	10 L&H 20	1917
Þórarinsson v. Iceland II	H. 1918-30	10 L&H 601	1918
– also reported in		UfR.1918.953H	1918
Zoëga v. Iceland II	H. 1918-141	10 L&H 603	1918
– also reported in		UfR.1918.957H	1918
Reykjavík v. Knudsen	H. 1942-059	Hrd.1943.154	1943
Hrafnkatla	H. 1942-118	Hrd.1943.237	1943
Svarfaðardalshreppur v. Jónsson	H. 1945-077	Hrd.1946.345	1946
Kampmann v. Strandgata	H. 1951-041	Hrd.1951.268	1951
Víðir v. Iceland	H. 1952-190	Hrd.1952.142	1952
Alfons Jónsson v. Iceland	H. 1953-005	Hrd.1954.073	1954

Hamar v. Iceland	H. 1953-051	Hrd.1954.093	1954
Guðmundsson & Víðir v. Iceland	H. 1958-116	Hrd.1958.753	1958
Kristinsson v. Iceland (Hrd.1985.1290)	H. 1985-077	Hrd.1985.1290	1985
Sverrisson v. Iceland	H. 1986-273	Hrd.1987.0356	1987
Þorgeirsson v. Iceland	H. 1986-272	Hrd.1987.1280	1987
Ægisson v. Iceland	H. 1989-120	Hrd.1990.0002	1990
Gunnarsson v. Iceland	H. 1991-494	Hrd.1992.0174	1992
Guðmundsson v. Frami	H. 1993-124	Hrd.1993.1217	1993
Ólafsson v. Iceland	H. 1999-065		1999
Social Security I	H. 2000-125		2000
M v. K	H. 2000-419		2000
Öryrkjabandalag v. Iceland	H. 2001-397		2001
Vigfússon v. Iceland	H. 2001-461		2001
Óskarsson v. Iceland	H. 2002-156		2002
Alþýðusamband v. Iceland (H. 2002-167)	H. 2002-167		2002
H. I. Guðmundsson v. Iceland	H. 2002-338		2002
Jónas Guðmundsson v. Iceland	H. 2002-499		2002
Mathiesen v. Hafsteinsson	H. 2003-036		2003
SÍ v. LÍÚ	H. 2003-046		2003
Júlíusson v. Iceland	H. 2003-112		2003
X v. Iceland	H. 2004-460		2004
Sveinsdóttir v. Áshreppur	H. 2005-051		2005
Shelton v. Þorláksson	H. 2005-181		2005
Reykjavík v. Jónsdóttir	H. 2005-248		2005

ECHR Cases by Year

Case names are shortened; applicant party names usually to one surname, respondent State to shortest convenient name.

When a case appears in the text for the first time, ECHR appears in brackets to indicate an ECHR case. No report citation is given in the text, as ECHR cases are sensibly referred to with party names. Further references can be found in the table below.

Cases can be found on the on-line report of www.echr.coe.int, more specifically at http://cmiskp.echr.coe.int/tkp197/search.asp?skin=hudoc-en.

Case Name or Parties	Case no.	Report no.	Year
Kjeldsen v. Denmark	5095/71		1976
Sporrong and Lönnroth v. Sweden			1984
Rasmussen v. Denmark	8777/79		1984
Nielsen v. Denmark	10929/84		1988
Hauschildt v. Denmark (ECHR 1989)	11/1987/134/188		1989
Barfod v. Denmark (E)	11508/85		1989
Georgsson v. Iceland	12170/86		1989
Kristinsson v. Iceland (ECHR 1989)	12170/86		1989
B. N. v. Denmark	13557/88		1989
Sverrisson v. Iceland	12170/86		1990
Zvi Goll v. Denmark	14169/88		1990
Thorgeirson v. Iceland	13778/88		1992
W. M. v. Denmark	17392/90		1992
Jersild v. Denmark	36/1993/431/510		1994
E v. Norway	12/1989/172/228		1995
PROSA v. Denmark	20005/92		1996
Johansen v. Norway (E)	24/1995/530/616		1996
A v. Denmark	60/1995/566/652		1996
Eriksen v. Norway	102/1995/608/696		1997
Bladet Tromsø v. Norway	21980/93		1999
Nielsen and Johnsen v. Norway	23118/93		1999
Ninn-Hansen v. Denmark	28972/95		1999
Bergens Tidende v. Norway	26132/95		2000
Hansen v. Denmark	28971/95		2000
Kurt Nielsen v. Denmark	33488/96		2000
Siglfirðingur v. Iceland	34142/96		2000
Hamdi Sari v. Demark & Turkey			2001
Kristinsson v. Iceland (ECHR 1989)	12170/86		1989
B. N. v. Denmark	13557/88		1989
Sverrisson v. Iceland	12170/86		1990
Zvi Goll v. Denmark	14169/88		1990
Thorgeirson v. Iceland	13778/88		1992
W. M. v. Denmark	17392/90		1992
Jersild v. Denmark	36/1993/431/510		1994
E v. Norway	12/1989/172/228		1995
PROSA v. Denmark	20005/92		1996
Johansen v. Norway (E)	24/1995/530/616		1996
A v. Denmark	60/1995/566/652		1996
Eriksen v. Norway	102/1995/608/696		1997
Bladet Tromsø v. Norway	21980/93		1999
Nielsen and Johnsen v. Norway	23118/93		1999

Ninn-Hansen v. Denmark	28972/95	1999
Bergens Tidende v. Norway	26132/95	2000
Hansen v. Denmark	28971/95	2000
Kurt Nielsen v. Denmark	33488/96	2000
Siglfirðingur v. Iceland	34142/96	2000
Hamdi Sari v. Demark & Turkey		2001
Beck v. Norway	26390/95	2001
Amrollahi v. Denmark		2002
Ringvold v. Norway	34964/97	2003
Watson v. Norway	37372/97	2003
Sigurðsson v. Iceland	39731/98	2003
Vasileva v. Denmark	52792/99	2003
Y v. Norway	56568/00	2003
Pedersen & Baadsgaard v. Denmark	49017/99	2004
Ásmundsson v. Iceland	60669/00	2004
Pedersen & xxx v. Denmark	68693/01	2004
Rohde v. Denmark	69332/01	2005
Sørensen v. Denmark	52562/99	2006
Moesgaard Petersen v. Denmark	32848/06	2008
Orr v. Norway	31283/04	2008
A. and E. Riis v. Norway; No. 2	16468/05	2008
Hasslund v. Denmark	36244/06	2008
Valentin v. Denmark	26461/06	2009
Nielsen v. Denmark	44034/07	2009
Christensen v. Denmark	247/07	2009
Egeland and Hanseid v. Norway	34438/04	2009
Björk Eiðsdóttir v. Iceland	46443/09	2012
Erla Hlynsdóttir v. Iceland	43380/10	2012
TV VEST & Rogaland Pensjonistparti v. Norway	21132/05	2008
Vörður Ólafsson v. Iceland	20161/06	2010
Lindheim and others v. Norway	13221/08, 2139/10	2012

Other Cases by Year

Jurisdiction indicates the polity in which the decision was made.

Case Name or Parties	Jurisdiction	Report no.	Year
Faroe Islands v. Starvsmannafelagið		Unreported	
Klaksvík Fishermen v. Faroes	Faroe Islands	UfR. 1958.170H	
Marbury v. Madison	United States	5 U.S. 137 (1803)	1803

van Gend en Loos v. Netherlands	European Union	ECJ Case 22/62	1963
Van Duyn	European Union	ECJ Case 41/74	1974
Von Colson	European Union	ECJ Case 14/83	1984
Marleasing	European Union	ECJ Case C-106/89	1990
Francovitch	European Union	ECJ Cases C-6, 9/90	1991
Griswold v. Connecticut	United States	381 U.S. 479 (1965)	1965
Roe v. Wade	United States	410 U.S. 113 (1973)	1973
Defrenne v. SABENA	European Union	ECJ Case 43/75	1976
CCD Case 82-146	France	Case 2001-454	1982
Werner Larsen v. Faroe	Faroe Islands	UfR.1983.986Ø	1983
Chevron v. NRDC	United States	467 U.S. 837 (1984)	1984
Bowers v. Hardwick	United States	478 U.S. 186 (1986)	1986
FAG v. FA	Faroe Islands	UfR.1986.314H	1986
Elektron v. Faroe Islands	Faroe Islands	Unreported	2000
CCD Case 2001-454	France	Case 2001-454	2002
Perorsaasut v. Paamiut	Greenland	UfR.2002.2591Ø	2002
Lawrence v. Texas	United States	000 U.S. 02-102 (2003)	2003
Confiscation case	Denmark	UfR.2005.261Ø	2005
Greenland Bankruptcy case	Greenland	UfR.2012.2360/2H	2012

Index

363